The Best of The Virginia Writers Club
Centennial Anthology
1918-2018

Edited by Betsy Ashton

Snowy Day Publications

Hardy, VA

Dedication

Thanks to all Virginia writers, from our founder, James Branch Cabell, to those writing today, for keeping the literary arts flourishing in Virginia.

Foreword

Dear Readers,

Prepare to be amazed.

A few years ago, when I first joined the Board of Governors of the Virginia Writers Club (VWC), talk of our centennial year was just that, talk. However, the more we talked, the more we knew we needed to commemorate the status of being one of the oldest, ongoing writer organizations in the country. What better way to do that than highlight members' writing in an anthology?

When we opened for submissions, we were almost overwhelmed by the response. As President of the VWC, I was heartened by the interest, and when I reviewed some of the submissions, I was thrilled at the depth and breadth of talent among VWC members. I knew this anthology would be one for the ages, not merely here in the Commonwealth of Virginia but beyond.

I have to express my extreme gratitude to former VWC President Betsy Ashton for taking on the duties not only of organizing our centennial celebrations in 2018, but also for managing the details of amassing work for an anthology and editing every single submission. Without her dedication, our centennial would have passed with little notice—and you wouldn't be holding this magnificent anthology in your hands.

Thanks, as well, to VWC member Chuck Lumpkin for formatting the interior and Janell E. Robisch for designing not one but three possible covers for our members to chose from. The final, as you see, is representative of what we are: writers.

Thank you to all who submitted. Your entries made selecting the stories, essays, and poems included here very difficult. The result is what we talked about in our long-ago centennial discussions: the best of Virginia writers.

Make your favorite beverage, snuggle up before a cozy, roaring fire with this good book, and prepare to be amazed.

Phyllis A. "Maggie" Duncan
President
Virginia Writers Club

Poetry

§

TABLE OF CONTENTS

396 DAYS

Betsy Ashton

Plague arrived unannounced,
infecting men in their prime,
odd symptoms never before
seen together.

Diagnosis struck fear,
carried a death sentence
to be executed
within 396 days.

From deep in Africa,
its various names meant death,
rejection
by friends and family,
as if Plague were their fault.

Men terrified of discovery,
of death,
yellow and purple, alone
at the darkest moment of life.

They died in agony.
too little compassion,
too little love.

Was it God's judgment?
No matter. Mankind loses
with each victim.

My first friend died on Day 302.

STONE OF HOPE, 2011

Betsy Ashton

Granite statue gazes outward,
seeks proof the dream
continues

I have a dream

looks for footprints
on the path to freedom

that one day on the red hills of Georgia

laments ridicule of a president
with the audacity to dream

the sons of former slaves

sees a country
broken by religious hatred

and the sons of former slave owners

hears uncivil discord not
peaceful civil disobedience

will be able to sit down together

wonders what happened
to embracing differences

at the table of brotherhood.

abandons hope of government
for all people.

I had a dream.

Granite statue gazes outward and weeps

ALZHEIMER'S

Judy Light Ayyildiz

I don't find time to use the teapot
these days. On the back shelf
of the pantry, cold and different
from everything else. The one
who gave it was taken away,
and even quit writing.
Hardly, anymore,
can we talk on the phone
let alone have a cup,
unfinished what we took
in together half-full,
half-empty, with or without.

Friend, will you ever get well,
buy me some matching cups?
Do you like where you store
your bags these days,
and do you still take
one lump or two?

Stirring words around
on the swollen tongue
of your medication Saturday
when I set up a visit,
I heard you say,
Yes, if you please,
I donuh mine. If I do
not say this, I'll choke
on the strain.
You were never that
polite, and oh,
my dear, how
I miss the tang.

REQUIEM, AUSCHWITZ 1985

Judy Light Ayyildiz

—Auschwitz 1985

Forty years of winds have not cleared the air
laden with unfinished chains, minor modes
that steel against the grain of brick
and mortar made as sanctum for the massive
freight. "Arbeit macht frei", words
in the gate. Requiem aeternam dona eis Domine.

An iron slab rolls back into the crematorium,
the host is heaved upon it. Three million
candles cannot rekindle even one
bright eye gone ash out that furious
tunnel into night.
Hair spins into blankets, tons of twisted
threads genuflect. All sorts, sizes of unpaired
shoes pile empty against the wall,
strings tied upon the tongues.
Kyrie eleison, Lord, have mercy, boxcar
loads. —Sanctus. Sanctus
freezing flesh huddled in the courtyard.
In the guts of a gray building,
a three-foot cubicle confined three. One
etched an eagle in the corner
with a nail, a final litany. Amen.

Forty years of rains have not cleansed
the firing block. Fresh flowers laid
against the boards burn
their incense. Sun cuts through
the gallows noose. The horseless cart
stands steady on the hard earth.

VIEW FROM THE TOP

Judy Light Ayyildiz

Istanbul, October downpour

The last light call to prayers shudders space against this
dying under dragon-bellied rain clouds
washing rivers into streets below,
mooring ferryboats to their docks,
suspending the bridges that span the strait.

The seagulls—hieroglyphics
across the sharp-edged vista between
high rises and apartment buildings,
appear to be swarming portents vaulting
up from the sea to this hill,

loosely-wound tornadoes breaking apart to dispersion.
They fan, glide the thick wet currents,
sweep up between the down drafts,
some filtering low onto red-tiled roofs.
These sit like hens facing East in oneness, all in rows.

Yet, now one comes head up, fluttering like a frantic angel
peering in at me writing about it
as one come with a message in all this mess,
and then, it's up over the top, an indefinite other.
Rain thrashes against the panes. A thousand lights glitter

as fixed wingless points, voiceless, nameless.
And gulls that care less which corners they cut
continue their phantasms, flamenco folding
into the mix above and gracing the eclectic
architecture of our separate noise between.

BROWN EYED WORLD

Madalin E. Bickel

No one ever said
I had mama's eyes;
no one ever said
I had daddy's eyes, either.
Truth be told
Aunt Wanda looked the
most like me.
At least there was
evidence I was
related by
blood…

When your mama passes
all sorts of crazy
memories jump into
your head, flash across your
eyes like a movie
preview in reverse.
Those memories
tempted me to look back;
revisit the past, but
why?

What if my blue eyes
didn't belong in our
brown eyed family?
Mirrors don't lie,
families do.

WINTER'S DETRITUS

Madalin E. Bickel

Walking makes a crunching sound,
footprints in mud angle off leading
someone somewhere around gray
remains of last week's snow.

Mud flaps are aptly named, but
still the grunge hits windshields
leaving smudges of grime, ghosts of
yesterday's efforts to clear roads.

Tracks of once abandoned autos
veer from concrete lanes to be
filled with black water set to
refreeze when darkness unveils.

A lone white cross sits to the right
reminiscent of last year's winter
blight and a parent's lost child,
left behind with memories and

winter's detritus.

FLOWERS BRUISE TOO EASILY

Cindy Brookshire

Some women are bred slim
And delicate as blossoms
Groomed hair, glossed lips
Pencil skirts with ankle tattoos
Appealing to impulsive men
The kind in suits who race
Into the grocery store after work
To grab a cellophaned bouquet
From the refrigerator case
And a twenty-dollar bottle of pizza wine
Scanning them in the self-checkout
Along with a pack of condoms.
These women have good teeth
They live to be 90 because
Men take their risks.

Other women raise themselves up
From the earth, bovine, sturdy-backed
Reeking of the mop and bucket
Breeding and nursing babies like
Chain smokers light butt to butt
One latched to the teat
Until the next one is born
They bake fruit-filled pies
With buttery crusts
Live in trailer parks and
Trample everything in Dollar General.
Ignorant of their own mortality
Until they are suddenly culled
While bending to pick tomatoes
In the hot August garden.

Best to keep the two kinds apart
Especially mother and daughter-in law.
Bruised petals never heal.
And the last thick slice of pie
Reveals a plate older than both of them
A rose pattern cracked with time and wear.

SHAKEN AND STIRRED

Peggy Clutz

I hold the can of spray paint
And gently wave the valve over
This precious porch furniture
Watching the instant change which
Causes the corners of my mouth to curve
At feeling sad to cover the old paint
On the worn 80-year-old sofas and chairs
Made shiny from repeated contact with arms
And fingers unthinkingly stroking the wood
Whilst immersed in deep conversation
With all the people who have sat down
To enjoy a comfortable seat and a
Lazy summer drink and conversation
With friends and family on a hot July Day,
The humidity high and the cicadas
Singing their song from tree to tree
All catching up on their lives
And gossiping about neighbors,
Relatives not present, and faraway
World affairs, which seem millions
And millions of miles away from
The safety of this wonderful summer
Porch and the security of people who care

TEETH

Carol L. Covin

Take it back, I thought to myself.
I don't want your advice.
"My mother used a soft toothbrush," he told me.
"She used a special mouthwash," he said.Before chemo,
Before surgery,
Before radiation,
Friends were already trying to help me.
My teeth?! My brain screamed silently.
Breast cancer will affect my teeth?!
I bought the soft toothbrush,
The special mouthwash,
Talismans to fight off death.
The big "C" retreated in front of them,
Scared by my baby soft toothbrush,
As I had been of cancer.

OH, XENIA, OH SO SWEET

John Cowgill

Her name is Xenia, a woman who is so sweet
She is a woman you would want to meet
The shirt and her jeans that she wears are so neat
She wears no shoes on her beautiful bare feet
She likes to take a walk down the street
She goes over to take a seat
That she finds next to the street
She feels the extreme heat
On her lovely bare feet
As she puts them onto the seat
She begins to eat
Her snack made from wheat
As she sits on the seat
That is next to the street
Where she feels the heat
On her beautiful bare feet
But here comes her friend Pete
He sits next to her on the seat
And he rubs his hands on her beautiful bare feet
It was here where she first saw Pete
He saw that she was neat
A beautiful woman who had beautiful bare feet
From that day, he knew where to meet
A beautiful woman named Xenia who is so sweet.

IN HONOR OF SPACES BETWEEN

Carol Cutler

The spaces between stars,
The space between thoughts,
The resting potential of a neuron,
The emptiness of the Buddha mind,
Spaces in Gibran's togetherness
The interstitial space of cells,
The pause of before inhalation
The space before the lub of heartbeat
The silent sweep of eyelash,
The space in genetic material,
That isn't ATGC
The pause after the firefly's light
The rest in a musical score
The point of cresting wave
The something between
The before and after
Is a calm that generates power.
The rests, pauses, and nothings
Are spaces that hold potential.
And any dentist will tell you to
Floss the space between your teeth.

NON-NUCLEAR EXCHANGE 2017

Carol Cutler

Fourteen countries are up to date
With 15,000 nuclear warheads.
US, UK, China, Russia, and France
Have promised non-proliferation.
North Korea, Pakistan, Israel, India,
And others, holding, waiting,
With no promises made.
To assure the balance,
Up to the minute and
Strategically placed,
Non-nuclear countries,
Turkey, Germany, Italy,
The Netherlands
Host warheads on their soil.
Who gets to decide
 When to throw the first rock?
Or what will be done with
The reckless, the hateful,
The show-offs, the bullies?
Poets and artists all,
With music, painting, writing,
Offer a mass proliferation
For what could better be exchanged.

SILENCE

Danielle Dayney

Ink is silent, without wording.
Thoughts on tongues which cannot wag.
Gears are stuck, no longer turning.
Flowing words have caught a snag.
Eyes are glazed, and minds are searching.
Visions have been choked and gagged.

COUNTY RONDEAU STAFFORD

James Gaines

Ice thickens on twigs
All the way down White Oak Road
Winter stalks back in
How can it help remind me
You are weeks away

Winter stalks back in
Magic conjures in darkness
Ice thickens on twigs
Broadway in sudden headlights
Not a thing to sell

You are weeks away
How can it help remind me
Time coats me like ice
Mummifies my bright yearning
Winter stalks back in

THE QUILT

Linda Hudson Hoagland

I spread the handmade quilt on my bed.
I had only good thoughts in my mind
As I rubbed my hand gently across
Bright calico and some solid prints.

The feel of the elegant cottons
All tacked down with brightly colored yarns
Ignited sparks of fire in my thoughts
Bringing the old memories to life.

Calico patterns were my mama's
And mine if she forced me to wear them.
She sewed all of my homemade dresses
Spending time to make them so pretty.

Solid colors were from white to black
With blues, green, and yellows added, too.
My eyes fell on the darkest black block
Focusing on an unhappy time.

I sat on the front porch watching cars
Pass by as I wiped away tears from
My red cheeks since I could not travel to
School and choir because I had no ride.

The light blue gauzy fabric filled me
With tears of bitterness and anger.
Not to be a girl scout like my friends,
Instead, you made a doll dress of blue.

White with beige and pink centered flowers
A dress I truly hated to wear
I tried to ruin it many times
It survived the torment and torture.

The paisley print upset me so much
That I closed my eyes trying to block
The urge to heave up my light breakfast
Reminded me of my pregnant days.

The quilt is making me remember
Events I would much rather forget
I have to remove it from my bed
So I won't revisit my regrets.

IN GENEVA

Esther Whitman Johnson

on the twenty-sixth day of December, just miles from the UN,
the World Council of Churches, the Red Cross and High Commission

for Refugees, past the outdoor Christmas Mart where merchants
sell their wares—artisan chocolate, Italian nougat, sweets in powdered

sugar and golden syrup—in the Rue de la Croix, a man plays his guitar,
sings a Caribbean tune, his dreads soaked, cap on the walk empty—

not a franc, not a euro. Past Philippe Patek with watches for millionaires,
past Louis Vuitton where the doorman tips his top hat and swings wide

the bronze door, past Cartier where diamonds gleam and red-lipped
socialites totter in high-heeled boots, against a stone wall, beneath

a plaque that reads GENEVE CITÉ DE REFUGE, an old woman
huddles, hips wrapped in thin striped cloth, her hand out.

SECRET MESSAGE

Amanda Judd

It was a simple note
and nothing more,
except for the hidden message
that it bore.

To any other
but mine eyes,
the symbol might not have been noticed,
And surely not recognized!

And, I must admit that, at first,
even I hadn't a clue
he had cleverly typed in my letter,
a secret "I love you."

MIRACLE FLOWER

Carolyn Kreiter-Foronda

After Georgia O'Keeffe's <u>Jimson Weed,</u> 1936

Jimson Weed, Devil's Snare,
poisonous as lust,
release your beauty

into shadows, lure me
under your spell.
Pricklyburr, Thorn Apple

odorous as oil, extend
your green stems
and strong-scented leaves.

Unfurl your alabaster petals,
restless as snow.
I don't need to taste

your venom – your
small black seeds –
to walk among spirits

or commune with deities.
Stunned, I watch you
wilt in the flare of day –

you, delirious for twilight,
your night blooms –
a palace of desire.

With green and golden
swirls, I stylize
your floral centers,

outline with nectar
your angular lips
until translucent

with venerable heart,
you fan out rapturous
in desert moon.

"MIRACLE FLOWER" originally published in CROSSWINDS
POETRY JOURNAL, Vol. 1, Spring 2016.

AFTER I WAKE AT DAWN, A WHILE, I TURN

Jeanne Larsen

on radio, trying to drown a lapping tide. Already
muggy. A piece on Coyner Springs [the local
potter's field]: generosities of a funeral parlor,

gratitude of the beat-down son. Waves in air
against a drum-skin. I manage to drowse. Watch a reed
hut by a charnel ground rise up. Its penitent hag

creaks into dance: the poet Komachi [perhaps not
childless], each long silk sleeve, her hair, a passionate
cascade of nerve-fire, in colors to no one visible. All,

rags laid off [with beauty, words] in the drawn-out rain
of aging. I see suitors, no matter now. Cast
loose. Dead. As she is near 12 centuries interred,

or burnt. Sure, gone today, that leafy savor in her
of a green medicine called *tea*, or the Kyōto summer's
sticky warmth. Gone the stirring *hiss-sh-shush*

that made of sliding papered doors, a secret visitor.
Gone, when sun awakes, or consciousness has passed
beyond. But—how do they rise, what neuro-rōshis

name *qualia*, from synapses' glimmering Indra's
-net. How do I see in a tepid dusk-like room [my old
mother 12 years dead] Komachi dancing [or yours, or

any] in that field. How exists the morticians' gift. How
the gratitude, how *gratitude*, of one who grieves
and hears a radio. Reads Komachi. Tastes this tea.

HERE'S THE THING

Jeanne Larsen

you and I don't want
to forget: yellow tiger
     swallowtails on light
pink blooming shrubs,
dimorphic, hale,
     and continual
-ly fanning blue-tipped
wings. [Nan-yue: *Zen is*
     not about sitting
or lying down.] And how
one sudden morning [2
     weeks of diminishing
passed], they are [along
that tall old double-lane
     of boxwoods, small
leaved, moss black] re
-placed by a foggy
     flight of spider
hammocks, each [Master Ma,
in his turn: *It is*
     just this.] specific
to its outstretched circum
-stantial twigs, moment
     on moment apparent, *a*

mirror, each *originally the others*, and craft
     -ily self-engineered.

HISTORY [A BOOK REVIEW] IS MOSTLY

Jeanne Larsen

made of trash. Face it. That footslog monk,
heart set on wakening, is, seeking scripture, lost

to us: diligent name erased, map blanked
by dunes. An overlander heading west
[not this west], he walks, belly empty, thinking

the far-off holy places, his homely east,
are one. Across a *sandy necroscape*
[the review again], unreal, unresting, angsty,

the monk inscribes a palimpsest on bleak spaces
made of *motion embodied*, like [on palm-leaf,
leather, clay, wood] all the wrecked, un-spurious

libraries brushed by traders, novices, refugees.
Soon, hot-eyed plunderers of those *cave-archives*
[traducer-scholars, archeologist-thieves]

make fictions of a *space of exchange*, spun from garbage,
sheer zeal, murky faith. They unroll and hand on
scrolls where you and I see graffito-markings.

There is no *Silk Road*, really. A German invention,
recent, embroidered by a worm-reeling globe
scared of its voids, its sticky webs, uncertain

of all things. Uncertain in Sanskrit, Khotanese,
Gāndhārī, Sogdian, Hebrew, Uighur, in time
in French et cet. For the spacey monk, in glib Han

script. Unfaithful chronicles, his, yours, mine.
Yet in fact, the monk slogs. As if there were paradigms.

SHAMANIC SUNSET

Louise M. Mitchell

I'm cut loose, a convict escaped,
Fleeing the simmering Piedmont.
A lone, whirring cicada
Seasonally attuned
Slipped his shell, clinging
Empty and stiff to bark.
I'm parched as cicada's crunchy shell.

Survival instincts free me
To a higher perch in the Blue Ridge.
From a stone wall on the crest,
Legs dangle into oblivion.
The sun slips lower
In a Massanutten-Alleghany meltaway.

My head in the sky of diminishing day,
Magic and wonder return.
In a hail farewell at the horizon,
Sun tosses a burst of red light.
A sun-bear flies to within my reach
And we merge! "Huh!"
It is ecstasy and exhalation.
A higher voice interprets,
You are a shining ball of light,
From head to toe.

The message echoes within, encouraging
Comprehension as diminishing light
Takes the cacophony of day.
Trees covering mountainsides
Withdraw to their roots.
Air cools. Insects and butterflies retire.
The only sound in the panorama
An uplifting nocturne chirped in duet.
Moon takes center stage.
Day is done.
No longer a wizened Piedmont shell.
Homebound, full, nestled in fleece.

THE SPIRIT OF SHENANDOAH

Louise M. Mitchell

The rhythm of my boots, irregular
Up the Apple Trail.
Under oak-hickory canopies,
Wildflowers wave in the draft.

My consciousness opens with a vision
Of the Spirit Shenandoe.
Her radiance burns through gossamer fog.
Framed by long, lustrous silver locks,
A face ancient and ageless.

Soft chuckling crosses my intrigue.
The voice of skarn and moss,
That's right. Give it to me, my darling.
Ground yourself with each step.
Send me your angst and limitations from earthly life.
That's it. Send it down to me with each step. Ha Ha!

Her arms reach up through layers of crust,
Take energy from my soles
—cleansing and purifying!
I trod on across rock with
My ethereal companion.

Acorns clunk through branches,
Roll on the ground, startling my reverie.
Her image strengthens. She mothers me,
Restore yourself to gentleness.
Take the gentleness of nature
Back to your people.

A soft breeze catches her hair
And whispers through my heart.
AAH, Shenandoe, delivering
Endless joy.
Endless.
Joy.

AMONG VIRGINIA'S PINES

James W. Morrison

No luster of New England in Virginia.
No Adamses, Kennedys, or Frosts.
Stopping by a Virginia woods on a snowy evening,
don't look for white birches from which to swing.

In Virginia, you won't find rich, black soil,
only red-orange clay, capable of growing little more
than a Washington, Jefferson, Madison and
the most beautiful white pines in nature.

Spare me wintry New England. Give me, instead,
a warm afternoon among Virginia's pines.

Let me gaze at the soft, dark-green needles
and crusty, light-brown trunks and limbs.
Let me smell the resin sweetening the air,
sticking to my fingers when I touch the trees.

Let me feel the warm breeze as it stirs the boughs
and hear the "whooo" of the wind passing through.

Let me experience euphoria.

Though I, too, have miles to go
and promises to keep,
on the soft bed of needles
I lie down to sleep.

"AMONG VIRGINIA'S PINES" was originally published in *FIT TO PRINT: THE 1998 SAMPLER,* an anthology of the Valley Writers Chapter of the Virginia Writers Club (VWC), Roanoke, summer 1998, and later in *REFLECTIONS ON SMITH MOUNTAIN LAKE,* an anthology of the Lake Writers, a sub-group of the VWC and literary arts arm of the Smith Mountain Arts Council, 2015.

MAGICIANS AND POETS

James W. Morrison

Magicians are not to be trusted,
we are told, indeed, we know.
They are masters of illusion,
using smoke and mirrors,
slights of hand, ruses,
even magic words
to deceive us into
seeing images
that do not
exist in
reality.

Poets
are, to the
contrary, well-
intentioned, even
honest, so they say,
would have us believe.
They are dedicated, they
claim, to elevating our minds,
indeed, ennobling our very spirits.
But, they, also try to create images,
ones founded not on illusion, but allusion.
They work to capture our eyes, minds, hearts,
using words, meters, metaphors, and even rhymes,
                                    sometimes.
And why, if their motivations are so pure and fine, do they,
like magicians, take immense pride, when all is said and done,
                                    in keeping us guessing?

AUNT MAUDIE

Becky Mushko

Settling herself in a split-bottom chair
on the remnants of her front porch,
her hands weather-beaten as the porch rail
she grips to steady herself,
she leans forward. With age weighing
heavy on her like a winter shawl,
she says, "When you got land, you got something.
Clothes, fancy things—they don't last.
Husbands run off; children grow
up and away from you.
Land, it's always there."

Her land lies too close to town
To be much account for serious farming;
Not close in enough to fetch top dollar,
even if she'd consider selling.

A run-down trailer park leans so close
against her, she shuts her front door
in summer to keep out
the brassy voices of women
shrilling at drunken husbands
who drink to escape
the brassy voices.

Over the past seventy years,
what was her grandpa's five hundred acres
was chopped off, whittled down, doled out
to one heir or another: razor thin slices
like her grandma's smokehouse ham
served to hungry-eyed young'uns
til the plate was only a slice
away from being licked clean.

The one slice left is hers;
Unlike the others, she'd not been tempted
("Not by love nor money!" she brags)
to sell herself out.

"Well, I don't need much," she allows.
"I'll make do with enough for a garden plot
long as I can find somebody to come plow."

From under her sun-bonnet, she squints
Past other people's laundry flapping
on rusty clotheslines, and sees the farm
the way it was when she was a girl:
Traffic noise transforms
to lowing cows or clanking trace chains;
her spindly tomato plants
fighting each other for sun against the fence
become a crop spreading green
over too many acres
to look at all at once.

Every so often,
after a rain, she smells
the sweetness of wet earth,
new-plowed and waiting.

"You ain't got land," she says,
her voice rich with conviction,
"you ain't got nothin'."

THREE SIDES OF THE STETHOSCOPE

Jan Rayl

You, me and family makes three
Three sides of the stethoscope

I am the one in the bed
The Patient
The one that is scared and crying
I know it is my heart
I feel that beat, no wait did I feel something
I am gasping for breath
I feel the pain
I know I am fading, Dory am I dying?

I am the one beside you
The Nurse
Holding your hand while giving the medicine in your IV
Looking at the cardiac monitor
Knowing your rate is irregular and too fast
I saw the beat, I saw the skipped beat
I am fearless
I got this
No you are not dying it only feels like you are

I am by your bed, in the waiting room, on the other end of the
phone
The family, your friend
I don't know what is happening
Why is your heart rate all over the place
I hold my breath
I am scared
I hurt for you
I cry

I have been all of these I must remember
I have been the nurse
I have been the patient
I have been the daughter
I have been the friend
I have been the granddaughter

When I care for you in the bed
I am the nurse, I must remember there are more than two sides
of the stethoscope
I must recall how scared I was when I was in that bed
I still see Linda the Cardiac Nurse, she fixed my heart
I still hear Dory the EMT she assured me I was not dying

I must recall how exhausted and helpless I was as the family
When Grandma was in Hospice I was there
Brenda the aide gave me a hug and told me I was a wonderful
Granddaughter
She brought me tea as I sat with Mom for days holding Grand-
mas hands as she lie dying

When Mom was in Critical Care
JoJo the ICU Nurse came in and reminded me I am the daughter
not the nurse
All the while JoJo let me be the nurse and help turn my Mom
For me, the nurse daughter that was a gift JoJo gave me

Kelly the ICU Nurse was honest and said Mom was too unstable
to transfer but she would do her best to make her stable
Kelly was there when Mom was finally stable and the helicopter
for transfer came

Karen the nurse in the next ICU brought water, juice and snacks
for the family as I read the Bible to Mom for hours as she died.

These are my colleagues, my friends, they allowed me to be the
daughter
They allowed me to be a granddaughter
They allowed me to be the nurse
They allowed me to be the patient
They showed me there are more than two sides to the stetho-
scope

THE BALLAD OF THE HANGSTER'S WIFE
A Tale Which Might Be True *

Richard Raymond

Hangman, Hangman, slack your rope, slack it for a while—
I think I see my father comin', ridin' many a mile.
O Father, have you brought me gold, to pay my hangin'-fee?"
O no, I've come to see you hang upon the gallows-tree."
-- Old ballad

There was a lass in Tennessee, and she was far from fair,
Few lovers came to call on her, she gave them all the air.
The years went by, her Ma did cry, O Ellie, won't you wed?
But no, said she, for all these boys, I'd be a nun instead.

At last there came a bonny lad, who pressed her for her hand,
(Though what he mought have seen in her she'd never understand),
They married, and she served him true, yet doubting all the while,
loved her, and their children two, he wore a charming smile.

A county Sheriff Albert was, who kept the county jail,
But when lung-sickness took his life, her heart ne'er ceased to wail.
Depression sickened all the land, and larders went for bare,
How to support her fine strong boys? She wept, and prayed a
prayer.

For there stood Ellie, widowed now, with children to be fed—
She begged to serve the Sheriff's term, to function in his stead.
The council then appointed her, and deputies obeyed
This fragile woman with a badge, so seeming-unafraid.

Now in that town there lived a wife, and Celia was her name,
As a young maid she'd laughed and played the old Dumb-Supper
game,

With seven friends set out a meal, who'd see their husbands first?
(For superstitious mountain folk, it seemed a thing accurst.)

In time she wed, despite her dread, a painter fine was he,
Yet little fortune came their way, they lived in poverty.

Till on the mountain, one cold day, she posed for photograph--
He pushed her down, a thousand feet, and gave a horrid laugh.

Not long before the Sheriff came, to cast him into jail,
No lawyer would take up his case, and none to make his bail—
Two witnesses had seen the deed, no use for him to lie,
The trial lasted but a day, he was condemned to die.

But O! what mournful duty weighed on Ellie's kindly soul—
None but the Sheriff was obliged to fill a hangman's role,
Then carpenters, with plank and nail, they built a scaffold high,
While Ellie greased the hanging-rope by which he was to die.

The dark day dawned, as set by law, and folk from far and near
Arrived in hundreds, some to weep, and some (alas!) to cheer.
Out of the jail, with pastor first, the small procession went,
Deputies round the prisoner, a rescue to prevent.

The trap was tested, while the rope swung gently to and fro,
A prayer was said, upon his head a black hood was to go,
And as the village clock rang nine, a firm hand sprung the trap—
Down Lonnie fell, clear as the bell they heard his neck-bone snap!

But Ellie stood, as carved in wood—she had not moved a mite—
A *deputy* had done the deed, to spare her from that sight!
A sigh of long-held breath went up from the surrounding crowd,
But Ellie said, "Be sure he's dead. At least *that* law's allowed."

Thus Ellie Robbins stands alone—one woman in that state
To do the task which otherwise had fallen to her mate,
Yet ever, on some stormy nights, with thunder overhead,
She'd wake and wonder, Can it be that he's not truly dead?

6-2-16

* In *Prayers the Devil Answers,* her fictionalized version of this tale,
the noted Appalachian author Sharyn McCrumb explores the state of mind of
Ellie Robbins, a woman faced with a grim task, but strong in a sense of duty.

LOUISIANA SWAMPWATER

Sara Robinson

When you are born, you are old enough
to drink in Louisiana. You don't need
your momma's milk when you can drink
distilled spirits down by the bayou.

Your Momma rubs your teeth with kudzu
and wraps you in Spanish moss where
you learn how red bugs bite.

You can take your hot sauces and pour
them liberally over crawfish before you
can walk. The small bottles fit perfectly
in toddlers' hands. Get those fingers
gripping at an early age will fend off

the arthritis, don't you know. It is
impossible to pass up alcohol in this
strategically located gulf state. Anything
that ends in -ol can be found on

land and in the air. It's a legacy
to come into the world from a
state where one can drink so young.

You have to get a head start, build
up your tolerance levels, get the
internal organs prepped to receive
those holy spirits. It's the alcohol,
baby. The hot sauce is simply

the chaser. Everything else
in the swamps is collateral damage.

SENJARAY, AFGHANISTAN

Sara Robinson

The book, found, dusty and torn
still had its pages intact.
Leftover from the old library
it would start the new one.
Pages as seeds for a new oasis for ideas.

A school closed for years had a chance to open for the winter.
The fighting groups battled tough through a hot summer-the violent season.
Grenades that had found young bodies and abandoned houses were silent.
The school's role as fortress was finished-walls rested with secrets and bullets.

Daily threats of mortars and small arms attacks kept parents and neighbors panicked.
Children, dimmed and desperate, fought everyone as enemy.
They used guns too big to handle, too heavy to aim, but it didn't matter.
Their chests absorbed blasts and kicks—killed by those that knowledge threatens.

They have barely the winter to get the school back in order.
Teachers will come, the leader said. I have money and can pay them
to live right here, where they will teach our own.
Our village will have smart kids to fight the enemy with stealth and tactics.

Back along a shattered wall, shelves leaning but in place,
a soldier put the found book on its side next to a dented helmet.
Using his blood-stained scarf, he gave a gentle wipe to the cover.

War and Peace

At last, somewhere it might be read.

THE EYEBALL STEALERS

Victor Rook

It lurks on streets and inside cars
On sunny beaches and darkened bars
From the U.S. to France and Pakistan
It will find its home on any land

It sneaks inside women's purses
When it's found it often curses
With shrilling sounds or rippling beats
Just some ways in which it greets

You cannot move once it's seen
Your eyes affix upon its screen
No one near can break the spell
For they are often trapped as well

It preys upon your lonely life
To mask out all your daily strife
And swallows up your idle time
For this is part of its design

To make you laugh or form a grin
Though it's the one that scores the win
When people near take second place
To the eyeball stealers in your face

The conversations you once knew
Swapped for this attention glue
Replaced with games and spitting text
Who knows what will suffer next

Books and art have been sucked in
Music, too, now fills its bin
A giant mouth consumes it all
To keep you hooked and at a stall
No need to explore or walk about
To greet the land with a shout
To mingle with your human kind
And share what's on your open mind

For it is closed by the stealers
Trapped within their many feelers
Wrapping you so very tight
Freeing will take all your might

But they do bear an Achilles heel
When they no longer blindly steal
For once discharged they're mostly dead
And you can remove them from your head

A TRUTH

Richard L. Rose

Immense in a tiny back yard
the oak with its terrifying crown
a frozen dance of dryad arms
slowly shakes everything in reach.
What is this tangle, this individual?
A record of its own life in splay
of paths, spray of leaves
thrown out in all directions,
raking the sky, here is proof
being centered is untroubled travel,
unlike the pinched face beneath it
of the house with stained roof
which suffers from the idea
it is alone and cannot move.

LUCRETIUS

Richard L. Rose

So, did the costume of that gospel we are bit
players battered, blown, and always losing something
that we may later need become a creed too tight
fitting, like all uniforms, though, fear of hell
dispelled, the gods and death itself were shown the exit?

You, who portrayed your holy book, interpreted
stagecraft, lined out scenes, and wrapped the universe
in one scheme, cutting even into love's sloughed image,
you could not take poison, potion, or position
conditioned on delusion. You had too clear a head.

This stage, this world's the pattern we inhabit, so
careless in our play of wills that we've forgotten
the plotting has been done, ourselves the consequence.
Dissolution waits. We try on hope, convince
ourselves, and relish, if we're wise, that we can know.

DRIVING THE BLUE RIDGE IN OCTOBER

Ann Skelton

Morning light plays in the forest.
All is quiet.
Bouquets of trees wave at my passing
Showing off.
A canopy ablaze with leaves of red of orange of palest green.

Rolls of hay, giant and motionless, testify:
Harvest is in.
Everywhere I turn beauty pierces my heart.

Time is passing.

Not again shall I know the joy of first things:
Plunging fearful into a rocky river,
My first dance.
Never again, moments of motherhood so fleeting.

Memory assails my heart.

Once I had a boy-child I sang to sleep at night.
Once I had a girl-child twirling in my flowing skirts.
Once I had a child who held my hand so tight.
Once, and again, they come to me in sleep.
No need for mother's comfort now.

Time is passing.

Blue Ridge autumn stirs memories.
Long ago we read before a fire.
We hoped for news that school would close
And then we built a snowman and his snowdog.
And after, wrapped in blankets on the couch to read aloud.

Would a Greek chorus lament for me?
That time together, when I was Mother.
Who will grieve October in a Mother's heart?

Time past.

A MILLION STARS

Ann Skelton

The past outruns me.
Hunts me down all unsuspecting
Summons hidden moments, still alive.

'Enjoy your children' my prophet-mother said,
'While you can. While they're young.'
What does that mean?
How does one?
What should I feel?
When is there time?

Surely she meant, 'love them more.'
Does she know about the times I failed?
Allowed hurt in their paths.
Saw them wince from pain.
Pushed them crying from my bed.

Or did she foresee a moment?
Prophets do, you know,
When all alone with one dear babe,
Blanketed together against the night
We looked over the mountain
And there -- above us in the silent dark
We saw a million stars.

A SENSE OF PLACE

Ann Skelton

I thought it was the house I loved
Surrounded by sweet clover in the spring.
Cherry trees bloomed on my birthday,
A perfect gift
Before their day-long shower of pink.

Then bleeding hearts demanded thought,
Delicate but magnificent red in their blooming
The fireplace, too -- after snowfalls,
The deer who once birthed her young in my woods
That expanse of green and giant trees fixed in memory.
Birthdays happened there and dogs scouted for bits of cake.

I mourned the house and the moments left behind
Until, oh yes, I saw it was the swing I missed.
Its long rope flung over a burly oak limb.
Much tested for the slightest hint of danger.

Yes. Yes, it was the swing imbued with laughter.
Sheepdog barking after flying feet.
"Hold on,"
"Go higher, once more, please."
"My turn!"
Oh yes, the swing carried all the smiling faces.

We left it behind,
Hanging motionless from the oak.
We left my bleeding hearts as well.
But then, we brought the laughter with us.

TRAIL OF TEARS*
(A Rannaigheacht Ghairid)

Elizabeth Spencer Spragins

Fairy stones**
Mark the graveless broken bones
Deep beneath the Trail of Tears.
Splintered spears and ghosts of crones

Cannot hold
Ancestral lands veined with gold.
Driven west through snow and mire,
People of the Fire grow cold.

Lullabies
Cannot soothe the hungry cries
Of babes in the arms of death—
One last breath breaks earthly ties.

Spirits roam,
Searching for blue hills of home.

Keepers of the sacred flame

Cannot tame the dark at gloam.***

Priest intones
Prayers for wounded earth that groans.
In dark shafts no gold appears—
Crystal tears yield fairy stones.

~Fairy Stone State Park, Stuart, Virginia
*The discovery of gold in Dahlonega, Georgia, generated a flood
of prospectors eager to mine the land populated by the Cherokee.
The United States Army forcibly removed the Cherokee Nation
from its ancestral territory over the years 1838-1839. According to
some estimates, approximately 4000 of the 16,000 Cherokee died
on the westward march they call the "Trail of Tears."
**Staurolite crystals that form a distinctive cross.

***An archaic term for twilight.

EMERGE

Sofia M. Starnes

At times this brings a stork, past rains, abandoning
a tower; at times a bubble dying
in a pond. I hear the word *emerge* and see a fern

or a feather; the first one wild and wispy,
to cure a wound, the role of ancient grasses; the other,
trail of a bird, slim fan or lady's purse—

the kind fairy tales gather.
Does not your heart, weary from things apparent,
ask what each storyline will tell,

which words carry their roots with candor?
Secrets would hunker down, safe in their winter castles,
were it not—

for the prophetic stem, weighty with beans
that rides its pole for air, for what we sense of seeds,
soft inches down, fussing our veins awake,

for every bone that pulls the body alert, to learn
its fragile face. But what about our hands,
the ones we excuse from light, deep in our pockets?

With chambers dark, I think, the dark is change, is key.

From *The Consequence of Moonlight*, Paraclete Press (forthcoming);
first published in *The William and Mary Review*, 2015

THE MONUMENT RESTORER

Sofia M. Starnes

Between storms,
an obelisk, a man, and the oils
of a late sun, streaming. He toils
away in the heart-cavity
of a field. A yard or so

from our ankles,
he soft-brushes the dead.
Lion-mane, luminous head;
hands, bristly as paws, tease up
the earth: five years in still

company.
They're everywhere—
foot over flat foot, hair
wisp on hair, shoe buckle and
loosed linen: Sheol, Sheol.

Lord, how we bury, bless,
commend them to oak groans
and wonder: the universe owns.
Could it be otherwise?
We, swallowing the world, it

and the withering stars,
the carbon dissolution of a place
so intended. Once out of the race—
we, with a brush on the bricks,
leveling ages.
Sweethearts and weeds,
the man and his broom,
the obelisk and the small room
under, where no one lies,
sleeps, waits. I'd swear

a lost locket appears simply
from loving—gold in the crook

of his arm where dusk leaks. Look!
Full are the man and the field,
full are we under the sun.

From *Fully Into Ashes*, Wings Press, 2011; first published in *The Southern Poetry Review*, 2002

THE SOUL'S LANDSCAPE

Sofia M. Starnes

Ah, what the soul gives for shape –
    to be handled head-first
at the temple, to be cumbered
    with cotton, white puffs

from plantations in heat; what it gives,
    for the flick, flick elastic
on wrists, loose-leaf palms it befriends,
    at its youngest – for the sake

of all this, and this place.
    Love me now with your
hands (says the soul, half-exploring its
    landscape), better me

with embodiment; come, angle the ribs
    where they beach into
longing; come, finger the oval description
    of death, smallest hope

for cessation. When the room is redundant
    of space, and its walls
wish for closure, thumb my corners
    up, inward, wade your lips

through the ridge where they meet,
    to allow recollection.
I must love with the tissue and the gloss
    that embody: cellule, elegy,

ghost, danger, languish... all those words
    out of context for souls,
god-forsaken, whiplash of the neck –
Interim

that's the word I would use the most
cautiously; how precarious
its hum, ear to earth, plumbing earth,
earthwise.

From *A Commerce of Moments*, Pavement Saw Press, 2003; first published in *The Pavement Saw Literary Journal*, 2001

STILL THEY RISE

William E. Sypher

To my Creative Writing class, Muscat, Oman,
(with Apologies to Maya Angelou's "Still I Rise")

"Sir, we're lost.
We need examples.
Must it rhyme?
Have a certain meter to a line?"

I'd heard it all before,
the little lamb refrain.
Oh, they were bleating,
"Is it good
to have a line repeating?"
I could see it
in their anxious eyes.
Could they rise?

So I gave it out, reluctant,
gave them "Still I Rise."
Only meant to be a model,
illustrating a refrain,
could they rise above it?
Could they rise?

Maya showed
the sway of repetition
bound with hurt, with inspiration.
I chose it only as example,
not a meal, just a sample.
Not quite unleavened bread,
just slightly yeasty,
Could they rise?

Yes, I knew the perils:
model morphs to rigid mold
into which they'd pour their thoughts
like muffin batter and out they'd come
too close to Maya's:

hot and golden, butterscotch.

Oh lord, she had them
in her grasp.
I should have known.
I've reaped clichés
from what I've sown:
refrain too potent to dismiss.
It showed up in their eyes,
on their pages, in their lines,
Maya's muse far too compelling.
Should I now resort to yelling
or simply stop to realize:
some works transcend their telling.

Now the class has ended.
Outside, a half-baked chorus
floats warmly down the hall.
They bask in borrowed brilliance.
You can see it in their eyes.
"We rise, sir. We rise."

BALKAN BEES AT WAR

William E. Sypher

The war to oust Milosovic ended
long ago, but for a year or more
strife still ruled the Balkans.
Beehives were war-torn,
still noisy, as expected,
but not a vintage year for honey
that year in Macedonia.

Buzzing work songs in the hives
calm bees who, after all,
live limited lives.
Not so, the buzzing in the skies--
the din of Allied warplanes
had rankled bee digestion
and crimped production.
Balkan bees were under stress.

NATO bombs were dropped
to crush the Serbian war machine
not to rile the bees and
stanch the fragrant flow of honey.
But, as is the way of modern man,
the keepers of the combs
sought compensation:
the strangest claim of collateral damage
ever entered in the books of war.

More than the flow of honey was at stake.
Just as bombs can madden men
and push them to aggression,
shrieking warplanes roiled bees
and triggered biting frenzies.
But vengeful bees could not sting
their long gone aerial tormenters;
who'd' flown back home to safety.
No, bees were targeting civilians.
and that might draw the interest
of The Hague War Crimes Tribunal.

Indeed, the honey enterprise is strange:
bees make food to feed their young
then forfeit it to men in netted masks
who steal it in a cloud of smoke:
micro- fogs of war.
Imagine if it were reversed:
if bees stole baby food from men,
stripped baby pantries bare—
we'ed be up in arms.

Soft, sweet human thieves,
you're spared such raids.
It's not in the genome plan. You see,
bees know well our tastes and theirs
and scorn our baby food as bland,
the way our babies do.

SUCCESS REDEFINED

Larry Turner

As starting physicist I was so wise.
I thought my Nobel Prize as good as won.
But now I'm satisfied to realize
I did some things nobody else had done.

Upon the poets' ladder, where's my rung?
I've always been obsessed by where I stand.
But I am now content to be among
The million finest poets in the land.

My goals have changed, and at this point I ask:
As a father, how high is my score?
I do not want the world to rate this task.
To me the judgment of my sons means more.

Moreover as a husband I'll not grouse,
If I have the approval of my spouse

DISORIENTED:
A sonnet

Rodney Vanderhoof

My hope goes 'way in murky black of night,
I tremble now at many words I said.
I brood on how to make my conflict right,
and hate the horrid spin within my head.

I dread my nightly fear of aimless death,
of frantic terror lurking just behind.
I struggle hard to gain my final breath,
to heal the gray cells of an angry mind.

Ahead, I see blue sky devoid of strife,
a time to speak above the madding crowd—
a springtime verse to reconnect with life,
a voice to claim, to shout, and cry aloud,

to rise and soar atop the vicious wrath,
a chance to guide, through hordes, a clear-cut path.

COMMENDATION

Erin Newton Wells

These wrist bones I commend
to the placidity of morning

when they are rested from the night
and move liquidly again.

And I commend them to the air
which moves back in surprise

to say, *Ah! It is you. I thought
you were gone.*

And to the water which warms them
and lets them delight in lyric,

each small plate sliding in unison
and equilibrium,

I say, Alleluia, mother of bones,
renewer of melodies.

I say, Bring these bones into the kingdom
they dreamed last night,

the mountain with its head
hidden in a cloud.

Let them ascend and know it
and rejoice.

And let them clap there
forever.

("Commendation" originally published in *The Sow's Ear Poetry Reveiw*, Vol. XXVI, No. 2, Summer, 2016, and a finalist in the *Sow's Ear* Poetry Contest 2015.)

DANCE

Erin Newton Wells

You again. It's only you
making a sloppy rhythm on the shore
where the sand is immigrant. Who knows

where it comes from? Every color
of the world is here in particles. Waves
scrape into the ribs of cliffs, the flanks of bays.

I want, is what they say.
I want. And you always return,
bringing no tune but the tune of the surf,

its crash and roll, the hollow
suck drawn back into its underworld.
Who knows how deep it goes or if it wanders?

Your footprints slur
and will not hold a shape in the sand.
They slide into the dance but lose the steps.

You are made of these minerals.
Each time you come up from the sea,
it wants you back.

("Dance" originally published in *Poetry South*, 2015.)

AFIRE

Judy Whitehill Witt

In Cleveland
the Cuyahoga River
was frequently afire
from the city's ooze.
I never understood
how they could quench
a flaming river
with water

or in a classroom
how a smug *Of course,*
you're damned to Hell
could be spitballed
at the lone Jewish boy
by a guaranteed Christian
hot with righteous zeal
and the knife be met
with numb silence
of both the damned lamb
and the dazed flock.

They'll need
Cleveland's firemen
in that Heaven

END OF DAYS

Sally Zakariya

Cheerleaders for the end times
dressing in bright satin in the ladies' room
they come out twirling batons
    banners studded with strange symbols
revving up for revelation

We're hustled out the cafeteria door
before the fun begins, wondering
    at the spectacle to come
not for us the ecstasy, the devotion
    the altered states of angels

Handmaidens they call themselves
not a word I'd use now
    or on the last day

On that day let me be an eagle
or a mourning dove – I'll want the wings

Let the handmaids dance on the day
earth cracks open, spews hellfire and damned souls
    back into the universe

What will their banners and batons
avail them then

"End of Days" originally published in published in *Poetry Quarterly*,
Winter 2015

GRANDFATHER'S BED

Sally Zakariya

The owl looks down from the headboard,
keeping watch as I sleep on the walnut bed
my grandfather slept in.

No, not really an owl, just fanciful swoops
and swirls of Victorian carving – still
sometimes I see two wise wooden eyes
trained steadily on me.

I never met grandfather. He died young
when appendicitis grabbed him in the
Maine woods and wouldn't let go.

I like to think that somewhere in the trees
an owl was watching him, silently sharing
a deep understanding of the natural
end of things.Grandfather's Bed
Sally Zakariya

The owl looks down from the headboard,
keeping watch as I sleep on the walnut bed
my grandfather slept in.

No, not really an owl, just fanciful swoops
and swirls of Victorian carving – still
sometimes I see two wise wooden eyes
trained steadily on me.
I never met grandfather. He died young
when appendicitis grabbed him in the
Maine woods and wouldn't let go.

I like to think that somewhere in the trees
an owl was watching him, silently sharing
a deep understanding of the natural
end of things.

Non-Fiction

§

TABLE OF CONTENTS

NICU

Judy Light Ayyildiz

1 AM, Sunday, 7/6, 1986

I am still awake. Half of me can't move. Trapped in this bed, I stare up at spider-web cracks in the plaster, splintered lines like strings of nerves.

An eerie violence creeps through my body. A guerrilla army has ambushed, captured my nerve-system. The doctors mention blood plasma transplant. Then say they're not sure it helps. Would my blood be removed, altered, and put back? They speak in calm, professional voices so I'll feel safe. Like when Dr. Miller brought up respiratory failure. Heart and lungs use muscles, too. He's ready to put me on a respirator. What if I get to where I can't breathe? Is this paralysis permanent? If it gets worse, will I be able to talk? Could I go into a coma? Die?

Thirty-nine hours ago I walked up the hill to my house. Fourth of July fireworks shattered against the night sky. Less than a day later I'm hooked to machines. The one time it would be handy to have a husband who is a doctor, he's out of the country.

The guy in the bed on the right side of me is almost gone. I hear their voices while they work on his body: "Had a stroke two weeks ago. No change yet." Whispering, as if he could hear. He and the woman on the other side of me don't ever wake. I don't sleep. I can't raise up. My brain is juiced up. Like these florescent lights that stay on all the time. My mind jumps from one image to the next like some high-energy drug propels my thoughts, though they haven't even given me an aspirin.

The wall clock rules this space. Calls the doctor, regulates the nurses' methodical brush from beds, to desk, to door, floating white caps checking our radiant vital signs, angels with charts. A gray-haired nurse has worked evening into night on the old man. Up-dating, mixing, injecting measured units of hope. When he inhales, it's a wobbling tone, a bass violin being tuned. His exhales whap. String breaks. He drones on and on.

The woman's jaw flutters when she breathes. Gives me the willies. From the desk I heard, "... and brain tumor." I eavesdrop on their pity. They can't operate. Her feathery rasp could be a bat flapping out of a cave. Must always be night wherever she is. If she's having an out-of-the-body experience, she knows I'm spying.

I must stay conscious. This paralysis moved in on me last night while I slept. My legs seem attached to my torso like dead-weight, rolls of sausage. My toes tent the sheets like a pyramid.

Yesterday, my thirteen-year-old Karen stood in the driveway when the attendant wheeled me to the ambulance. Her eyes, wide as a spooked cat. Looked like an abandoned waif the way her jaw was clinched, and one arm was holding the other. I was leaning back off the litter as they carted me away telling her not to worry, I'd be fine.

I hear the rustling of Linda's starched uniform before I see her. Black curls trickle from her cap. Cherry lipstick shines. Lips pucker like some Forties' movie star. She hums, "Amazing Grace." Linda sees me staring and stops mid-song, casually pulling her hands behind her back. I note the yellow blotch on her lapel that was not there thirty minutes ago and guess she had a sandwich with mustard. She smiles, studies the monitor, and then looks down at me. "Hi," she says. I mumble back.

"Who are you, my friend?" she asks. I take a deep breath. They know who I am. I scrunch my lips like hers then answer, "Judy."

"Where are you?" She shakes a finger. I cross my arms, carefully. The pull of the IV throbs. She waits.

"OK, Judy." I am judging her restraint. The same round of questioning, every half hour since five o'clock last evening. "We have to chart your physical and mental responses," she repeats.

I give up. "I'm in the NICU, University Medical Center, Charlottesville, Virginia."

I like Linda. We've talked. We're both from West Virginia. She adjusts my pillow. "Do you know what day it is?"

Green-eyed Sally brings me the bedpan. She never stops chattering with the two interns, who rattle off questions to me while they once again probe and tap my arms and legs. The three of them lift me like a piece of furniture, slide the porcelain pan under my butt, and pull the sheet back up to my neck. My toilet. Then, as if it is an outhouse with a door and sides, they stand waiting and talking as if I am not even here.

The hefty intern is asking Sally a question. "Did you try that new pineapple cheesecake down at the snack bar?" Green-eyes licks her lips. "It's fantastic!"

Now, the shapely female intern wants to know, "Is it real or frozen?"

We could be at a bus stop. I don't know where to look. Am I supposed to be a part of the group or invisible? I close my eyes and pretend I am a telephone pole. I can't tell if anything is doing until the odor mingles with astringents and talcum.

The lower half of me seems as if it's vanished, except for a deep heaviness. My legs are cool concrete. But I could feel that burning cold of the bedpan rim.

Beyond the pea green tent over my toes, 1:30 AM glares from the black-clawed clock. I shut my eyes, and the clock leers from behind my lids. Time feels suspended, but those claws move from digit to digit, number and number, every second a nervous twitch, round and round. If I had a rubber arm, I could stop that clock.

Will I see my kids again? My husband, my mother?

Don't begin imagining Mother seeing me here.

Closing my eyes again, I force myself to see phosphorescent colors encircling my toes, blue-green energy spiraling my legs, curling up until I'm cocooned in colors and healing lights. I imagine gathering hundreds of sparkles of golds and greens and sucking them to my lungs. The sparkles are healing energy, flashing warriors now charging throughout my system.

It must be time for my husband to board his plane back from Istanbul. And he hasn't a clue what's going on with me. I'm glad I wouldn't let them call him. What could he do but worry the whole flight home?

Two weeks ago, Karen and I were on our way to California. Our mother-daughter adventure. Not that it turned out that well. I expected too much. Yeah, so I didn't plan it quite right, like the ritzy hotel in San Diego when we should have taken one on the beach where she would have met some teen types. Maybe we should have gone to Turkey with her father, after all. But what if I had awakened paralyzed in some Anatolian village? If the doctors at this university center know so little about my condition, what would doctors know on the Asian plains?

Time holds the answers. Negative draws negative. Focus on positive. When you're in a dark place, look up. *It's always darkest before the dawn.* Now, I'm really in a pit. The NICU. The nurse said that most patients in here rarely care how long the night gets, said my talking is a novelty.

I strain to listen past the doorway. The hallways out there are a tunneled maze. Every so often, I hear laughter. It seems to flare up like a whirlwind. The maze must be full of cackles and croons and clangs. Stainless steel instruments against the tile would toll like a bell. All over this hospital, machines gasp and sputter. Sudden legs race to keep up with the clock. Blithe spirits in white cotton soft-sole shuffle back and forth on their trained feet. And people stand and walk off without having to think of telling their legs to move, their legs carrying their bodies like magic.

I can't believe I'm here. Yesterday afternoon the ambulance rushed up the Interstate from Roanoke to Charlottesville. Then, I was on the litter in a corner of the emergency room somewhere downstairs.

The old nurse pattered up to me. She looked burnt-out, probably from years of overwork. She methodically took my pulse and temperature, jotted it on scrap paper and pinned it to my pillow with a safety pin.

"What's your problem?"

"Don't know, just can't move my legs."

She looked at me a few seconds. "Did you fall?"

"No."

She took a step back. "Well, did you lift something? Do you have any pain?"

When I said, "Not really," she must have decided I wasn't urgent. I saw the look. How many times I've heard a nurse or doctor's story about hypochondriac patients. I felt baffled and a bit embarrassed about my whole situation.

"Stay put, and we'll get to you soon as we can." She nodded, and then shunted off down the hall toward some commotion.

I was there for an hour. I suppose my chart got laid aside or overlooked in the circus of stab wounds and overdoses. I just lay there like a dummy, not making a fuss. There seemed to be so many coming in down the hall that were really sick.

My nurses bathe and dress me skillfully as undertakers. When they're bored, I get massaged. Since I can't sit, they fluff my linens, feed me broth. I tell jokes, anything to distract, tales about my childhood, my three kids, can't seem to stop talking, whether aloud or in my mind. Can't let myself fall into the black hole. I got paralyzed in my sleep.

Linda is patting my arm. I smile back like she is right. "...even though you tell a lot of stories—" Is she hinting that my stories are getting on her nerves? The IV aches like an impacted tooth. I make a fist with the other hand, raise my arm and bend my elbow. "My arms are still working fine, see?"

"I see, and, yes, you look good. Anything you need?"

I could give Linda a list, but I answer her in a nice southern voice. "Not a thing right at this moment."

"Fine and dandy." Linda turns, takes three steps over to the white desk under the clock, writes on my chart, replaces the chart in its slot, and she's out the door.

OK, I'll just close my lids, won't go to sleep, will try to relax, do a dead man's float on a wide, placid river—going where, it doesn't matter. Scenes from the last three days begin to pass in my mind like a movie reel: Friday, almost two days ago, July 4th. I am bouncing around, shopping for furniture, fresh tomatoes, beans, and corn from the Farmers' Market. After I come home, I am cooking for the street party this evening, then climbing up into the attic over the garage to get the metal table for the picnic. Do I strain my back? No, no pain. I lug the table to the opening at the steps, lean against the railing, ease it over a bit, then step down backwards.

Is there an answer for me in that garage? Concentrate. Did I hurt my back when I carried that table down that ladder in the garage? My limbs are on the thin side. But they're wiry, strong. I learned back in West Virginia the proper way to lift heavy objects. When my boys were small I moved a piano out the front door of the house we lived in, around the hill and down to the rec. room. I was 120 pounds then, before my baby girl was born. The old man next door stood on the hill and watched me for the hour and half it took me to do it. Yard by yard, with rugs, ropes, and boards, I lugged that spinet around the house and in through the French doors at the back. I was determined to show my darling husband,

Vedi, I'd get that piano moved downstairs in spite of his saying we didn't need to have a moving company out, that the piano served as a perfectly good piece of furniture in the living room. But it was mine, and I wanted it to be where I wanted it to be. Nobody played it but me. He said, "Leave it until we can get a couch." I finally got it down the bank by using the big oak tree on the side as leverage. The old man had been standing all that time in his flower garden, watching. When I finished, he spoke. "Little girl, I never saw anything like that in my life. Must be because you are a redhead." People always think redheads are gutsy. If it's not that, it's the freckles. I tell them it's really because I'm an independent-minded Scotch-Irish poet. Seeing Vedi's surprised face that evening was worth the effort. More ways to skin a cat than one.

Rewind. Friday, yes, an active day with no signs of illness, not even throughout Friday evening as I climb the hill with neighbors to watch fireworks explode over Roanoke. All the neighborhood kids run ahead. We amble around the bend and up the grade. A breeze dries the sweat from my neck. On the knoll, we sip drinks. Celebrations. Wildflowers bursting above layers of purpled mountains. I sit, bathed in the artificial glow from below and the star shine overhead. It's cool and serene.

"Mom, can I spend the night with Missy?"

"Sure, Karen, if her mom says so."

"You don't mind staying alone tonight?"

"No, Honey. Go ahead. I'd best enjoy the quiet. Those two brothers of yours will be home from camping Monday."

"And Dad comes home Sunday, right?"

"Yes, Vedi will come with a trunk full of presents, maybe those exotic earrings."

"And lots of pictures of Turkish relatives."

Karen's reply had made me miss Vedi's mother, and I knew she would tuck a treasure for me into his luggage. But he'll be glad to get back. When he's in the States, memories of Istanbul take on a romantic luster. When he gets over there in Turkey, he longs for the Blue Ridge.

The clock says 3:45 AM. He'll land in eight hours. Life will get back to normal. When he phones home, they'll tell him where to find me.

5:45 AM.

Did I do something to make myself paralyzed? When Kevin and Kent were small, if they got hurt, I felt responsible. There's no reason I should feel guilty for being ill. Yet something nags at me, saying, "Oh yes, but you're always doing too much, never content. Now you've made yourself sick." That's Mother's voice. I can see Mother standing in some doorway with tears in her blue eyes, looking hurt and scared, having lived her whole life fearing the unknown and what the neighbors think. She stayed with Daddy all those years when he drank. Dad was the indisputable head. We didn't share personal feelings much and never let outsiders know what was going on inside. "You just have to get through hard times the best you can, then forget it," Mother said. She said that over and over. Yet, I've learned that not only do you have to dig up the past, you have to sort through it like an archeologist.

That moment two nights ago is stuck in my mind: 11:00 PM, after the fireworks, standing at my bedroom closet looking down at my tennis shoes, no socks. I didn't untie them but balanced on the right foot while my hand steadied against the wall as I pushed the heel with the toe of the left. My right foot pulled up, but the shoe seemed to want to suck it back. I kicked away the right shoe, then the left, paused to rub my soles against the carpet, and noticed a tingling on the bottoms of my feet, which I figured was from running around all day in tennis shoes.

Later, a dream: Exhausted me was trying to take an inventory of a huge warehouse but couldn't get my legs to move down the aisles fast enough, and I seemed to be running out of time. I awoke in a sweat, threw back the covers and sat on the side of the bed. 2:00 AM. Had to pee.

I stumbled, caught myself against the nightstand. My feet felt like they had gone to sleep. No wonder the dream. Went to the bathroom unsteadily, then back to bed.

Next, it was 6:00 AM. Slung first one leg then the other over the side of the bed. When I put my weight on my legs, I collapsed to the floor on top of my numb and heavy legs.

Shocked, I sat there with a pang of memory: my feet last night. What was going on? I rubbed my soles on the carpet, pinched my calves, then tried to get up by pulling on the mattress; but my legs wouldn't cooperate.

I crawled to the desk. My arms couldn't lift my body. I slipped, hit my shoulder. No strength in my lower legs. Impossible. Mind tricks? Nothing like this had ever happened to me. I had to get moving. Lying on my side, I lugged my hips and legs, elbows skinning against the carpet.

Finally, I was in the bathroom wrestling with the commode. No way could I pull my hips up onto the seat. After ten minutes, my belly was stretched across the top. I dangled, figuring how to turn over and straighten up. The water beneath my abdomen was cool, but I was stranded in my heaviness.

My hips thudded against the tile when I let my weight pull me from the commode. Anger, big tears, and a howl didn't help. I imagined amused powers watching me and yelled at them. "O.K., this is enough!" No response. "I won't give in. I have to go, but I will not pee on the floor!" The air sighed from the floor vents.

I hauled weight to the bathtub, grabbed the water spout with my right hand, and pushed against the side with the left until the top half of me was juggled onto the rim of the tub. I yanked at my right leg until it was up and over. Inch by inch, I lowered my body inside.

Pulling myself into sitting was easy, but turning to face the spout was another matter. My arms were cranes, lifting and positioning, first the left leg, then the right, as I pivoted on my tailbone. Grunting and heaving for breath, I wrenched my nightgown from under my butt, then rolled it and held it up with my chin while I turned on the water. Splashing my abdomen, I relieved my bladder. Maybe the water would revive me. When I shut off the water, I sat in a chill. My legs were still lifeless, and now my nightgown was wet. The thought of what it would take to get dressed was overwhelming.

My heart was racing. The clock by the sink told me a whole hour had gone by. I dug back out over the tub, letting upper torso pull the lower. Yanking a towel from a rung on the wall, I dried off, taking account of the sore places on my body. They would be bruises. My elbows were near bleeding. When I saw that the skin on the top of my feet was scraped raw, a realization creamed over me: I hadn't been feeling the damage to my feet. Sitting there in a damp nightgown pondering wouldn't solve anything. Move!

Scrunching and wiggling like a snail got me to the bedroom.

The waterbed stretched before me like a plateau that I desperately wanted. Back in bed, I could figure out how to handle this attack of whatever it was. The challenge was to get up there.

I grabbed the bottom of the desk chair and tugged it to the bed, then pulled and heaved until my torso was belly-down across its armless seat. I rolled over onto the bobbing bed. The warm softness of the covers soaked my skin like lotion.

Thoughts had to get organized, self, gotten together. There had to be some way for me to comprehend this nonsense. Calm, I had to steady my breathing, steadily, like I was pulling a cord to slow a train. I concentrated on an image of a peaceful surface, a mountain lake shimmering in a coral sunset, where I forced myself to glide into the center. The engine in my chest slowed.

Gradually the reality of my situation came clear: <u>paralysis</u>. My body went to sleep last night, and my legs didn't wake up. *Oh, my dear spirit, help my body.*

I opened my eyes.

Excerpt from: NICU, Chapter 1, from memoir, *Nothing but Time*. Originally published by Xlibris Corporation, Copyright 2000 Judy Light Ayyildiz

FIRST ENCOUNTER

John D. Broadwater

I twist my body to peer through the tiny viewport. The cobalt blue Gulf Stream water darkens to ever-deeper shades as we descend toward the sea floor. Huddled in a cramped aluminum cylinder, I'm struggling to control my fear of close spaces. I have to stay focused, because I am sealed in the dive chamber of the *Johnson-Sea-Link*, an incredible research submersible that can reach depths of 1,000 feet. Even though we aren't going nearly that deep, my claustrophobia leapt out as soon as the hatch closed.

Across the chamber, my dive tender, Don Liberatore, is concentrating on the sub's gauges, digital numbers, and lights, but I know he's also keeping a close eye on me. Don will make sure I don't get into trouble today, since this will be my first deep sub dive. He is an experienced research diver with the Harbor Branch Foundation, the Florida-based oceanographic institution that designed, built, and operates this sub. Don clearly senses my apprehension, gives me a confident grin and quips, "Well, you're finally going to see her, John."

I grin back, because that's the reason I'm willing to stuff myself into this little dive chamber, which I described to my friends as "a 55-gallon drum with a hatch." I'm getting ready to dive on the famous Civil War ironclad USS *Monitor*. As a boy, I built a plastic model of it; as an archaeologist I searched for it, and in 1974 I helped produce a mosaic photograph of its remains. Now, five years later, I am one of a small team of archaeologists and research divers that will explore it in person, 240 feet below, sixteen miles offshore of Cape Hatteras, North Carolina.

"Bottom in sight," reports Roger Cook from the pilot sphere forward of us. Roger is Harbor Branch's mission director and our sub pilot.

"Bottom in sight," Don responds into his headset.

A flash of light catches my eye, and I see a large fish just outside the viewport.

"There's the amberjacks," Don says, "The *Monitor* must be pretty close." Apparently, the jacks hear the sub's thruster motors and see its floodlights, so they've ventured out from the wreck to see who's come to visit.

"Wreck in sight," Roger calls out, right on cue.

"Roger, wreck in sight," Don acknowledges. "Better get ready, John."

High-pitched whirring sounds from the thrusters signal us that Roger is crabbing the sub into the current, which almost always flows over the wreck. Another sound, higher in pitch and longer in duration, reverberates off the chamber walls. From our training dives, I know that's the sub communicating with the mother ship on the surface through hydrophones. It's Roger reporting our status to the mission coordinator on the bridge.

As I zip up my wet suit jacket, Don taps me on the shoulder and points out the starboard viewport. At first I can't see anything, but as I lean closer to the port I detect a dark shape. As the sub moves forward the shape materializes into a recognizable image: it's *Monitor*'s bow. The unique circular anchor well is clearly visible, and I can see anchor chain draped over the side of the armor belt and disappearing into the sand.

A slender vertical shape comes into view; it's the plastic pipe that our archaeological director, Gordon Watts, installed yesterday. My job is to complete the installation of two more reference pipes, one near the turret and one at the bow. Our goal is to install a row of four survey pipes, parallel to *Monitor*'s hull, which we will use for mapping the wreck.

Roger expertly settles the sub onto the seabed near *Monitor*'s port side, in the lee of the Gulf Stream's flow. "On bottom."

Don acknowledges, and Roger reports poor visibility, only 20-30 feet, adding that the sub is positioned near *Monitor*'s amidships bulkhead, facing the turret. Gordon thoroughly briefed me on my assignment, and I understand exactly what I am to do. I'm just a bit apprehensive—I've been this deep before, just never with all this equipment and all the procedures associated with diving from a submersible.

Don undogs the exit hatch, which is being held tightly in place by the outside water pressure. Next he carefully checks all my equipment and asks if I'm ready. Trying to appear confident, I muster a firm "roger." With that, Don opens a valve. A hissing roar fills the chamber as a mixture of helium and oxygen gasses rushes in from a storage tank, raising the pressure inside the chamber. I can feel the pressure on my eardrums, reminding me that I need to pinch my nose and blow forcefully to balance the pressure on both sides of my eardrums. The medical term is the "Valsalva maneuver," but most divers call it "equalizing."

Don calls out, "Fifty feet," but his voice is two octaves higher. A combination of increasing pressure and the helium in our breathing gas makes him sound like Alvin the chipmunk. He's giving me the "okay" signal, which I return to indicate that he can keep pressurizing the chamber. Pulling on my band mask—which covers my whole face and includes a gas regulator and communications gear—I hear Don calls out "Hatch open."

Sure enough, I look down, and I'm staring at the Atlantic Ocean! The pressure inside has reached the same as that outside, letting the hatch drop open. I know that's how it works, of course, but somehow it seems more dramatic now that we're in such deep water.

I tighten the straps on my band mask and take a breath. The regulator's hiss is followed by a comforting inrush of cool gas. My squeaky "Comms check" comes across as a real surprise. During our training dives we didn't breathe helium, so it's the first time I've sounded like one of the chipmunks.

After sliding my feet down through the hatch I get one last checkout from Don. He gives me a shoulder tap, and I hear him report, "Diver leaving the sub." I push myself down and onto the seabed. I'm out. I crawl out from beneath the sub and stand up next to the armor belt. I'm seeing everything in deep shades of blue. I turn to face the pilot sphere, a thick acrylic bubble that gives the two people inside a panoramic view of the scene. I give them an "okay" sign, then pull the water hose off the sub and start walking (we don't wear fins on this project). Don feeds my umbilical out through the hatch and asks if I'm okay. I reply, "okay." I am. In fact, I'm very excited to finally be here. Walking aft, following the armor belt and the guide rope that Gordon set in place yesterday, I pass the first plastic pipe. Ahead I can barely see the faint shape of the pipe I am assigned to install.

I reach the pipe, a ten-foot-long section of white, thick-walled

PVC pipe, lying in the sand next to the reference marker that tells me where to install it. Following my dive plan, I secure a "leveling collar" around the center of the pipe. This device, fitted with two bubble levels set at right angles to one another, will ensure that I keep the pipe vertical as I sink it into the seabed. I then insert the jetting tube that will force high-pressure water through the pipe, thus washing out a hole that will let the pipe slide into the seabed.

Suddenly, my focus leaps from the task at hand to the surrounding scene. I've just become acutely aware that I'm standing next to the USS *Monitor*, America's first modern warship. I am only a few feet from *Monitor's* most iconic feature: its armored gun turret. I look back toward the sub. The water hose and my umbilical trail off along the bottom, but the sub is lost in the blue haze. Yielding to a nearly irresistible urge, I set down the water hose and walk to the turret.

Twenty-two feet in diameter and nine feet high, the turret towers over me, covered with more than a century of corrosion and marine growth. I reach out and gently place the palm of my hand against the turret. I can almost sense the flow of history into my body. This is why I became an archaeologist, why I love investigating shipwrecks. My mind is reeling with images of *Monitor's* battle with CSS *Virginia* (ex-*Merrimack*) in 1862, of shot and shell crashing against this very iron, of that terrible night when *Monitor* sank out here, taking sixteen men to the bottom.

"Ready for me to turn on the water, John?" It's Roger trying to keep me on schedule. I only have a few minutes before I must return to the protection of the sub and begin the slow ascent to the surface. Quickly, I return to the pipe, raise it to vertical, and call out, "Ready."

The rest of the dive was fairly routine. I was able to jet the reference pipe the desired five feet into the sediment before moving to the pipe at the bow. The operation began well, but after sinking only three feet, the pipe struck a hard surface and wouldn't go deeper. I kept pushing the pipe until my dive time was up, and Roger was telling me to return to the sub immediately. I barely made it back into the sub before the maximum dive time of 60 minutes. Beyond that limit, Don and I would have been subjected to a much longer decompression time because of the extra gasses our bodies would have absorbed under pressure.

As I stowed my band mask, I heard Roger call out, "Leaving bottom."

I also heard gas hissing as Richard Roesch, in the forward sphere with Roger, began methodically reducing the pressure in our dive chamber to begin the decompression process, just as the pressure would have decreased had we been ascending to the surface as swimmers. I watched as the sub was recovered from the sea and "mated" (docked) with a hatch on the ship's deck. When pressures were equalized, our hatch opened again, and we slid through a short metal trunk into a large decompression chamber where we ate a hot meal and completed our return to atmospheric pressure.

My first encounter with *Monitor*'s turret will remain a vivid memory that I will cherish for the rest of my life. And, although I didn't know it at the time, I was to have many more visits with *Monitor* in the coming years.

"First Encounter With a Shipwreck" was originally published as the prologue in the book USS Monitor: A Historic Ship Completes Its Final Voyage, Texas A&M University Press, 2012.

THE SOLDIER

Peggy Callison

She saw him hurrying down the hallway to class, and she knew that he was going to say it again. He said it every day. The moment that she finished determining who was absent, he would say it.

She followed the last ninth-grade student into her classroom and closed the door. As usual, the students did not fall silent and bow their heads in reverence as she approached the podium where her grade book, lesson plan, and a copy of *The Red Badge of Courage*, which lay waiting. As usual, it was as noisy in the classroom as it had been in the hallway. She wondered why she had failed so miserably as a tyrant. Even though she was a rookie, and this was her first year of teaching, she wished her "Class Management" course in college had been more helpful. She wondered why the busy little creatures did not fear her as she had feared her teachers when she was their age.

He sat in the very first seat in the row just beneath the podium, and while she called the roll, he smiled that brilliant smile that matched the brilliance of his sparkling blue eyes. He was such a happy child, and she wished her smile looked as perfect on her face as his smile looked on his "Tom Sawyer" face. She finished the roll call. She held her breath. And he said it.

"Mrs. Freeman, what are we gonna do today?"

She rolled her eyes toward the ceiling for help as the irritation... even anger...filtered through her emotional system. Her annoyance at opening the lesson every day with that same question never lessened because she knew how the dialogue was going to go...

"Josh, I have planned some very interesting things to do today. Why don't you wait and see what we are going to do?"

"I don't want to do any of that stuff. Let's talk about other stuff. I want to talk about the movie I saw last night. It was awesome!"

If he didn't want to talk about the movie he saw last night, he wanted to talk about a television show he had seen....or a ball game he had attended...or a conversation he had in the lunch room...or a fight he had witnessed...or a fight he himself had with another student...or a date he had with his girlfriend...or couldn't we just "take the day off" and let everybody talk to each other??? Josh had an endless list of suggestions and a hundred lesson plans of his own, but they all began with the original question..."Mrs. Freeman, what are we gonna do today?"

"Today, Josh, we are going to begin reading *The Red Badge of Courage*. I think you will like it. It is about a young man who goes off to war. It is the kind of story that you might find interesting since you are a young man, and there is a lot of action and adventure in the novel. I will begin reading, and each day we will read more and discuss what we have read. Each day we will also have a brief review before we begin to read again." She thought she saw a flash of fear in his blue eyes, but since there was nothing to fear, she attributed his expression to disappointment.

She began to read the novel. She read aloud, adding the drama to the reading that her double major in English and drama had prepared her to do. Actually, you could say that she "performed" the novel. They listened and watched as she dropped behind a desk, aiming her yardstick musket across the meadow into the stand of trees beyond the last row of desks where enemy soldiers waited to return fire. The rag she wore around her head with the stage-blood stain was a popular item that they all wanted to try on or to wear while she read. Josh was most often wearing the head band, and magically, they were all lost in the story of the war and the lives of the characters.

Amazingly enough, Josh's question at the beginning of class changed to an excited,

"Mrs. Freeman, are we readin' today??? And every day Josh wanted to present the review of the story at the beginning of class. He left no detail out. With the precision and accuracy of one who had read the novel a hundred times, he presented the review. Josh's classmates marveled at this, declaring that Josh must have BEEN THERE to know the story so well. He would smile that dazzling smile as he sat there with that red-badge-of-courage rag across his forehead and accepted all compliment graciously. Josh had "arrived" as a scholar in the eyes of his classmates and his teacher.

Finally, she had read the entire novel to the class except for the final two paragraphs. Proudly, she announced, "Because Josh has helped to teach Crane's work, he will read the last two paragraphs for us."

Josh's face lifted to meet hers with an expression of one who has been totally exposed to onlookers. There was no sparkle in the terrified, darkness of his eyes.

"Go ahead, Josh. Read for us," she encouraged, misunderstanding his fear.

Josh dropped his head and stared at the page before him. Slowly, he read until the word "trudged"...he stumbled...he tried again... she pronounced the word for him, only to hear him stumble again at "blood." She repeated the word for him, still not understanding, still caught up in the honor she was paying a student who had given his all to this study.

Suddenly, there was a different silence, and she looked down as Josh raised his bandaged head to look her full in the face. With all the courage and dignity of a defeated soldier, he sadly declared, "Mrs. Freeman, I can't read. I ain't never learned how to read."

She fought to control her tears as she realized what she had done to Josh, and she suddenly understood that his daily question was his attempt to hide his inability to read. He desperately needed to control what happened in class. He was a pass-along. Yet he was very bright.

"Josh, sometimes learning to read is kinda like going to war. It's a tough battle. But this year, you and I will fight that battle, and we will win! Are you ready?"

"Yes ma'am! Can I wear the bandage?"

"Yes, sir!" she shouted as she saluted him.

Suddenly, she realized there may be other pass-alongs in class. "Anybody else want to go to war with Josh and me?"

From various places in the room came a chorus of, "Me!" "Me!" "Me, too!"

Josh became her hero. He met the enemy...illiteracy...and the victory was his.

MAGIC FISHING PANTIES

Kimberly Dalferes

The boat rocks up and down as the waves roll across the top of the ocean in an unrelenting waltz. It's a good day to be on the water; today Mother Nature is in a peaceful mood. I've been here more times than I would've ever expected. I'm no stranger to the ocean. When you grow up in Florida, the beach and the sea are as second nature to you as breathing or laughing. However, this, *this* is different.

This is Alaska.

Back in 2005, I shocked the majority of my gal pals by announcing I would be heading to Alaska to go...wait for it...fishing. This crazy Southern Irish gal is a bit of a weird hybrid: loves pretty pedicures, but will also happily get downright muddy in the garden; will rabidly watch a football game, followed by her favorite DIY show on Home and Garden Television; is as comfortable wearing a frilly dress as she is relaxing in torn jeans and a sweatshirt. However, fishing?!

A little background: Nine years ago, the women in our family stomped our collective feet and demanded we be included in the annual Alaskan fishing trip. We had heard so many wonderful stories from the boys—husbands, fathers, brothers, and sons, all blissfully sharing descriptions of beautiful Alaska. They told tall tales of monster halibuts and ferocious king salmon, of breaching whales, giant sea lions, and lush, rugged coastal terrain.

We gals wanted our fair shot at the glory. The pushback was in fun, but a little serious, too: There would be no girly girls allowed. You had to pull your own weight, be down on the dock at oh-dark-thirty—no time for hair or make-up—manage your own pole, and "woman up." Game on.

I'm happy to share that all these years later the gals are still going strong. Trust me, I'm the last person who thought I would come to appreciate and look forward to an annual fishing trip. Have I gotten sea sick? Yep, but only once, and I was a trooper and jumped right back to my pole after I cleaned myself off. Have I been miserably cold, hunched over in the icy rain, and wondering how the hell I got talked into doing this more than once? You bet. I've been so exhausted after a day's fishing I've sunk fully clothed onto the bed and fallen fast asleep, even with the eternal daylight of Alaskan summer beating through the window. And still, I keep going back.

Over the years I've come to master the Alaskan fishing lingo. This is a must in order to handle yourself on the boat and pull your own weight. Here's a brief tutorial, a cheat sheet if you will, highlighting commonly heard expressions on an Alaskan fishing boat:

King. The biggest of the salmon. Puts up the best fight. Also known as a Chinook.

Trophy. A big king.

King Slayer. Common nickname of Kim Dalferes.

Silver. Another species of salmon. Also known as Coho. Superb eating; most often used to fill the fish boxes.

Pink or Pinky. These little suckers can put up a fight! But they're throwbacks. Hang out near the surface of the water. What's used for the canned salmon you purchase at the grocery store. You don't want to travel all the way to Alaska to bring these back home.

It's a Dog. When you land a chum or dog salmon. Toss 'em back.

Brown or Black Bombers. Rockfish, so named because they hang out near the bottom of the ocean. Can be a bugger to reel all the way to the top. Make great fish tacos.

Flatty, Chicken, or Butts. Slang terms for halibuts.

Parking Lot. A common fishing hole where fishing boats hang out together.

Fish On. Shouted when you have a fish on your line. Also known as a "hook-up."

A Double. Two fishermen with fish on their lines at the same time.

A Triple. A rare event. Three fishermen with fish on their lines at the same time. Often followed by…

An "Oh S***" Moment. Lines crossing, going over and under each other; fish making runs all around the boat; a general sense of chaos. Usually wicked fun.

In the Boat. When your fish is netted and brought into the boat. If it doesn't make it into the boat, it doesn't count.

Comin' in Hot. No net, no gaffe (which are used for halibuts), just horsing the fish into the boat. Not recommended, but sometimes necessary if you are having an "Oh S***" moment.

Bird's Nest. There is an art to casting and reeling. Fail to master your technique, and you could end up with a bird's nest—when the fishing line spools out of control up and around the reel, coming to resemble a bird's nest. Happens to everyone; embarrassing to admit.

Thumb It. To guide the line as you're casting and releasing your line, you gently glide your thumb back and forth across the reel. Do this incorrectly, and you end up with a bird's nest.

Derby. Fishing competition, mostly friendly. Winning the annual family derby bestows upon you the right to brag incessantly for a year. Except if you are my husband; then you need to drop it. Right, honey?

Mooching and Jigging. Fishing techniques. Too complicated to explain the difference; you'll just have to take my word.

Keep Your Tip Up. Often yelled at fishermen when the mates are trying to net your fish and get it into the boat.

Gettin' the Stink Off the Boat. Describes some mornings when it takes a long time to get the first fish into the boat.

Man-gina. A device which is strapped around your waist to provide support for your rod if you are having a tough time bringing in a large halibut. Warning: Don't ever ask for the man-gina. Right, honey?

This Ain't My First Rodeo. Term often used by kid brother Scotty when the women on the boat are getting too bossy.

There is a magical feeling when you land a king. The pull on the line is heavy and immediate. The line makes a unique zinging sound when a king grabs your bait and works to plunge down into deeper waters. As your pole bends under the weight, even the way the fish shake their heads is a distinctive alert to the captain and first mate you've got a king on the line.

I've learned to let the fish play out. Your instinct might be to reel down hard and horse or drag the king to the boat. This rarely works and does nothing more than wear you out. The real trick is to keep the line taunt and let the fish go up and down as often as it needs to. When it's time to reel him up to the boat, you'll know it. Even I, often the girliest of girls, have come to love the distinctive tug of a king.

Here's a little secret that might explain my affection for the annual trek.

Each year, on our last day out, the fishing lodge hosts a girls-only boat. This has become the favorite day of the year for us. The captain and first mate have their hands full working to manage a boat full of gals, but we sure do keep them smiling. It should be noted that not all the boat captains over the years have fully embraced our gaggle of gal pal fisherwomen. Most—such as Captains Kevin, Guch, and Bones—have tolerated and even enjoyed our propensity for fun and some silliness. I can clearly recall one ol' salty dog who made no attempt to hide his displeasure about being saddled with, of all things, women who fish. Little Bro Scotty immediately christened this brusque naysayer *Pecker Ted*. To this day, if you are behaving surly in my family, you are often greeted with "don't go acting like a Pecker Ted."

What I've come to appreciate about girls-only day is that we sincerely don't care how many fish we catch, which probably contributes to our frequent landing of the biggest catch of the day among the boats. Maybe laughter is not only the best medicine, it's also the best fish bait. We women also have a secret weapon discovered during, of all things, a bathroom break.

We gals possess one distinctive disadvantage out on the fishing boats. It's the head. For the guys, their need to relieve themselves is accomplished by a quick pit stop over the bow of the boat. For the gals, well, our equipment doesn't work that way. A woman's use of the bathroom on a fishing boat is a time-consuming process. I use the term "bathroom" here with a bit of poetic license. Often, the facilities are nothing more than a bucket. You can take as many countermeasures as possible: limit the coffee consumption and definitely go at the lodge before you get on the boat. But, eventually, you gotta go.

How to Pee on the Sea

Step 1: The captain clears out the cabin for a little semblance of privacy.

Step 2: Layers of clothing (gloves, hat, scarf, rain slicker) are removed.

Step 3: The bibs must be unhooked, but—and this is important—you mustn't remove them fully because this would entail also removing your boots.

Step 4: Shuffle over to the cubby area under the bow. You're lucky if there is a cubby area.

Step 5: Back in, derriere first, drop the bib tops you've been holding up, unzip and drop your pants, followed by your underwear, and attempt to squat/land upon the toilet/bucket.

Step 6: Pull across the battered blue plastic sheet that is supposed to provide some modicum of cover.

Step 7: Pray the toilet paper is somewhere within reach.

Step 8: Anchor your hands and feet against the sides of the cubby to steady yourself as the boat sways and rocks.

Step 9: Proceed with, well, you know.

Step 10: Attempt to rise, remaining in a somewhat stooped position in order to avoid bumping your head. (I did not forget about the use of the toilet paper; I'm trying to keep this classy.)

Step 11: While remaining hunched over, attempt to pull up your underwear and your pants in the cubby. Damn near impossible.

Step 12: Pull back the blue plastic sheet and while once again attempting to hold up your pants and bibs, turnaround, bend over, and pull the lever which evacuates the contents of bowl.

Step 13: Turn back around, continue to hold up your bibs, and shuffle back out into the main cabin.

Step 14: Refasten your pants and your bibs, put back on all your clothing—rain gear, hat, gloves, and scarf—and head back out to fishing.

What could possibly go wrong?

My stepmom, Mary, had held out as long as she could. However, eventually, nature called. She mastered steps one through twelve with aplomb, but upon reentering the cabin, her bibs caught on her boot, also tugging on her yet-to-be-fastened pants. As Mary stumbled and reached down to untangle the orange slicker fabric from the top of the brown rubber sole, she proceeded to bend over and show off her...panties.

As we heard her exclaim "Oh, shoot!" we all turned and were presented with her leopard print undies. Not exactly the granny panties you expect your mother to be wearing.

"Mom!" exclaimed sister Chris, "What are you wearing?!"

Mary abruptly stood up straight, hiked up her pants and her bibs, and with a wonderfully wide smile responded,

"Oh, these ol' things? They're my magical power fishing panties."

"Well there's something you don't hear on the boat every day," snorted Captain Kevin.

"Why do you think I'm so lucky each year?" replied a still grinning Mary. "Because I've got my power fishing panties on. Tell you what, I'll get all you gals a pair for next year."

True to her word, the next Christmas all the girls in our group received a pair of magic fishing panties in our stockings. Somehow, Mary had managed to not only find leopard print undies for all of us, but they also were purple! I ask you, how could they not be magical? Each year, without fail, we all wear our magic undies under all our gear as we head out on our girls-only day of fishing. These silly little slips of silk have become our girl-power symbol and have indeed brought us great luck and good fortune.

Sorry, boys, but I don't think you could ever handle the power of the purple leopard print. The gals respect the enchanted properties of our magic undies and have vowed to use their charms for good, not evil. Above all else, we sincerely enjoy winning the fishing derby; go find your own damn mojo.

Often, we women are told there are things we cannot do. We are too old, too weak, not pretty enough, not smart enough … all of it absolute horse hockey. My posse of fishing women issues this call to action to the sisterhood:

Hitch up your magic fishing panties and get on the boat.

My lucky fishin' hat and magical panties sit perched on a coveted shelf in the middle of my closet, patiently waiting to be packed and ready to leave the lower forty-eight for another Alaskan adventure. Who's with me?

Fish on!

Magic Fishing Panties originally published in *Magic Fishing Panties* (book by same name) by Mill Park Publishing, 2016. Reprinted with permissions.

EPIPHANIES WITH FRIED EGGS

Diane Fanning

I was just thirteen on that sunny day in 1963 when my twenty-one-year-old Uncle Harold was thrown from a pick-up truck to his death. Family harmony also died that afternoon. The instrument of Harold's demise was his brother-in-law Burn. In a drunken stupor, he had driven the wrong way up a one-way street, causing the ensuing collision.

The members of this thirteen-sibling family were scattered far and wide from California to Massachusetts to Germany. They all converged in Baltimore to pay their last respects, filling the houses of those who still lived there. Overfilling my house, as a matter of fact: I had to move next door for the duration.

In the evenings while bunking with my fifteen-year-old neighbor, an aspiring beatnik-communist, I was introduced to Joan Baez, Buffy St. Marie, and Peter, Paul and Mary. I read Karl Marx, Fanny Hill, and a number of beat poets.

In the mornings, I learned the varieties of fried eggs. No two uncles wanted eggs the same way. One liked them basted in butter, another fried in bacon grease. Another insisted on once-over-light. Just about all of them wanted a perfect, whole, runny yoke surrounded by a firm, completely cooked egg white—not an easy feat for a novice like me.

Among all these picky connoisseurs, one uncle requested a broken yolk, ever so slightly scrambled into the edge of the egg white and cooked hard. He ended up with all my mistakes. At the time, I didn't think he knew that. Looking back, I do believe he planned it that way.

Of course, the uncles also wanted big mugs of coffee to wash down those eggs. The mistake I made was setting a steaming mug in front of Uncle Ed, the Mormon from California. That eared me a lecture about polluting my body, the Temple of God, with that evil stimulant caffeine.

Uncle Harold was a Navy man, and I remember uniforms and American flags as the backdrop to the unfolding drama of the funeral. Muttered whispers of disapproval rippled around me as the presence of a certain woman became known. I heard hesitant movements and a gentle sobbing that built to a keening wail. The unknown woman suddenly rushed forward and threw herself prostrate on my uncle's closed coffins. She was disheveled, her clothes tawdry. Her face was tired, worldly, defeated.

My heart was pounding. Who was this woman? Why was everyone acting so disgusted? Why was her sorrow treated with disdain? Why was the most obviously heartbroken person at the funeral being led away in disgrace?

The muttering voices around me explained.

"Just a whore from The Block."

"He had one in every port."

"What an indecent display!"

"She's just sorry she lost a customer."

Part of me wanted to stand up and scream in her defense. "Even a whore can fall in love!" Another part of me wanted to run to this Mary Magdalene and wrap my arms around her. Instead, I dutifully kept my seat, quietly trying to understand the adults who had taught me to "do onto others as you would have them do unto you" and "let those among you without sin cast the first stone."

Later at the graveside, a Baptist minister said the final prayer. He expressed the hope that Harold had, during his fatal flight from the pick-up to the roadside, asked Jesus for forgiveness for his sins, and that Harold was now rejoicing in heaven rather than suffering in hell.

At this, my Mormon uncle launched himself forward to the graveside, looked the preacher in the eye, and shouted: "How dare you? There is no such place as hell, and I am deeply offended that you would desecrate the memory of my brother and insult every member of this family by suggesting he could possibly be there."

A moment of tense silence followed until the cowed minister was able to intone diplomatically, "Let us all take a moment for silent prayer." When the air was clear, the preacher said "Amen," and we all shuffled off to get on with grieving for Harold.

For me, the entire week was a turning point—an epiphany. I learned volumes about life, death, and the fine art of frying eggs.

THIS OLD DOG AND I

June Forte

Megan edges gingerly toward me; her cataract-clouded eyes aim downward, trying to gauge the exactness of her steps. She lifts each oversized paw and slowly places it some predetermined inches from where it had its start. I've watched her perfect this regimental march for months now, maneuvering across the living room, listening to an internal cadence that only she can hear. The drill is repetitious and unyielding and sets an intricate path circumventing tables, chairs, even throw rugs. A harsh, imagined punishment must lay wait should she be remiss in rounding the coffee table each and every time she crosses the room. Megan draws comfort from routine. These are my familiar old friend's last acts.

She stops mid-step and looks to me. I am easy to find in my usual spot at the kitchen table, a cup of fresh-brewed tea steaming in my hand. This is my routine, and I'm pleased to be her destination.

Reaching me, she slides her bony head into my ample lap, nosing up the cushion of my free hand and gently nudging it to her brow. She waits, anticipating. I reward her with scratches on the knob of her head. She closes her eyes and burrows down into my lap. My hand passes over the wen above her ear.

"Nothing to worry about," the vet assured.

"A cyst?"

"Perhaps."

What there is to worry about goes unspoken. Megan is dying. The vet knows it. I know it. We've known it for months. There's nothing we can do to make her stop. She is losing weight, two to three pounds at a stretch, a total of fifteen pounds in five months. She's all bones, no meat. Her body is starving. To operate, to find out why, would kill her. For this old dog, the vet recommends "nothing."

Helpless and in denial, I do little more than nothing. I massage her tired bones. More bare spots have surface in her coat. I feed her puppy food, some recommended supplements, and a few choice table scraps. Rather than plumping up, she loses ground.

This morning, I sit, stroke Megan quietly, and talk to her. "Remember when you were a puppy, and I came to take you home?" She lifts her head bumping against my paused hand, her way of saying please continue. I stroke her skeletal back. In her wasted form, there lurks the lank and loose-jointed shadow of her puppyhood.

"I almost took your sister, you know. You were a marbled dark-brown piglet. Definitely not my first choice." Megan yawns. I can't get a rise. Perhaps she remembers, too.

The scene comes sweeping back. I lifted the brindle-colored puppy to my face for a better look. She wound her paws around my neck and dug in. "Take me. Please, please take me," those golden doe-shaped eyes seemed to plead. What choice did I have? I took her home.

Home, at the time, was the eastern slope of the Rocky Mountains, southwest of Pueblo by fifty miles. A spread of forty semi-arid acres allowed an isolation we both sorely miss. Megan and I surrounded by nature in the Colorado foothills. We thrived. There was wildlife all around us, cattle and sheep in the pastures, and there were horses, magnificent herds that dotted the landscape in every direction.

The pasture to the back of our property was home to a pair of Morgan horses. Megan was not yet knee-high when she raced to challenge the behemoths. She circled the pair and raised a cautious battle cry. Unmoved, the Morgans continued to graze, tails flicking. Gathering courage, Megan darted in and out at them, coming inches closer and decibels louder with each pass. Bored or perhaps amused, the larger of these giants stepped a shod foot forward and stretched his mooselike head down to sniff the essence of this noisy pest. Megan's ever-expressive eyes rounded in terror. Jumping vertically into the air, she tucked her compact rump to her underbelly and shot off to the safety of the porch. From that day forward, although I'd catch her glancing at them sideways on occasion, she never again acknowledged the Morgans' existence.

Colorado was our adventure. Together we raised turkeys and goats and a barn full of kittens. "Such a gentle dog you are, Megan," I say, rising from the chair. While I start my day in earnest, she labors to her bed for a nap. I pause in the middle of sorting clothes and think back again to Colorado. Litters of kittens come scrambling to mind. A neighbor's mother cat used Megan as a day-care center, dropping in at feeding time, and then disappearing for hours. If I hadn't been an eye-witness, I'd find it hard to believe Megan would have put up with those miniature acrobats. They'd crawl on her back, do balancing acts on the top of her head and scratch her nose for good measure on the way down to the ground. They'd bat her ears and bite her tail. Megan spent days lying patiently on the porch, enduring the pain of sharp teeth and claws, waiting to be rewarded by the warmth of furry bodies kneading contentedly against her tummy.

A new job moved us to San Antonio and a neighborhood of tract-homes. Our backyard shrunk from a never-ending expanse of mountain beauty to a 16' x 20' fenced plot. We made the best of it.

Shortly after our move, I was raking the leaves while Megan circled the perimeter of the yard at a lope, running off some steam. On her final sweep past the corner oak, I watched her scoop her favored yellow tennis ball into her mouth. Her face contorted in disbelief. She spat the ball to the ground like a spent wad of tobacco. Still grimacing and trying to get the taste out of her mouth, she stopped short under the tree. It took a moment for me to realize that the pale-yellow ball was actually a fledgling that had fallen from the tree.

In a spectacular display of avian air power, the resident mocking bird left her cover and dive bombed into the confused Megan who took off for the safety of the house. But not before the angry bird had given her what-for, unjustly flailing her about the neck with beak and wing. In the aftermath, the fledgling eventually made its way back to the safety of its nest, surviving the traumatic experience of momentarily being inside a pit bull's mouth. It took a few days for all of us to recover from the shock and for Megan and the mother bird to return to their relationship of mutual disinterest.

I look up from my chores. My window frames a northern-Virginia landscape, another job, another house. There is a yard, but its size is of no importance to Megan now. She can barely make it down the back steps.

It's been a while since I checked on her. She's in her bed, lying flat on her side, stiff, like road kill. I step close, straining to hear her breathe. Ever so slightly, her chest rises and falls. I breathe easier.

Sometimes, I probe her gently with my toe to make sure she's still alive. It wasn't so very long ago that Megan barked a warning at the slightest sound. Now she's deaf. Strangely, I don't accept the fact that deaf does not mean silent. I'm startled when she barks. It's rare and always unexpected. Now, people come and go, doors bang, the phone rings; Megan goes on sleeping. She's always tired.

I'm tired too—tired of her dying. Like Megan, I need to rest from this painful journey. Hers has almost ended. For me, the memories will remain, nudging me gently like a probing toe. We're a pair, this old dog and I.

MY INTRODUCTION TO JANIS JOPLIN

Linda Hudson Hoagland

A Night with Janis Joplin was a performance at the Barter Theatre in Abingdon, Virginia. I was never a Janis Joplin fan, but I felt I really needed to see that show.

Going alone was the result of my husband passing away seven years earlier. I was sure that my son and his wife who lived about eight miles away from me would not be interested in an old, rock star who died in 1970 at the age of twenty-seven. My youngest son and his wife lived in Nebraska, so there was no hope there that they might attend the performance with me.

I sat before the computer and purchased my front row seat for forty dollars and change. When I printed out my ticket all I had to do was wait for the days to fly by.

My need to see this musical performance stemmed from the fact that I had seen the real Janis Joplin over forty-five years earlier. As it turned out, it was about six months before she died of an overdose of drugs.

It had not been my utmost desire to see the real Janis Joplin, but it was part of the first date adventure with my heart throb, Joe Stevens.

I had been starving myself for months, getting down to a size twelve, when Joe asked me out for the long dreamed of date.

We had become talking friends and were coworkers at the steel company in Cleveland, Ohio. His position in the company relegated him to the warehouse where he worked among the men that loaded the trucks that hauled the steel bars, rods, and plates to other companies where they would be ground or cut into workable pieces for tools.

I was secretary for the boss, who was president of the company, so I had reason, quite often, to make a run to the warehouse.

When I first met Joe, he was so nice and polite that I wanted to speak with him again and again. My necessary trips to the warehouse multiplied, and my need to lose fifty pounds took precedence over everything in my life.

On one of those absolutely necessary trips to the warehouse,

Joe said, "Linda, do you want to go with me on this coming Saturday to the new Akron Outdoor Pavilion? I have a friend who will be performing there in a band called Faces."

There was no mention of Janis Joplin being the headliner.

Faces was the only reason for Joe to see the performance because he had a friend, a fellow guitarist, who was a member of the band. As far as Joe was concerned, Janis Joplin was a 'so what.'

My interest was not in any of the performers. All I cared about was the fact that he had asked me out on a date. The fifty-pound weight loss with me eating only a can of green beans each day was worth every painful moment of starvation when I head those long awaited words of invitation.

I was living in Cleveland at the time in an area that had been derogatorily labeled the 'inner city.'

"I hope he can find the house," I mumbled as I paced back and forth from the living room to the kitchen.

"Sit down, Linda. It's not even six o'clock yet. You said he was going to pick you up at 6:30 pm. Stop that pacing. You're making me nervous," said my mother who was almost as excited as I was.

I was so worried that he might not find our old, two-story house hidden behind another one on West 11th Street. Actually, there were three houses back there, and ours was in the middle located right next to my aunt's house.

My Aunt Bessie and Uncle Walter were the ones who owned four houses. The one in front of us and the double family home in front of Aunt Bessie's house. Dad paid Aunt Bessie rent, and we had the privilege of freezing in the winter and burning up in the summer. The house we lived in had a centrally located gas space heater on the first floor and, of course, there was no central air conditioning. Many days during the winter, I would wake up in my bedroom on the second floor, and the glass of water I had placed beside my bed when I went to bed would be frozen solid. Heat rises, but it never quite made it to my bedroom.

I looked out the front bedroom, window watching for his black convertible to pull into the driveway that was in the shape of a U that circled in front of our house

I worried, also, about how my dad would react when he saw Joe.

Joe had shoulder length, brown hair along with a well-maintained beard and moustache. He wore gold-rimmed glasses and dressed in fringed clothing with a gold medallion around his neck, which was the clothing of the day for rock musicians.

I was sure Dad would call him a hippie. I knew Joe wasn't a hippie, but his manner of dress said otherwise. Joe was a musician and had to look the part for the band he had formed.

Joe arrived quietly without stirring the dust on the graveled driveway. He knocked gently and waited for me to open the screen door.

"Would you like to meet my mom and dad?" I asked as I fervently hoped he wouldn't want to do that.

"Just to say hi because we have a long drive ahead of us, and I don't want to be late for the opening act," he answered.

That was exactly what we did.

"Mom, Dad, this is Joe. We've got to go so we won't be late," I said and turned to walk to the door as quickly as I could leaving my parents, both of them, standing there with their mouths open.

When we walked to the car, Joe held the door for me to slide in, and I was impressed.

The convertible top was down, and my hair blew around in the wind. It felt wonderful and scary at the same time, because I was really living a dream, and I knew it had to come to an end.

His convertible had a wide, front, bench seat that separated us by a couple of feet because I was sitting as close to the door as I could get. When he spoke, I could barely hear him in the wind that encircled us both.

"Move over here, Linda," Joe said as he patted the empty part of the seat next to his thigh.

I felt myself blush, because I had been wishing for him to ask me to move next to him.

He started talking and never stopped. He had found a good listener in me, and I was hanging onto each and every word that left his mouth.

When we arrived at the outdoor pavilion, we had to park on a grassy field that was a long walk from our destination.

I had worn my new black pants with that gold trimmed laces up each side toward the front and a black long sleeve blouse that matched the pants to a tee. I also wore a gold medallion and gold hoop earrings. Unfortunately, I was wearing a pair of dressy shoes that had a little spiked heel, and it was difficult navigating the terrain without twisting an ankle or falling flat on my face, because Joe was moving rapidly so he wouldn't miss the opening band.

We didn't bring a blanket to sit on the grass of the hill surrounding the pavilion, so we opted to find a couple of seats beneath the pavilion roof where we sat down to enjoy the show.

Joe was happy to see his friend performing and that lasted for about thirty minutes. There was an intermission while the equipment for Janis Joplin was set into place and the instruments and equipment for the opening act were removed.

Janis Joplin was on the stage with a chair and a microphone. Her band members were elsewhere. I think they were below the stage in the pit, and she was front and center with her bottle of Southern Comfort.

Janis Joplin appeared on stage without make-up which was a good thing, because she probably would have sweat it off in the heat. Her long, brown hair was stringy and unkempt. Her clothes were dirty, peasant style. I was not impressed.

When she started singing, you fully recognized her as Janis Joplin with the gravely, throaty versions of music spiked with outrageous screams.

The entertainment concluded, and we started the trek back to the car.

I removed my shoes and walked through the grass with my bare feet. I was trying to force the walk into a slow, leisurely pace, because I didn't want the night to end.

Joe started talking as soon as we climbed into his car with me sitting as close to him as I possibly could manage. He regaled me about his life as a struggling musician and told me of all of the rock stars he had seen or met. Again, I was impressed.

The night was warm, stars were shining in the sky as well as my eyes, and the moon was a brightly lit balloon hanging in the darkness. The breeze blowing through my hair made me feel light as a feather and pretty. It had been a long time since I had felt pretty, if I ever had. I really didn't ever remember feeling that way before my date with Joe.

Sadly, we arrived on my street, and he turned into my driveway.

I lived with my parents, so I knew there was no real privacy to be had in my house. As soon as he opened his car door, he ran around to my side, so I could climb out. I had to do something to let this might continue.

"Come in for a while, Joe. My parents are in bed. They won't bother us," I said softly.

He came inside, and the flowing love started. My heart was running over with the need to let him know what I thought of him. After a few nervous kisses, Joe jumped up and started for the door.

His parting words were, "I'll see you at work on Monday."

That was my one and only date with Joe Stevens and my introduction to Janis Joplin.

He later explained to me that there couldn't have been a second date because he was falling for me and he couldn't allow that to happen. He didn't want any road blocks to his musical success, and he was afraid the two of us together would be an obstacle.

As I watched the performance of the role of Janis Joplin, I remembered that wonderful evening, and the smile never left my face during the performance.

THE TRIP BACK

John P. Hornung

In 1955, the Beauregard District Senior Scouts, (Sea, Air, and Explorer Scout units), were having their annual camporee on March 5 and 6 at Camp Salmon, Louisiana. Camp Salmon was a very large camp run by the New Orleans District of the Boy Scouts of America. It was located across Lake Pontchartrain from New Orleans. Bayou Liberty ran thru the camp and emptied into the north shore of Lake Pontchartrain. Six Sea Scout Units (Ships) were attending the camporee. Three Ships brought their twenty-five-foot Coast Guard light patrol boats, and two Ships brought the Pine Tree Jim, a thirty-five-foot lake boat. One Ship traveled by land. Our Ship #12 with its crew of three, Jack, Tommy and me, left early Friday morning on March 4 aboard our patrol boat. The trip to Camp Salmon took us across eighteen-and-a-half miles of open water, as the crow flies, and then five and a half miles up Bayou Liberty. The trip over was, for the most part, uneventful.

Early Saturday morning we were awakened to a bugle blaring out reveille. We made our beds, cleaned the cabin, attended the flag raising ceremony, and headed for the chow hall. After breakfast, we gathered our gear for the various competitive events and headed off. The three of us in Ship #12 did well in the events we entered. That evening we attended the ceremonial bonfire, listened to stories, and sang scouting songs.

Sunday morning, all Sea, Air, and Explorer Scouts dressed in their formal uniforms. The awards ceremony was held at 11:00 AM. After the awards we change to casual uniforms, collect our gear, and prepare our boat for the trip home.

The skippers of the Sea Scout flotilla gathered to coordinate the cruise back to New Orleans. Their behavior told me there was uncertainty in deciding if we should delay our departure or leave immediately. A check on the weather report stated we were to expect partly cloudy skies with scattered showers, and the temperature would be turning colder in the late afternoon. The winds were to be moderate too fresh, southerly, and shifting too northerly in the late afternoon. It was 1:00 PM by the time the skippers made the decision to leave and to stay together for the duration of the cruise home.

At 1:30 PM, units of the three twenty-six-foot patrol boats and the two units on the thirty-five-foot Pine Tree Jim were ready to depart. Jack took the helm, started the engine, and let it idle for a few minutes. Skipper Claudino wished us a good sail as we pulled the anchor from the sandy bottom of Bayou Liberty. Jack backed the boat into the center of the bayou, put the gear leaver forward, and the boat began to respond to the increase in the throttle. The three other boats repeated the departure sequence, and we were on our way. Half way down the bayou we reached the rotating bridge. The bridge was too low to pass under. This was a do-it-yourself bridge that was a scant single lane wide. It was supported by a column in the center of the bayou. A large circular hand crank was attached to the center of the bridge. Jack pulled the boat up to a small landing on the starboard shoreline fifty feet from the bridge. I went ashore, walked to the dirt road, and got to the center of the bridge. I cranked the wheel and the bridge began to swing open on its center column. Once fully open, I remained on the bridge and allowed our boat and the three others to pass through. I cranked the bridge closed and walked the path to the second landing where Jack and Tommy were waiting. As I scampered aboard, Jack put the boat in gear and increased the throttle. In a short distance we joined the other units, and we continued our exit of the bayou. We reached the mouth of the bayou at about 2:30. The waves were two feet high and the wind was ten knots out of the northwest. We followed the channel markers in a southeasterly direction, rounded the last marker too starboard, and headed southwest to New Orleans.

The wind and waves slowly increased in strength and height. After a half hour, conditions began to get rough. None of the boats in the flotilla were equipped with marine radios. Communication between boats was done by hand signals or the use of voice megaphones. I could see a couple of boats draw close to one another, and the skippers were yelling to each other. One of them broke away and slowed to drop back closer to us. Once we were within hailing range, the skipper shouted that we are to go to Mandeville and wait out the weather. Mandeville was twenty miles west and a little north of our location. It was a very small town on the north shore of Lake Pontchartrain directly across the lake from New Orleans. They were separated by twenty-four miles of open water. Jack turned to starboard and steered a course of 280 degrees. After a half hour, the temperature had fallen from the mid-eighties into the high fifties. The winds increased significantly and were now coming out of the north. The waves were six to eight feet, and we were traveling almost parallel with them. Our boats were pitching and rolling severely. Waves were beginning to come over the starboard side of the back deck. The scupper drains on the deck enabled the water to exit the sides and transom. Tommy, Jack and I stayed in the wheelhouse.

Things were just as bad on the southern shore of Lake Pontchartrain. Sunday morning brought beautiful boating weather for the yachting community of New Orleans. The waters along the shore had enjoyed the company of a large number of sailboats and motor craft. However, boaters were unaware of the change in the weather yet to come. In the early afternoon the beautiful skies suddenly changed without warning. The temperature plummeted from 83 degrees at 3 PM to 55 degrees by 4:30 PM. The fleet of water craft found itself in survival mode as the wind and waves began tossing boats in all directions. Many were able to make a dash to the safety of the harbor. Sailboats lowered their sails or reefed them to reduce the force of the wind. Motor craft began their swift return home. A number of the boats were too far out to make the trip to the harbor an easy one. The Coast Guard and the New Orleans Marine Police found themselves in the midst of a rescue mission that looked like a wild western roundup. They rescued many boats, but were eventually outnumbered by the task at hand. Yachts and other water craft began to be driven against the harbor's breakwater and up onto the concrete seawall. The Coast Guard and the Marine Police struggled to save as many craft and crew as they could. There were heroic efforts performed by them and other yachtsmen. However, the rescue boats of the Coast Guard and Police were claimed by the storm. The storm dashed them onto the seawall along with the other craft that couldn't make it to safety. Luckily, no lives were lost.

Twenty-three miles away on the north end of the lake, our flotilla of four boats was now struggling to maintain a course to Mandeville and was being beaten sideways by the waves. The boats had to steer in a northwesterly direction to maintain their western movement. We could only see the tops of other boats just above the waves. After two hours of fighting the weather, we had not made much headway. The waves were now over eight feet, and we could not push through them. Tommy spotted two of the boats heading to the southwest. Their skippers realized we could not make it to Mandeville. I could see one of the crew of the two boats arm signaling they were now heading for New Orleans. Jack turned to port and asked Tommy for a heading for New Orleans. Tommy reviewed the nautical chart and called out, "Jack, that would be 220 degrees. But, I think we should take a heading of 265 degrees to offset the winds." Jack turned the boat to 265 degrees. Our rolling became less severe. However, our pitching was just as bad and now we had a following sea 50 degrees starboard off our transom. The waves were still increasing. They were constantly breaching over our starboard deck and transom. Jack said to me, "Johnny! Take over the wheel for a while". I slid from the center standing position to the left, and Jack took my place. I began the struggle of keeping the boat headed in the right direction. I quickly discovered I had to turn the wheel to the right going down the front of a wave and to the left going up the back of the next wave to maintain our direction. "I better go out and check the bilge for water," said Tommy. He slid by Jack and me and cautiously opened the door onto the deck. Jack kept an eye on Tommy, as he struggled over to the bilge hatch in the deck. He opened it and discovered we have been taking on water. He hollered to Jack, "Give me a hand. We need to pump out the bilge." Jack made his way out the door. This task was done by the use of an old fashion portable hand pump. Jack retrieved the pump lying below the deck. He lowered it through the bilge hatch and began long up and down strokes with its internal rod. On the fourth stroke, water began to flow from the spout near the top of the long cylindrical metal tube. Tommy hung on to Jack and a hand grip attached to the cabin. Waves continued to come over the starboard side and transom. The scuppers did the job of releasing the wash off the deck. I steered the boat in a direction that lowered the pitch, roll, and yaw. After struggling for a while, Jack and Tommy concluded their pumping. Tommy stowed the pump, closed the deck hatch, and the two made their way back into the wheelhouse. They were cold and soaked. The temperature had dropped significantly. I turned the boat to put us back on course.

After a half hour, the waves had gotten huge. We could only see another boat when we and the other boat were simultaneously on the crest of waves. A boat in a wave's trough would be hidden from view. When our boat was in a trough, we could see nothing but angry sea all around us. We were now experiencing new phenomena. When the boat crested atop a wave, the engine would rev up considerably. The waves were throwing the boat high enough that the prop was coming out of the water. While I fought the wheel, Jack and Tommy watched for the other boats. As we crested the waves, we could see the rear of other boats coming clear out of the water. It was getting toward dusk, and the waves continued to build. As I steered down a wave, the boat would propel itself directly into its trough. I notice a change in the troughs, as the waves became more intense. I wasn't sure if what I was seeing was real. I said, "What do you think is in the trough?" Tommy stared into the next trough as we zip down a wave. Jack was alarmed and said, "It looks like sand! The lake bottom is being churned up." The depth of the lake ranged from 12 to 14 feet deep. I could tell from the lack of conversation my fellow crew members were thinking the same thing, if we go any deeper into the sandy trough the bow would crash into the bottom of the lake. This sleigh ride from hell continued for another hour or so. It was pitch black, cold, and we had no idea where the other boats were.

It was time to check the bilge and change the wheel-man. Tommy took over the wheel as Jack and I tried to make our way onto the deck. We opened the cabin door and instantly got hit by a huge wave. The weather was so bad we had to abandon our attempt to pump the bilge. We could now see the lights from the city reflecting off the storm clouds above. With a minor correction to port, we took aim in the direction of the harbor. Tommy was doing a great job at the wheel, and we continued on. The wind and waves did not relent. Another hour went by and we began to identify features of the shoreline. At about two miles from shore, we could see lights shining out into the lake where we estimated the mouth of the harbor should be located. I took a look through the binoculars. I could make out the rhythmic pulse of the lighthouse above the Coast Guard station. It was on the left edge of the lights shining out into the lake. I could not see the red navigation light on the end of the seawall marking the starboard entrance to the harbor. It was critical that we knew where the entrance was. If we went to the right of the light, we would be thrown up onto the huge rocks on the breakwater. Too far left and we would not make the entrance due to the force of the waves and wind coming from the right. Jack took a look through the binoculars. In a concerned voice, he said, "It looks like the lights shining into the lake are from several cars parked at the turnaround at the harbor's entrance. That's why we can't see the navigation light. Man! This is going to be tricky."

It was pitch black, and there was no sight of the other boats in our flotilla. We had taken the best possible course to position ourselves for a run at the entrance to the harbor. The problem we faced was the harbor's entrance was 200 feet wide, but it ran perpendicular to the shoreline. The wind and waves were driving us directly towards the shore and sideways to the entrance. We would have to hit the opening just right and make a quick starboard turn to clear both sides of the entrance. As we approached within four blocks of the entrance, the lights from the cars began to obscure our vision. The waves were huge, and we were being tossed from starboard stern to port bow. They were hitting the seawall and disappearing over the top. Tommy said in a warning tone, "We have to get the people on the breakwater to turn out their lights so we can see the navigation light." "I'll try to get on the deck to signal them," I said. I slowly opened the door and worked my way out onto the aft deck. While hanging on for dear life, I waved and placed my hand over my eyes. I repeat this three times with no results. They could see us. However, they wouldn't turn out their darn lights. Just then the engine sputtered and died. Tommy frantically tried to get it started. Nothing! Jack made his way out onto the deck with a flashlight. I held onto him and the boat as he stretched to reach the engine cover in the center of the aft deck. He lifted it slightly and shined the light into the engine compartment. The water had risen to the level of the coil and shorted out the engine. By the time it would take us to bail out the engine, the waves would have thrown us against the seawall. Tommy started blowing the horn to let the Coast Guard know we are in trouble. He gave a series of three blasts over and over. We could clearly see the Coast Guard station 250 feet away. Jack raced back into the wheelhouse and down into the storage area in the bow. I noticed that the emergency survival craft was being readied at the Coast Guard dock. Jack reappeared from the cabin with the long through-line with a weight tied to the end. We rolled down into a trough, got swamped by a wave, and rose up again. The Coast Guard rescue boat now moved from its dock and slowly plodded towards us. Then we noticed the rescue boat turn around and head back to the Coast Guard dock. What the heck! We were now moving sideways toward the twelve-foot high concrete seawall. After the entire struggle with the storm, we weren't going to make it. Jack looked to our starboard and yelled, "One of our boats is on the way in!" It was a one of the patrol boats. It was pitching heavily. We began waving our arms like mad. They were taking their one possible shot at the harbor's entrance. "They see us!" Tommy yelled. If they turned in our direction, they would miss the entrance and end up on the seawall with us. It appeared the skipper at the controls knew this. Their boat was almost a hundred feet from us and beginning to cross our starboard bow. It was the Cartagena with Ship #2 aboard. The Cartagena began its run for the harbor's entrance. Jack was already wheeling the throw line attached to our bow tow rope. The weight at the end was circling the air. He let it fly. The line and weight could clearly be seen in the bright light coming from the cars at the entrance. Holy cow! The line flew right over the top of the cabin of the Cartagena. One of its crew grabbed it while hanging on to the back of the cabin. We continued to be slammed toward the seawall. We lost sight of the back half of the Cartagena as a wave covered its stern. We continued to slide sideways. The Cartagena pitched forward down a large wave just as we began moving backwards into a trough. The tow rope flew up and shivered through the waves between us. Both boats came to a complete standstill. The sudden stop slammed the skipper of the Cartagena into the ship's wheel, badly injuring his chest. One by one the waves overtook the transom of the Cartagena. Suddenly, our boat got a slight, firm pull forward. "They got us hitched," Tommy yelled. The two boats began to slowly pick up forward movement. Tommy turned the wheel to starboard to stop our sliding to port. The Cartagena's engine was straining to its limits. The storm began to reluctantly release the two boats from its grip. We were now at half speed. We slipped pass the Coast Guard station to our port and into the mouth of the harbor. The noise of the storm softened as we moved behind the breakwater to our right. We could hear the parents of Sea Scouts standing next to their cars yelling at us. They were joyful of our rescue. We waved and yelled in unison, "Turn out your lights! We can't see the entrance!" and glided further into the safety of the harbor.

The Cartagena throttled back, and pulled us over to the Power Squadron barge. We were set adrift and Tommy guided the boat to our docking area. We gave the crew of the Cartagena grateful thanks as they pulled away. We took a short pause of relief. We then opened the cover to the engine. The water was up to the sparkplugs. We casually began the task of manually pumping the water from the bilge. After fifteen minutes, we noticed the Pine Tree Jim rounding the marina channel and heading in our direction. As Jack continued to pump out the bilge the Pine Tree Jim did a "U" turn and docked with its stern facing us. We continued our pumping. There was unintelligible conversation on the Pine Tree Jim for about ten minutes. The boat was running well and looked fine. Then the engine went silent. The Pine Tree Jim sank in four feet of water in five minutes.

During the storm we were in open water for seven hours. We traveled a total of 25.6 miles at 3.6 miles per hour. What saved us? Not the Coast Guard. It was our determination and dedication to the Scout motto, Be Prepared! Two months after surviving the storm I jumped ship, to Ship #2. Ship #2 owned the Cartagena.

A CARETAKER, A DHOBI, A WIFE

Urmilla Khanna

When my husband Kris went in for his shower, I raced into his room to tidy up and make his bed. As I straightened the linen, it smelled moist. There were patches of grey on the otherwise pale-blue sheets. I looked a little closer, and I knew. Today, not just the sheets but the mattress protector would also have to be stripped and washed. I had other sheets to make his bed, but not a back-up mattress protector. This was the first time I could have used one. My morning chore of doing the laundry and getting it out of the way became more than what I had anticipated.

Kris was diagnosed with Parkinson's disease (PD) almost thirteen years ago. Over time, we acknowledged the diagnosis and found our own private ways of conquering his illness. We jocularly crafted it into a ghost-like figure who shamelessly invaded our privacy. We called him Mr. Parkinson, the unwanted guest who refused to leave. Gradually, the guest became an integral part of our family, and I learned to accept his presence graciously. Today, he was challenging my strength.

I dumped the arm full of clothes on the laundry-room floor and stood motionless as I looked at the mammoth pile. I can do this. I am strong, I thought. The Whirlpool's lid was open, ready to receive the load and go to work silently and mercifully. However, one look at that mountain in front of me, and I lost all control. My legs became weak, and I wilted into the mass. I drew my arms and knees under me and breathed deeply.

I must not cry.

The very next moment, torrential tears were gushing from my eyes and nose. I could hear the shower upstairs. Kris was doing everything at the slow pace of a Parkinsonian these days. By the time he gets done, I will be strong again. He will never know. For now, I wanted to let myself go. I sobbed incessantly.

I was startled when I heard heavy footsteps coming rapidly down to the laundry-room.

"What's the matter?" Kris said as he helped me back on my feet.

Then he saw it. And I saw that childish look of shame on his face.

"I know you are very tired," he said. "I create so much extra work. You must get exhausted." His tremulous, shaking hands held me at my shoulders as he stood staring at and beyond me. Then taking me into his arms, he said, "Don't worry about it. You don't have to do it all right now. Come, let us have breakfast. I will help you after that." He led me up the stairs to the kitchen.

While I was in the laundry-room and had a few quiet moments to cry, I had relived a segment of my childhood, amazing myself at the clarity of my thoughts and the speed of travel through time and space.

I was in our bungalow in Jabalpur, India. It was laundry day. Mother had asked Babulal, the day-servant, to collect all the laundry and bring it to the courtyard. Babulal stripped all the beds and refreshed them with crisp white sheets and pillowslips embroidered with red and yellow roses. He emptied the clothes hamper, which had collected the family's soiled clothing of over two weeks. Tablecloths, kitchen towels, and other sundry clothing from every room of our five-bedroom bungalow were brought out and dumped into the pile. It was a mammoth pile and I loved jumping on it and playing hide and seek, my small body disappearing between the masses of sheets.

The servant in charge of washing clothes, our *dhobi*, finally arrived around eleven o'clock. He sorted the clothes and put them into several smaller piles. Mother pulled up a chair and sat down beside him, making notes in her small diary. He counted the items. Towel 6, sheet 7, pillowcase 10, lady blouse 6, sari 4, baby frock 4. On and on he went with the count, Mother's eyes following the movement of the clothes from one pile to the other. She had him shake each piece of clothing a second time just to make sure that he was not pilfering an item or two. With her primitive arithmetic skills, she slowly did a grand total on her page, while the *dhobi* counted the clothes on the floor for the final tally. This accomplished, the *dhobi* used one of the larger sheets and tied all the clothes into a tight bundle. Babulal helped him hoist the bundle on his head. He centered it, checked his balance, and walked away with a slow, waddling gait. The laundry would be delivered back to us, washed, ironed, and smelling of the tropical sun in three days or three or four weeks, depending on how the weather would co-operate. During the monsoons, it rained for two and three weeks at a stretch. and Mother had to be patient and understanding.

As a child, that is what I envisioned to be a laundry day. Some-day when I am married, I will have my own *dhobi*. I made dream-like plans of how I would be different. I would be much more organized. Unlike Mother, I would be clear and precise in my accounting. The *dhobi* was paid by the number of items he had washed. In his mind, a handkerchief was equivalent to a sheet or a sari. In Mother's eye, it was a bonus she deserved. After all, she was giving him so much business. Moreover, he was living rent-free in our servant's quarters.

"You should consider yourself lucky," she would say to him as she handed him his dues. I could never comprehend the *hungama* created over the payment for the washing of those handkerchiefs and kitchen towels. But I saw him as a lucky man, just as Mother said.

My thoughts hovered over the life of our *dhobi*. How hard he had to work for the petty reimbursements. He took all the clothes to the banks of a nearby stream, rubbed each piece with a bar soap and beat it with a paddle until it was clean. The wash was given its final rinse in a pail of water tinted blue with a pinch of the refresh-ing Neel. Piece by piece he rung the clothes and spread them on nearby rocks and boulders. After a whole day's toil, he finished the ironing in the fading twilight, using an oil lamp and a coal-fed iron. However, at the end of the day contentment shone through his small brown eyes as he joined the other servants and shared his *bidhies* and the day's gossip.

Letting my emotions roam freely in the solitude of my laun-dry-room in Virginia, USA, I sobbed and wished I could start all over again. What would I change? Did I wish I could disappear under those sheets and be reborn to the leisurely life of a *dhobi*? How contented he appeared in my memory. Or, did I want to be a mem-sahib and live in the comforts of having a *dhobi*? No, it was none of that.

Life had been perfect up until now. Both Kris and I had ac-cepted our unwanted guest, Mr. Parkinson, and, together we had built a happy life around him. I was Kris's wife, friend, and companion. I was a retired pediatrician, and he a retired scientist. We were content with our lot in life. And yet, today something was gnawing deep inside of me.

When Kris and I came to the kitchen, Kris had me sit down. "Let me first fix you a cup of tea," he said and proceeded to boil some water.

I watched the turn-table in the microwave go around and around with a Pyrex cup of water while I drew circles with my tears as they fell on the breakfast table.

"What has come over you? You are never like this," Kris said as he poured the hot water into a cup. "Now stop crying, and tell me what is bothering you. You are my strength. You can't just crumble like this." He appeared annoyed at his helplessness of consoling me.

"It is not the work at all. I am strong and healthy and everything takes just a few minutes with all these machines and gadgets," I said.

"Then, what is it?"

"It's not the extra work." I said with emphasis. I fumbled for words. I tried to compose myself. "I am crying because I feel I am no longer your wife."

With a pounding heart, I had finally said it.

"What do you mean, you are no longer my wife? What has come over you? You always were and will always be my wife," he said.

He removed the teabag from the cup and added milk and sugar. His tremors caused sugar to spill all over the counter. His willingness to help had created another clean-up job for me and a miniscule smile escaped from the corners of my lips. Seeing that smile of resignation, something clicked in his brain. He walked across the room, stood behind my chair, and, wrapping his arms around me, planted kisses of reassurance on my head.

"Aren't you going to say something?" he asked.

"I did not like the support group meeting that I attended yesterday," I said and felt the raging fire that was burning inside of me come alive.

"What?" he said, amazed.

Just the day before, I had attended a Parkinson's disease support group. While Kris was dropped off for a workout with the PD exercise group, all the spouses met in a separate room. Hesitatingly, I walked in with them. I had never gone to a support group of any sort. I had counseled many patients in times of their need but had never sat on the other side of the table. I did not know how I was supposed to behave, or how I was supposed to feel. I pulled up a chair and sat down, closing the circle.

The moderator, himself afflicted with early onset PD, was a trained social worker, and a remarkable man. I admired him for his soft-spoken demeanor and the courage with which he faced life.

The meeting began with the introduction of the new members in the group and the usual exchange of pleasantries. Then the counselor went around, asking each one of us to talk about our concerns. One woman talked about the constant anger in her spouse, and another spoke about her spouse being downright lazy. Another woman said that eight years after the diagnosis, her husband refuses to believe that he has Parkinson's.

I had nothing to say. I listened.

As each one rambled on, the counsellor began to refer to us as a care partner, interchanging the word with caregiver and caretaker as he spoke. He was very casual about the use of this terminology and yet, at that moment something changed inside me. His words hit me like an arrow aimed directly at me. I mulled over them the rest of that day and all through the night. I repeated them many times silently.

Gosh, not only do I do all the work around the house, but I am not Kris's wife anymore. I am a god-damn caretaker.

The unexpected extra work the following morning was like adding kindling to a fire that was already smoldering inside me. There we go, I said to myself as I stood in front of the pile of laundry, I am indeed a caretaker, a *dhobi*.

Sitting at the kitchen table, sipping the cold syrupy tea, and looking at my husband's placid expression, my nerves relaxed, and I began to talk. I told him about my experience at the meeting that I had attended the previous day. I told him about the resurgence of my childhood memories. He listened patiently, his tremors subsiding slowly. When I finished telling him my lengthy saga, he was smiling.

"So you are angry with the counselor. What is he supposed to do? Invent new words? That is not his job."

Indeed, our lives had not changed overnight. I had merely attended a support group meeting. The counselor had done his job. For some strange reason his words had jabbed me at the very core of my being. My future suddenly appeared bleak and worthless.

"We all have weak moments," Kris said, as he wiped the lingering tears off my cheeks, and we launched into our usual breakfast table dialogues.

A single word uttered by a well-meaning counsellor had caught my attention and triggered a host of buried memories and momentarily turned my life upside down.

We discussed about the inefficiency of language—a caregiver, a caretaker, a care partner, a care recipient. Where, when, and how does this change take place? What happens to the years of spousal relationship? Was I now a caretaker like our *dhobi* who took care of our clothes? Our *chaukidar* who guarded our bungalow against burglars and riff-raffs? Or was I a care recipient for all the moral support I received from Kris.

We talked about our vulnerability when we are weak. We talked about our needs to vent. We talked and talked and talked.

"Gosh, it is well past the time for your morning pills," I said at last and brought the seven-day pillbox to the table.

I looked at Kris as he swallowed a handful of his pills. How patiently he had accepted every aspect of his disease. He never complained about the past nor did he paint a gloomy future. I, on the other hand, had become a victim of my own fears. I needed to conquer that enemy.

"I think I am going to make cream of wheat for breakfast," I said. "Would you like that?"

"Sure," he said.

MARTHA LEE'S CHINESE CRACKERS
A FIVE-YEAR RECIPE

Julie Leverenz

No, it doesn't take five years to make these crackers. Martha Lee made them in an afternoon. But prying the complete recipe out of her? Five Christmases—count them. She didn't do it on purpose; my mother-in-law was a genuine gray-coiffed southern sweetie. But still.

The first Thanksgiving after her son, Les, and I married in 1989, Martha Lee brought us a tin of her legendary "cheese crackers." These pecan-topped goodies look like sweet cookies, but one taste reveals a cheesy, buttery, salty melt-in-your mouth treat that makes you reach for another one, then another. The tin soon emptied; Les told me between bites that these crackers had been a holiday staple in his Eastern North Carolina family for as long as he could remember.

Because Les was clearly smitten by them—not to mention the serious waistline willpower they sparked in me—I asked Martha Lee when we saw her at Christmas if she would share the recipe. With a pleased smile, she said, "Of course." I grabbed paper and a pen and she recited from memory: "It's very simple. You take a pound of butter, a pound of cheese and a pound of flour, mix it up, roll it into logs, chill, cut into slices, top each one with a pecan half and bake."

"How many logs?" I asked. "How thick are the slices? Bake at what temperature? How long?" I had taken cooking lessons as a student in Paris, so I figured I knew a thing or two, and I suspected there were some holes in this recipe. Fortunately, Martha Lee was inexplicably grateful that her forty-something PhD only child was being looked after at last, even if by a Yankee, and took the time to explain the techniques that were second-nature to her.

Piece of cake, I thought as Les and I drove home to Virginia. So what if the cooking lessons I took in Paris were in a neighborhood program for domestic-help wannabes. I could do this.

The following December, I set about making Martha Lee's cheese crackers. I was on a low-salt binge that year, so I bought unsalted butter and a couple of eight-ounce blocks of cheddar cheese, brought them home and let them sit out until they came to room temperature. Then, I took my Mouli Grater and cranked chunks of the cheese into a big mixing bowl, added four cups of all-purpose flour, and the pound of soft butter, and squished it all together with my hands. After one squish, I thought of the rule my mother drilled into my young head back in New Jersey: "Never take off your rings. Never. Not to wash, not to garden, not ever. Well, you can take them off when you make meatloaf." Clearly, this cheese-cracker goo qualified as meatloaf. I scraped the crumbly cheese-butter-flour bits off my fingers as best I could, washed my hands, took my rings off and set them in a saucer, then went back to squishing.

When the mixture was uniformly blended, it was easy to spatula it into a smooth, semi-firm yellow blob. I turned the blob out onto a cutting board, shaped it into a loaf, and cut the loaf into six more-or-less even chunks. One by one, I took the chunks and rolled them back and forth on the cutting board with my fingers until they splayed out into logs about one inch in diameter and seven or eight inches long. Then, I rolled up each log in a rectangle of wax paper and placed it carefully on a shelf in the door of the refrigerator.

I don't know where Martha Lee chilled hers, but the door shelf seemed to be the safest place to keep the soft rolls from getting mashed or bent. Of course, to make room I had to move some things to the dead space on the bottom shelf of the main refrigerator: the mint jelly that had been in the fridge since I made lamb chops and found out my husband didn't like lamb; the maraschino cherries we bought for a visitor who liked Old Fashioneds; the little yellow lemon-shaped squeeze thingy that still had a few drops left in it; the graying horseradish from the one time I made cocktail sauce from scratch; the oversized jar of pimento-stuffed olives that I bought on sale. The lemon thingy rolled into a corner and wouldn't be found again until the following June, but that's another story.

A few hours later, I preheated the oven to 425 degrees. Taking a now-firm roll out of the refrigerator, I unwrapped it and sliced it into quarter-inch thick rounds. After placing the rounds on an ungreased cookie sheet, I gently pressed a pecan half onto each one, slid the pan into the oven and set the timer for ten minutes, just as Martha Lee instructed.

Rule Number One when making somebody else's recipe for the first time: Watch it. I pulled those babies out after eight minutes, just before they burned. I set them on paper towels to cool— and spent the evening soaping the butter spots off my countertop. There is a *lot* of butter in this recipe.

Les had been hovering in the kitchen from the moment the first whiff of toasted pecan and cheese drew him out of the study. He claimed taste-test privileges, and I waited expectantly, more than a little nervous, as he tossed a hot cracker from hand to hand to cool it, then popped it into his mouth.

"Good!" he declared. I exhaled.

"But," he said.

Uh oh, I thought, and braced myself. "It's not quite right," he said. "Kind of bland." He looked apologetic. "It's not that I won't eat them." He took another one and ate it. "They're not bad. But not quite right."

I sampled one. Les was right. These were not the same as the cheese crackers Martha Lee made. The toasted pecans were delicious, but the cheese cracker underneath lacked…something.

"Oh," I groaned. "Of course. It's my fault. I never should have used unsalted butter."

That night, something felt wrong when I washed my face— oh no, my rings! I rushed downstairs to the kitchen and searched, frantic. I found them, still in the saucer, hidden behind the flour canister. Trudging back upstairs with the rings securely on my fingers, I remembered the treasure that I found deep in the sand on a beach in Massachusetts when I was ten. Mom said its tiny heart-shaped ruby and gold setting were probably real, and I loved how it shined on my hand. On the drive back to New Jersey, I set it on the edge of the sink to wash my hands in a gas station restroom. We were half an hour down the road before I missed it, and Mom and Dad refused to turn back. Lesson learned: Never take off your rings.

Fast forward to the next year, Les's and my third Christmas together. I told Martha Lee about my mistake with the butter, and we had a good laugh. She cautioned me never to use margarine, either. This time, I bought regular butter, set the timer for eight minutes and cooled the crackers on a paper grocery bag under the paper towels.

Les could barely contain himself when the first batch came out of the oven.

"Good!" he pronounced with his mouth full. "Much better."

"But?" I said.

"No 'but'," he said. I grinned.

Then Les finished chewing and looked thoughtful.

Uh oh.

He picked up another one and examined it. "Are they cooked enough?" he said.

"I'm pretty sure," I said. "They're good and brown on the bottom, and the pecan is toasted."

He handed the cracker to me, and I tasted it. "Does it seem cooked in the middle to you?" he asked.

"Hm, I see what you mean," I said. "I'll try cooking the next batch longer."

"But don't burn them," he said.

I gave him The Look. He raised his hands in surrender, grabbed another cracker, and hustled out of range.

With trial and error over the rest of the batches, I found the right balance of time and temperature. I dropped the temperature from 425 to 375 degrees and increased the cooking time to Martha Lee's original ten minutes. Or eleven minutes—remember Rule Number One when you try this at home.

When we were halfway through the last, perfectly cooked batch of cheese crackers, Les got up his courage and said, "Would you kill me if I said these still aren't right?"

My eyes narrowed. "Yes," I said. "But tell me anyway."

He winced, then sighed. "They're still not quite... they're still kind of bland."

I spared the messenger and telephoned Martha Lee. "Martha Lee," I said, "I made your cheese crackers, but I must not be doing something right. They're kind of bland."

"Oh dear," she said in her lovely, low drawl. "I can't imagine what could go wrong. Did you use regular butter this time?"

"Yes, regular butter, cheddar cheese..."

"Sharp cheddar?"

"Oh, *sharp* cheddar," I said. "Of course! That would add an extra zing. Thank you."

"Not at all," she said. "It's such a simple recipe. I'm sure they'll be delicious."

So the next year, for Christmas Number Four, I bought regular butter and, not to take any chances, extra sharp New York triple-zing cheddar cheese. And lowered the oven temperature and used paper grocery bags. Confident that I finally had everything right, I greeted Les when he came home from a business trip one weekend with a little plate of his favorite cheese crackers. "Ta dah," I said.

"Cheese crackers? Oh boy!" He gave me a quick kiss and wolfed down a cracker. "Mmm," he mumbled through the crumbs, then reached for another.

"At last, huh?" I said. "Only took four years to get it right."

"Mmmm." He savored the second cracker. Then I saw his eyes become thoughtful.

Uh oh.

"But," he said.

I gave his arm a playful punch. "Kidder. Don't do that."

His thoughtful expression turned into resolute appreciation. "They're fine. Really."

I studied his face. "They're really not, are they."

He looked at me warily.

"Come on, tell me," I said. "I'm going to get these things right if it's the last thing I do."

"Well," he said, "they're still lacking something. They should have a little extra kick." He looked miserable. "I wish I could tell you what it was."

My shoulders slumped. He put his arm around me. "But they're almost there," he said. "And they definitely won't go to waste." To prove it, he took two more crackers.

A week later, we celebrated Christmas with Martha Lee in her garden apartment in Goldsboro, North Carolina. After we had opened presents and enjoyed the incomparable pork, slaw and hush puppies we had brought over from Wilber's Barbecue, I helped Martha Lee clean up the kitchen.

"Martha Lee," I said, standing at her old-fashioned porcelain sink, "I'm still not getting your cheese crackers right."

She handed me a cut glass tumbler to wash. "I can't imagine

why." She looked mystified. "I've told you everything."

I put the glass in the rubber-footed rack on the laminate countertop, making a mental note to get her a mat so the drips would drain into the sink, not onto the counter's faded turquoise starbursts. "Well, let me tell you what I did, and maybe you can find something I'm not doing right." While I washed and she dried, I walked her through the whole process, from the ingredients to the mixing, shaping, cutting, pressing and baking.

She stowed the forks in the drawer in the kitchen table. "I sprinkle them with powdered sugar after they've cooled," she said.

"I know," I said. "But that wouldn't account for what Les says is a missing 'kick' or something."

Suddenly Martha Lee's face cleared. She gave me a wide-open smile. "Oh, you forgot the cayenne pepper," she said.

"Cayenne pepper," I repeated through clenched teeth. *How could I forget the cayenne pepper when I never knew about the cayenne pepper?* "Ha ha," I trilled, trying to keep my voice light. "Of course. And how much pepper was that?"

"Oh, I don't know. A little; a pinch or so."

For Christmas Number Five, I bought regular butter and extra sharp cheddar, lowered the oven temperature and used paper grocery bags. And added two pinches of cayenne pepper.

They tasted fine to me. Perfect, in fact.

But: "I can barely taste the pepper," Les said after eating four crackers from the first batch. "Maybe you should use a little more."

Okay, I thought grimly, if he wants cayenne pepper, he's going to get cayenne pepper. I took the remaining rolls out of the fridge, brought them to room temperature, dumped them in a mixing bowl, added a whopping teaspoon of cayenne pepper and re-kneaded, re-formed and re-chilled.

Les tasted the second batch. "You got it!" he crowed. "These are great!"

He was thrilled, but they were way too spicy for me. And so, as all good married couples do, we compromised. Now I make the recipe with half a teaspoon of cayenne pepper.

Here, at last, is the complete recipe for Martha Lee's cheese crackers. I assure you, it was worth the five-year wait.

MARTHA LEE'S CHEESE CRACKERS

Mix with hands in large bowl:

1 lb butter, softened

1 lb extra sharp cheddar cheese, grated

1 lb all purpose flour (4 cups sifted)

Cayenne pepper to taste (¼ to 1 tsp)

Shape into one-inch diameter rolls, wrap in wax paper and chill.

Slice into ¼ inch slices and place on ungreased cookie sheet, about 2 inches apart

Press a pecan half into the top of each round

Bake at 375 degrees for 10-11 minutes, or until lightly browned.

Remove from cookie sheet and cool on absorbent paper (I use paper grocery bags topped with paper towels)

Sprinkle cooled crackers with confectioner's sugar (optional)

Makes about 14 dozen cheese crackers.

(Note: the rolls keep for a week or two in the refrigerator. And if I am not entertaining or giving tins of them as gifts, I often make a half recipe)

MARTHA LEE'S CHEESE CRACKERS – A FIVE-YEAR RECIPE originally published in CHRISTMAS BELLS, CHRIST-MAS TALES, November 24, 2012

THE DAY I RAN OVER A BLACK CAT

James W. Morrison

Let me say at the outset, I would never intentionally run over a cat. Indeed, if I had seen this black cat in time, I would have tried to stop the car, and probably even turned around and taken another street home.

There is a principle here. The French probably have a saying for it--*n'ecrasez pas les chats noire* (don't run over black cats). The French have sayings for almost everything, or so they claim. I hadn't thought of it before, but, on reflection, there are similarities between Frenchmen and cats—an aura of independence and superiority and an unwillingness to pay attention to you unless you speak their language.

Most people either love cats or hate them. As for me, I just don't like them very much.

I'm allergic to cats. I remember going with my wife to someone's house for dinner. We were greeted by two large, gray cats. They looked like Siamese twins, but the hosts informed us that they were Burmese, cousins to the Siamese. I hoped they were very distant cousins, as I had once had a severe allergic reaction to a single, Siamese cat. They must have been kissing cousins, as I had another terrible attack—eyes tearing, nose running, and lungs wheezing. We had to leave early. The cats probably got my salmon steak.

Catologists, or whatever one calls those who study felines, say the allergic reaction stems not from the cat's fur or dander but saliva the cat has licked on itself and spread all over the house. I think my allergic reaction is physical, but it could be partly psychological. I'm really not turned on by the idea of sitting around in dried cat spit.

Cat lovers will probably disagree, but, to me, cats seem aloof. They don't come running and wagging their tails, as dogs do. Oh, they'll come and rub themselves against my leg, but they probably just sense my discomfort and are playing with me.

My father didn't care much for cats either, especially black cats. As an attorney, he was generally a man of reason, but, if he were driving down the street and a black cat ran across the street, he would stop the car and try to turn around and find another route. If he couldn't turn around, and if he were wearing a hat, he would drive across the cat's path and then spit in his hat, a ritual to erase any bad luck. If not wearing a hat, he would spit in his hand. I won't go so far as spitting, but I'm enough of my father's son that I try not to cross a black cat's path.

Well, let me get back to my story. It was a mild, winter day when I received a call at my office in Washington, D.C. My daughter was on the line, calling from her temporary job. She had the flu and asked if I could come take her home. I picked her up in my car, and we drove toward home in the Virginia suburbs.

Reaching our neighborhood, we turned onto a quiet, narrow street lined with shrubs. I was driving along about 20 mph when suddenly I saw something out of the corner of my left eye. It was only a black blur, and it dashed out into the street and under my door. Then I heard a thump. I braked and stopped the car in about twenty-five feet.

My daughter sat up and said, "What was that?"

I responded, "It must have been a squirrel." When I looked in the rear view mirror, however, I said, "Oh, no. It's a cat—a black cat."

I pulled the car over, and we walked back to the cat. It lay on its side in the middle of the street, writhing in pain, blood dripping from its mouth. It tried to crawl away on its side but couldn't move far. We didn't want to move the cat for fear of hurting it more. It wore a collar, but there was no identification tag.

While my daughter stayed with the cat, I went to find the owner. I knocked on the doors of several houses, but no one answered.

Just then a car came down the street and stopped. A neighborhood couple got out and joined us in the street by the cat. I had met the couple once at a party but knew them only by their last name. They were neat people—I mean immaculate. They actually vacuumed their yard, and I often saw them washing and polishing their cars.

I told them I hadn't been able to locate the owner. The wife, appearing distressed, said that they had a cat of their own and knew a feline veterinary clinic a few miles away. They told me the name of the clinic and said they would take the cat there. I thanked them and said I would continue to try to find the owner. The husband got a towel from the trunk of the car, and the wife picked the cat up in the towel. He opened the passenger door of the BMW, the wife slid into the yellow leather seat holding the bleeding, squirming cat in the towel, and off they drove.

After knocking on the doors of five or six more houses and getting no answer, I took our daughter home, gave her some medicine, and sent her to bed. I then telephoned the cat clinic to inform them that the neighbors were on the way with a cat I had hit. I left my name and phone numbers for my home and office. Next, I called the home of the neighbor from whose yard the cat had run. I got their answering machine and left a message.

I finally decided to go back to my office. On the way, I got to thinking. Running over a black cat could mean only one thing—bad luck! But wait a minute. While I'm not a lawyer, I am the black sheep in a family of lawyers, and I know enough to argue a case on technicalities. It's bad luck only if you cross a black cat's path. The cat in question had run under the left side of my car, right under the driver's door, between the left front and left rear wheels. Perhaps only my left rear wheel had crossed the cat's path. That would mean that three wheels—three-fourths of the total—had not crossed its path. Moreover, the cat had run right under where I was sitting. We had reached the same point at the same time. I hadn't crossed its path, and it hadn't crossed mine.

Back at the office, I got a call from my good Samaritan neighbors who were at the clinic. They were going to leave the cat at the veterinarian's. There were going to be some costs. Would I share them? *Costs?* This was the first I had thought of costs. It began to sound more and more like bad luck.

I hesitated a second and then said the only thing I could say, "Sure, I'll share the costs." Then, on reflection, I added, "Actually, I don't think you should have to pay any of the expenses. You only came along after the accident, and you've already been very helpful." I thanked them again for taking the cat and said I would continue to try to find its owner. We said we'd stay in touch. I began to think more seriously about the costs of treating the cat.

I called my wife, who was just about to leave her office for the day. I explained the situation and asked her to try to find the cat's owner by going around the neighborhood and knocking on doors.

Next, I called my automobile insurance company. The news was not good. My policy wouldn't cover the expenses of treating a cat.

Then I received a return call from the neighbor whom I thought might have been the cat's owner. More bad news. The cat wasn't his. He had seen it sometimes in his yard harassing birds around his birdfeeder, but he didn't know who the owner was.

I then called the clinic and inquired about the cat. The receptionist put the doctor on the phone. He expressed appreciation for my concern and explained that the cat had suffered trauma to the head. Because of swelling, he wasn't able to determine the extent of injury to the head or other parts. He had stabilized the cat and had it hooked up to an IV. He wanted to wait until the swelling went down to determine if X-rays or other procedures were necessary to find out how badly injured the cat was and what course of treatment should be pursued. As the doctor talked, I began to wonder if the neighbors had taken the cat to the county hospital, not a veterinary clinic. Dollar signs began to flash in my head.

My next call was to the police department, where an officer finally gave me some good news. While the county didn't require that cats be kept on leashes, the owner of the cat, in letting it run loose, had to assume liability. The officer said that from my description of the incident I was not at fault and should not be liable.

I then called the county animal shelter. A woman explained that if I had first called the animal shelter, they would have come and picked up the animal and treated it at county expense. Now, however, they could not intervene and take the cat away from the veterinarian. The cat was going to have to stay at the cat clinic, presumably with me listed as its guardian and benefactor.

Toward the end of the day, I called back to the clinic. The veterinarian's assistant said the cat's condition was about the same. I raised the issue of costs and asked what the bill was so far and how long the cat might need care. The assistant said she understood my concern but couldn't say what further treatment might be necessary or how long the cat might need the veterinarian's care. The cost for the first half day was $200. I gulped but held my tongue, thinking that that was close to what one might pay for a full day's stay in a human hospital.

When I mentioned this to some of my office colleagues, they

were sympathetic and told stories about having their animals treated by veterinarians. One mentioned running up a $3,000 bill for his dog. At this point, I hoped the veterinarian could make the cat whole again, but I didn't want it to cost what it took to reconstruct the $6 million dollar bionic man.

When I got home that night, my wife told me she had some good news. She had talked to the good Samaritan couple, and they had located the cat's owners, a family that lived one street over from the scene of the accident.

From calls to the owner and the clinic that evening and the next day, I received more good news. The owners had gone to the clinic to see the cat. Despite the veterinarian's recommendation that he keep the cat for further observation, the owners had paid the $200 bill and taken the cat home.

Somewhere it had been judged that I had not crossed the black cat's path. There would be no bad luck, not that day.

Looking back at the incident, I think what happened was that the wheel of the car did not run over the cat, but the cat ran between the wheels of the car, and some part of the undercarriage of the car hit the cat's head and caused trauma to its head. The cat and I were both lucky, the cat probably more so than I.

After the incident, I used to see the cat from time-to-time in our neighborhood. Sometimes, I almost thought it smiled at me. Whenever I saw it, I slowed the car down and stayed as far away as possible. The odds, after all, were against me. I had only one life, which I wished to live peacefully, while this cat had eight more lives to go.

"THE DAY I RAN OVER A BLACK CAT" was originally published in *VOICES FROM SMITH MOUNTAIN LAKE,* an anthology of the Lake Writers, a sub-group of the Virginia Writers Club and literary arts arm of the Smith Mountain Arts Council, 2013.

BESS AND ROY

Madelyn Rohrer

Bess and Roy grew up together in Memphis, Tennessee—same neighborhood, same schools, same friends. They even dated on and off during their high school years. But it wasn't until Roy joined the Navy and left Memphis that they both realized how much they truly cared for each other. They decided to get married when Roy was finished with his four-year stint in the Navy; he had a little over a year to go.

Then Bess got thinking about where Roy was stationed—Hawaii. *Wouldn't that be a great place for a honeymoon,* she thought. They changed their plans and decided to get married the next time Roy was home on leave. After the wedding, Roy went back to his base in Hawaii, and Bess followed three weeks later aboard one of the Matson Lines luxurious ships. Oh, it was such a beautiful ship—certainly the biggest one she had ever been on. She felt like a princess going off to meet her prince.

They rented an apartment in a private home on a hillside overlooking the harbor. From the back porch (lanai), the view was stunning. There were pineapple groves and sugar cane fields on the hillside below; further below and off to the left was the city of Honolulu; and straight ahead were the beautiful, sparkling waters of Pearl Harbor. It was like having a "balcony seat over paradise."

Roy was assigned to the battleship USS Pennsylvania and, on a beautiful day in December, the Pennsylvania was put into dry dock for some routine maintenance. It was expected to take just a day, but there were delays, and it had to remain in dry dock until the next morning. Roy was able to come home that night, but he had to be back early the next day as the ship was prepared for its return to Battleship Row.

That next day was….

Sunday, December 7, 1941
It dawned a beautiful day – a gentle breeze, blue sky, puffy white clouds. It was shortly after 6:00 a.m. when Bess walked out

to the street with Roy to wait for his ride that would take him down to the harbor. Then she went back to bed. She was expecting their first child and mornings were not kind to her. An hour and a half later, she awoke to the sound of guns.

Big guns.

Ships' guns.

Bess had heard those sounds before. The Navy routinely cleaned their guns by firing them out over the open water...but they had never done it so early in the morning, and certainly never on a Sunday. Something didn't seem right.

She went out onto the lanai and looked down on the harbor—planes were swooping low over the water, and there was the unmistakable sound of gunfire. *Were they having some kind of military exercise?* She hurried back into the house and grabbed her binoculars—then she saw more planes, *many* more planes. She saw big red circles on them—*Japanese* planes. They were diving and shooting at the ships. She could hear the boom of the ships' guns, and she saw red flashes coming from the ends of the guns as the ships returned fire.

But why? How could this be? We're not at war. Bess could not believe what she was seeing.

Her landlady came running out of the house. "What in the world is going on," she sputtered. "They don't need to be cleaning those guns on a Sunday morning. They can do that anytime."

"I don't think they're cleaning the guns," said Bess. "I think we're being attacked."

But even as she said that, she didn't believe it. They both stood there in total shock, their minds not believing what their eyes were seeing.

A shell hit the hillside below them and shook the ground. Another one sailed directly over the house, exploding somewhere behind them. They both turned and ran back into the house—they didn't know if they should be inside or outside. Another shell hit somewhere nearby, and the house shook. They ran back outside and continued to watch in horror, realizing that the shells flying all around them were *not* from enemy planes—they were from our own ships. The ships were firing at the planes and shells that missed their targets were hitting unintended targets.

Bess watched through her binoculars as wave after wave of Japanese planes flew over the harbor, some high, some low. She watched bombs dropping—bombs that looked like small black pellets against the clear blue sky. She watched as one solitary bomb was dropped over the USS Arizona, disappearing into its stack, seconds later erupting into an enormous fountain of fire as the ammunition in the magazine exploded. Black smoke billowed into the air. The planes kept coming.

The USS Nevada managed to get underway and headed for the mouth of the harbor, but ran aground just before it got there.

Then it was over—the planes were gone. Bess's mind flashed to the Pennsylvania. She couldn't see the dry dock area from the house. Had it been hit? Roy! Was he alright?

A wave of nausea swept over her—was it morning nausea... or was it from what she had just seen? Bess's landlady insisted that she go inside and make herself something to eat so she wouldn't be sick. She went into the kitchen to fix herself an egg and tripped over something. It was the feet of the landlady's maid, Kyoko, who was sitting on the floor under the kitchen table, back up against the wall with just her feet sticking out. She had been fixing breakfast for the landlady when the attack came and now she was terrified—crying and shaking.

"Are they gone, Miss Bess? Are they gone?"

"Yes, Kyoko, they are gone."

Bess was almost finished cooking her egg when the second attack came. She ran outside, only to realize she still had the frying pan in her hand. She ran inside, gulped down her egg, and ran back outside as the nightmare continued.

Once again, she watched the horrifying scenario unfold—planes swooping down, strafing the ships and the buildings in the harbor, bombs falling, explosions, fires. Only now it seemed that more of the ships were shooting back. There was more return fire; the element of surprise was over. Fiery planes were crashing into the water and into the ships. One burning plane crashed into the field below, filling the air beneath them with black smoke.

Bess watched as the Oklahoma was hit, capsizing, turning over on its side. More and more billows of black smoke and fire filled the harbor and the air.

Once again, it was over. The planes were gone. Bess and her

landlady stood together on the hillside in frustrating helplessness, wanting to do something but not knowing what to do. How long would it be before the planes returned? Maybe they should go down to the harbor and try to help. No, that would be foolish, they decided. They waited. Minutes seemed like hours; and hours like days.

Then, they heard loud speakers. Vehicles were driving through the neighborhood telling everyone: "Stay inside—do not come out. Turn on your radios and wait for instructions."

Bess's landlady had a radio. They turned it on, but there was nothing being broadcast. Others joined them—a couple more Navy wives whose husbands were on the Pennsylvania, plus several neighbors. They waited; they prayed; they consoled each other.

Finally, the radio crackled out a message. There was reason to believe, they were told, that the Japanese could be back that night for another attack and possible occupation of the island. They were instructed to pack a small bag, stay by their radios, and be ready to evacuate. If the Japanese invaded the island, they would be informed and should proceed to designated gathering places where they would be picked up and moved inland.

They all went home, packed their bags, and returned to the landlady's house to sit by the radio.

A total black-out condition was in effect—any and all lights would be shot out by sentries. As daylight dwindled and darkness set in, they realized their radio had a little green light in it that became more and more visible as it got darker. They covered the radio with towels to hide the light, and they waited.

Gunfire. They froze as they heard gunfire from several directions. Had a ground invasion started, or were the sentries shooting out lights as they said they would? Then, someone said they thought they heard the sound of planes in the distance.

There was dead silence in the room. Yes—it *was* the sound of planes. Were they going to be bombed? Were they going to be obliterated? Would they be taken prisoners by ground forces and put into concentration camps?

The radio came on with just three words: *"Planes are approaching."*

Never had Bess known fear like this. Her heart pounded so hard it hurt her chest. Someone held her hand; heads were bowed in prayer as the sound of the planes got closer and closer.

The radio came alive with three more words: *"They are ours!"*

Cries of relief flooded the room. There were tears and hugs. And even though the radio remained silent for the rest of the night, sleep would not come easy as they remained huddled around the radio.

The rest of the night was filled with strange noises. There was sporadic gunfire once again coming from different directions, which they found out later *was* from sentries shooting out lights.

And there was another sound…drilling—coming from just one direction, on and off for most of the night. Days later they found out it was coming from a nearby cemetery where the Navy was cutting trenches in the cool ground as temporary holding areas for all the bodies.

§

It was the morning after the attack—Monday. Bess *had* to know about Roy. She decided to go down to the harbor, find the Pennsylvania, and look for Roy. She walked past the bus stop; there were no buses running, of course. She began to make her way down the road leading to the harbor.

A kind neighbor woman stopped and gave her a ride. She was also on her way to the harbor to take supplies to her husband, a Navy diver. She told Bess that the divers had been working constantly since the attack, down in the water listening for pings and taps—any noise at all. "There are many men trapped inside watertight compartments of the ships," she said. "The divers have rescued a lot of them." Bess cringed with claustrophobic chills at the thought of being trapped inside one of those compartments. It would be an image and a fear she would carry with her the rest of her life.

Her neighbor let her out on the road that ran along the shore of the harbor. Everywhere she looked was devastation—smoldering ships and buildings, piles of debris, ashes, smoke. People and vehicles moved about, some slowly, some hurriedly. She looked out at the Arizona. It was broken in half with both ends sticking out of the water like a "V." Smoke was still pouring out of it.

The Pennsylvania was nowhere in sight; maybe it was still in dry dock. As Bess walked through the carnage toward the dry dock area, nothing seemed real. It was like being transported through a nightmare. She kept expecting someone to stop her and tell her she couldn't be there, but no one did. She just kept walking.

There it was. The Pennsylvania **was** still in dry dock. It had damage—she could see holes in the side. The masts had been shot down and were crossed. She could see men moving around high up on the deck. *Oh, please let one of them be Roy!* She waved, hoping he would see her. But as she got closer, a sentry *did* stop her. "You don't want to go any further, ma'am. They're taking bodies off."

Bess went numb as the cold reality that Roy could be hurt or dead penetrated her heart. She could do nothing except turn around and head back along the water toward the road that would take her home.

She fought back tears as she walked along, barely hearing the strange sounds in the harbor next to her—depth charges. She learned later that the Navy divers had discovered small, two-man submarines hiding under some of the ships. They were being brought to the surface, and Japanese sailors who were still alive were being forced out and were begging to be shot, as capture was a disgrace.

She started up the hill. Another neighbor stopped and picked her up and brought her home. There was nothing she could do except wait. Bess knew she should call or send a wire to her parents and to Roy's parents, but she just couldn't bring herself to do it until she knew about Roy. The rest of Monday and all day Tuesday were just a blur in time as she waited.

Wednesday brought the first glimmer of hope that Roy was alive. A friend whose husband was in Communications told her that Roy's name was *not* on any of the lists of confirmed dead or wounded.

§

Thursday Roy came home—exhausted. He slept for four hours and then went back to the harbor. He had been on deck when the attack came. The Chaplain had been just about ready to start an 8:00 service prior to the Pennsylvania's move from dry dock back to Battleship Row. All systems were up and running; so when the attack came, the Pennsylvania was one of the first ships to be able to return fire.

But as the men ran to their battle stations, two enemy planes flew over, strafing both sides of the ship. Roy's life was saved by a huge iron hoisting crane that was sitting on the dock next to the ship. The plane that strafed that side of the ship had to fly a little higher because of the crane and those who were in its shadow were spared as the bullets hit the crane. Most of the men on the other side of the ship were killed.

Oddly enough, as history would later document, the Japanese pilots had lost track of the Pennsylvania. It was not where their intelligence said it was supposed to be—on Battleship Row. They actually thought they had sunk it. When they finally did discover it, however, they tried vigorously to destroy it, only to hit the two ships in front of it, the Cassin and the Downes. So even though the Pennsylvania sustained damage, it was repairable.

Roy wasn't home much after the attack, maybe just two or three hours a couple times during the week. Finally, he was scheduled to have a weekend off. Bess was so relieved and looking forward to having her husband home for a couple of days. She planned a lovely dinner out on the lanai that evening. As she waited, she picked up her binoculars and looked out over the harbor, as she did so often now—and her heart sank as she saw three ships leaving port and heading out to sea: the Tennessee, the Maryland, and the Pennsylvania.

She tried for days to find out where the ships were headed. Someone told her the South Pacific; someone else said Midway; but no one knew for sure. Once again, there was nothing to do but wait.

A notice was sent to all of the military families that a flotilla of ships was going to be leaving Pearl Harbor for San Francisco in a few days. They could put their names on a list to go back to The States, or they could stay. Bess didn't know what to do. She didn't know where Roy was, how long he would be gone, or even if he would be coming back to Honolulu.

She also never got the telegram Roy sent her that said, "Stay there. It is too dangerous to travel right now. I will come back for you. Stay there." But she didn't know. She made the decision to return home to Memphis and wait there for Roy. She went down to the harbor and put her name on the departure list.

They left on Christmas morning. The Navy had commandeered three of the Matson ships—one for Navy and Marine families and wounded, another for Army families and wounded, and a third for civilians. They were nothing like the beautiful ship she had arrived on. They were no longer luxurious. They had been stripped of everything that was not necessary to make room for as many cots and hammocks as possible.

Someone handed out Christmas wreaths to throw in the water as they departed. It was a Hawaiian custom for all who left by ship to toss wreaths into the water and say "aloha." It was meant to be good luck…something that would someday bring visitors back to their island paradise. The "alohas" that day were half-hearted, sad, almost bitter as the wreaths floated away in the oily water.

As they headed out to sea, they were joined by three Navy destroyers and two cruisers that kept circling the Matson ships, keeping them close together.

On the second night out, Bess awoke because of *the absence of sound*. It was deathly quiet. She went up on deck and started to ask a sentry why the engines weren't running, but he motioned to her to stay quiet and not move. Then she heard the noise she had heard only one time before—the sound of depth charges!

"We've had submarine contact," he told her, and once again, the cold reality of imminent danger swept over her. It happened again later that night and again the next night.

§

The mainland at last! Never had that big old San Francisco Bridge been such a welcome sight to so many as it was that day. People cheered as they pulled in. Bess looked off in the distance as they were docking and saw a ship that looked a lot like the Pennsylvania the way the bow was damaged, but she knew it wasn't—the Pennsylvania was somewhere out in the Pacific.

Oh, but it was! As she got off the ship, the Chaplain from the Pennsylvania was waiting for her and another woman. "Your husbands are waiting for you," he told them.

It was in that moment of realizing she was finally in a safe place and knowing her husband was near, that Bess allowed herself to break down. Everything she had bottled up inside of her—the stress, the fear, the horror of war, and what she had been through—spilled over. She put her head down on the Chaplain's chest and sobbed (or in her words, "I just blubbered all over his coat."). But he didn't care; no one cared—it was finally okay to cry.

Yes, Bess thought Roy was somewhere in the South Pacific;

Roy thought Bess was still in Hawaii; and *somehow* they both ended up together again in San Francisco.

§

Life changed for Bess and Roy—war has a way of doing that. Roy's four-year stint in the Navy turned into a twenty-year career. They were blessed with two sons, and they cherished each and every day they had together as a family. Any struggle they would ever face would pale in comparison with what they had already been through.

Bess and Roy *did* go back to Hawaii, many years later—for a vacation. They drove up the hill to that first home they had shared and once again looked down over the hillside from their "balcony seat over paradise." The pineapple groves and the sugar cane fields were still there. Honolulu was much bigger than they had remembered.

And straight ahead were the beautiful, sparkling waters of Pearl Harbor.

This is a true story that has been entrusted to me by my friend, Bess Caraway Twaddle. It is her story as she remembered it, and is told with her permission.

USING MY KARATE CHOPS IN NURSING

Susan Schwartz

Having been summoned to the control desk in the Operating Room at the beginning of my shift, I wondered what mischief I had caused this time. As I arrived, I saw a group of nurses talking and pointing in my direction. A couple of the staff knew I took Tang Soo Do, a Korean martial art, and they suggested that I could be of valuable assistance. Now, I know what you are thinking. We had a belligerent patient whom I needed to subdue to save another staff member. It could be a patient just waking up from anesthesia causing issues for the nursing staff. Maybe it was a hostage situation, and I had to go in like Chuck Norris and save the day with my famous roundhouse kick. It was actually something I had never imagined.

She was a sweet eighty-seven-year old Korean lady who spoke no English. Her daughter was with her in the preop area trying to help until a translator could arrive. Since I knew enough Korean from my martial arts to be dangerous, I tried to assist in keeping them as comfortable as possible before her procedure while waiting for a translator.

"*Annyeong-hashimnikka.*" (Formal Hello in Korean) I said as I stepped into the lady's room. She grinned and waved at me. She started to talk very quickly, and I explained to her daughter that although I was not fluent in Korean, I did know a few words and phrases. I wanted to try to help her mother through the procedure without her feeling all alone in a strange place. The daughter was very grateful that I would take the time to do such a time consuming task for her mother. I told her that no patient should ever feel alone, especially in an OR. When it was time to head for her surgery, I walked back to the OR repeating "*Shio.*" (Relax, be calm.)

When we arrived in the OR, we got the beds lined up perfectly with the wheels locked in place. The CRNA looked at me and said, "Do your magic."

I patted the OR table and told the lady, "*Ahn Jo.*" (Sit here)

She slid over to the table as I directed her to move her "*Pahl,*" then her "*Bahl.*" (Move her arms at the top, then her feet at the bottom to scoot over to the OR table.) When she was on the table and situated, I again said, "*Shio.*" She smiled and nodded.

Until they got her off to sleep, I stayed with her and held her hand reminding her to "*Shio*" throughout the procedure. She chatted with me the whole time, and although I have no idea what she was saying, I could tell she was happy to have someone that could speak to her and give her simple directions she could understand. She went off to sleep quite easily.

After the procedure, I went back to be there when she awoke. She remembered me and smiled. I again said "*Annyeong-hashimnik-ka. Shio.*" The CRNA took time to get her completely awake so she would be ready for her daughter to come to recovery and stay with her as well as the translator. Until then, I stayed with her and held her hand. She was sleepy from the anesthesia, but she seemed at peace knowing we were going to take good care of her and keep her safe.

After she arrived in recovery, her daughter came to sit with her, and I explained what had happened in the interim. Her mother had been through a frightening situation with someone who only spoke a little of her language. I went back to check her about an hour later, and she was getting ready to return home. She stood up and with a deep bow said, "*Ko Map Sum Ni Da.*" (Thank you very much)

I returned her bow with "*Chomane Yo.*" (You're Welcome)

I learned that even the smallest thing we do for a patient will sometimes be of the greatest help. This patient was able to go through an important and frightening procedure with a nurse who could only communicate with her using a few words learned in a karate class. It made all the difference in the world.

THE TURTLES OF RAS AL-JINNS

William E. Sypher

Amid-October evening above the beach at Ras al-Jinns on the Indian Ocean, halfway down the coast of Oman. In the brilliant light of a full moon, the ocean waves glitter as if home to a million frenzied, phosphorescent fish. Each wave breaks with a hiss and then a roar; its dancing lights suddenly go out as it sends a shallow flood onto the beach. Fifteen campers sit silently on a sandy ridge about thirty yards from the shoreline, all fixated on the water's edge. On this night, their patience will be rewarded. A shiny black hemisphere, topped by a bright yellow-white spot, the reflection of the moon, protrudes from the shallows. It is a giant greenback turtle coming ashore to lay its eggs in the sand, as it has from July to November for the past twelve million years. In our hurried, unstable world, such a predictable, slow-moving act is comforting.

Coming ashore? It is far too cavalier a term. In the sea, the greenbacks, like all marine turtles, swim powerfully and gracefully, propelled by four flippers, an aquatic version of four-wheel drive. On land, they are hopelessly clumsy. Lacking legs, they can only launch themselves in spasms, digging their flippers into the sand at a sharp angle and then pushing off these webbed supports, flopping their bodies forward a few inches at a time. Their flippers leave tracks like the cleated wheels of a four-foot-wide garden tractor; their dragging tail leaves a shallow central trough. On land they are clearly out of their depth; surely, they are a colossal evolutionary mistake—fish and land-based turtles need cope with only one medium. Yet, to watch these two hundred-plus pound animals struggle to reach places beyond the water line where they can safely lay their eggs is to ignore gaps in the Grand Design and to be inspired and filled with questions. How far have they come? Are they already exhausted from swimming hundreds of miles? What has impelled them to come ashore? How do they know it is time? Apart from distance and time, how do they know to come unerringly each year to lay their eggs in the place where they were hatched and first crawled into the sea? Surely these great lumbering creatures do not navigate by the stars; their eyes are designed for looking aside and ahead, not to the skies. They must be imprinted with some magnetic or electric fields from birth, internal compasses which guide them.

The beaches at Ras al-Jinns (in Arabic, *a point of land where spirits dwell*) and neighboring Ras al-Haad are considered national treasures by the Omani government. They are zealously guarded by rangers, all business in their tan-colored robes, cinched at the waist with a gun belt, and a gun in the holster. The greenbacks are endangered, and Oman is determined to preserve them. No one is allowed to go unescorted to the nesting beaches. Each evening through the nesting season, at around nine-thirty, the guards summon campers and escort them in small groups to various points along the beach. Every effort is made not to intrude openly on this critical phase of the reproductive cycle. Flash photography is forbidden, and as it is dark, all photography is virtually ruled out. A few campers have come equipped with night-vision binoculars, which must impose an eerie, redundant green on the great green amphibians we have come to see.

We sit quietly for a few minutes, then our ranger gestures for us to approach slowly and quietly. As we draw near the nesting sites, we walk over loose sand that is cratered with cone-shaped depressions about two feet deep and four feet in diameter at ground level. This is what remains after a mother turtle's work is done. Thus, many egg clutches lie buried beneath our footsteps, with eggs in various stages of incubation. The guard spots a nest under construction and gestures vigorously, palms down, for us to sit. We are only ten feet away. All are quiet. We have come to witness a miracle.

After perhaps a half hour's tortuous progress up the gently sloping beach, the hulking greenbacks have mounted the sandy shelf near where we are sitting and have chosen a spot of deep, loose sand where they have begun digging with their flippers. The sand is fittingly egg-shell in color—an incubating sand which must stand in for the massive, absentee mothers either too big to sit on the eggs as protective, lightweight birds do, or too dim-witted to imagine the fate of unguarded eggs. As they dig they sink slowly, ironically, into the sand, as if they are digging their own grave, but this is an act to propagate life not end it. After perhaps fifteen minutes, they have sunk one to two feet below ground level and are covered with the sand. From the depression where they are hard at work, double volleys of sand, the size of small shovels full, spew out in opposite directions. Like bursts from a long dormant but now awakened volcano, they continue to be flung from the hole spasmodically for a half hour or more. Under their posteriors, the mother turtles are digging a separate chamber with their back flippers, twelve-sixteen inches deeper than the three-foot-wide hole they have dug for themselves.

Unmistakable yelps of foxes in the distance go almost unnoticed, their role in the nightly drama not yet recognized by those bent on seeing turtles. Volleys of sand, less frequent now, continue to spray from the nest. The ranger crawls on his belly toward the edge of the nest to get a close view without disturbing the process. He watches intently, then turns to us and gestures for us to approach slowly and silently. Some of us crawl on our hands and knees to the edge of the nest.

The guard has trained a flashlight onto the turtle's posterior. He lifts her right flipper, exposing her protruding egg tube, a kind of proboscis. The off-white, elliptical eggs are emerging from the tube, one to three at a time, interspersed with spurts of milky fluid, which lubricate the egg tract. As the eggs are leathery and flexible, they are in no danger of breaking when they fall into the small chamber. One observer at the front of the turtle hears an audible sigh from time to time and reports tears running down the face of the mother, most likely the result of sand irritating her eyes. A typical female might lay up to 300 eggs in the space of fifteen minutes. After she is finished, she remains in the same position and artfully fills the hole with sand, using only her back flippers. It is all done blindly; only her tactile sense guides her. When the hole is mostly filled, she works her way out of the depression, the sand cascading off her back, and launches herself back down the slope to the dark water.

By daylight the scene, with turquoise waves breaking on eggshell white sand, while still pretty, is less romantic than when seen in moonlight. It is even chilling. Turtles come ashore only under cover of darkness, and they are well-advised to do so. As we walk across the cratered sand, around tens of nests, we see ominous signs of fresh digging and a fox paw print. One nest lies exposed to the air and sun. In the incubation chamber, an egg lies open, its yellow yolk spilled out. Surprisingly, other eggs lie undisturbed. A curious fox, like the Dr. Seuss character, has sampled the "green" eggs and decided he doesn't like them. No matter, the remaining eggs, exposed to the open air and other predators, are doomed. Outside the nest, what appears to be a greenish turtle embryo lies dead in the sun. The turtles are in constant danger from the moment they are released as eggs from their mother. If the eggs are not taken by foxes or snakes, the hatchlings face terrifying airborne predators on their awkward lurch to the sea. Falcons, gulls, and osprey can snatch and eat their fill of the helpless wanderers. Even in the sea, a medium comfortable to them, the young are gobbled by large fish. Thus, on land, in the sea and in the air, they are hunted relentlessly. It is estimated that only one in 300 eggs, the maximum output of one mother turtle, will survive to adulthood. That grim statistic makes seeing a full-grown adult a small miracle in itself. That one has beaten desperately unfavorable odds.

Nest-robbing is sad but predictable, and perhaps essential to the survival of foxes and other wildlife. And it is only fair to point out that on this beach we are presented with a one-sided picture of nature. We do not see the giant greenbacks feasting on other mother's babies in the ocean. We are all linked not only in the Great Chain of Being but in a great chain of non-being, the food chain.

On this balmy, moonlight evening on the western shore of the Indian Ocean, time is marked only by nature's graceful, unhurried units: the circadian rhythm of night and day, the lunar cycle lighting the night and pulling the tides, orbiting planets defining the seasons, and the reproductive cycle urging greenbacks to go ashore. We could be watching this yesterday, tomorrow, or a million years ago. All that we see has always been here; nothing we see has been crafted by us. We are gloriously incidental to the shadowy movements on the sand. It is at once humbling and wondrous and shall remain so.

THE RITES OF SPRING

Erin Newton Wells

May is the month that says all is finally well. Warmth and color return after a winter of snow, a March and April of false starts. It is the friend you can trust. But years ago I learned of a shadowed part that hides toward the end of this favored month behind the blooms and blue sky. It is never welcome, always a surprise. Just when things couldn't be better, it steps out to demand its due and break the hearts of so many people.

I stand before a small group of high school students on the first of May.

"Who knows what day this is?" I ask them, as I have asked their predecessors over the years.

"Monday?" someone finally offers.

"No, I mean what's the significance of the day?"

The less polite visibly roll their eyes. The rest do so inwardly. But no one ever gives the answer I seek. They hunker down, waiting to get back to the lesson.

But, of course, this is the lesson. Officially, our time together is listed as Art on their schedules. And yet I forever point out to them that my seemingly random wanderings are going somewhere of importance. When they ask what they should study to prepare for a career in art, I answer, "Everything. Everything." Nothing is too small or unrelated.

"It's May Day," I say, supplying the answer one more time.

More blank looks. So I begin to tell them of its history, far back when people were in touch with the land and were truly exuberant as the season of growing returned. They spent the day outdoors, sang, feasted, danced around a May pole, made garlands of flowers and crowned a Queen of the May. Literature has numerous references to it, and many customs descend from it. It often appears in art. It is part of what makes us a species with a remembered culture.

"Did any of you make May baskets when you were younger?" I ask. But I already know the answer.

They look up, preceded by the snapping of cell phones under the table. Use of the phones is forbidden. It is like asking them not to breathe.

"When I was a little girl, we made baskets of a piece of paper rolled into a cone. A paper strip was attached for a handle."

The heads drop down again. In earlier times this posture would indicate guilt or extreme humility. Now, it is the pose of texting. Fleeting smiles pass across faces as they check gnomic postings from virtual friends.

"We gathered flowers from our yards to put in the baskets," I continue, "then hung them on the front door knobs of neighbors. We rang the bell and hid to watch as they found the gift."

At least one girl gazes into space, as if she might be thinking about what I said.

"This simple custom comes from those earlier times," I conclude. "It ties us to those people."

Her head drops. One of them asks permission to go to the bathroom. The others start shuffling materials, setting up their drawing boards. It's the same as having the vaudeville cane reach out and pull me off the stage. Vaudeville. Another topic they don't know.

I put the example of a standing figure on a display easel. I haven't told them yet about the complete reversal of the old May Day to the May Day parades of the Cold War era. The Soviet Union's marching soldiers and rolling stock of missiles and tanks turned it into a celebration of military might, not the joy of spring.

There's the May festival of my childhood, too. We danced at a ribboned May pole in the school yard. I want to tell them this. But as I look at these gifted children sprawled around the table, I see the high school of my senior year, and the shadow hovers at the edges of the room. If only I could push it back until it never came out again.

These days the school year often runs into June. But May was the end in my school days, the month of graduation. We had no air-conditioning in the schools then, and I grew up in the South, in the state as far south as you can go without bumping into Mexico or sliding into the Gulf. School finished by Memorial Day of necessity, before the miasma of real summer set in.

Along with graduation came prom night in the latter half of

May. We felt relief we would soon be free. It was time to celebrate. But there were always some who let it get out of control.

At least where I lived, we didn't have those contained after-prom parties now offered by many communities. Groups of us hosted our own parties or went somewhere to celebrate together, like the famous pizzeria in town. But there were also carloads that traveled the short distance across the border of our dry state into the neighboring wet one. This meant a lot of teenagers behind the wheel with their minds on anything but safety. Returning late that night or in the dark hours of the next morning, their minds were even less capable of concentrating on the road.

I'll call her Marion, like the Queen of the May in Robin Hood's forest. Every school has a Marion. This group in front of me, for instance, surely can name someone like her. She is pretty, sweet, takes part in everything, makes top grades, a class leader, and the most likely to succeed at being Marion forever.

The Marion of my senior year was in Latin Club with me and in Honor Society, too. But she kept going where I left off. A class officer, a member of the homecoming court, she had it all, including Deke. I'll call him Deke, the basketball star, math whiz. They'd been the perfect couple all through high school. We expected to see them happily married someday and leaders of the community.

At the pizza palace after the prom, some of the others persuaded Marion and Deke to go along with them over the state line. Anyone could see they didn't want to. But, hey, the others said. Once in a lifetime have some fun. They left, and the restaurant emptied out a bit.

I look at my superior students who have made it all this way through school. They are at work drawing figures in motion, and they check proportions with their fingers the way I've taught them. They use the unit of a person's head to plot the body. They learn to ask themselves how many heads it takes to measure someone. When people who don't know me ask what I teach, I tell them Life. It is what makes the figures move as these students sketch. Hang onto Life, I say. It is an important subject. You will need it.

If they would listen, I would like to tell them that the story turned out well. I would like to say that all of us met up again at school on Monday to laugh and wink as we shared tales of the magic May night. But it didn't work that way at all. The shadow hiding among the blooms at the end of spring stepped out and named its price.

The car carrying Marion and Deke swerved on a country road, coming back from across the border. Maybe it turned to avoid a dog or to miss a slick stretch after a light rain. Or there was fog. Or the driver didn't notice anything at all by that time, and his hands just turned and turned the wheel any which way, once in a lifetime.

It was Marion and Deke in the backseat who were thrown from the car and killed when it swung around and slammed the rear end on a pole. No one had seat belts back then.

There was no joy that Monday, after we heard the news. The May queen was dead, along with her king. Innocence went directly out of my life. Two were missing at the graduation ceremony that year. How many seniors does it take to equal a graduating class? How many Marions and Dekes to make the world go round again?

Almost every year since then, usually in May or close to it, I will hear of another tragedy like this. Sometimes, it is in the town where I live now. But it can be found in news notices from all over this country, those brief statements of names we don't know and places we haven't been. Teenagers joyriding after proms or graduation parties meet up with the same shadow we all have learned to know so well and wish we did not.

I want to pound on the table to get the attention of these bright students in front of me, some of them about to graduate this year and the others not far behind. I want to tell them to put their assignments aside for a moment, to let their thumbs be silent on the messages they think I don't see them making below eye level. Let the brain static not interfere with what I have to say.

Continue through this May, I would tell them if they would listen. Outlast it, and another and another spring, until you are old enough to see a younger generation roll its eyes at the stories you tell of your own youth. Do not be consumed this year by the rites of spring, I would say.

("The Rites of Spring" originally published in *Skyline 2016,* and the recipient of First

Place in nonfiction in the *Skyline* spring-themed contest, 2015.)

WHAT HE KNEW WHEN HE WROTE THE LETTER

Robin Williams

I am holding in my hands a seventy-two-year-old letter that my father sent to his parents from Burma in 1944 in which he says he expects to be home from the war "around the first part of the year." It is fascinating to think about where he was and what was happening when he wrote the letter—things I know as I read the letter but things he didn't know as he wrote it.

My father, nicknamed "Bo," wrote the letter on November 11, while sitting in a house made entirely of teak deep in the exotic world of north Burma. A week earlier, he and his unit had crossed the Irrawaddy River on bamboo rafts propelled with 60 hp Evinrude engines that had been dropped by parachute from low-flying cargo planes. So well-packaged were the engines that only one of the sixteen was damaged. The quartermaster had learned how to package and drop supplies so well that troops in the field sometimes received fresh eggs and live pigs.

After nearly a year of battles and firefights in the dark labyrinth of the jungle, broken by only a few clearings and the miserable, burned bamboo huts of abandoned villages, Bo and his unit had entered a more populous and resource-rich region south of the Irrawaddy. Here, the towering trees consisted of royal coconut palms and massive teak groves. The hills held not just Japanese fortifications but jewel mines of rubies and jade. Poking up above the green canopy of the jungle like tent poles were ornate graceful peaks of Buddhist temples, often covered in gilt.

"I've seen sights that are hard to describe," Bo wrote. "I'm on some kind of mission that just doesn't have arrangements made for [the mail]. I stay busy all the time and it's the most fun I've had since I've been overseas. This is really something to tell about when I get back."

As he wrote home, he could see that the tide had turned and, inexorably, the Allies were pushing the Japanese out of Burma and the Germans out of France. The war was not yet won, but there was a growing sense that the forces of Good would eventually vanquish Evil. After perforce living one day at a time, Bo had begun to let himself think about the future.

"My count calls for 18 more days over here but that's all wet. I expect to be here a few months yet."

Always optimistic, even in war, Bo sounded upbeat in his letter, excited by the mission he was on but also seeing a realistic end to his two years of overseas duty.

Elsewhere in the world, the Allied command prepared for the final push to Berlin—only to be shocked by Hitler's desperate counteroffensive, a senseless attack that would do nothing but multiply human suffering and death in the winter of '44-'45: The Battle of the Bulge.

But Bo didn't know that when he wrote. He didn't know when he wrote and joked about getting home before his brother, Joe, who was serving as a doctor with the 20th Engineers, that the fighting had begun in the snow and cold in places like Hurtgen Forest. And he didn't know when he wrote that Joe had been injured, that he had stayed at the front to care for other wounded men, covering them with tree boughs to shelter them from the snow. Bo didn't know, as he smoked a Pall Mall cigarette and thought of his family, that Joe had defied his commanding officer and stayed with his men, that Joe had been killed three days before he wrote his upbeat letter.

"What's the news of Joe?"

Winner, 2016 Richmond Writers Club Golden Pen Award for NF

3d, 2016 Virginia Writers Club Golden Pen Award for NF

FICTION

§

TABLE OF CONTENTS

DECEMBER 1910: CHRISTMAS AGAIN

Jo Allison

Nurse was pushing her toward the hallway that looked out on the sanitarium's courtyard. Sarah Upton often thought she would like to go into the courtyard, but it hadn't happened yet, and now it wouldn't happen until spring. She had tried to tell Mother about the courtyard in the spring, but Mother had started crying and cut short that particular visit.

Today, though, as Nurse turned the wheelchair into the hallway with its large windows, Sarah caught sight of snow falling. The large flakes were covering the ground, and Sarah waved toward the windows, excited by a memory of snow-covered ground. She managed to say, "It's Christmas."

"No, dearie," Nurse said. "Christmas isn't for more than a fortnight yet."

Sarah's tears started. She needed to look at the snow longer. The memory was getting away from her, and she couldn't stop the chair, couldn't explain, couldn't go back to the windows.

Was it something about School? She'd enjoyed the children's excitement building and the few days of vacation at Christmas. But whatever was calling to her seemed like a memory more important than School, and she couldn't locate it.

Nurse stopped the wheelchair in the visiting room and pulled a straight back chair close. Sarah heard Nurse sigh. "Now, dearie, don't cry, You said it was okay if this woman came to see you."

Sarah took a sharp breath and twitched toward the door. What woman? When would she have said that? She didn't want a visitor. She wanted to watch the snow and find the memory that might be a good one. It had the feel of a good memory. She couldn't waste the effort to explain that, so she jabbed a finger at the one window in the visiting room. The sigh was even louder as Nurse turned her toward the window and adjusted the other chair accordingly.

"You don't want to stare out the window while she's trying to talk to you, now," Nurse said. She wiped the tears without further comment, put the handkerchief back in Sarah's lap, and left Sarah's immediate circle of attention.

That was good. If Nurse wasn't right next to her, treating her like a child, that was good. Sarah had wondered early on if Nurse didn't know that Sarah was a respected teacher, moving up to assistant principal by her mid-thirties, the youngest woman in the system to do that. Maybe Nurse thought she was a loose woman who had had syphilis for years, instead of a respectably married—if recently married—woman. Now, though, Sarah had ceased to care what Nurse thought. At the moment, she'd ceased to care that she wouldn't reach forty. What she cared about just now was the snow.

It occurred to Sarah that she would like to get up and walk to the window, pull aside the sheer panel beneath the heavy drape, and—oh, this would be wonderful—lean her forehead against the cold pane as she watched the snow. She could will the memory back if she could stand and walk and watch the snow from inches away.

She put her hands on the arms of the chair and pushed. Nothing happened in terms of standing, but pain erupted in palms and soles and joints. And she'd already had her laudanum that morning. More movement meant more pain, and no way to get more relief. She paused with her hands in place, wondering if another effort was worth it.

A voice said, "Can I help you?" and Sarah knew it couldn't be Nurse. But, she didn't want to look around, to break her fantasy about walking to the window to discover the memory.

"Mrs. Upton?"

Goodness. No one here called her that. No visitor called her that, but, of course, visitors these days were only Mother and, less often now, Father. There had been others, but not for . . . Sarah couldn't remember how long that had been.

So, she let her hands fall back into her lap and turned to look at a visitor who would call her Mrs. Upton.

Sarah knew she didn't see as well as she once had. She took her time looking over the young woman who stood before her. Maybe it wasn't her vision. Maybe it was her sense of time. She took in the details of the woman's appearance. The woman was slender and wearing what Sarah remembered as the new style: no corset to change her posture, no petticoats to fill out a full skirt. This woman wore a skirt that dropped straight and stopped several inches from the floor, with a jacket that bloused the skirt in an easy sort of way. A school teacher couldn't wear anything like that. The woman's hair wasn't on top of her head; it must be in a bun or some other unconventional do. Sarah had the oddest feeling that she could look like this now, having lost so much weight and not being able to put her hair up if she had cared to.

The woman was smiling slightly and looking at Sarah in return. Sarah heard herself make the mewing noise she knew she made when she was distressed, because of pain or forgetfulness or vision loss or the wound that gaped beside her mouth. It was the sound she made when she knew someone was seeing all that in her.

"I'm Julia McConnell." The woman sat down in the difficult straight skirt. "I've come to talk to you about your house, Mrs. Upton."

Sarah jerked in her seat. The house. Yes. The house was the memory: she and Richard walking in the snow at Christmas to see their new house, not yet completed inside, but the picture of modernness on the outside. The fine little bungalow was situated there in the snow to house them and the child she had just found out she was carrying. Sarah looked toward the windows as if she could see the house there, in the snow of the courtyard. She knew she was saying "my house," although she didn't know if the woman could understand her.

"Yes, Mrs. Upton. Your father is selling the house, you know, and my husband and I are considering buying it."

Sarah turned to look at her more closely, at this bearer of unthinkable news. Sell their house? Father would sell their house? Meaning she couldn't go back to it. Or course, she knew that if she thought about it. If she couldn't go to the courtyard, she couldn't go back to her house. But, it was still her house, and Father had said the puppy was there, staying in the garage, because the sanitarium wouldn't allow it. Would he sell the puppy as well? Or turn it out? And what would someone else do with the empty bedroom? The one that was supposed to be the baby's.

"My house?" It came out almost a squeal, the sound escaping through the wound near her mouth.

The woman—had she said her name was Julia?—was alarmed. The nurses and her mother called the place on her mouth a chancre. But it felt like a hole, and Sarah suspected it was the most off-putting of her various sores and disabilities. Sarah thought of it as *the wound*, symbol of all she had lost and was losing.

The woman breathed deeply and said, "Yes. Your house on Humphrey Street. We know about it because my husband worked with Richard at the *Globe*."

Sarah was stunned. She got one hand up and waved it and thought the woman was reaching for it, but she couldn't see her well. The woman, Julia, must be backing off because Nurse was close; Sarah smelled disinfectant. Also, she heard Nurse say, "We don't usually talk about Mr. Upton."

Sarah ignored both women, feeling Richard's arm around her shoulders as they looked at the house in the snow. She explored all around inside that memory but turned to find the woman still there, simply looking at her. Nurse had moved away.

"I know why you're here, in the sanitarium, Mrs. Upton, and what has happened." The woman spoke quietly, and Sarah was surprised she could hear her so clearly. Maybe it was because the woman was speaking directly to her. Most visitors, even Mother, looked away. "As a matter of fact, my husband feels guilty. He knew, the whole newsroom did, about Richard's disease. William, my husband, said Richard boasted of taking a cure, but—apparently not. William felt he should have said more. I am so sorry, Mrs. Upton. So sorry it's happened so quickly and gone so badly."

Sarah's tears flowed again. One tear irritated a sore near her nose, and she raised a hand to wipe at it. The woman picked up the handkerchief for her, and Sarah clutched it.

Back to the question. Sarah recognized amazing clarity in herself in knowing that there was a question at hand. She would have smiled if she could have. "My house?"

"Yes, Mrs. Upton. Other potential buyers may not know your story, but I do. And I won't live there, much as I love it, without your blessing."

"My house." That came out so loud. Sarah didn't know she could still generate so much volume. She still had the wind to say, "the puppy."

"The puppy—Queenie, right?—goes with the house, and we'll take good care of her. If we buy."

"My house." The emphasis was on the word *my*, and Sarah saw the woman react, maybe take that as an answer. Sarah watched closely, struck by the woman's slow nod, a personal sadness growing on top of her sadness for Sarah.

"I understand, Mrs. Upton. It's your house, and I won't live there if—"

Sarah sobbed loudly, and the woman stopped talking. She stood, probably to leave, and Sarah realized she—Julia, wasn't it?—was saying she would give up living in Sarah's house.

Who would live there, then? Not Sarah and not this Julia, who knew about her and about Richard and maybe about the empty bedroom that had been a nursery and about where Richard was now. In his own, different sanitarium, suffering different wounds. Sarah couldn't begin to say all that. But it was clear what she needed to say: better this Julia live in the house than someone who didn't know.

"No," Sarah said, although that always came out *oh*. She rocked forward in the wheelchair as if she could move closer and keep the woman from leaving.

It worked in that the woman managed to take Sarah's hand, without Nurse there to stop her.

"What would you like to have happen with the house, Mrs. Upton?"

Sarah managed more words than she would have thought possible. "You live there. The bungalow in the snow. Take care of Queenie." Her voice broke, and more tears slipped down her face. The woman let go of her hand and dabbed at Sarah's face with the handkerchief.

"May I call you Sarah?" she asked.

Sarah sniffed and nodded.

"I promise you, Sarah, I will take good care of the house and good care of Queenie."

Sarah could barely see Julia. She reached out but couldn't find a hand to squeeze. She tried nodding again, as hard as she could. And then she smelled Nurse. Nurse was saying the visit was tiring Sarah. Sarah should object to that, but it must be true. Nothing else would come from her mouth, except the mewing. She could barely hear Julia as the woman said, "God bless you, Sarah."

Nurse turned Sarah's chair away, and Sarah assumed the woman was leaving. Sarah kept the image of this Julia, tall and straight in the skinny suit, as the chair rolled. Nurse pushed Sarah to a window in the hallway and left her there.

When Sarah got back to realizing what she was doing, she found she had given up on the image of the woman and was counting snowflakes, the big ones. She had taught so many children to count, and now it was the numbers themselves she loved, not caring how many of the flakes she actually identified.

Sarah stopped counting when the numbers got too large to say to herself and let her head rest on the chair back. She enjoyed the satisfaction that was the odd victory these days. Not so tired after all that she couldn't see to her house and the puppy. Not so wounded she couldn't remember that she had loved Richard and carried his child. Not so far gone that she didn't know Christmas when she saw it.

TOAD

Betsy Ashton

Toad lay in his bed while the world woke up around him. He heard his dad drive his pickup through the gate to travel the twenty miles up the highway to his job selling appliances at Montgomery Ward. His mother wrestled his eight-year-old brother into her own truck. Jimmy howled because he had to get up early, because he had to stay all day with his mother at the doctor's office where she worked in town, and most of all because he had to walk next door to the dentist for his annual teeth cleaning. Toad lay still until his brother's bellowing faded away with the sound of the truck engine. He hadn't heard the clang of the chain link gate shut behind her, so he knew his mother had left the gate open. Again.

She harped on him to lock the gate, but at least twice a week she ran late and skipped the task, making her the worst offender in the family. Even if he didn't know the rules, he would always lock the gate to keep his dog safe.

On his first day living in the trailer compound, even before he unpacked his boxes of clothes, books and writing tablets, his grandfather gathered the family together to talk about rattlesnakes.

"They like to sun themselves near our steps." He pointed to several places where he'd seen rattlers. "There, there and there."

Jimmy's eyes grew round as a hubcap. "Gee!"

"Never get close to one, because they strike faster than you can imagine."

"I can outrun anything." At eight, Jimmy had infinite faith in his ability to get away from danger.

Their grandfather laughed and ruffled Jimmy's hair. He showed the family how to use the forked sticks he'd hung on hooks beside each exit, where he kept the machetes nearby and how to pin the snake to the ground before chopping off its head.

"Now, don't get near the mouth. The fangs are still full of poison even after the snake is dead."

"I want a rattle." Jimmy's eyes glowed with love for his grandfather.

The old man reached up to a shelf near the steps and handed dried rattles to each of the boys.

"Wow!" Toad breathed.

"Yippee!" Jimmy shouted.

I can't believe my good luck. I have the whole day to myself.

For once, he wasn't in charge of his younger brother. At ten, Toad's parents said he was responsible enough to be left at the trailer compound, with or without his brother.

Jimmy's okay, but he's a scaredy-cat and a tattletale.

Today, Toad had privacy. He wanted to explore, go out to a forbidden place. Something wondrous had entered his world, and he had, just had, to know what it was.

Today I'm going further west than ever, out where the spaceship landed.

For more than a week, new loud noises carried across the open desert from the higher plateau beyond the dry wash. White trails filled the sky. It had to be a spaceship.

"What else could it be?" Toad muttered. He wondered if the white trails were a sign that spacemen were building a landing spot or a city nearby. "I bet they're bringing supplies from a huge ship hiding in the shadow of the moon." Could a smaller ship have already landed? Was it burying itself under the sand? It could be a scouting ship with spacemen who wanted to see if we are friendly.

He had tried to tell his parents about this stupendous event.

"Hey, Dad. I think a spaceship landed out in the desert," he said one night at dinner.

Jimmy squealed and leaped out of his chair. "Let's go find it."

His father's long arm stopped him in mid leap. "Sit." He took a long swallow from his beer can. "What's this nonsense about a spaceship?"

Toad told him about the strange noises coming from the west. He hadn't see it land, but the animals were behaving oddly. "I'm positive it's a spaceship."

His father laughed. "You have quite an imagination, young man."

"Yeah," said Jimmy. "You make stuff up all the time." If he couldn't search for the spaceship, he could try stealing Toad's thunder. Toad made up his mind that Jimmy would never meet the spacemen.

"Maybe you should become a writer," his mother said.

"But I want to learn to fly," Toad said.

"Ha," said his father

Let them eat their words. I'll find the spaceship. They'll be sorry when I become famous.

Toad bounded out to where his German Shepherd waited. He filled his dish with kibble and put down fresh water before he trotted across the barren ground between living area and gate. After just a few weeks, he no longer found it odd that he lived in a three-trailer compound in the middle of the desert instead of a suburb outside a mid-sized city.

He scampered across the platform between his trailer and his parents' and pushed through the screen door into the kitchen where he found a bowl of cereal waiting for milk.

"Oh boy, Rice Krispies."

"It's a good day for you to find the spaceship," said Snap, Crackle and Pop.

A quick swipe at his teeth, and he was ready for his big adventure. He stuffed a peanut butter sandwich his mom had left for his lunch in his pants pocket, fastened his canteen to his belt and left the trailer. He checked for snakes before stepping off the platform into the dirt surrounding his home.

He had already killed his first snake, much to Jimmy's dismay. The younger boy wanted, no needed, to kill his own snake and keep the rattle in his pocket.

"That's not fair. You should have let me kill the snake." Jimmy whined.

"You went to town with Mom to swim. I couldn't let the snake get away." Used as he was to Jimmy's always feeling like a younger brother and therefore inferior, Toad promised the next snake was his brother's, if his brother was at home.

Some nights Toad slept alone in his trailer. He liked to read late into the night, but he couldn't if he was out on the platform. When his father was ready for bed, he forbid any lights on outside. After Jimmy dropped off to sleep, his parents would talk. They acted as if they didn't know Toad could hear every word.

"When we got married, I never figured we'd be living in three trailers connected by a covered outdoor platform on a dirt road in the middle of nowhere." His mother never let his father forget he'd lost the family's money when his business failed.

"Right now, we don't have a choice. This place is free, and we need to save money to get back on our feet." His father sounded resigned to their situation.

His grandfather owned the hundred-acre plot off Route 66 but no longer lived there. When his grandfather's health declined, he moved into town to be closer to the hospital.

"I just wish your father had told us what to expect." His mother complained often about the difficulty of their lives in the compound. "He should have told us everything about this place before we moved up here."

The power company had run lines along the highway years before, so the trailers had electricity. One even had a small window air conditioner, a necessity because that was where his mother cooked. Toad and Jimmy had to make do with a fan in their trailer. Most nights the whole family slept outside on cots on the covered platform. A television antenna on the top of the largest trailer brought in three black-and-white stations. Evening viewing centered on what his parents wanted to watch. During the summer the television was outside, but Toad suspected that when the weather changed, his father would move it into the main trailer, because that was also where his parents would sleep.

What the compound lacked was running water, hence the outhouses. His mother took large water bottles to work with her once a week to fill at a public tap.

"What could be better than not having to take a bath every night," Jimmy said.

Sun heated water in a large outdoor tank. During the week, the boys took sponge baths every night; on Saturday a full washtub bath was the rule.

Toad had grown brown and sturdy under the relentless sun. He was no longer the pasty stick-boy he had been when his family left the city for a new beginning in the desert.

Rex sat patiently, tongue hanging out, tail sending up small plumes of sandy dust with each wag. Toad pulled Rex's ear and gave him a scratch under the chin. In a pen at the far side of the compound, adjacent to a pair of outhouses, Shorty thrust her head over the rail and blew softly. When he walked up to the gate, she nuzzled his pocket for a treat. He clipped a lead to her halter, opened the gate and led her through the main opening in the perimeter fence. His parents trusted him to leave the compound to play and explore as long as he took Shorty and Rex with him. Usually, Jimmy tagged along. When he became too tired to walk, Toad would boost him onto Shorty's broad back. He hooked and locked the gate behind him to keep wild animals and strangers out. With only two wooden houses on his dirt road and no children except his brother, these animals were Toad's best friends.

Behind him came the whoosh of big rigs running north. Toad headed toward the end of the world far away from the rising sun and the highway. This had become his daily routine since the family moved in May after school ended. Rex took a couple of steps toward the highway and whined. Toad whistled.

"No, boy. Not that way. I don't want you to get hit by a truck."

Thirty minutes after he started walking, Toad noticed a slight shift in the sand near his foot. He froze, stooped and saw a tiny dinosaur sunning itself beside a rock. He picked up the horny toad and stroked its armored head and spiny back.

"You just stay here and warm yourself," Toad said to the dinosaur. "I can't play with you today. I got bigger things on my mind. I have to meet the spacemen."

Toad put the reptile back on the ground where it burrowed itself halfway into the sand. He continued his hike toward the spaceship. Behind him, half asleep, Shorty bobbed her long-eared head. Rex flushed a rabbit but lost it down a hole and barked at a snake on a patch of sand. Toad turned away from the snake, but kept marching toward a low rise. He saw a scurry of activity when a striped head with two shiny black eyes popped out of a hole. He squatted in the sand and held out his hand. A striped body and short bushy tail followed the head out of the hole and into Toad's hand.

"Hey, Chip. Where's Dale?" Toad stroked the little critter, which rewarded him with a chirp and a couple of pellets of poop in his hand. Toad had named the chipmunks Chip and Dale after his favorite comic book characters right around the time he made friends with them.

Dale ran out of a different burrow a couple of yards away. He chattered as if complaining that Toad wasn't petting him.

"You're such little beggars. I'll save some of my sandwich. You can have it when I get back," Toad promised. He played with them until they jumped out of his hand, and with twin swishes of their tails disappeared into their holes.

Ever since his family moved into the compound, Toad had spent his days exploring and daydreaming. At first, he didn't know anything about this new world. To keep him safe, his father and grandfather taught him and his brother how to identify snake trails, ant nests, clouds on the distant horizon, and plants that bit if you touched them. Toad forgot about the plants once and came home one afternoon full of sharp spines. It hurt like heck when his mother pulled jumping cactus out with tweezers.

He had no idea how much land he had to roam in. He and Jimmy started close to the fenced perimeter of the compound, gradually working their way outward.

"What do you want to play today?" Toad asked every morning.

"Cowboys and Indians."

But sometimes when Toad grew tired of cowboys and Indians, they dug a shallow fort and played war. What one boy couldn't dream up, the other could.

Not only was Toad more imaginative, he was also the braver one. Jimmy followed his father's instructions to the letter, even when they got in the way of a grand adventure. Toad thought those instructions were suggestions for good behavior, not orders to be blindly obeyed.

"You are never, ever, to go into the dry wash. It could flood in minutes if there's a storm to the north," his father had warned. "It's the most dangerous place around here. Other than the highway, that is."

What could be more exciting, more dangerous than finding spacemen? Natural hazards had nothing on the possibility of a real spaceship.

Toad had crossed the wash a few times before. Jimmy tattled on him once. His father spanked him; he ate dinner standing up. Well, his brother couldn't tattle today.

Today, Toad decided he knew better than his father. Some rare and wondrous adventure lay over the low rise, across the dry wash and up onto the higher plateau. He approached the rim; the new thing, the spaceship, was on the other side.

"Whaddya think, Shorty? Should we cross?"

Shorty lowered her head, shook her ears and snorted. Rex barked and bounded down the trail, tail wagging, nose scenting the air. He stopped at the bottom, looked up at Toad and Shorty and barked again.

"Okay."

Toad checked north, saw no clouds, and led Shorty down one side of the wash, across the deep sandy bottom, and up the rocky far side. His heart thumped by the time he climbed out. Rex led the way, until he took off after a jack rabbit and disappeared behind a clump of Joshua trees.

"We won't tell anyone where we went. Okay?"

Shorty blew warm breath on his face. By the time he reached the rim of the wash, he was thirsty and stopped to rest. He threw himself on the ground.

"We must have come at least a hundred miles," he said to his animals.

He took a swig of warm water from the canteen, thought about the peanut butter sandwich squished in his pocket, and decided to save it. Shorty rested her head on Toad's shoulder and nuzzled his shirt pocket for another treat.

"Is food all you think about? It's no wonder you're so round."

Toad pulled her gray ears, patted her fuzzy forehead and surrendered a treat. Rex loped back, panting, to flop in Shorty's shade. Once again, the jack rabbit was safe. Toad watched a tarantula make its awkward way across a small patch of scree. Unusual for it to be out in the daylight, he assumed something strange had disrupted its normal hunting patterns. The spider didn't rear up in a threatening manner, but Toad knew better than to provoke it. He'd been bitten the first week at the compound. The bite hurt less than a bee sting, but it had left a red lump for a couple of days. He reached out and touched a hairy leg.

"If you walked on me, I bet you'd tickle." He wasn't afraid of spiders like Jimmy was. He was much too old for such nonsense.

He shifted sand between his fingers and put a bit of green bottle glass and a couple of rose quartz rocks into his pocket. Not the one with the peanut butter sandwich, the one on the other side.

"I wish I could fly."

Lying on the warm sand, Toad watched contrails loop, spread and fade in the jet stream.

"Way above that cloud into the sky."

He pointed to a puffy cotton ball, which appeared out of no-where. Rex and Shorty ignored him. Rex put his head on his paws and snoozed; Shorty rested her weight on three hooves, eyes half-closed, ears flicking to keep flies from landing.

More contrails crisscrossed the bright blue sky. He dreamed of riding one to a distant land where wonders not yet imagined awaited. Could a contrail take him to the moon or even beyond? Could they be from supply ships traveling between a large space-ship and the city spacemen were building? He dozed in the heat of the midday sun and dreamed of flying away.

Toad woke when Shorty nudged his nose and Rex licked his sweaty face. If he was going to finish his big adventure before his parents came home from work, he had to get moving. He ate the melted sandwich, not even noticing that the bread was soggy and the peanut butter slick. He remembered to save a bit of the crust for the chipmunks.

He brushed sand from the seat of his pants and picked up Shorty's lead. Even though she wouldn't stray, he felt responsible for her. Once more, Rex bounded away, nose to the ground, tail parallel and wagging. For another half hour, Toad neither saw nor heard anything out of the ordinary. The wind moaned softly, but otherwise the land was so silent and empty he might have been the only little boy on earth. Nothing stirred on the ground since he left the tarantula.

"I wonder where all the animals are. Could they be hiding from something?"

He'd never come this far before. He tried not to be afraid, but deep inside his chest, his heart thumped.

Toad stooped and picked up a piece of lava. "Cool. Another one for my collection." Then he found a black snake skin, coiled it up and wrapped it in the waxed paper that once covered his sand-wich. He put the skin into his pocket too. This side of the wash was loaded with treasures.

Finally, Toad heard a low rumble, the same noise almost ev-ery day for two weeks, a noise made by no one and nothing. He squinted against the glare.

"It's just gotta be spacemen."

Shorty's head shot up, and she yanked back on the lead, which slipped through his fingers. Rex whined and clamped his tail between his legs.

The rumble got louder. The spaceship was headed right toward him.

Whoosh! The noise knocked Toad on his butt, his chest too tight to breathe. Shorty brayed and took off for home, followed by a yipping Rex. Toad couldn't move. More whooshes. Then, a silver-gray jet roared one hundred feet above Toad's head. Upside down.

Toad sat and stared. Other jets followed. Some soared upward and disappeared, leaving only contrails behind. Four flew wingtip to wingtip. Then all disappeared with little more than the normal midafternoon wind to mark their passage, dust devils replacing clouds of sand from the low-flying jets.

Toad still couldn't move. He sat and grinned and grinned and grinned.

Later, when it was obvious neither the jets nor his four-legged friends would return, Toad picked his way to the edge of the wash, down the rocky trail and up the other side. An hour of steady marching brought him to the gate where Rex and Shorty waited as if nothing unusual had happened. Shorty flicked her tail and shook her head; Rex lay in the dust and panted.

"Hey, you're the 'fraidy cats. You ran off and left me behind. Remember?" He petted each of his best friends.

He let them in, fed and watered both and ran a brush across Shorty's rough coat. He returned to the platform and threw himself on a ratty sofa, which should have long ago made its way to the town dump. Too restless to take a nap and forbidden to watch television during the day, he searched for a spare tablet and began to write his first short story: "The Day My World Changed Forever."

Maybe, just maybe, Toad thought, he hadn't heard a spaceship after all. Maybe, just maybe, they were jet planes. If he couldn't fly like the pilots he'd seen, he could write a story about them. Maybe, just maybe, his mother was right.

This time, anyway.

A version of this story appeared on the Roses of Prose blog and on my website, www.betsy-ashton.com.

SEPARATION

Judy Light Ayyildiz

Nuri had been expecting his mother to die for a long time, but somehow pictured her as being alive forever. These past two years, I'd stir as Nuri eased out of bed in the middle of the night to dial his mother across the oceans. In the last six months, Adalet's voice had sounded hoarse, but she was in her full mind until the end. "Did Lee finish my book yet?" she'd ask him. "Still sharp as a tack," Nuri would say, climbing back into bed. Two nights ago, that jarring ring startled us.

Istanbul, September 1993

At some signal I don't catch, the mourners all at once make a surge toward the wall. My husband, Nuri, tugs our son's shoulder and says, "Over there." I follow them to join the rows of bodies quickly forming at the base of the concrete platform.

The heavy-bearded imam appears in a white cap and black robe to conduct the rites. Stationed above and behind the bier, he raises his hands toward the cloud-straggled sky. As a breeze furls his gown, he looks like Moses in *The Ten Commandments*. His oboe voice waffles over the concrete pedestal and across the compound's garden. A gust ruffles the Arabic script on the green and white mantles draped across the coffin. The recital mingles with Istanbul's engines and horns.

"People don't understand Arabic," Mother Adalet said a year and a half ago, telling me how her leader changed the prayer calls to Turkish after he became president of the new republic and how they were later changed back to the old language in the sixties.

She clapped her hands beneath a toothless grin and added, "Ataturk was our everything." After that, she brought her palms to her face, whispered a prayer into them, winged her hands out and up, and then continued just as if she hadn't paused. "Why should Turks pray in a foreign tongue? Allah understands Turkish."

"Leee—no! Come!" Nuri's youngest sister is gripping me by the arm.

"What?" I yelp, dumbfounded and tugging loose.

When I turn, I see I'm stalled between men at the altar and women clumped back under some trees.

The sister, grabbing and propelling me with an air of authority, flicks her head as she indicates my place with the females. I am doubly stunned with confusion and jet lag but am irritated at the idea of being siphoned-off because of my sex. I yank back against her pull, cross my arms and give her a message in international body language by my stance: I'm an American. Your rules don't count for me. She tightens her lips. But, of course, they do. Remember where you are. I shrug and uncross my arms and turn, facing the bier. But I don't take a step; stay stuck between the two groups. I hear the swish of her skirt as she leaves me. I'm silently calling after her, *What happened to "Justice," the literal meaning of your dead mother's name—and equality, the reason she gave for joining the revolution? Is the reform warped and withered inside that box?* I stare at my husband's back. He's unaware of my dilemma. They say that the older women usually stay home from funerals. Small wonder.

Across my shoulder at the edge of the courtyard, my eyes are drawn again to the concrete hut, where earlier today, a woman had cleansed Adalet's body. At noon, after we drove in from the airport, the family was together. For the first time, the reunion was sad, clustering around that hut. Nuri and I along with our twenty-seven-year-old son, Kurt, joined the nieces and nephews and the middle sister and her husband. The older sisters didn't come then, either. When the woman finished, the females were invited inside to view the body. The nieces pulled back and the younger sister walked away crying.

"I'll go," I said.

I went to the niece in from the States, a professor who has taught economics there for ten years. She was sitting on the steps with her sister. "Come with me to see your grandmother," I said, knowing that if any one of them would go, it would be her. The red-eyed and silent others weren't moving.

"I'm afraid to see her this way," she told me.

I tightened my gaze on her sun-glassed eyes. She took a breath and wiped her eyes under her glasses. "There are not enough women like Grandmother in the whole world," she said, taking my arm. We walked toward the heavy wooden door with the green paint scabbing on it. Only a few years after she came to the States, she was teaching undergraduates at Purdue. This was her first trip back.

The hut felt as damp and cool as a springhouse. Adalet's body lay bound in white linen with only her face exposed. Extra strips were tied at her legs and beneath her breast. She looked as if she was meditating, as if she was some Egyptian bird goddess lost in a trance. Perfumed oils, soap, dank walls and mildew mingled in the gray light of a naked bulb hung at the end of a black wire. Her cheeks were drawn, eyelids dark and shallow, nose rigid and protruding like a beak above her shriveled mouth. Her spirit was not in that place. There was just her wrapped-up form looking too small to really be hers. The peasant woman caring for the body lowered her head and whispered, "Allah give you grace."

I ran my fingertips over the sheet at the outline of Adalet's hands, remembering them soft as dough. The lump was cold and set.

"I can't touch her," my niece whispered in a foggy voice. "But don't you think she will know I made this trip back for her?"

I couldn't answer but nodded yes. She stepped away and ducked out the open door, her black ponytail swishing back and forth.

A white muslin scarf framed the ruddy face of the peasant woman, the ends tied in a knot at the top, the same as my Virginia mother used to wear for cleaning, and a style common for Adalet in the house. To show that she was sharing the grief, the woman swayed side to side three times, then paused, waiting. Still red and puffy from the cleansing, her hands rested, cupped on her abdomen. I remembered when I had washed Adalet's bent back:

Summer before last, I had come home to the apartment after an all-day jaunt with one of my friends. We had gone up to the village beach at Kilyos on the lip of the Black Sea where it enters the Bosphorus Strait. On the way back from the beach, I spotted Ottoman wooden stools with woven hemp tops scattered around tables in front of a shop.

When Adalet was on her new bath stool ready to be lathered in olive oil soap, she whispered to me, "My body is old. Don't look."

"Your body is very good," I answered. Adalet loved getting bathed. She had me shampoo and rinse her hair three times, just like they'd done in the old hamams. I scrubbed her gnarled hump with a rubbing cloth until it was as red as tomatoes.

As the Arabic preaching goes on and on, I loosen my stance and wander back under the tendrils of the willow, feeling the women's eyes on me. I rub the arm where Sister caught me, thinking: Sure, the unbeliever—the Gentile—embarrassing the family in front of the guests.

I stare across the yard to the wall of jackets. The men arch their necks. The imam looms above the coffin. A few of the men have on skullcaps, but most of the heads are bare. It feels wrong that patriarchy should dominate an equal-minded woman's final ritual. But, either way, she is gone. Adalet's prayers for all of us five times a day are sunk into a hush. Her strong will, her chuckle, and my earthly bond with her. I envision her and me on a couch in our den years ago eating popcorn and watching a Hallmark special of *King Lear*, both of us weeping in all of the right places. Back then, her bulky frame moved in a grace of subdued slow motion, though she could dart after a child at the drop of a hat. Adalet was forever down on her plump knees swashing the floor with a rag. Or concocting at the stove, her straight hair wound into a loose salt and pepper colored bun. Always hoping company might drop in, the guest, a gift from God. The hump that developed over the next twenty-some years was hardly noticeable then. Only her smooth skin never changed—and the light in her eyes. Dead, as gone as those fresh figs we bought from the side of a road: *quickly peeled and slurped up while Nuri drove down that bumpy Anatolian highway. Splitting back the miles. Slinging purple skins out the windows. Above the Aegean Sea. Transparent wind and sun. The leaves of the olive groves making sparkling mirrors on the hillsides.* Finding ourselves out of those famous Smyrna figs, we turned and retraced our route until we found them. Adalet insisted on it, saying that you hardly ever found something that good anymore. We missed the ferryboat at Bandirma landing and gave Nuri's younger brother Vedat a two-hour wait—although he heartily agreed with what we'd done and didn't mind when we let him share the figs.

Staring over to the coffin, I tell myself that it's a blessing to die at age 92 when your body's completely worn out. And then, I recall with a jarring reality check that my slender husband standing across the court has lost his dear mother. Glancing at him, I feel a wavering in my stomach. I have her oral memoir in my office back home. But, how can that ever come close to being the same as her voice? Adalet and I managed to connect in spite of our broken languages—and on a level that the people in this yard could find confusing. A mixture of broken Turkish and English along with lots of gestures. That was our way. The others around might think that I'm making too much of my grief, like the professional mourners do. Mothers-in-law are not exactly treasured subjects by their daughters-in-law here. Through the years with our coming and going and Adalet's visiting us in Virginia, I've told myself that I've absorbed Nuri's culture. But, what do I know, really? For instance, I'm at a loss to know how to deal with this Muslim funeral. When I asked Nuri's youngest sister why the service is held here in the courtyard, I was politely informed, "Well, of course, death is not taken into a mosque. Mosque is for life." Sure will be strange to return to this country from now on without Adalet's pillowed giggles warding off the wounds of travel.

As I loosen the knot under my chin, I think, Headscarves—in this stifling heat. I dug Adalet's headscarf out of a drawer at the apartment today. We arrived from the airport one minute and were told the next that we had to hurry to the compound to view the body. They told me to grab a scarf.

The women are restless. One niece has her hands linked behind her back, scanning the others' shoes as if she is ready to make an offer on a pair. So much Arabic that few of them understand seems forced. Catholics do it. We say the Latin's ethereal. It's all what you're used to.

The chant staggers across the courtyard. Eyes closed, I can almost hear Adalet's thin voice chirping, chiming the stories of her life to me a summer ago, laughing about love and loss, faltering on her husband, Burhan's, name, claiming how she never really cared that much for him and then admitting yes, she guessed she did. Even after the shock that he'd really leave her flat after she'd had to go away from him for the sake of the children so many times before—and yet, of all that she'd lost, one thing was clear to her. His leaving was not the worst.

A stirred-up breeze brushes against my face and I look up and see one of those little brown wrens, its claws surely holding it balanced on a willow branch. The wind swirls. My head tilts toward a wide sky beyond the skinny-leafed tree. The silk scarf slides down onto the back of my neck. Its embroidered tassels flick on my chin. The air lifts the sweat from my hair as I watch the single little female wren flit from the branch, away from the knoll and on out of sight.

From the novel, *Forty Thorns*, 1st and 2nd Editions published by Remzi Bookhouse, 2011-2012, Istanbul. Copyright Judy Light Ayyildiz since 2015

SNAKE SKIN

Lynn Bechdolt

Carol was cleaning up a patch of wild mint when she found it. At first, she thought it was a piece of gutter guard left over from the re-roofing last year. It certainly was the color and pattern of aluminum mesh. But it wasn't metal at all; it was snake skin.

She laughed when she picked it up. In her head, she could hear Professor Snape warning Harry Potter that his stores of "boomslang skin" had been raided and Harry must have been responsible. Here was "boomslang skin" for "polyjuice potion"!

From the size of the foot-long piece, it had come from a medium-sized snake which had used the tangle of old mint stalks to help it peel off this skin. As Carol worked, she found a few more little pieces. The skin must have been here for at least six weeks, probably longer, and become visible only as this summer's crop of mint had died back. She hoped the snake had found its way into the gopher holes in her yard and cleaned out the little pests. Last spring, they had eaten all her tulip bulbs.

As Carol pulled up another batch of dead mint, the skin caught her eye again. How beautiful it was—silvery, imprinted with scales as regular as print, paper thin, but tough enough to have survived 90-degree heat, rain, hail, and a hard freeze. It wasn't a very big piece, but just for fun she hung it on the chain link fence. There, that will get the neighbors in a tizzy.

Sure enough, a few days later, Carol's neighbor, Win was standing at their property line staring at the snake skin. He was a quiet man of indeterminate middle age, so average he was hard to describe other than his thinning hair and a Celtic accent that crept into his vowels sometimes.

"How do you like my 'boomslang' skin?" Carol said as she met Win at the mint bed.

"Is that what you call them here?"

She wanted to laugh, but she was struck by how seriously he considered the skin.

"This isn't the first one I've found," she said to see if he was afraid of snakes like most of the neighbors. If he was Irish, did he even know what snakes were? St. Patrick was supposed to have chased all the snakes out of Erie.

"More than one?" he asked, in wonder.

"They do shed more than once a year."

"Perhaps, but it's rare, rare indeed, that they ever leave you sheddings more than once. Boomslang, ey? There's a story to tell."

"What did you think it was?"

He shot her a piercing look. "Oh, nothing much."

"I think you know exactly what it is," she said, surprising herself.

For a moment, his eyes measured her. "Did you ever see one?"

Remembering the skink she had seen last spring, she said, "It was incredibly beautiful, electric blue, and so fast I wasn't sure what I had seen at first."

He sighed. "Yes, they are breath-taking. I've seen one turn from buttercup yellow to lavender then copy the foliage around her so perfectly she disappeared. This one likes you, or she would never have left you her perfect skin once, much less twice." He gazed at it longingly. "Had you thought of, ah, selling it?"

"Should I?" she asked. "How would 'she' feel about that?"

His eyes lit with alarm, searching her yard. "Oh, please, don't let her know that I asked. I wouldn't want to offend her. She meant for you to have it." He bowed slightly to her.

The hair on the back of Carol's neck stood up. She had been capricious, but Win truly believed the skin belonged to something far more than a simple black snake, something powerful, which could hear him. Was he schizophrenic?

"And, how should I care for this piece of skin?"

His face shifted, returning to the milquetoast mask. "It's something naturally beautiful, which is its power. Treat it with respect. I'll be getting back to Da now." Win nodded to her and began to walk away, his shoulders rounding and head sinking. "And, if you ever get sick, keep it close."

She knew his father was an invalid and that Win came regularly to care for him.

"Since I have more than one, would you like this piece to 'keep close' to your father?"

The man stopped in his tracks. "You were just playing with me, weren't you? You knew all along that her skin is powerful only if it's given, never taken."

"And only half powerful if sold?"

Turning, he strode toward her, with every step becoming a confident man of power. Without thinking, Carol delicately plucked the skin from the fence and offered it to him as though it was a mantel of gold.

He bowed as he accepted it with profound respect then said something to her in a language of twisted vowels and soft consonants. Seeing her confusion, he said, "Alwyn, son of Clewyn, on behalf of his father, thanks the lady so favored by the *derwen daragwen.*"

She stood watching him go, trying not to let her mouth hang open. Did he just say 'dragon'? But, it was just a snake skin, wasn't it?

SNAKE SKIN originally published in COUNTY LINES: A LITERARY JOURNAL 2017, rights reverted to author after publication.

CALENDAR GIRL

Madalin E. Bickel

What parents don't understand about moving to a new city almost every year is that it makes you the new girl in class. It means making new friends and trying to find a group to fit in. Being the new girl was sometimes okay, but most of the time it seemed more like a crutch. This September was the beginning of fifth grade. My parents had decided to move back home near family. They had finally bought a house, but we had no furniture. So while my mother worried about buying furniture, decorating our new house, and planning a house warming, I went to school.

The "new" school was brick and looked like an old four-room building, but it had a lower level with two more classrooms which became the cafeteria at lunch time. The fifth grade class was in the downstairs room farthest from the kitchen and was separated from the other classroom by a movable floor-to-ceiling wall. The desks were old wooden tables like first graders use. At my last school we had real desks in nice neat rows facing the blackboard, but in this room sitting at the tables made some of us sit with our backs to the teacher. Somebody was always twisting around during a lesson to see the board or Mrs. Fisher.

After a few months of school, our class had settled into a routine. The teacher knew who the strong students were and had chosen her favorites. We had reading groups. Even though I was in the group with better readers, they still read too slowly. More than once Mrs. Fisher caught me silently reading ahead. She scolded me if I didn't know where to begin when it was my turn to read aloud.

Mrs. Fisher looked older than my mother and reminded me of a dried prune. Her pinched lips would assign us difficult activities like diagramming sentences. When we didn't do well, she would get a gleam in her eyes. She rarely ever smiled at us.

When we came back to school from Christmas vacation, Mrs. Fisher greeted us with a handful of chocolate candy bars and a challenge. "Today, we are going to make calendars for 1957. You will not be able to look at any calendars for help. I will give you the day the new year begins, then you must draw each month's calendar and number the days for each month. You may add holidays and drawings. Those who complete the assignment with perfect accuracy will be rewarded."

After placing the candy in a basket on her desk, she handed out paper and rulers. We quietly got our pencils from the little storage places under our tables. When we had our materials ready, she looked around the room. "Today is Friday, January 4th. That means this month and the year began on Tuesday. You will now draw the calendar for the twelve months. You may begin."

I picked up my pencil and ruler and began measuring and dividing my paper into large squares for each month, then I divided each large square into columns and rows. January had thirty-one days. Because it began on Tuesday, I would need five rows. I labeled the top January and then labeled the day of each column beginning with Sunday. I carefully began numbering each small square beginning with Tuesday.

An elbow poked my left rib. I turned to see one of my two best friends, Sherry, looking at me. She whispered "I don't know how to do this. Can you help me?"

I looked at her blank paper, then at the teacher who was walking around the room. I whispered back, "Divide your paper like I have and draw squares for January. Fill in the little squares with numbers beginning with January 1 in the Tuesday block, then just keep going."

She picked up her pencil and ruler and began to draw lines. No measuring. She just began drawing lines. I stopped her. "You must measure to be sure you have enough lines and spaces."

Sherry turned her big brown eyes on me, "How?"

I sighed, took her pencil and ruler, and proceeded to draw all her blocks for twelve months. Just as I finished, my right rib received a jab. It was Leslie.

"Can you help me, too?"

I looked to see if the teacher was nearby. I saw her look at me.

With my head down, I completed numbering January on my calendar and began numbering February while mentally reciting 'Thirty days hath September, April, June, and November…' I needed to know how many days were in February. It was not a leap year, so February would have 28 days and begin on Friday. Another jab in my right rib got my attention.

"Mary-Margaret, please help me." It was Leslie again. She was small like me but not very bright. She was in the low reading group and was always needing help with her arithmetic.

I picked up her pencil and ruler and started blocking off her paper. "Begin with the first large square, January, divide it into thirty-one small squares and number them one through thirty-one beginning with Tuesday."

I watched as she slowly began writing her numbers then went back to my own. As I continued to work on my calendar, I would get whispers and jabs. The girls had never heard of the Thirty Days poem and had no idea how many days were in each month. I finally stopped my work and wrote on a piece of paper how many days were in each month. The girls then went back to filling in their squares.

Mrs. Fisher stood at the front of the room, "You have ten more minutes then we will go outside for recess. All calendars must be finished and given to me as you leave."

Sherry and Leslie were well on their way to completing their calendars. I still needed to draw a few squares. I looked at the school clock on the wall and knew I needed to hurry.

My paper was getting smudged as I quickly moved across each row. I mumbled the number of days in each month while trying to make sure I didn't skip a day as I moved from one month to the next. Just as I wrote December 31 into its square, Mrs. Fisher said, "Time."

I looked at my less than neat calendar and was disappointed with my work. I wrote my name at the top. With the other students, I cleaned up my area then got out of my seat and pushed in the chair. We silently handed in our papers and grabbed our jackets.

Outside the wind was blowing and it was cold. Sherry and Leslie ran off with some of the other girls to grab the swings. I leaned against the building's warm brick wall and thought about my calendar. I had wanted to made special drawings for the holidays and add some color. Instead, I had handed in a hurried-up, messy paper. My teacher would be disappointed in my work.

Soon, Mrs. Fisher came out and blew her whistle. Kids came running from around the graveled playground and lined up. "You may go to the restroom, then return to the classroom, hang up your jackets, and take your seats. I will return your papers and tell you who earned the candy bars. Won't it be fun?"

"Yes, ma'am," the class chimed. Sherry and Leslie had pushed their way to the front of the line. Mrs. Fisher looked down at them and actually smiled.

Good, I thought, maybe they will get a candy bar too and quit nagging me for help.

The classroom was quiet. We sat up straight in our little wooden chairs and looked at the teacher. She had the papers in her hand. "I am so proud of your work today. Many of you surprised me with your ability to make a calendar accurately. There were a few disappointments, but most of you earned a candy bar, and will receive your papers first."

Mrs. Fisher began walking around the room with our papers in her hand. "Sherry, I will begin with you. You did a marvelous job and earned a candy bar. You may help me give out the rewards. Please fetch the basket from my desk and place a candy bar at your seat. You may now follow me around and give out candy as I hand back the papers. Leslie, you are next. Congratulations."

Leslie beamed. I was pleased for her and watched as Sherry placed the candy on Leslie's calendar. Then, Mrs. Fisher with Sherry following behind her, continued around the room handing out calendars and candy. Billy and Jane of course earned one. They were good students like me.

Mrs. Fisher reached Freddy's desk and shook her head. "Freddy, I know you tried so hard, but you had a few mistakes." She handed Freddy his calendar and patted him on the head. He gave her a small smile.

Everyone had their papers but me. Sherry was out of candy bars and sat down beside me. She looked at me with a big ugly grin and then giggled. Mrs. Fisher paused by my chair, "Mary-Margaret, I was so disappointed in your calendar. It was smudged, and when you reached September, you started the month on the wrong day. So, September, October, November, and December were incorrect. I guess you don't know on what day your birthday falls in September this year. I really expected better from you."

She slapped my paper down in front of me then turned to go back to her desk. "Boys and girls, you may eat your candy bars. Mary will come around and collect your wrappers and place them in the trash."

Without looking up, I folded my paper and placed it in my desk. I heard Sherry and Leslie giggle while opening their candy bars. Sherry leaned across me, "Leslie, I do believe this is the best candy bar I have ever eaten. Don't you think so?"

"Delicious," Leslie replied and giggled again.

I did not look at either one of them. I thought they would share a bite with me, but instead they seemed to be enjoying eating in front of me. Mrs. Fisher looked my way. Tears were trying to squeeze through my eyes, but I stood up and pushed my chair in. I whispered loud enough for most of the class to hear, "Sherry, my birthday falls on Wednesday this year. My parents will have a party for me, but I don't think you will be invited."

The room fell silent as I walked over and picked up the trash can. I began circling the room and collecting the candy bar wrappers. Mrs. Fisher probably heard my whisper, but she sat at her desk with her head down grading some papers. She never saw me smile like a calendar girl.

SATURDAY MORNING SKATE

Cindy Brookshire

The inside of Skate City in Manassas is a dark refuge. Kara neglected to tell me, until I had a gift-wrapped Totally Hair Barbie shoved at me, that my custody visit would include taking our seven-year-old daughter Ginger to her friend Samantha's birthday party. I'd planned a movie at the Reb-Yank. Instead, here I am, headed to the rink's snack bar where the parents congregate. There's a table decorated with party-store plastic ware and helium balloons. I add the gift to the ever-growing pile and then inhale disinfectant from shelves of rental skates as I lace up a pair of size 13s.

Ginger's a great kid. She takes to sports full throttle. I watch her thrust herself into the cacophony of roller skaters. The music is pumping, and the floor is churning with colored lights. After a few circuits of the hardwood oval with her, I head to the snack bar again. Lindy, Samantha's mom, stands by the unboxed sheet cake, rocking to and fro as a baby nurses at her blanket-covered breast. This must be Number Three, since Number Two was nursing the last time I saw her two years ago. Lindy is my ex-wife's best friend. In the cold war of ex-spouses, I am The Bad Guy.

"How's the renovation going?" I ask.

She informs me they sold the Fairview Avenue house two years ago.

Not surprising. I never could say the right thing to her.

"Peter designed our new home in Nokesville," she adds. "Ginger loves fishing with Samantha on the pond. There's a treehouse for the girls, too."

"Great." I smile, then take my Loser self back on the skate floor, looking for Ginger. More adults have ventured out. A tall black dude, head shaved, silk shirt rippling against his broad chest, glides by on hockey-quality roller blades. Blades take commitment and cash – two things I'm short on.

A young woman, her white blouse tucked into tight jeans, and red hair piled up in a thick knot, passes me. Her hips sway gently as she scissors forward, and I imagine placing my hands at her waist.

I want her to throw back her head to laugh and lean into me, so I can feel her weight against me. But instead I veer off, setting my own pace. I can feel the adrenalin kicking in.

Ginger whizzes past, two laps to my one. I used to be able to shoot the duck and spin on either foot. Today, I stick to balancing and t-stops. Around me swirls a noisy mish-mash of gangly arms and A-frame legs, oversized t-shirts and cutoffs, bows and flounces, razor cuts and cornrows.

The D.J. announces a couples' skate.

"Daddy!" Ginger shouts from behind me. "I just made a friend!" Then she is off, arm in arm with another girl. The song is Michael Jackson's "Billie Jean." I watch her, all pigtails and pushing up glasses and bony knees. I vow to spend more time with her. I vow to teach her life skills. I vow…

Just then, she falls. Her friend helps her to the side rail, and onto the carpeted walkway.

"It hurts!" she cries in frustration.

"Let's take a break," I say.

We make our way to the party table, where a waitress balances two pitchers of soda pop in hands already bulging with napkins.

"Should've worn my own skates today," she says, whisking away empty pitchers, and returning to dole out pizza slices from a round tray, all part of a packaged party plan.

The D.J. plays the Rules of the Rink. The partiers are too busy talking, devouring pizza, draining drinks. By the time "Ghostbusters" cranks up, the children are out on the floor.

"Kara says you have a new job," says Lindy. I help her carry grease-stained plates and solo cups to a trash can.

"Yes. Sales."

"What do you sell?"

"Building supplies at Lowe's, until I can get back in my technology field. I may have to look outside the area."

"I hope not," she says, "Especially with the new contractor coming in to take over the semiconductor plant. Maybe you could get on there. Ginger's lucky to have you close by."

I look at her, carefully.

"You've been great with her. Kara says so."

The D.J. stops the music and calls the children into a big circle. "Let's give a big hand for Skator Gator!" he announces.

Out of the rink office skates an alligator mascot, his toothy mouth flapping up and down like flippers. First one child, then another, skates up to hug him about his padded middle; he encases them with his green arms.

Jeez, are my eyes stinging? I'm not going to lose it over a stuffed alligator. It's just an employee sweating inside a hot costume. But I can't help it. I've been there. Every soccer coach, scout leader or Sunday School teacher has – when they look up at you with the biggest eyes, and you feel like some towering god!

The children finish flapping their arms to the bird dance and wave goodbye to Skator Gator. A few stragglers stalk after him, trying to catch hold of his tail before he disappears into the rink office.

Samantha blows out the candles on her cake and rips through presents while the children bolt down forkfuls of confection.

The D.J. announces the last song, "Day-O." Then the rink empties from the morning session. Ginger's face is red with exertion. I peel off her sweat-soaked socks, and she puts on her sneakers without them. Samantha shouts goodbye, then charges for the door, her mother following with baby in arms, a stroller full of presents.

"My ankles are sore," says Ginger.

"How about a movie at Reb-Yank?" I offer.

"Yes!" she squeals.

I open the heavy metal door, my legs a bit wobbly. Sunlight streams in, blinding us for a second. Then we step into the world, hand in hand, together for the day.

THE SOCK MONKEY DOLL

Peggy Callison

Characters:

"Hittie"-- eleven-year-old protagonist
"Kate"-- Hittie's older sister; Miss Parker's caregiver
"Miss Parker" -- elderly invalid
"Beulah"-- housekeeper at sisters' home; confidante (speaks in dialect)
"Big Luke"-- Beulah's adult son; manager of Parker farm (speaks in dialect)
"Doc" -- physician
"Dax" -- moonshiner

Setting -- Southwest Virginia
Time – 1915

The sleigh moved swiftly over the snow to Miss Parker's house, while a troubled Hittie considered the very scary "what-ifs." What if something awful happened to Kate when the baby came? Her family would never forgive Beulah or Big Luke...or even her. She was afraid of her family's discovering Kate's secret...of their learning what Dax had done to Kate, and now she was expecting a baby. She tried to shake off her fears...telling herself that Kate couldn't be the only girl who ever had a baby without being married. She couldn't understand why the birth of a tiny baby was something to be ashamed of or why people would punish Kate if they knew. She understood why her daddy and her brothers would want to hurt Dax, and she understood that if they did hurt Dax, *they* would be punished. What if the people in town weren't the only people to dislike Kate for having a baby? What if Mother and Daddy didn't like Kate anymore? What if they didn't believe Kate's story? She couldn't bear that thought. She hoped she might figure it all out someday, but right now, she didn't feel ashamed that a baby was coming. She really wanted to hold it and just say, "Hi."

Suddenly, the sleigh was slowing in front of Miss Parker's porch.

Once stopped, Big Luke, with his usual brilliant smile, helped her down and pointed her toward the front door. He followed her in with a box of holiday dishes Beulah had prepared. Kate's smile was sunshine on a winter's day.

"Mama said we can all have Christmas dinner together if dat be alrite wid you, Miss Kate."

"Of course, it is, Luke. We'll have a great meal together!" Abruptly, her hand went to her stomach, and her lips thinned in pain.

"Miss Kate, is you alrite?"

"Yeeees." She paused. "I've been having these sudden jolts over the last couple of days. It goes away as fast as it comes. Doc says it's normal. He says I'm very close to my time. Guess the baby wants to come out and see the world. Doc says by his calculations I'm about a week past due, and things ought to get going about Tuesday. That's when we have a full moon." She laughed. "Doc says he doesn't know why that happens, but it does more often than not. Now, I'm going to put our supper on the table. You and Luke can sit by the fire. I'll call you when it's ready."

Hittie and Luke did as they were told. Settled on a large cushion on the floor, Hittie stared into the flames...a thousand "what-ifs" still in charge of her brain in spite of her efforts to squash them.

"Hey, Miss Hittie. Santa be comin' tomorrow nite! What you think he be bringin' you?"

She giggled. "He's bringing me the fun of not having to play the piano for church service tomorrow night! Mother will have to play the piece she picked for me!"

"Well, now, I think you needs to play fo us. Dey be a pianna by de door. How 'bout some Christmas songs?"

"Just for you, Luke! Just for you!" She stopped short, remembering Miss Parker upstairs. "Kate, is it okay to play the piano? Will it bother Miss Parker?"

"It's okay. Play softly."

She played, and for the moment, she felt they were all safe and happy. She had brought gifts of her own making for Kate and Luke, and tomorrow they would open them under the Christmas tree. Kate would read the Christmas story about a baby that was born many, many years ago in Bethlehem. And they would wait for a baby whose birthday wouldn't be celebrated. She hoped no one would be mad if she gave the baby her own favorite toy...her sock monkey doll. It was the doll Kate had made for her when she was a baby. It would keep Kate's baby warm, and the little one would have something of its mother with it when it was taken away. At least it would have one birthday present.

§

Wearing the new, flannel nightgown Kate gave her for Christmas two nights ago, Hittie was sleeping soundly as she lay curled into the feather bed in Miss Parker's guest room.

"Hittie, get up! Hurry! Get up!"

Hittie didn't recognize Kate's voice at first. It was strangely hoarse. Frightened, she sat straight up in the bed. When she saw Kate bending over at the waist and holding her stomach down low, she knew what was happening. "I'll go get Luke!" she said as she quickly threw back the covers and slid her legs over the side of the bed. Standing up, her bare feet landed in a puddle of liquid that she could only feel, not see. "Oh, Kate! What is this? Is this blood?!"

"No. It's not blood. My water broke. We have to get to Luke's house." Still bent over, she was already going toward the door.

"No! I'm supposed to go get Luke who is supposed to take you to his house."

"There's no time for that! I've been in labor for a while...the pains haven't been regular. Then my water broke. Please, Hittie, just get my coat and help me get it on! Get your own coat and shoes...but hurry, please hurry! We have to go to his house now!"

"It's too far for you to walk!"

"Please, Hittie. Just do as I say! I can't have this baby here. Miss Parker will hear all of it!"

Minutes later, through snow almost to Hittie's knees, they struggled to walk across the fields to Luke's by the light of a full moon. Both of them in coats over their night gowns. Kate's arm was around Hittie's shoulders for support, but she had to stop frequently to allow a pain to shudder through her. Hittie could see the fluid from Kate's body melting the snow beneath her as they moved slowly along. She accepted her pain in silence. She never once cried out. Closer to Luke's house, Hittie called out to him as loudly as she could.

"Luke! Help us! Luke!"

She heard Luke's dog bark just once, and a light came on in his bedroom, and then in his living room. The front door flew open, and he ran, as well as he could in the snow, to meet them. He picked Kate up and carried her into the house. He placed her on a bed he had obviously prepared for her earlier. Draped on a chair by the bed was a heavy quilt, and he covered a shivering Kate with it. A stack of flannel sheets were folded neatly on the dresser. Firewood was ready in the fireplace needing only a match which he supplied.

"Miss Hittie, you gots to git de wet clothes off Miss Kate and yousef. Mama put a gown in de dresser drawer fo her. Gits you one of my shirts frum de chest by de door. I got to git Doc and Mama now. Miss Kate, you gonna' be alrite 'till we git back?"

"Yes, Luke. Oh, thank you, Luke. I..." She wanted to say something else, but another pain prevented it. Luke took a long look at her, sizing up the situation, and then, he hurried away.

Hittie immediately went to work helping Kate change her gown and making sure the bed was dry. She found some towels to catch the slowing flow of Kate's water.

"Hittie, I'm worried about Miss Parker. If she woke up while we were leaving, she might be upset that I haven't come into the room. You have to go back to the house to see if she's all right. Get that wet gown off and put on one of Luke's shirts before you go. Are you afraid to go back by yourself? Take Luke's dog with you."

"No." Hittie lied. "I'll go. I'll leave the dog here by your bed. He might bark and wake Miss Parker if he goes with me. Will you be okay until I get back?"

"Yes, but you have to hurry. I don't want you out in this weather by yourself for long. Now, go and come back as fast as you can."

Hittie stopped on Luke's front porch. The distance between where she was and where she was going suddenly seemed like miles. She tried to run, but the depth of the snow brought her down in a heap. She had to walk in the footprints she and Kate had just made. Constantly, she looked about her, jumping at every crack of a tree branch breaking from the weight of the heavy, wet snow. The only other sounds were her heart pounding in her ears, her labored breathing, and the crunching noise her steps made in the snow. She looked up to see her goal...the Parker house. It loomed before her...only the usual tiny light in Miss Parker's up-stairs bedroom could be seen. She was too distracted to notice that Kate had turned the lights off as they passed the switches. Why? Why!? Then, she knew. A well-lighted house at two o'clock at night would certainly draw attention for some distance. No need to attract visitors now. Then, she remembered Dax...and that horrible night. She stopped at the foot of the back porch steps... How could she go into that dark house!? Suddenly, the sound of what she thought was a faraway scream drifted across the night air. Did she really hear it? She thought she heard it. Was it an animal? Was it Kate!? Was the baby coming with no one there to help!? Was it Miss Parker? Would she have to stay with Miss Parker and not go back to be with Kate? She bolted up the steps and into the dark kitchen. She stopped to remove her shoes, and then she ran on tiptoe through the house to the stairs. Mounting them in record time, she was at Miss Parker's door. Slowly...quietly, she opened it. To her great relief, Miss Parker was sleeping peacefully. Her relief was short lived, when she remembered the scream she thought she heard. She had to get back to Kate! Stopping only to grab yesterday's clothes she had left on the chair by her bed, she was out of the room and at the head of the stairs when she remembered...the sock monkey doll. She had to go back for it. It took only seconds, and she was down the steps and out the back door. Again, that eerie sound of a far-off scream met her ears. "Oh, Jesus, help us! Please help Kate! Please let Luke and Beulah and Doc come soon!" she prayed aloud as she traced her steps back across the moonlit path. The closer she got to the house, the clearer Kate's screams were. Terrified, Hittie stopped on Luke's porch. "Oh, Jesus, I can't go in! Help me! Help Kate! Don't let Kate die! Don't let the baby die! Please send Doc and Beulah! Please! I'm so scared!"

She heard a low guttural sound from Kate. She hated her fear of going in to confront what was happening in that bedroom. But she had to help. Quickly, she was by Kate's bed.

"Oh, Hittie! The baby's coming...the baby's coming! Help me...help me!" cried Kate, her eyes wild with fear and pain.

"How, Kate, what do I do? Tell me what to do?" She could feel the hot tears running down her face. She couldn't see! She had to stop crying! She had to see!

"The baby is going to come out! You have to catch its head.

Oh, God in Heaven, let its head be first! Hold its head, Hittie! Catch the baby! Oh, God, help me! Help me!" she screamed.

Hittie ran from one side of the bed to the other. Her arms were not long enough to stand beside the bed and reach the baby. She threw back the covers, grabbed some sheets from the stack on the dresser, and crawled onto the bed. She placed the sheets below Kate where she thought the baby would be. She went down on her knees, sat back on her heels, and waited...too frightened to breathe. She tried to remember how it went with the puppies she had seen born. Another guttural groan came as Kate pushed. Suddenly, Hittie saw a different color of red appear. It was not the color of blood!! It was...it was the color of Kate's hair! The baby's head suddenly slid out, stopping just at its shoulders! It had Kate's beautiful red hair! Its eyes opened, looked up at Hittie, and began to cry before it was fully delivered.

"It's not all the way out! You have to make it come out!!" Hittie cried frantically.

Kate heard the baby cry, and another push brought the perfect little boy into Hittie's waiting arms. She wrapped it quickly in a sheet while Kate, exhausted, fell back on the bed. Suddenly, Big Luke's dog barked in recognition of his master. Off in the distance, they heard horses' hooves pounding hard, meaning Luke was running them at racing speed. They were approaching fast. Help was near.

Hittie sat back on her heels again and held the baby close, listening to its tiny cry, and marveling at its perfection. Besides the hair, it had Kate's nose and eyes. She was still sitting on her heels on the bed... holding the baby...when Doc and Beulah rushed into the room. Luke stayed in the kitchen.

"Lord have mercy, dat chile done delivered dat baby! Why she's jes shy of 'leven, and she done been de midwife! You be tryin' to git my job, Chile?"

Hittie couldn't speak. She was so relieved to see them that she could only hold them with her eyes...afraid if she looked away, she would find herself alone again.

Doc came straight to Kate, and Hittie relinquished the baby to him. She slid off the bed on the opposite side and rushed to sit alone by the fire. She felt very tired and very cold even though the room had to be quite warm. She began to shake, so she drew closer and closer to the fire. Doc finished the delivery while Beulah bustled about cleaning and swaddling the tiny new person.

"Young lady, you did a fine job delivering this baby. One of these days, I'll just have to hire you on as a regular helper. Now, you go wash your hands and arms up to your elbows," said Doc.

"Thank you, Sir. I just want to give him my sock monkey doll to take with him when he leaves."

Kate began to cry quietly. There was no rejoicing at this birth. No one spoke about how beautiful the baby was or how lively he was, or how cute he was trying to suck his little fist when Beulah was swaddling him. Instead, they talked about how brave Hittie was and what a good job she had done. They talked about how fast the baby had come and said that happened sometimes when the water broke. Their voices seemed surreal as Hittie waited for the most important moment of all...when they would walk away with the baby that belonged to her family, and she would never see it again.

"I want to see the baby," said Kate.

"Oh, no, Miss Kate, you doan wanna' do dat."

"If you do, giving it up will be very difficult. I don't recommend it," said Doc.

"I heard Hittie say 'him' so I know it's a boy. I want to see the baby. If it looks like Dax, it might be easier. Please, let me see him."

Doc and Beulah exchanged a momentary glance. Doc nodded permission.

Beulah brought the baby to Kate and placed him in her arms. Kate's stunned expression conveyed the shock of seeing herself in the tiny face of her first-born son. There was nothing of Dax to see in this child. It was as if he had had no part in his creation. The baby's little hand wiggled out of the blanket, clasped Kate's finger and held on.

"Oh, Beulah! Oh, God, Beulah, I can't!!! I can't give him away!!" came through sobs of anguish.

"Miss Kate, you knows what you gots to do. The Good Lord heps us do what we gots to do. He doan puts mo on us den we can carry. Dat's what de Good Book says. He be hepin' you. He be hepin' all of us," Beulah offered through her own tears.

"The baby will be fine, Kate. I'll take good care of him. He'll be cared for and loved. I'll educate him. I'll not adopt him out.

Miss Ellen and Bob are like my own family, and I'll do right by all of you. The decisions you have made are the right decisions. You have to understand, though, that you can't come looking for him at the house. You must have a clean break. Beulah, wrap the baby up in a couple of quilts for the trip back. It's time to go."

Beulah approached Kate to take the child. "Not yet, Beulah, please not yet," Kate cried.

"It gots to be now, Chile. It gots to be. Doc gots to be back fo daylight," Beulah took the baby as Kate tried to get out of the bed...her arms outstretched, reaching for her baby.

"Now, Kate, stay in that bed! You've got to settle down for your own good. I'll be back in a couple of days to check on you. You must rest now," scolded Doc. "Beulah, remember to bind her breasts tightly. We don't want the milk to come in."

"Yes, Doc. I knows 'bout dat."

Quickly, Beulah wrapped the baby for the trip back. Hittie ran to Beulah and stuck the sock monkey doll into the folds of the quilt. Beulah handed the baby to Doc who picked up his black bag, turned, and, with head bowed, left the house.

Through the doorway, Hittie saw Luke waiting at the sleigh. Beulah closed the door and went to the kitchen while Luke took Doc and the baby away. Kate's baby would simply vanish from their lives. She heard Kate's weeping and wished she knew how to comfort her. She realized then that tears were running quite freely down her own face. Slowly, she approached the bed and knelt down to Kate's level.

"Kate, I gave my sock monkey doll to the baby. I wish I had another one for you. I always felt better when it was around to hold onto."

"Oh, Hittie, you are my sock monkey doll. You've stayed by me. You've kept my awful secret. You've delivered my baby. You've never judged me. You're the best sister in the whole world, and I love you so very much." Kate raised herself and clasped her little sister in her arms.

"I'm glad I got to see the baby. I'll never forget him," said Hittie.

"Nor will I," said Kate, and her sobs came again.

Hittie had said all she knew to say. She pulled away from Kate's arms and went to the washstand where she poured water from a pitcher into a small pan. She lathered her hands and arms up to her elbows as Doc had said to do. Standing on tiptoe, she leaned forward and rinsed every trace of the delivery into the pan. She dried herself with a small towel, picked up the pan and carried it to the edge of the front porch. She stopped and stared into the discolored water. She knew that when she threw the water into the snow, every trace of that beautiful baby she held and loved instantly would be gone forever. She couldn't understand how such things could be. Slowly, she poured the water into the snow. The ground would welcome it, and somehow that seemed a comfort to her. She leveled the empty pan before her, saw that all was, in fact, gone, and returned it to its rightful place.

Beulah made hot tea for everyone, and she made Hittie a pallet near the fire. Staring into the flames, she wondered if she really wanted to grow up. She wasn't so sure that being an adult was going to be all that much fun. She knew Kate had a really nice boyfriend and that she was going to be married in the spring, but she didn't think she wanted anything to do with boys. She knew that when morning came, life would begin again, but with a wound inside of her and her sister that would never heal. Every trace of Kate's long ordeal was gone save that.

THE PERIL OF GRETEL

John Cowgill

It was a very late bitterly cold evening outside of the village of Povost. The people were gathered to watch a young woman named Gretel wearing thick brown coat and shabby green dress with white frills standing barefoot on a wooden stool that was sitting on a bale of hay. A rope was strung around a tree with the noose around her neck. The people were shouting, "Kill the witch! Kill the witch!"

Tears were rolling down her face as she felt the insults towards her. The village leader walked up and stood at the edge of the hay bales in front of her.

"Gretel," he said, "you are guilty of witchcraft."

"I am innocent," she wept.

"So," he quickly interrupted, "you continue with your lies. I condemn you to a brutal death."

"I am not a witch," she pleaded as two men carrying torches approached her. "You have no witnesses, just accusations."

The two men lit the hay on fire, and the hay began to burn. Tears continued to roll down her face as she felt helpless as she saw the fire grow and as the people continued to insult her.

Two men came walking out carrying a wooden window frame with the shutters closed. They set the window frame down behind her, and they walked away. The people continued to shout out insults. The window shutters opened, and a man stepped out with a fire hose hosing down the fire until it was completely out. The people were silenced.

"Kill him!" the village shouted pointing at him.

The people took out their swords, and they charged the man. The man just stood there as three combat soldiers jumped out of the window. They took their AK-47s, and they shot up all of the village people, not leaving one standing. Gretel was astounded at what she just saw. The man laid down the hose. He climbed up to Gretel.

"You are safe now," he said as he removed her noose from her neck.

Gretel was speechless.

"I am George of Sand Sop," he said shaking her hand. "I could not see these people condemning you for a crime you did not commit. Therefore, I came to change the story."

"You… ah…" Gretel pondered.

"I must be going now," George smiled. "We have other outcomes to rescue."

George began to go to the window.

"How did you…?" Gretel tried to ask as she saw George and the three combat soldiers climb into the window, pulling the shutters closed behind them.

Two men came, and they began to carry the window away. She walked up to the two men.

"What just happened?" she asked them.

"That which just happened," the one man said as they were walking away.

"Can you explain what just happened?" she pleaded.

The two men went into the ground. She could not believe what she just saw. She looked back, and she saw that the village was gone along with the bodies of the people. She looked around her, and she found herself standing on a mountain. She looked down and saw the line of trees below her. She took a step, and she stepped onto a tiny sharp rock that cut into the bottom of her foot. She started hobbling around to a fallen log, and she sat down. She looked at the bottom of her foot, and she saw the gash near her big toe with blood flowing out. A large nearby rock rolls away, and a man wearing a doctor's cloak walks over to her.

"Gladly to introduce myself," the man quickly shook her hand. "I am the doctor."

"Where did you come from?" Gretel looked around, wondering how he got there.

He picked up her foot.

"That is a very bad cut. It looks like the piggy that went to the market will survive."

He took out a band aid, and he put it over the cut.

"That should take care of it. Have a good day," he said as he walked away.

"But where did you come from?" she asked as the rock rolled back over the doctor.

She looked at the bottom of her foot, and she saw the band aid. She felt a cold strong wind. She saw herself in an icy crevice, and she was sitting on a block of ice. She stood up, and she looked at the high icy cliffs above her. She took a step and another and another until she slipped, and she found herself sliding down an icy slope. She looked ahead, and she saw that she was about to go over a cliff into a very deep ravine, but she landed into a soft bed. She sat up, and she looked around, but she felt something around her feet. She lifted up the blanket, and she saw a rattlesnake wrapped around her foot. She shook with extreme fear. The rattle-snake turned to look at her. It hissed and wildly rattled its tail. A maid snatched the snake and threw it away.

"Sorry about that," the maid said. "Is there anything I can take care of?"

Gretel was terrified as she shook in fear. She looked at her feet, and she wiggled her toes.

"I will let you rest." The maid smiled at her. "Just call if you need me."

The maid walked out of the room, and she pulled the door behind her.

Gretel looked around and saw herself in an upscale hotel room. She moved to sit at the side of the bed, and her bare foot touched the velvet carpet on the floor. She stood up, and she saw the curtains closed on the window. She walked towards the window, and she began to free fall very fast as she saw herself in a ravine with rocky cliffs on each side. She saw that she was about to come upon the sharp rocks at the bottom.

"Stop!" a man shouted, and she stopped in the air just above the rocks. She looked below her, and she was very confused.

"Gladly to introduce myself." The man shook her hand. "I am George Dyingson, the great explorer who had never been exploring in his life."

She stood up, and her feet touched the rocks.

"I hope that you are fine," George Dyingson said. "I will move on."

George Dyingson walked away. Gretel sat down on a rock, and she felt sand between her toes. She looked around and found her-self sitting on a beach chair at a tropical beach. She took off her coat. She stood up, and walked to the water. The waves crashed over her feet, and it made her smile.

"Prepare to walk the plank," a pirate said with a sword to her neck.

"Where am I?" Gretel looked around and saw that she was standing on a plank. "How did I get here? Who are you?"

"That is not your concern." The pirate nudged his sword against her neck. "Now walk!"

She slowly stepped on the plank until she came to the end. The pirate pushed, and she fell, and she kept falling in the air. A skydiver grabbed her.

"I got you!" The skydiver gripped her very tight. He opened the parachute, and they freefell onto a grassy field. She turned to look at him.

"Glad you're safe." The skydiver waved. "Have a good day." He took off his chute and walked away.

She looked over and saw her house. She began to walk towards the house, and it began to rain hard. Mud was building up between her toes. She stepped through the mud, and the rain turned into snow. She arrived at the house. She stepped onto the porch, and it became bright and sunny. She peeked down at her feet and saw that they were clean. The door opened, and a man in a white suit appeared.

"Come in," he said. "We have been waiting for you."

She saw herself in a shiny white laced dress. She looked down at her toes and moved them around. She looked at the man, and she went inside.

ABSENTEE COUSINS

Carol Cutler

Dean Goff, a fit man in his fifties, was cozying up with a beer when Monica called. "A meth lab? Good grief." Dean was the youngest of three cousins who leased land for gas extraction in western Virginia.

Monica, his oldest cousin, lived across the state in Brunswick County. She'd just returned from Buchanan County, having gone with the forester to assess conservation of the timber and soil reclaimed from strip-mining a decade ago on 150 acres of family land.

"Yes, maybe behind a hunting cabin," Monica said. "The forester is going to call the sheriff. It's just a rumor at this point. I went with him to check on the logging job—I talked with him about goals for timber management on the Dry Fork tract."

"Behind what hunting cabin? Okay. I'll call Lonnie and find out what he knows about it." Dean ignored the rest.

"We'd get more people involved watching our land if some of the younger folks were better informed," Monica said.

"Well, you know Lonnie. He's not inclined to talk much."

"Won't talk to me. There's another problem with the logging job besides the cabin. There were water violations."

"Uh, oh," he said. *Monica is on the wacky side with her ideas about the environment—last time she called it was about protecting the wild turkey, elk, deer, a variety of smaller mammals, birds, and the fish on the property. Who really cares besides tree-hugger Monica?*

"The logger's responsible for fixing it. And he was cutting timber on the wrong property and got accused of timber theft," Monica said.

"That's all on the logger."

"Yes, but we could help him out by giving him an accurate map."

Dean yawned. His dulled and apathetic attitude was par for the course when he talked to Monica. He cared little about what he called the worthless land except for gas drilling.

"He's supposed to check out the boundaries by the deed and

maps in the courthouse," Dean reminded her.

Dean hung up. He immediately called Lonnie.

"Monica's been trying to call you," Dean said.

"I put her on my blocked caller list," Lonnie said. He was just finishing dinner after coming home from his part-time job as a used car salesman.

"So much for being available to stockholders, Lonnie, when you are the president. Isn't that a little immature—to just shut out whoever doesn't agree with you?"

"Well, I don't want her butting in. My mother said to keep Julie out of the business. She didn't like her questions that amount to snooping around what didn't need to come out."

"What do you mean 'what didn't need to come out'? She's been in the business a lot longer than you."

"Might be some things people would question as illegal. We're not sure of a lot of what we own and some property the coal company says we own, but we don't have a deed."

"What the hell? Well, we'll get to that at some point. We have a problem. Can you meet me tomorrow in Perryville?"

Perryville was halfway between Tonto, where Dean lived, and Cumberland where Lonnie lived. The men ordered coffee and a sandwich at the restaurant.

"How come you didn't tell me they changed the timbering site?" Dean asked Lonnie. *Why do I let Lonnie make all the decisions about the property? Why wasn't it Lonnie instead of Julie calling him about problems on the property, anyway?*

"They switched to the Garden Creek tract since they couldn't cut what they expected on Dry Fork." Lonnie said. He took a big bite of his sandwich, his eyes on his food.

"Because of being on the wrong property," Dean said dryly.

"Yeah, the maps aren't very accurate so I had that section surveyed," Lonnie said, still focusing on his sandwich. Dean sensed Lonnie knew about the logger's error and wanted to avoid discussing it. Dean had begun to realize just how unilateral Lonnie's decisions were.

"It's about time we did that anyway. Look, Monica's been up there with the forester to do some assessments of the timber. We should go up there and check out what the logger says is going on at the top of the Dry Fork ridge," Dean said.

"Check out what? Getting accurate boundaries and maps for the property?"

"The logger you hired says there is a hunting cabin up there."

"Well, I guess we might do that," Lonnie said, uninterested, not asking how Dean knew about a hunting cabin.

"What do you mean, you guess? Don't you think it matters?"

"Oh, sure. But it's just a rumor, right?" Lonnie said off-handedly.

Dean thought to himself, *I know I'm lazy sometimes, but this wins the prize.* "What about a key? Can you get a key to the gate? Last time the family wanted to go up there you didn't have a key."

"I still don't have one," said Lonnie. "The other thing is taking your car up that road. You'll ruin it."

"Look, Lonnie," Dean said, "I think it's time we got keys to our own property."

"Omega doesn't want people going up there."

"But we own the surface property, Lonnie. Hell, get the key or I will. And we'll take your SUV." Dean raised his voice. "What about the sheriff? Are you going to call him, or do I?"

"I'm not going to call him about Monica's rumor," Lonnie said.

"Get over it, Lonnie. This is not about Monica. It's about what's going on right under your nose that needs to be looked into."

§

Sheriff Sam Blankenship needed to reach the owners of the property Andrew Marshall had called him about and the only contact information he had was Monica's. The forester had given him her number.

"Ms. Simmons, this is Sam Blankenship, sheriff down here in Buchanan County. Andrew Marshall gave me your number—said you all got a tip about a drug problem over there in Dry Fork hollow."

"That's right. Glad you called." She sat down, relieved the forester had followed through on calling the sheriff promptly.

"He said you all are absentee owners of the property. Can you tell me, Ms. Simmons, who exactly owns that particular property?"

"The I. C. Clapper heirs, Sheriff. My grandfather started a corporation and his heirs run the Big Skeggs business. Lonnie Wyatt is designated president and is usually the contact person for our coal, gas, and timbering leases."

"What exactly were you doing on the property, Ms. Simmons?"

"I'm having some of the tracts assessed for natural resources—that is, besides the coal and gas. I do volunteer work with Virginia naturalist group—wildlife surveys, conservation projects. Forester Andrew Marshall is allowing me to go look at the property when he goes up there."

"Are you the one responsible for the property or not?"

"Oh, no, not just me. I'm just one of about twenty stockholders. I'm preparing a proposal for our stockholders about marking boundaries and securing the timber. I don't make decisions on land use by myself."

"Hm, marking boundaries isn't a bad idea with the timbering and hunting that goes on around here."

"My cousins are supposed to oversee the property but no one shows up there half the time."

"How do you know that?"

"I mean no family members. I don't think so because, in the first place, my cousin Lonnie Wyatt told me last time I talked to him a year ago, we don't even have a key to the property. There's supposed to be an annual inspection of the land, but we never get any kind of report. So the family isn't very informed about what goes on our property."

"I see."

"I've asked my cousin many times to walk the property with me. He says he's busy, and there's nothing to see. Anyway, here's Lonnie Wyatt's phone and email. He's doesn't return my calls."

"Sounds like there may be something besides trees up on that ridge."

"It does, and I am not sure it's safe to go up there, Sheriff." Julie said.

"No problem. I'll check it out."

After Sam Blankenship hung up, he called Lonnie.

"I talked to your cousin Monica, she gave me your number."

"How did you run into her? She lives in Brunswick County."

"She was with the forester on your family's Dry Fork property yesterday. The logger up there said there might be a meth lab in the woods at the ridge."

"I was going to call you, Sheriff. I just heard a rumor about a hunting cabin up there. Now you're saying there's a meth lab, too?"

Lonnie said. "I'll call the logger, Mr. Smith, to get more details on what was told to him."

"Ms. Simmons says you're the designated head of the corporation of the Clapper heirs."

"Yes, we have a few hundred acres in Buchanan County."

"Well, I need you to show me where that tract is so we can check this out. Can you meet me at the office in Sommerville on Thursday and we'll ride up there together?"

§

After he talked to the sheriff, Lonnie called the man who checked the wells on the Dry Fork property for Omega Gas, Harley Jones.

"Harley, who owns the mineral rights on the Dry Fork property you lease with us?"

"The tract that you all have the surface rights on? The coal and mineral owner is listed as Pocahontas Coal—OMEGA bought them out twenty years ago, but they haven't changed the deed in the courthouse. Why do you want to know?" Harley drawled, his voice a slow twang.

"You all have about ten gas wells there that we've leased to you. Do you know anything about a hunting cabin up there on the ridge?" Lonnie asked.

"You mean the 150-acre tract? No, no hunting cabin that I know of. We go up there to check on the gas wells once a month. Someone trespassing, eh?"

"How many wells do you have up there now?" Lonnie asked

"About fifteen wells up that road," he said.

"I thought we'd just leased for ten." *Wonder if that was what Monica was talking about at the annual meeting last year, about Omega Gas putting in extra wells without permission? Or it could have been in the amended lease in the courthouse records to add more wells that she said she'd found. She's always snooping around the courthouse when she's not looking over my shoulder*

"Didn't you get the notice of the amended lease?"

"I guess not," Lonnie said. He knew he should pay more attention to the mail.

"I can meet you at the gate on Thursday at 11am to let you in," Harley said.

"I'll call you back if that time doesn't suit the sheriff. He wants to go with us."

§

The sheriff's County of Buchanan truck was parked out front of his office near the courthouse when Lonnie and Dean arrived Thursday morning. Lonnie's belly hung over his jeans with the buttons straining on his tucked-in plaid shirt as he walked over to the sheriff. He eyed the brown uniform and sheriff badge and holstered gun cinched on the last hole of a large belt. Sheriff Blankenship was 5'10", broad shouldered, and solidly built. He had dark, curly hair and wore rugged outdoor boots.

"Sam Blankenship," he said, extending his hand to Lonnie who jumped slightly.

"Lonnie Wyatt, Sheriff, and this is my cousin, Dean Goff, from Tonto."

Dean smiled, his blue eyes looking directly at Sam. He shook Sam's hand. "Thanks for driving, Sheriff. I don't think our cars would make it up that hill." Dean was dressed in hiking pants and mesh and leather hiking shoes with rubber soles. He had a baseball hat on and a water bottle hung from his belt.

"You boys call me Sam. Well, I'm glad to drive. We need to check this out."

Lonnie sat in front beside the sheriff. Dean climbed in the narrow seat behind them. They got underway on Route 460, headed east, on the widened road. The traffic flow was improved when the Army Corp of Engineers moved the town across the Levisa River five years ago, but the new road was heavily traveled with coal trucks and gas drilling rigs.

Lonnie told the sheriff, "I'm interested in leaving the property in a fairly primitive state. I don't really want to do any development or forest management."

"There's something to be said for that. What kind of work do you do, Mr. Wyatt?"

"I used to teach at the high school. Retired now. Sell some used cars. I'm president of a leasing business, Big Skeggs. I just renew leases and sign new ones. Once in a while, there are land disputes and law suits to deal with over who owns the mineral, coal, or surface rights."

"No one knows who owns what around here," Sam said. "What about you, Mr. Goff?"

"Call me Dean, Sam.," he told the sheriff. "My mother left me her fifteen shares in the business. She and her sisters pretty much let the coal and gasmen take care of things for the last fifty years."

"Speaking of meth labs. They broke up about thirty over in Wythe County. Well, I'm glad to know you all. I'm running for sheriff again and the election's next week. It's been a really busy time."

We weren't exactly talking about meth labs right this minute, Dean thought.

"Our grandfather was in politics," Lonnie said. "Represented Russell and Buchanan counties in the legislature years ago. He bought all this land for investment back in the early 1900s."

"Is that so?" Sam made a mental note to talk to Lonnie about it later.

"Look, there's the gas guy already parked by the gate," Lonnie said as they went around the curve in the road, and the clearing on the side of the hill came into sight.

After Sam parked, they stepped out of the truck, and the Omega man greeted them.

A woman who lived at the trailer across the road watched them from her yard. A brown dog was barking.

"Howdy, Ma'am," the sheriff called, smiled, and nodded his head.

'Howdy, Sheriff." she called back from her spot across the road. She didn't see him often, but she had voted for Sam Blankenship for the last three terms and planned to again.

"I think we can all fit into this truck," Halsey, the Omega man, said.

"I'll need to take my vehicle. Thanks anyway. The boys can ride with me."

Dean smiled at the expression "the boys."

"I'll lead the way up, then. But I need to check on the wells as we go," Halsey said. The two trucks started up the hill. Even through the motors were loud, they could still hear the dog barking.

The early spring air was crisp as they headed up the steep road, green leaves shook in the trees, a few drifted down in the soft morning wind.

"Looks to be cloudin' up." Sam craned his neck to look at the sky.

The Omega man pulled over at the first gas well and waved them on. The sheriff, Dean, and Lonnie drove up the hill, past the first landing of the logging operation, to the top of the ridge. Logs were piled up and a few timbering vehicles were parked but no loggers in sight.

"The logger said the men weren't going to work up here today since it might rain.

I called him yesterday. He said the hunting cabin was about a quarter of a mile back from the road," Lonnie said.

They hiked off the road through a path in the woods.

"If someone wanted to, they could conceal just about anything in these woods. Just like marijuana patches, you don't want to go stumbling into something that's going on." Sam said.

They walked silently through the tough briars and underbrush, leaves from winter crunching under their boots. A fresh canopy of green leaves of the poplar, oaks, and maples were above them. Brown leaves that had once been the autumn carpet of red, gold, rust, and yellow from at least ten species of ancient hardwoods just a few months ago.

They came within sight of the hunting cabin. Its tin roof was hanging over boards loosely nailed together; a metal pipe was sticking out of the roof.

"Y'all sure this is your property?" The sheriff asked, lowering his voice.

"Reasonably so," Lonnie said. "As much as any of the old deeds make clear."

"I hope so. We pay taxes on it," Dean said. *Wonder if we actually have a deed?*

"Mr. Smith said the loggers didn't go in the cabin. It looked like it was deserted, about to fall down," Lonnie said. "It looks like it from here."

"That's smart," Sam said. "If there's a business is goin' on here, there could be toxic chemicals 'round."

"I don't think anything's really goin' on," said Lonnie, "but I am looking for shotgun cases on the ground just in case."

"I wouldn't know what to look for," said Dean

"We should be getting' a whiff if something's going on."

"What's it smell like?" asked Dean.

"Sulfuric acid, lead acetate, lithium batteries melting—highly toxic stuff."

They walked along in silence up to the makeshift cabin.

"Hunting cabin, huh? Look at that trash in there," Sam looked in the window. "Bottles, cups. There's what looks like a gas burner attached to a propane tank. This is or has been a crystal meth lab if I ever saw one. There's some syringes over in that corner."

Lonnie's hands shook as he tried to open the door. "I'm going in."

"No, you're not," said the sheriff. "Someone's been cooking something inside for sure. Let's look around back."

The three men walked around the back of the ramshackle cabin.

"I'll be damned," Lonnie said.

Under a green tarp in the woods behind the cabin they found more glass bottles, tubes, empty boxes of pseudoephedrine, and blister packs. A 30-gallon rusted drum stood near the trees.

"What a mess." Dean said. "I can't believe this."

"Don't touch any of that," said the sheriff.

The sheriff tried to call the DEA, but the call didn't go through.

"No cell reception up here. Let's get out of here, boys."

As they walked back to the truck, the sheriff said to Lonnie and Dean,

"Y'all may not have known 'bout this, but I got to fine you. You've got hazardous material and illegal activity going on your property. The by-products of the chemicals create a very dangerous situation for the loggers, the foresters, hunters, whoever comes up here."

Dean looked at Lonnie and shook his head. His face was twisted in concern. *I'm responsible, too, and just leaving Big Skeggs up to Lonnie, showing up once a year or so, will have to change.*

"Y'all might want to contact a lawyer," Sam said. "It's not personal, boys, but we have to investigate this further."

"Of course," Lonnie said. He didn't say what a wake-up call this was for him.

"We'll help in every way we can," Dean said, furious at himself with his part in the neglect of their property. *We will be lucky to get a fine and not be charged.*

Back at the sheriff's truck, Sam Blankenship said, "How about let's stop for a cup of coffee before you pick up your cars at the office."

And we don't even vote in this county, thought Dean. *He is one nice fellow.* "That's good for me. How about you, Lonnie?"

"No problem," Lonnie said, uncomfortably tight in the truck's cab.

"Will you all be notifying the other family member—your other cousin?" the sheriff asked.

"Other family member?" Lonnie asked, as if that were a remote concept.

"Monica called you about it and left a message. She called me," Dean said.

"Oh, good grief," Lonnie said. "Why don't you do it, Dean? Or come to think about it, I will."

GATHERING AT LE BOURGET AEROPORT

Patricia Daly-Lipe

April, 1927

We had only been in Paris a short time when Michael and I were invited to a reception by Philippe de Beau, an amateur pilot Michael had met at Le Bourget Airstrip. The party was to honor and christen Count de Beau's new aeroplane. Unusual in itself, for us, it was even more unusual and exciting since this was the first party we had been invited to since arriving in Paris. For the drive to the aerodrome, Michael borrowed a 1925 Alpha Romeo called a Tipo-6C-1500. Bright red with two bucket seats, a windshield that turned down flat, and wire wheels, it was a snappy little sports car. I didn't ask where he found it or who was lending it to us.

"This car is the prototype of the famous Alpha Romeo P2 Grand Prix car," Michael explained. I had no idea what he was talking about, but it was great fun setting out to the country in such style. The seats were deep and covered with pillowy cushions filled with hair, upholstered in long-grain leather. A walnut-paneled tonneau cowl was rolled up behind.

The cool, refreshing wind tried to tease the scarf from my neck, but my blond hair, now bobbed short in the modern style was secure under a yellow cloche crammed well over my forehead. This was secured with one of mother's precious jeweled hairpins. She had given it to me in a moment of rare affection. Michael was also fashionably attired with his foulard flapping in the breeze as we drove out of the city of Paris and into the country. City streets became poplar-lined lanes and the fumes of Paris were replaced by fragrances of early spring. Flowers were in full bloom and the green grasses were swaying in a light breeze. Shadows cast by stately old trees with alternating patterns of light, dark, light, dark were almost hypnotic. The wind created the only conversation as the comfy car rolled through the scenic countryside.

All too soon, we arrived at the big field that was Le Bourget Airstrip. Windsocks indicating the wind direction flew from each corner of the field. Michael explained that all planes land into the wind and the flag designation helped pilots determine their landing pattern. More fluttering flags representing different countries, Switzerland, Belgium, The Netherlands, Italy, Jugo-Slavia, Bulgaria, Czechoslovakia, Estonia, Latvia, Lithuania, Poland, Spain and Portugal adorned the facades of various aeronautical clubs whose small lightweight aeroplanes lined up in rows at the other side of the field. Michael drove toward an area where a smartly dressed group had gathered. I could see heads turn as he pulled the dashing little Alpha next to a low slung Cadillac Phaeton. Unlike our little sports car, this automobile had a rumble seat in the rear, classic chrome bumpers, and twin-mounted headlamps jutting out below the winged hood ornament. "Why would anyone want such a monster car?" I asked recognizing only size and opulence.

"Some people prefer those heavy giants because of their powerful V8 engines," he replied crisply.

"To me, they are simply big, noisy, and flashy."

Michael maneuvered the little roadster carefully avoiding the protruding running boards of the *pleasure mobile*.

"Why are you parking here, Michael?"

"So I can keep this car blocked from the dust that is blowing across the field." So the big Cadillac would serve another purpose, securing us from the dirt.

As I slid out of my seat, my high heels sank onto the soft soil. I realized how difficult it was going to be to walk. Perhaps I had not dressed appropriately after all. To make maneuvering even worse, the wind had picked up, determined to whisk off my hat. Michael was eager to go ahead and mingle and was less than gracious about having to wait for me to hobble across the dirt field.

Approaching the gathering, we were greeted with a loud din punctuated by an occasional high-pitched twitter. It sounded as if everyone was talking at once whether anyone else listened or not. Michael was visibly thrilled to be around people who loved the sport of flight, but I was excited just to be out and about socially. Apparently, the big news was that the Brevoort and Lafayette Hotel Group in New York was offering a $25,000 prize for the first pilot to cross the Atlantic Ocean nonstop. The conversation was in French, and I had no problem understanding what was being said. The hope, of course, was that a French pilot would win the coveted prize. There was some misgiving that an American group was coming up with the funds, but the French sought the prospect of enhancing their aeronautical industry. Winning would be most helpful.

Michael could not understand what was being said, nor was he tuned into the tension that existed between the French and Americans. I was torn, sympathizing with the French, recognizing their need for recognition after the horrors they had been subjected to during the war. However, I was an American. Besides, since I was invited to this gathering only because I was Michael's wife, I decided to voice my opinion.

"Perhaps this will be a way to bridge the gap between the French and the Americans?" I suggested in French.

"*Au contraire*," retorted a tall mustached gentleman in the group. "We've had quite enough of these wild and reckless New World people."

Michael, not understanding, murmured something about flying across the ocean. The mustached gentleman turned bright scarlet. "Oh, I am so terribly sorry. I did not realize you were Americans," he said in pleasant *cocktail* English. "Your wife has such a perfect accent and I, well, I only ..." *Poor Michael. He was going to have to become used to this sort of thing.* Graciously excusing ourselves from that group, we went to find our host.

It was not difficult to locate Philippe de Beau. He was leaning against the fuselage of his new toy, one arm patting it like a soft puppy, the other hand gesticulating as he spoke. Though not terribly tall, maybe five feet nine, he gave the impression of being a big man. He was also, I thought, quite handsome. His hair was dark brown and slicked back from his wide intelligent-looking forehead. His eyes were brown with flecks of gold, and they sparkled when he smiled. The pipe between his teeth added to his jaunty air. Several people stood around him, smiling, eager to hear whatever he was saying.

"Do you remember the small planes at the beginning of the war? The pilot's job was to spy on the enemy's positions and report back to a courier soldier who would then jump on his horse or motorcycle and report to the officer in charge. Can you believe the pilots from the opposing sides would pass each other in the air and wave? It was the chivalrous thing to do. 'Hello there, having a nice spy?'" Philippe laughed heartily and the group laughed with him.

I was captivated, not so much by the conversation, but by the man. I didn't realize my feelings showered my face.

"What are you grinning about?" whispered Michael.

Embarrassed, I began to quietly translate Philippe's anecdotes to distract Michael.

"Of course, they eventually smartened up and armed the planes with grenades, that is, after trying handguns. The planes also had machine guns, but first they had to find ways to shoot *through* the propellers so they didn't shoot the propeller off," Philippe explained with a giggle. "But with the grenades, they had little darts to toss off, aiming at the other spy planes. Then there were bigger aerial darts we called *flechettes*. The Germans call them *fiegerpfeile*. The planes would fly over the opposing troops only long enough to toss out some of these *flechettes* and, should anyone get hit, well, I wouldn't want to describe the gory picture."

"The French are …" I began, but Michael cut me off demanding that I pay attention and translate later.

"These aerial darts were clumsy but most effective. They were dropped in clusters and reached a velocity of 200 meters per second," Philippe added, then paused to take a puff from his pipe giving me time to translate for Michael.

"How much did these *flechettes* weigh?" asked a thin, serious looking gentleman with horn-rimmed glasses and a white broad brimmed hat.

"They weighed about twenty grams and were approximately twenty-five mm long with a caliber of 5.67 mm."

"That's about 1/4 of an inch," Michael whispered. He didn't want to interrupt Philippe, but he was making it difficult for me to listen and continue the translation.

"They had a sharp pointed nose on the striking end and a fin on the tail. Both sides used thousands of them. You can still find them all over the countryside where the battles were fought."

"We found some in Germany when I went there with my parents," I added to my interpreting to Michael. "They were on the ground near the spot where we picnicked."

"Did the pilots use these aerial darts to kill the other pilots, too?" asked a masculine looking woman with an absurd little red hat perched atop her straight short brown hair.

"What did she ask?" Michael wanted to know. I translated. Clearly, my husband was fascinated with the discussion. I was fascinated with our host.

"No," continued Philippe, replying to the last question. "These darts are only effective at high speeds. If you put one in an air gun, it could kill. However, you would need to create a force strong enough to initiate a high velocity and a proper projectile to reach a moving target. Much too difficult, especially since the pilot had to fly the plane as well. Nevertheless, your thinking is right on target with the military intelligence." This brought a huge grin to the red-hatted lady's face. "Soon after the invention of the *flechettes*, the planes were equipped with mounted guns. This time the pilot could line up with the opponent spy plane and shoot. Unfortunately, the first plane equipped that way fell to its demise when the gun shot off one of its propellers."

The group tittered.

"Oh, there you are, *mon ami*," Philippe called out to Michael, disentangling himself from his audience. He gave Michael the perfunctory *baiser* on both cheeks. I was left behind with no introduction.

Michael could not wait to add his knowledge. "I hate to disagree with you, my dear friend," my husband, the serious student of history, began. "But this was not the first attempt. It was Roland Giros, the Frenchman, who had devised the first mounted gun."

"Ah, *oui*," he said making a sweeping gesture with his hand. "Leave it to the French to make such a stupid mistake."

Such a gentleman, I thought.

"You misunderstand me, my friend. Monsieur Giros mounted the gun but put metal deflectors on the propeller. He was successful on six missions."

"*Ah, bon.*"

At that point, I wished Michael would stop, but I knew that he was persistent when making a point.

"Yes, well on the seventh mission, he wasn't so lucky. The deflector gave way and he shot himself down. Unfortunately, he was behind enemy lines."

"So you see how it is with the French?" Philippe added cheerfully, not the least perturbed by Michael's intrusion into his discussion.

"But do consider that after 1910, most development and racing of early high-speed aircraft has been concentrated in France," Michael continued, not understanding his host's simple good manners.

Philippe, however, had by now clearly lost interest in the conversation. He stared directly at me for a second before he said, "Michael, I assume this is your lovely wife you have finally brought for me to meet." I could feel my face turning red. Michael never looked at me with eyes like that. Philippe was not only looking at me, he was looking through me, as if probing my very soul.

"*Enchantée*, Monsieur de Beau," I mumbled hoping to (yet fearful that I might) receive the traditional kiss on both cheeks. But he did not kiss me. Much worse. He put his hands on both of my shoulders and held me in place as though I would try to escape his gaze. In French he whispered, "Madame, you are absolutely beautiful." There was silence as he continued to stare. I completely forgot my husband standing beside me. Michael, on the other hand, was utterly unaware of any impropriety. I was sure of that since he had already turned away to seek other flying buddies. I could feel my face heat up but I could not take my eyes away from his. Fortunately for me, another of Philippe's friends arrived and the chatter recommenced.

I found Michael and together we mingled amongst the guests. From time to time I caught Philippe glancing my way. Each time, my face tingled with schoolgirl embarrassment.

Waiters carrying trays with glasses of wine and hors d'oeuvres scurried around the guests. Ardent conversations continued. The theme was universal.

"Do you really think it is possible that a man will be able to fly across the Atlantic? So many have already died making the attempt."

"What about lasting that long with no *toilette*?" This came from a coquettish young lady brandishing a long cigarette holder.

"Don't be ridiculous, my dear," replied an athletic looking man sporting the latest chic, rakish white hat with a black band. "We are discussing something quite serious here."

While I was listening to this banter, Michael had wandered off to join a group of men standing to the side of one of the hangars. They were having a serious conversation of their own. It was apparent that he was well acquainted with this clique and appeared much more at ease with them than he had been with the chitchat of the mixed group. Watching his behavior again made me wonder what the future would hold for us. Was he really going to make a career out of aviation? Would I be left alone most of the time? Or would I be included in his adventures? Looking around Le Bourget aerodrome, I examined again the dozens of small, private company banners and flags and the many small, sporty planes. Obviously, the private sector was very involved in flying. Perhaps Michael was right. There might be a great future in aviation.

Out of the blue, a feminine voice broke my reverie. "How do you do? My name is Pamela," she said, her English clip and precise.

The lady who had come up behind me was certainly more suitably dressed for the dusty field than I. Wearing jodhpurs and slim brown riding boots, she was tall and elegant and had the unmistakable look of an English equestrienne. Under her brown brimmed Tyrolean hat with its jaunty green feather, her deep blue eyes impressed me with their sharp, penetrating gaze. I did not intend to be rude and hoped she would consider my hesitancy a mark of formality.

"Er, oh, how do you do, Pamela? I'm Libby."

"Short for Elizabeth. Yes, I know. Your husband has told me all about you."

Now I was on the defensive. *Michael knows this woman?* She appeared a bit older than I but was certainly an attractive lady, athletic looking and slender.

"We met at the Morgan Bank," she replied answering my naked look of surprise. "My husband is Director of the bank. Michael came in wishing to set up an account."

I had to smile. So this is not a romantic liaison after all.

"I happened to be there, in my husband's office that is, arranging for a dinner party. You know, telephone service can be so erratic these days. I think your husband assumed I was Victor's personal secretary. Now he doesn't recognize me in my hunting attire."

"But you look too clean to have been riding," I blurted out before realizing how gauche that must have sounded.

"I haven't been riding. I am more comfortable in pants, and this is the only acceptable way I can wear them."

I was a bit confused.

"I consider myself a modern woman. Victor and I try to behave as equals. This is one of the ways I express myself. He has no problem with my behavior. I rather think he enjoys it. Moreover, I love to shock people. I detest common behavior. Don't you?"

I didn't know how to reply.

"Oh dear, now I think I have rather shocked you."

"Yes, no, I mean, I admire your courage," I stammered. Pamela appeared pleased with my observation, and I began to relax in her company. Deciding to be daring in my own way, I elected to state my opinions on a subject I had never before discussed with anyone.

"I believe in the equality of the sexes, too." Now where had that come from? This conversation was opening up thoughts that I must have locked up in my mind for years. "However," I brazenly continued, "in the United States, women only won national suffrage a few years ago, in 1920." Remembering the many conversations about politics that I had with my father, never my mother, I reasoned that I was more of a modern woman than I had realized. Boldly, I continued. "Don't get me started. I have a passion for politics, but my family does not feel it is appropriate for ladies to talk about such things."

"My family is more liberal. Maybe that is the difference between the British and the Americans?" Pamela giggled.

Her easy manner made me feel more relaxed. Still, I was amazed at her outspokenness. At the same time, I was enjoying the freedom of conversation we were having.

Pamela continued. "Isn't this grand? Being at Le Bourget, I mean. We are taking part in the making of history. Don't you agree? Everyone is talking about transatlantic flight. Can you imagine being able to fly to your home in America? The trip would take hours instead of days. Why, great ocean liners could become history."

I shuddered, remembering only too clearly my honeymoon experience. Yes, flying across the Atlantic would be nice, but I wondered if that could ever become a reality.

"They have to make the planes a bit larger," she added nodding at the collection of small planes lined up on the side of the field. "These flimsy machines don't look terribly safe, do they? And, of course being so small, there wouldn't be the amusements and the camaraderie you experience on the big ships. I do so love their grand dinners." It was an odd comment from one so slender. She didn't look as if she could finish even half a regular meal.

"I don't suppose you would be able to eat at all or even get up and walk around, would you?" I asked, glancing at our host's little plane parked not far from where we stood.

"Can you imagine reading a book on a plane? It would be difficult with all the bouncing and bumping, wouldn't it?" We both stared at the little plane, in thought. "Consider crossing the whole Atlantic Ocean with absolutely nothing to do, sitting for hours and hours. I, for one, simply could not do it," She declared emphatically.

I had to laugh. A true Brit, this lady had brought the whole amazing feat down to the bare bones. And honestly, I could not see this vivacious woman sitting still that long either.

"Well, well, I see you two are getting along nicely."

I swirled around and was face to face with Philippe. Immediately, I blushed. Most assuredly, Pamela noticed.

"Please allow me to show you two lovely ladies my new Puss Moth monoplane."

Although little, it appeared quite impressive until we were next to it. Up close, my doubts about the joy of flying increased. The two cockpits looked small, tight and uncomfortable. On the other hand, with the beautiful wings spreading out, I could conjure up the feeling a bird must have of soaring, gliding. The wind, the sensation of being closer to the sun, warm caressing rays wrapping around my shoulders ... . Philippe took me by the hand and suddenly I realized, he had been talking, and I hadn't heard a word.

" ... called a barnstormer. But while a friend is helping me work on this Puss Moth monoplane, I still really love my original biplane." He took us over to another plane. Tapping the lower wing fondly, he told us, "She flew in the Great War." Pamela and I marveled at the sight of this quaint little plane.

"I did have to make some necessary modifications," he continued with pride. "For one, I have installed a second cockpit."

He looked unabashedly at me. I could not meet his eyes afraid that I might blush again, so I continued to look at the cockpits. It *would* be worth the discomfort of being cramped in such a tight place, flying with the wind in your hair, up into and through the clouds, dancing with the gods.

"There is a nice long exhaust stack to warm your hands on along the starboard side of the fuselage," he stated as if he thought I was thinking about the cold. Of course, I had no idea what an exhaust stack was, but warm hands sounded good. The plane's off-white metallic paint glistened in the late afternoon sun.

Philippe's enthusiasm was transporting me to a place I had never been. Looking at the complexity of his aeroplanes, I was sure that flying was out of the question for me, although I was glad to share his hopes and dreams. I was honored and it seemed Pamela was also that he was taking the time out from his other guests to speak with us.

The afternoon drifted into evening. Already, it was starting to grow cool. I hadn't thought to bring a coat, especially with an open-air car ride back to Paris. Pamela came to the rescue.

"Let's all go to the *Château Madrid*," she suggested. "We can take several people in our Duesenberg. Surely Michael can find someone to accompany him in the Alpha." As the word spread among the remaining guests, everyone thought it a splendid idea. I had never been to the famed *Château Madrid*, but heard it was a restaurant favored by artists, mainly because it was supposed to be reasonably priced. It was reputedly *"irrefutably sumptuous in its cuisine,"* at least, this is how Pamela described it.

Laughing and chattering, everyone headed for the motor cars. Michael was only too happy to follow in the little Alpha and had no trouble soliciting a fellow to accompany him.

I found myself seated in the back of Pamela's ritzy Duesenberg between two robust Frenchmen who smelled of cigars and cologne and talked and laughed nonstop. I was warming up both physically and emotionally. The mood was contagious. I laughed and even contributed once or twice to the gay conversation.

Because the ride had been so entertaining, before I knew it, we had arrived. In fact, I was having so much fun that I never questioned being without my husband and with people I barely knew. One of the traveling companions took my hand to help me descend from the car. I was grateful not only to keep from falling, but the crowd in front of the *Château Madrid* Restaurant was so huge, it could have easily consumed me.

We had to shove our way in. I was in the middle of our group getting jostled and tapped. Once I had the feeling of someone pinching me from behind, but when I turned around, I could only see a blur of faces also pushing their way in. Was it Michael? Or perhaps Philippe? I hoped it was Philippe. Such a thought. I surprised myself. Truly, this evening had developed into more than I could have imagined.

Once inside, I became acutely aware of the noise. Corks popped, glasses clinked, and people laughed and called to each other across the room. Smoke filled the air. There was decadence in the *devil-may-care* atmosphere. It reminded me how little enjoyment I had experienced since my wedding.

Once accustomed to the noise, I could make out the tinkling of a piano in the background. Pamela grabbed me by the hand and waltzed me through the crowd to a table in the rear. "We're going to have fun this evening." Pamela smiled at me.

This was the real Paris, and I was finally part of it. I could feel myself becoming someone I had never known before and it was thrilling. "Dance with me, *chérie?*"

It was Philippe. I rose and followed him in a trance to a crowded spot where couples were already dancing.

"You need a drink. You're a bit tense."

A glass materialized. Standing with Philippe beside the dance floor, I obediently sipped the smooth red wine. My body warmed, and my inhibitions began relaxing. A smile literally exploded across my face.

"That's more like it!" Taking the glass and placing it on a nearby table, he spun me around in a Charleston. "*C'est très excitant, n'est-ce pas?*" he laughed.

My feet hardly touched the floor as I bounced and swirled in time to the lively rag. I never danced to these tunes during my debut, but here I was and it was fun. Time and space dissolved. I was flying around and around, up and down. A little more wine and the room, the lights, the rhythm spun me round and round. When I finally sat back down next to Pamela, I was tipsy, not just from the wine but from sheer bliss.

By now the table was covered with food. We began with the first course. Two platters gave us a choice of *boeuf à la mode, or fillets de sole bonne femme* accompanied by *caneton aux navets, champignons farcis* and other vegetables cooked as only the French can. Then the waiters cleared away the plates and brought new dishes for the *salade* followed by cheeses. One way or another, the guests were able to continue the flow of conversation and eat at the same time because, in what seemed like mere minutes, the platters were bare. A different wine accompanied each course. The finale consisted of an assortment of tarts and *crème caramel* accompanied by coffee and a bottle of *Sainte Estèphe*.

Only when I had finished and was a little too full, did I realize that I had not seen Michael since leaving the aerodrome. Nor had I missed him.

Originally published in *A Cruel Calm*, New Edition, 2014

CANNONBALL

Wendi Dass

Gunny jumped off the nearby floating dock shouting, "Cannonball!"

The feathery evergreens around the lake swallowed the sound. The cool water nipped my toes, the sand turning gritty between them. I looked back over the water: Gunny's inner tube floated precariously on its side, the sun bouncing off its soft curves. That's when I felt it first. The urge to capture the moment.

I was seventeen, scrawny, and as thrilled to be on a family vacation as a slug in a foot race.

"Hey, Jen! Look at me!" Gunny catapulted off the dock, but my attention wasn't on him.

I pulled my clunky camera from my backpack, feeling the warmth of black molded plastic under my fingers. The sun blinded me through the lens, and I crouched. The fishy-smelling wake soaked my cuffed jeans, but I didn't care. Purples and violets streamed off the soft curves, dancing on the rippled water. I adjusted the shutter speed, hoping to catch the motion of the bobbing inner tube. I clicked again. I clicked until the whole roll was full.

At the one-hour photo, I spent the rest of my birthday money. Gunny paced the shop, standing on his tippy-toes to reach the shoulder of a life-size cut-out of Michael Jackson.

"Ya think Mom'll let us go to the movies?" He stepped back from the cardboard, snapping his gum.

"I dunno, Gun. Maybe *Elephant Man*." I leaned forward on the counter, straining to see the picture that dropped from the machine.

"Is that like *Babar*?"

"No, stupid. It's like …" I squinted, the vinegary chemicals permeating the air. "Just ask Mom."

Gunny scrunched his nose up.

I drummed my fingers on the counter. "Well, if we use our allowance maybe they'll let us pick."

Gunny ran to my side and yanked my shirt. "I wanna see *Cad-dyShack*. Let's go ask Mom and Dad. Please?"

His pleading sounded more like a five-year-old than a twelve-year-old, but I was used to it. I rolled my eyes. "Right, like they're gonna let us see an R-rated movie." The clerk picked up my photos and placed them in a paper envelope. My pulse thudded in my ears, and Gunny's voice faded. He handed me the photos, and immediately I dumped them onto the counter. I spread them out, the warm photos like tacky flypaper left in the sun.

Gunny continued to pull on my shirt, but I couldn't take my eyes off the photos. I sorted through blurry shots, shadowed shots, shots where the glare of the sun whited out the image.

Then, there it was, beneath a cropped picture of me sprawled out on a towel on the beach. I'd taken it with arms outstretched, hoping I wouldn't chop off my head. But I didn't care that my head was fully intact. I cared about the photo sticking to the back. The moment still fresh in my mind lay vivid in front of me: the ripples of the water, the bouncing inner tube.

I scrounged the rest of my money from my pockets and ordered two more copies.

I looked down at Gunny, suddenly feeling like I'd just drank a cup of Mom's coffee. "You know what, Gun?" I tousled his hair. "If you don't tell Mom what we see, I won't either."

§

Years later, I stare at a print in a flimsy frame — from the dollar store, I'm sure — hanging on a drab wall in Gunny's room. How can an artist be proud of that? But who am I to judge? Photography somehow lost its novelty around the time my grandkids started taking selfies two decades ago. About the same time, I'd guess, that Gunny's kids put him in this place. A glorified nursing home whose choice in artwork is on par with the care for the patients.

I leave the print, making a mental note to replace it with one of Gunny's album covers — *ACDC* would bring some life to the place. I take a seat next to Gunny and squeeze his hand.

"Gun?" Gunny's eyelids twitch just enough so that I know he's listening. "Do you remember that time you went with me to develop my film? At the Lake?"

Gunny turns his head, the remaining strands of his once full head of hair, now white, stick to the pillow. His eyes question me with foggy listlessness. "Grammy?"

I sink into my plastic chair, my old bones aching against firmness. I smile but don't correct him. I do look a lot like Grammy with my wrinkly, spotted skin, my grey hair cut short like she used to wear it. I pull a deck of cards from my purse and start to shuffle.

"Rummy?" I deal us each seven cards and place the remaining cards in a stack on the makeshift table between us.

Gunny picks up his hand. Regardless of the faces he forgets, he remembers our games. I pour us each a glass of lemonade. Real lemonade I made from scratch and packed in a thermos.

Surveying my pair of jacks, I sip the lemonade, and for the moment, I'm back on the beach, Mom's homemade lemonade in my hand, Gunny ramping for another takeoff. Card games with Gunny made nights in the sticky, air-conditioned cabin pass quicker. I lean back in my chair, imagining I'm on the lounge chair on the cabin's front porch, Gunny ranking the pictures from the roll from best to worst. I choke on a laugh. Gunny was adamant on first place, which wasn't even a picture I took. It was a picture Mom took of Gunny ambushing me with water balloons.

"Bingo!" Gunny's roommate, another Alzheimer's patient, shouts.

I pick up a card from the deck. It's another Jack. I grin and throw down my set. But Gunny has me.

"I'm out." He lays down the fourth Jack and gulps the rest of his drink. He slaps the glass on his nightstand.

I tally up the points and sigh. Never could beat my kid brother at cards.

An attendant comes in with a meal that looks as appetizing as balloon filled with sand, and I prepare to leave.

"Salisbury steak," the young lady in scrubs announces, dropping the tray on a table along the far wall.

Gunny moves over to the table, and I pack up my cards. I pick up Gunny's empty cup from the nightstand, to fill it with the last of the lemonade, and something catches my eye. A tattered photo of an inner tube. Gunny's inner tube.

I pick it up. "Where did this come from?" I ask the attendant.

She shrugs, tucks a napkin on Gunny's lap, and leaves.

I hold the picture in my hand, the same sensation of warmth radiates through me as the moment I removed it from the envelope sixty years ago. Something inside me clicks, like the roll on my 35-mm camera. I reach into my purse and pull out my smartphone, a device I hardly know how to use but one my kids make me carry nonetheless. I fumble to pull up the camera. I know the results won't be as good as my SLR at home, but it will have to do.

Gunny's hand moves the plastic fork up and down, the gravy of his Salisbury steak slowly dripping off. I press the circle on the screen, trying to catch the brown goo falling, but the shutter is too slow. I press again. I pinch the screen, using a motion my grandkids had to teach me, to zoom in. I press again. An energy pulses through me, and even though I know I can see the footage now, I don't. Where's the fun in that?

After a few more takes, I put the phone back in my purse. I fill Gunny's glass with lemonade and place it next to his dinner. I slide the tattered picture of the inner tube in front of Gunny's plate.

"See you next week." I kiss his temple and turn to go.

His voice stops me when I get to the door.

"Cannonball!"

I look back, and I know by the clarity in his eyes that he knows who I am.

MORNING FLIGHT

Danielle Dayney

The rising sun had yet to meet the sky, and hues of pink changed the clouds to delicious cotton candy. She shut the door quietly, trying not to wake her father, then flipped yesterday's braids behind her, and tiptoed quickly off the deck.

Wet grass slipped between her bare toes, as she ran toward the towering tree.

Once there, her small hands tugged at the ropes, pulling herself to sit on the wood, hand-carved by her papa. She tipped her head, purple nightgown soaring behind her like a cape, and toes touched the commanding sky.

She often dreamt of flying.

Morning Flight originally published on https://danielledayney.com, July 19, 2016

WISHFUL THINKING

Phyllis A. Duncan

1

The Depression was pretty much over, people said. In the real world, that might be the case, but, in step-daddy's mind, why hire farmhands when you had stepsons working for free?

"Idle hands are the Devil's playground," step-daddy always said. He made certain none of them were idle for long.

What he didn't understand was farm work kept you occupied from summer dawn until summer dusk, and that left summer nights for hell-raising. Not that a couple of teenagers and their twelve-year-old sister could do much in a county where every sheriff's deputy knew their step-daddy too well.

They hadn't had any say about getting a step-daddy. He was there, all of a sudden it seemed, and not long after their father had died. The man who had been the farm manager had become the farm owner because of a wedding.

Everyone told Freddie he was too young to remember their father, but he did. Or maybe it was how his older brothers and sisters talked of Daddy, but Freddie had his image firmly in mind. Or maybe he stared too much at Daddy's portrait, which had hung over the fireplace in the parlor of the rambling farmhouse and which now sat gathering dust in a closet.

To Freddie, no one rose to the level of his father, certainly not the pig-eyed man his mother had married. Of all the siblings, only Freddie and his next-older brother J.M. had noticed the way their stepfather looked at their youngest sister, Fee. They made sure he was never alone with her, but that became too obvious. They decided they had to talk to her.

§

"Jesus, Freddie, we can't do this," J.M. said.

The two brothers whispered to each other in the hallway down from their sister's room.

"We're the only ones who can. You know well enough if we go to Momma, she'll say we're lying because we don't like him. Mary and 'Lizabeth only care about those two boys they're seeing. We've got to explain to Fee why she can't sit on that old man's lap."

Freddie and J.M. came into Fee's room without knocking. None of the children still living in the house could close their doors. Step-daddy's rule.

"Hey," Fee said. "What y'all want?"

"We got to talk to you," Freddie said. "J.M., stand by the door and tell me if anyone's coming."

J.M. looked relieved. Sometimes he lorded the older brother status—all of eleven months—over Freddie, but for this he let Freddie do the talking.

Freddie pulled a chair up beside the bed. Fee had been reading. The girl loved to read anything she could get her hands on. Tall and gangly, she was a tomboy, to their momma's regret. The youngest of ten siblings, she, J.M., and Freddie had bonded with each other more than with their older siblings after their father died.

"What're we going to do tonight?" she asked.

"In a minute. I said we got to talk."

"About what?"

Jesus, Freddie thought, how the hell do I say this? He wanted to protect her, but he didn't want to scare her, either.

"Fee, uh, like us, you grew up on this farm, and you know, uh, you know about how the lambs and foals and calves get born," Freddie said.

"Of course. I even know how they get made."

Freddie and J.M. exchanged a wide-eyed look. Freddie swallowed hard and turned back to his sister.

"Well, uh, you know that the ewes and the mares and the cows don't get with, uh, young until they're old enough, right?"

"Yes. Brother Ed explained it."

"Well, the same is true for us, you know, people. People don't do, uh, things with, uh, each other until they're the right age."

"Mary and 'Lizabeth must be the right age, 'cause they go out with the Polk boys all the time."

"They're, uh, they're close to old enough, but what I'm trying to say is, you see, you're not."

"I ain't interested in no boys, Freddie." She rolled her eyes as if that were the stupidest thing he'd ever suggested.

"That'll probably change, Fee, but, uh, here's the thing. J.M.

and me, we want you to stay away from step-daddy. Don't go near him when there's nobody else around, and, for God's sake, don't get in his lap when he asks you."

"Why?"

"Because, because, uh, you're not old enough, like I said."

Fee frowned at him. She was usually sharp as a tack, but this puzzled her. "What's wrong with sitting on his lap? Sometimes, he gives me candy if I do."

"Just don't!" Freddie said, almost a shout. He looked over his shoulder at J.M., who peered down the hallway both ways. J.M. shook his head.

How the hell did you tell your twelve-year-old sister you'd seen step-daddy lure the young daughters of the tenant farmers into the barn with candy, that you'd seen those girls come out of the barn crying and bleeding between their legs? In a way, that might get her to understand better, but, damn it, he didn't want her to carry that image in her head.

"Fee, look, do it for me and J.M., okay? I'll explain more when you're older," Freddie said.

"You think step-daddy's going to do something bad to me?" she asked.

"Yes, we do."

She looked from Freddie to J.M. "Is it important to you?"

Both J.M. and Freddie nodded.

Fee thought for a while, shrugged, and said, "Okay."

"Don't forget, all right?"

"I won't."

"And if he tries to make you come somewhere with him, you come get J.M. or me."

"Okay. Now, what fun are we going to have tonight?"

Freddie sighed and wiped some sweat from his forehead. That talk had gone better than he'd hoped, and he hadn't had to get too embarrassing.

"Well, Fee," he said, "tonight, I thought it would be fun to ride the horses over Devil's Ridge and buy some of old man Bruce's liquor."

Her eyes brightened, but J.M. left watching the door and came into the room.

"Not with Fee along," he said.

"J.M., you act like I'm a baby and never had no moonshine before," Fee said.

"We are not buying 'shine with you along," J.M. said.

"Well, shoot." She pouted for a few seconds and smiled up at her brothers. "I got an idea for a trick we can play."

Fee's pranks were the best and by and large unexpected because she was so young.

"Let's hear it," Freddie said.

She sat up, cross-legged, on her bed and leaned toward them, lowering her voice.

"We ride to that crossroads with the big tree," she said. "We take some rope, and you two hang me from that branch overhanging the road right before the Culpeper to Charlottesville bus comes 'round the turn. All those folks on the bus will see me and piss their pants."

Freddie grinned; he liked it.

"Why on earth do you want to do that?" J.M. asked.

"It'll be fun," Fee said. "Come on. It's better than sitting here doing nothing."

"We are not hanging you from no tree," J.M. declared.

"Ease up, J.M.," Freddie said. "We're not gonna really hang her."

"I'll unbraid my hair, hang my head to one side, and let my tongue hang out," Fee said, and demonstrated.

Even J.M. laughed at the sight.

"I can make a sling with the rope that goes under her arms," Freddie said, "but it'll look like it's around her neck. She can wear a jacket over the rig, so's no one can see it. Fee, you know how you can make it better?"

"How?"

"Wear one of 'Lizabeth's skirts so it's obvious you're a girl."

"Do I hafta?"

"It'll be perfect."

§

A lot of headlights came from Culpeper towards the crossroads. They bounced and tossed their beams across the farmlands bordering the state road. More lights came on in houses, as people woke to see what the commotion was. A lot of people's sleep got disrupted, but that didn't matter much to Freddie. The fun was all that mattered, that and being away from step-daddy's reach for a few hours.

"Freddie, we've gone and done it now," J.M. said, almost a moan. As befitting an older brother, J.M. fretted over everything, like an old woman. He was the first one to like a good prank, but let there be a hint of getting caught, he was a nervous Nellie.

"Relax, J.M., we didn't do anything wrong."

"Freddie's right. Nothing we did was wrong," said Fee.

Freddie had to smile. This girl was truly the most adventurous of the three of them.

"There's two cop cars, Freddie. Dang it," J.M. said. "Let's get on the horses and get out of here."

When the Greyhound bus had barreled around the curve and its headlights fell on Fee hanging from that tree, Freddie and J.M. had almost peed their own pants from laughing. The driver went white as a ghost and slewed sideways trying to stop. The boys had laughed some more when the driver took forever to turn the bulky bus around in the narrow road. When its taillights were out of sight on its way back to Culpeper, he and J.M. lowered Fee to the ground and rolled up the rope.

"Lord, I almost busted a gut trying not to laugh," she'd said.

"All right, we had our fun. Let's go home," J.M. had said.

"J.M., don't be such an old biddy," Fee had told him. "We got to wait and see what happens."

What had happened was the arrival of the two state police cruisers, along with a whole bunch of people from town in jalopies and trucks, some even by wagon. They carried lanterns and rifles, the occasional pitchfork, ready to search for a poor young thing what got hung.

The three siblings watched the state cops shine their big, bright flashlights up into the tree and in the weeds on either side of the road. Freddie had hoped for this development. He'd coveted those big-lensed Rayovac flashlights for a long time, since he'd seen the state cops use them to direct traffic around a wreck on Rt. 29 weeks before.

"Fee," he whispered, "braid your hair and get your jeans back on. Mind you hide that skirt."

"What are we going to do?"

Freddie grinned at her. "We're going to join the hunt."

§

J.M. had stopped muttering by the time the siblings rode their horses into the chaotic scene of men, and a few women, thrashing through the fields on either side of the road.

"Who's there?" one of the state cops asked.

Faking breathlessness, Freddie said, "We was riding to get you! We saw the guy! He hung a woman and drug her down toward the river!"

"Which way?" the cop asked.

They pointed, thankfully all in the same direction. "We can help," said J.M., now fully into it. "We can cover a lot of ground on our horses."

One state cop shined his flashlight on their faces. "Who'd you say you were?"

"John Marshall Duncan and Frederick Winfrey Duncan," said Freddie. "This here's our sister Fiona."

The other state cop came up beside the first. "I know the family," he said. "The boys are a little wild, but we've never had any trouble from them."

Because you never caught us, Freddie thought. He smiled at the policemen. "Officers, we'll be happy to help you look, but we got no lanterns or flashlights on us."

"How were you planning to get home in the dark?" the first cop asked.

"Horses know the way," Freddie replied. "If you give us your flashlights, we'll search upriver while you search down."

The two cops looked at each other and shrugged. "All right," one of them said, "I got some spares." He walked to his cruiser and returned with two flashlights, handing one to Freddie and one to J.M.

Freddie hefted it, liking the weight of it, caused mostly by the dense, No. 2 batteries inside. Almost a foot long, the metal flashlight's handle was covered in ribbed, dark leather. The lens was thick glass, eight-sided. You could knock someone out with one of these and wouldn't have to swing that hard.

He smiled as he thought about showing Fee how to use it like a club.

"Thank you, officer," Freddie said.

"I'm loaning you those flashlights for an hour, understand?"

"Yes, sir," the three said, in unison.

"If you find something, get back here right away. Don't you try to apprehend the guy. Think of your sister," the cop said.

"Always, officer," Freddie replied.

§

Reins loose in their hands, the three let the horses pick the way back home. True to form, it didn't take long for J.M. to rue the fact they'd ridden off with the state cops' property.

"Thanks to you, big mouth Freddie, they know our names. What if they come to the house looking for these flashlights?" he said. "Step-daddy will beat the shit out of us for stealing them."

"We'll explain it got late, and we needed to get Fee home, and we planned on bringing them to the state police barracks, but we forgot," Freddie said.

"Don't include me in that," said Fee, "since you didn't get one of them fancy flashlights for me."

She'd hung back and not ridden abreast with him and J.M as usual, but Freddie hadn't realized it was because she felt left out. He slowed his horse until he and Fee were side-by-side.

"Don't worry, Fee. I'm giving you mine," he said.

"But why? You've always wanted one of them."

"Here, hold it."

Fee did, and her eyes widened. "Whoa, that's heavy!"

"Yeah, it is. I want you to hide it in your room and put it under your blankets before you go to sleep. Understand?"

"Why would I—"

"You remember what me and J.M. talked to you about?"

"Oh," she murmured. She smiled at her brother. "This would sure make him see stars, wouldn't it?"

It would probably cave in the old bastard's head if Freddie or J.M. hit him with it. Fee's spindly arms would only give step-daddy a headache, and maybe that was for the best.

As sometimes happened with him, a vision flashed before Freddie's eyes. He saw himself as clear as if he looked in a mirror, standing in the parlor of their house, rifle at his shoulder, and his stepfather in the sights. It faded almost as soon as it appeared.

My wishful thinking, he thought.

2

Six Months Later

Freddie had walked nine miles in the dark on cattle paths and over fences. He had ten miles to go. By midnight, Freddie would be at his dead father's house, where step-daddy was. Soon after midnight, step-daddy would be dead.

Long walks could cool tempers. Not for Freddie. His anger raged hotter during his trek, remembering how he'd overheard his oldest brother telling J.M. the story. Step-daddy had hit their mother for the offense of not having his dinner ready on time. No one had seen Freddie listening, and they hadn't seen him take the rifle from the rack or the ammunition from the drawer.

If I'd been there, Freddie thought, I'd have stopped the old bastard.

§

But he hadn't been there. He and his siblings no longer lived in the house they'd been born in—step-daddy's new rule. His older brothers and sisters were married and starting families in houses of their own. He and J.M. and Fee had eavesdropped from the hallway and heard the old man's bellowing to their mother on the day he kicked them out.

"By God, this is my house now! Only my children will live in it, not your brats with their high and mighty airs. Get them out!"

Freddie had looked to his mother to say something, to tell them to go through the motions until step-daddy slept the whiskey off, but she'd said nothing, done nothing to stop them packing their clothes.

Fee had gone to live with 'Lizabeth and her new husband. J.M. and Freddie had moved in with cousins. Even after he'd settled in, Freddie expected his mother to get him and the others, but she hadn't. She'd visit, asking about homework and schooling, but ignored his questions about when he, J.M., and Fee could come home.

One day, the three of them—well, it was Fee's idea—took matters into their own hands and showed up at the house. Step-daddy made them stand in the road because they were trespassing on his "private property."

§

Freddie reached the crest of the hill overlooking his father's house, his home. He paused only to catch his breath and to calm his pounding heart. He didn't want his hands shaking and spoiling his aim. In the farmhouse, a light shone in one window. The parlor, the place where step-daddy sat in his over-sized chair lording it over all of them, the place where he did his drinking, the place he'd tried to pull Fee into on the day he'd kicked them out.

Freddie and J.M. had gotten Fee loose from the old man's meaty grip. They'd all stared at each other, two boys on the edge of manhood and a man whose secret wasn't such anymore. He knew they knew, and that made the old man angrier than they'd ever seen. And they had to go.

Step-daddy would be sitting in the parlor, in that old, worn chair, drinking. Freddie's mother would be there, too. She couldn't rest until the old bastard passed out and she carried him to bed.

There was a teacher at school Freddie admired, a man who'd lost a leg in The Great War and who warned of another world war to come. His voice sounded in Freddie's head: "You're about to shoot a drunken man."

"No," Freddie murmured, "I'm about to shoot a drunken son of a bitch."

His breathing and heartbeat normal, Freddie drew a deep breath. "Let's get this over with," he told himself, and headed down the hill.

He didn't realize he was in the house until he blinked and found himself in the parlor.

Step-daddy sat in his chair, bottle of whiskey on a table beside it, a glass clutched in a fat hand. His face was crimson with the drink, his eyes bloodshot with it, too. When Freddie put the rifle at his shoulder, step-daddy laughed.

"Well, what you waiting for, boy? Shoot me."

Freddie lay his cheek against the rifle stock, sighting down the barrel.

"You don't have the balls, boy."

Don't answer. Don't talk. Get it done.

"Go ahead, boy. Shoot. Did you forget to load it?" Step-daddy laughed again.

Freddie focused on the aiming bead at the end of the rifle barrel, "setting" it in the notch of the sights. Step-daddy blurred as the sights came into focus, and Freddie's finger moved to the trigger.

Take a deep breath. Hold it. Squeeze, don't pull the trigger.

His finger tightened.

The hazy image of step-daddy disappeared, replaced by the floral print of a woman's dress. Freddie lifted his head. His mother stood between him and his target. The right side of her face showed a miserable bruise.

"Move, Momma," Freddie said, his voice losing the squeak of his adolescence.

"I can't let you do it," she said, her swollen lip making her hard to understand.

"Leave the room, then."

"And get what? A dead husband and a son in the electric chair? Put the gun down."

The rifle slid from his shoulder, useless now in his hands. He stopped fighting the tears he'd held in for so long.

"Why, Momma, why?"

"I was a young woman married to an old man. Now, I'm married to a man my age, a man who gives me what I need."

"Come away with me, please."

"I'm this man's wife. My place is here. You have your whole life ahead of you. You can't end it here."

"It's his life I'm ending. Not mine," Freddie said, tears hot on his face.

"The law won't see it that way. I want you to hold your children."

Freddie's hands tightened on the rifle. "At least I won't kick my children out of their own house!" he screamed.

The look his mother gave him showed him a woman he didn't know.

"You need to understand," she said, "I love my husband. You kill him, you kill me."

The tears came again, and Freddie didn't hold back the sobs. He threw the rifle across the room and fled a house he never would set foot in again by choice.

His stepfather's laugh followed him back to his cousin's in the cool, night air.

Forty years later, the life Freddie took was his own.

The End

Note: Part two of "Wishful Thinking" is adapted from the story, "Going Home," from *Fences and Other Stories*, published by the author.

THE LAST CHANCE PICNIC

Sydney Everson

There are places on Earth where time feels less settled. It's constant for the most part, but then, at given any moment, a light breeze stirs it into the air like grains of pollen that swirl and come together until you can almost see a faint green cloud before they scatter again. Avebury was one those places. Misshapen stone monoliths rose from the earth in a pattern too even to have been wrought by nature, and too abstract to reveal their ancient purpose. A dense, spring green carpet cushioned the steps of modern visitors who came to wander and wonder.

Blades of grass prickled my legs through the picnic blanket as James and I ate the sandwiches I'd packed for today's excursion. We didn't speak while we ate. After twenty years of marriage, it should have been a companionable silence, but it wasn't. It was the strained kind. The kind when you worry whether you're chewing too loudly. When you don't know where to rest your eyes and find yourself brushing invisible bread crumbs off the blanket just for somewhere to look. When you want to tell a lonely chirping starling to hush because his call only accentuates the absence of conversation that used to come so easily.

I focused on the stones and watched the grains of time swirl and blur, spread and coalesce. Twenty years. Twenty years of coming together, making a family, and building memories. Twenty years to forget why we came together and what we still have to hold us that way now that the children are grown and gone. Twenty years that are everything to me, but nothing to these stones, just a speck of dust in the air, a fleeting moment that twirls in the breeze and then is gone, blended with thousands of other fleeting moments.

"Looks like we may get a storm." James's voice interrupted my maudlin reverie. The wind chased my thoughts across the long grass as I glanced toward the heavy clouds. The air smelled damp and fresh, a prescient aroma of rain not yet fallen on earth. "Maybe we should pack up."

When I lowered my gaze from the sky, my eyes met his. I saw

his question lingering there. In his voice, it wasn't just his question; it was *the* question. The question that sent us on this whole trip in search of an answer. Should we pack it in? Throw our hands up and say, "Well, we had a good run, but it's over now," or is there a chance we could pull through this and somehow come out of it still together? The question laced itself through everything James said these days.

Maybe he heard it in my voice, too. "Why don't we take one more stroll around the stones before we head to the car?"

James nodded and together, working silently, we tidied our picnic supplies into the basket and walked toward the stones. James carried the basket in one hand while his empty hand hung limply at his side next to me. My hand stayed by my side, prickling with uncertainty. Do I take his? Will he take mine? Or do we not do that anymore? At some point, we'd stopped being that couple that held each other's hands as we walked. Instead, we were always holding little hands between us. When the little hands grew too big to be held, ours didn't find each other's again. Once more, the soft breeze ruffled the grass and sent grains of our past eddying around our uncertain present.

"It's amazing these stones still stand, even when the weather has worn them away." James's tone wasn't a question, but still I heard one.

I appraised the nearest stone, focusing on the narrow base where it disappeared into the ground. "I suppose, over time, they've settled too deeply into the earth to move."

James made thoughtful noise, a quiet "hmm" that was neither here nor there, and studied the base of the rock as though an answer might be buried there, too.

A cool droplet of water landed on my arm, followed by another. I glanced over at James and noticed dark spots on his light blue shirt where the drops had fallen on him. Maybe we should have packed it in after all.

The rain began in earnest. No gradual build-up, no slow escalation. The skies simply opened and dumped their contents as we turned toward the car. We took one look at each other and started to run. James' hand found mine as we hurried. Maybe he was worried he'd slip on the wet grass. Maybe he was worried I would. Maybe it was more than that. We ran hand in hand like children through the downpour until James stopped, pulling me to a halt.

He dropped the basket and bent over. At first, I feared he was having a heart attack or hurt somehow. What had we been thinking running like that? But then I heard it. James's laughter. A familiar sound I'd almost forgotten, and it was contagious. The laughter bubbled up out of me as I joined him bent over in the rain, hands on knees, laughing uncontrollably. I didn't even know why we were laughing, but it felt so good I didn't want to stop.

"Why," James asked, gasping for air, "are we running? It's not like we're going to get any less wet."

I wiped water away from my eyes. Rain or tears, from laughing or crying, I didn't know. "We're soaked to the bone!"

James stood as his laugh settled. "Do you remember that night in college?"

"When we got caught in a storm on the yard and ran all the way back to my dorm?" We were so young, so unburdened by the staggering weight of life.

He stepped toward me and looked at me, really looked at me. "I thought you were so beautiful that night." I heard the question again.

"I was drenched," I said, my laugh light as nerves tickled the edges of it.

"You were still beautiful. Just as you are now, Emily." His hand cupped my cheek. It wasn't the cheek of a twenty-year-old anymore, but there was truth in his eyes. Somehow, when he looked at me, he could still see the girl I was in the woman I'd aged into.

"James…" I didn't know what I wanted to say, but it didn't matter. James kissed me right there in the pouring rain. He was cautious at first, the question lacing itself through his kiss, but then, more sure, as though he'd found my answer.

When he pulled away, I searched his eyes for the confirmation I needed. It was there, along with so much more. He pulled me into a fierce hug. As I squeezed him back, a sob escaped me, fleeing my body, and taking with it the possibility of what almost was. I held my husband and looked through the rain at the stones around us, watching time swirl and fall away, our past scattering and coming together, forming a tenuous cloud that looked like our future, in an ancient place where time felt less settled than ought to be.

ALL IS NOT LOST

Diane Fanning

Tracy Carpenter sighed with relief as she stepped into the post office to complete the final to do item on her list. She picked up a parcel at the counter, returned to the lobby, and fished in her purse for her embroidery scissors. Catching a glimpse of herself in the overhead mirror, she laughed at her image: bedraggled hair, scuffed shoes, and a pooched-out blouse made a lie out of her neat and tidy reputation. She hoped she smelled better than she looked.

She tried to rip the tape on the package without success—she needed the scissors. Dragging her shopping bag on wheels over to a counter, she dumped out the contents of her pocketbook. Not there.

She remembered picking up her great grandmother's scissors off of her nightstand and dropping them into her purse that morning. Aside from a couple of photographs, those scissors were all she had of the white-haired woman who rocked her to sleep.

She wanted to go home and wrap her chilled fingers around a warm cup of tea. Instead, she trudged out of the post office retracing her steps. The scissors were beautiful with a crane etched into one side but, more importantly, they were used by three generations of women before her.

She returned first to the book store, inspecting the floor and the shelves. Inhaling the intoxicating scent of new books, she sighed and walked back outside. She continued her search at the wine shop, the computer store, the tea shop—no luck. She stopped in front of the Fig Leaf, the outdoor café where she'd met Margery for lunch. Now closed, the happy chatter and bustling wait staff were gone. A heavy chain ran through the chairs and tables securing them for the night.

She stepped high, weaving through the maze to her table. She spotted a billfold, bent toward it, and paused. She had a problem of her own. Did she really want to be distracted by someone else's misfortune? As soon as that thought materialized, she was appalled by the selfish impulse. She bent down and picked it up.

She saw a driver's license first with an address in the suburbs.

Then found a business card for a company downtown. She used her cell to reach the owner, promising to wait for him to walk over from his office.

He began expressing his gratitude while he was still half a block away. When she handed him the wallet, he pulled out a wad of bills and offered them to her. She refused his generosity. A flash of superstition overcame any twitch of greed—she didn't want to block any positive karma.

Arriving at the pharmacy, her shoulders slumped another inch. It was after five, and the drug store was closed. She crossed the street to the St. Francis Park where she'd rested earlier, laughing at squirrels cadging peanuts from walkers. Looking underneath the seat, she didn't spot the scissors but retrieved a bit of paper intending to discard it in the receptacle. Before she threw it away, though, she realized it was a letter and the address on the envelope had round, splotchy smears. Teardrops? she wondered. She pulled out the sheet of paper inside.

"Dear Jennifer," it read, "I can't tell you where I am stationed, but everywhere I go, I take you with me. Your face is the last thing I see before I fall asleep and when I wake each day, I can still feel the warmth of your body curled against mine."

She stopped reading, embarrassed by her inadvertent intrusion into a couple's privacy. She wanted to toss it out and continue her quest for her great-grandmother's scissors, but the contents and the tear stains tugged at her heart. The address on the front was only a block away. She sighed and headed to the high-rise apartments, just east of the shopping area.

She buzzed the button for the apartment. A sniffling woman answered, "Yes."

"Ma'am, I was in the park and I found..."

"You found my letter?"

"Yes, I..."

"I'll be right down."

Red-eyed and disheveled, a woman erupted from the door nearly knocking Tracy over with an enthusiastic hug. "I can never thank you enough. How can I repay you? What can I do?"

"It's nothing," Tracy insisted.

"It's everything to me. This is the last letter I received from my husband before he died in Iraq. Would you like to come up for coffee, tea, a drink? Anything?"

"No, I really need to get going," Tracy said, casting a nervous eye at the proximity of the sun to the horizon. As distressed as she was about losing the scissors, Tracy still smiled at the result of her side trip. She continued her quest, only one more place to look: the courtyard that jutted into a three-sided rectangle of shops. She sat on a bench chatting with a stranger that morning while they waited for the needlepoint shop to open. A memory clicked into place with an abrupt snap she could almost hear. She had shown the scissors to that woman.

She hurried up the sidewalk and went down on her knees looking through the monkey grass and the half-circle of pansies that arced around the seats. The mulch around the plants complicated the search. Absorbed in the task at hand, she was aware of nothing else until she heard the sound of heavy breathing.

The light of the day was fading fast. She was alone and vulnerable in this empty space. She wanted to run but couldn't make her muscles work. Her throat clutched tight, her mouth went dry. She turned toward the noise and something wet hit her nose. It took her a moment to register the source—the pink tongue of a furry little dog with hair flopping in front of his eyes. She laughed out loud. The little dog jumped back and barked at her, the tags on his collar jangling.

She coaxed him to her. He plopped down on his belly and crawled to her feet. She scooped him up in her arms and whispered to him as she read the information on the engraved metal. She called the veterinary office on the tag. The receptionist took her number and promised to contact the owner.

It wasn't easy pulling the rolling bag with one arm and holding the wiggling, licking dog with the other, but she couldn't stop laughing at his exuberance. She'd travelled a block when her phone rang. She stopped and reached into her pocket for her cell.

"Hello," the voice said, "are you the woman who found my dog?"

"Yes," Tracy said.

"Where are you?"

"I'm about four blocks north of Fig Leaf Café."

"I'm on the other side of St. Francis Park. Please, please wait for me at the café. I'll be there as fast as I can."

"Sure."

"Please," the woman pleaded. "I love my little Max so much."

"No problem. I'll be there." Tracy stowed her cell, grabbed the cart handle, and walked to the rendezvous.

Standing in front of the restaurant, Tracy saw a frantic woman rushing across the green space. Max saw her, too, yipping in excitement as he struggled to escape her grasp. Tracy was not about to take the chance he'd dash across the street even though traffic was now sparse.

Tracy grinned at the joyful reunion, nodding her head as Max's owner alternated between talking to her dog and saying "Thank you." Tracy excused herself, waved off the offered reward, and headed home in the descending darkness. By the time she reached her front door, she had to use touch instead of sight to guide the key into the knob.

She dropped her purse on the kitchen table and put the tea kettle on the stove to heat. She had a choice: she could dwell on the loss of her great-grandmother's scissors and the wasted time spent looking for them, or she could focus on what she did find. She chose the latter. Her search was not in vain—she made three people very happy. And if the cost of that was a pair of scissors, so be it.

She smiled as she pulled her purchases out of the bag—two new books, a bottle of wine, an antique china dog made in Occupied Japan, needlepoint yarn, toothpaste, aspirin, a dark, dark chocolate candy bar, and a bag of plum oolong tea.

The whistle shrieked the water's readiness. Tracy inhaled the fruity scent as she poured it over the new tea. While it steeped, she pushed down the handle of the rolling shopping bag and closed it shut for storage. As she did, she heard a dull clink. Her heart raced. Don't get your hopes up, she warned. She held her breath, and she pulled open the flaps where tiny gleam glinted at the bottom. She wrapped her fingers around it and felt the shape of scissors dig into her palm. She hesitated to believe the reality of the sensation until she opened her hand.

Her knees wobbled. She slipped into the nearest chair, closing her eyes to fight off tears.

THE PEP TALK

Pete Fanning

Tre sat on the trainer's table in the shadow of his grandfather's broad shoulders. His boots dangled freely, swallowing up his scrawny legs, but there was a slugger's stare in his eyes. Thomas wiped at his grandson's brow, then scooped up his fists. A drip in a dark corner near the lockers kept time like a clock.

"How you feeling?"

Tre nodded. "Good. I'm fine."

Thomas smiled. So much confidence now. Three years ago, the boy had come to him, roughed up after a scuffle with some kids. He'd been downcast and timid then since his father had died. Thomas took his hands then, just as he did now, and so began the routine.

Taping and gauzing, Thomas didn't rush, he savored these pre-fight moments. The kid hardly noticed, those boots kicking away under the table, brushing the old man's battered knees.

"You're going to be fine. Just remember. He's long, with the reach, so you need to get in and do damage. In and out. Don't linger, and don't try to slug it out with him, got it?"

"Yeah, Papa, I got it."

Thomas ripped a line of tape, tore it with his teeth. A sound that took him back to when he'd sat there, in that same room, a lifetime ago. Before the crowds, the bright lights, the managers. Before Marcus came along, and Thomas groomed him—harshly at times—to succeed in the family business. Father and son, within these same, smooth concrete walls. Walls that held as many layers of DNA as they did many layers of paint.

He had Tre take a few deep breaths. There wasn't much more to say about the qualifier. Tre was good. He was disciplined, and he knew what to expect. If he won tonight, it put him in a good spot. If he lost, well, they'd keep grinding.

Another stretch of tape, the kicking stopped. Tre's eyes on him. Almost brash. "Am I quicker than my dad?"

The tape hung from Thomas' mouth. He shot the kid a look. They needed so much assurance these days. So much hand-holding. In Thomas' day, you just went out there and slugged it out. "Why are you bringing that up?"

The kid shrugged, his gaze set proudly over Thomas' left shoulder. Thomas followed it to the picture of Marcus, primed to his peak, sculpted and beautiful. All the greats were up on there, including his own. But Thomas had been a brawler. Marcus had been flashier, a dazzler. They all wanted to be like Marcus. Thomas took a breath.

"Yeah, Tre, you got a step on him."

It was a small lie, harmless, too. The truth was that Thomas had never seen such speed and quickness that his son possessed. Nobody had. Marcus was lightning, in more ways than one. Could've been something, too, if he never had to leave the ring.

But Tre. This bright-eyed boy sitting in front of him, wanting so badly to believe it. "Really?"

"Yeah, I think so. Your Dad liked to play too much." *And it didn't matter. He still destroyed everything and everyone.*

The boy put his hands out. "Was he better than you?"

Thomas scooped up the gloves. "You got a lot of questions right before a fight. Let's worry about that kid across the ring from you. I'll bet he's not asking about old forgotten champions."

"You're not forgotten, Papa. They always talk about you at the park. Talk about who was better. Coach says Marcus was too quick for you. But you held the title. Was the belt heavy?"

"Nah, just shiny." Thomas motioned for the boy to hop down. Get him moving, get him focused. The kid danced around some, trying to mimic his father's pose. The last one on the wall. Undefeated. And dead.

"They say Dad would have been champ."

Champ. The boy loved that word. Thomas nodded.

A few sharp punches, the kid was crisp, at least. And he was good. Thomas hadn't wanted to take him on, not after Marcus. He'd been done with boxing. It was done with him. Like banging your head against a wall. Even if you were all right, and you somehow reached the top, there were too many vultures. Too many looking to make something off of your sweat. Then you lose a fight or two, and it's gone before you're forty. All that was left then was slurred speech and a letter from the IRS.

But this kid, he had something his father never had. He put in the work; he learned technique and took to coaching. Thomas hoped it would keep him off the streets and clear of the pitfalls. More than boxing had done for Marcus.

"This fight will be in the news," Tre was saying. Thomas shook his head. These young ones loved the publicity. Thomas had to lay down rules. No phones in the locker room. You didn't need to know what everyone was doing all the time. It was good to be in your own brain before a fight. A quick knock at the door.

"Two minutes, guys."

The door shut and Thomas straightened his back. "Over here, face me."

The kid sauntered over, rolling his shoulders, shiny and new. Thomas fixed on the headgear, then pawed the sides with a few playful jabs. The kid's grin lit up. At sixty-two, Thomas had refused sparring with him from day one. Never told him about the sessions with Marcus. Sessions that left his son in tears. Thomas was a different man now, a gentler man who'd learned from his losses.

He took the boy by the shoulders, breaths awake now. He wanted to tell his grandson the hard truth. *No kid, you aren't as quick as his father. You're not as tall or strong either. You won't be the champ, and there's a good chance you won't win tonight. But you got love in your heart and wise in your brain. You're a wonderful boy. Better than your dad and me put together. You got more than boxing. And you got me. I'll never leave your corner.*

Thomas was a brawler not a talker, an old man who knew that outside of this locker room the world was waiting to chew the boy up. But for now, right then, he had a hold of him. A drip in the corner.

"Just stay with me, okay? Keep your head, and stay with me out there."

"Yeah, Papa, come on."

Thomas nodded. Set his head against Tre's headgear. Clasped the sides with his big hands while they stared at the scuffed concrete floor. Where Thomas's boots had been, where Marcus's boots had been. Where Tre's boots were now.

"Let's get one for Marcus."

"Yeah, for Dad."

TEXAS TEARDROPS

June Forte

Gail Morgan was late. The Breen Foundation's board meeting ended over an hour ago, and her mother was not one to wait patiently, even for family. Gail exited the Interstate on the Commerce Street ramp and headed toward downtown San Antonio. The seesaw sweep of her wiper blades wasn't enough to erase the torrent of Texas rain that sheeted across the windshield. Dark skies and empty sidewalks made it seem even later than it was. Gail leaned forward and peered over the steering wheel hoping to see farther down the street. Shop lights reflected colorful swirls off the high-gloss hood of her Sting Ray.

Arriving at Alamo Plaza, Gail geared down and tapped the brake pedal. The car reined to a stop in front of the Menger Hotel. She sounded two short blasts on the horn.

Simon, the undersized doorman, looked up from his post and turned to Nora Breen with an offer of his arm. Emerging from the glow of the lobby, he snapped an oversized umbrella open over Nora's towering head and shepherded her to the car. Smiling at the sight of the mismatched twosome, Gail reached over the passenger seat and pushed the door open. Her collar-length, black hair swung back from her face, exposing a diamond-studded ear lobe as Nora slide into the seat.

"I wish you had just let me check into a room, Gail." Nora snatched the belt of her raincoat out of the closing car door. I don't like you driving in this weather."

"It's worse here than at the ranch, Mother. The radio said the storm is heading southeast toward the Gulf."

"I hate this car. It's not safe even on a sunny day. There are no seat belts. I feel like I'm sitting on the floor. I'm sorry I came to the meeting. We should just get a room here and wait for the rain to stop."

"We've seen worse, and I need to get home," Gail said.

"Well, don't blame me if we have to turn around and come back. This storm could easily wipe out the bridge, the whole ranch road for that matter. Look, the underpasses are already flooding."

"We'll be up on the highway in just a minute. It's a 'high' way, so we'll be okay."

"Be serious, Gail. It's the bridge at the ranch I'm worried about. It's so rickety. We should have replaced it years ago."

"It's stronger than you think. It will hold. It always has," Gail said.

"I should have moved into town when Daddy died. There's no need for me to live way out at the ranch. Your Olin is a good businessman, and Jake's been managing the cattle for years. I'm not useful there anymore."

They reached the highway and headed out of the city. "Just look at this rain. What in heaven's name kept you so long, Gail?"

"Anne Marie and I were at the mall when you called. The time just got away from us."

"Where is your sister now? No, let me guess, still shopping and in this weather. You and Anne Marie are always shopping. I wish you'd both take more interest in the foundation and a little less in haute couture." Nora removed the kidskin glove from her right hand and loosened the yellow silk scarf from around her neck. "The Breen Foundation will be your responsibility one day and…"

As they drove through the heavy rain, Nora kept a constant chatter. Between fussing about the weather and Gail's driving, she droned on about the foundation and the meeting she had just left. Uninterested and occupied with her own thoughts, Gail managed to nod and comment at the appropriate pauses. She knew her mother wanted her more involved with the family legacy, but she already had the life she wanted. She had Olin and her circle of friends, and she didn't need anything more. And why me? Olin's already a strong voice on the Board. Why not Olin? I'm not even the smart daughter. Anne Marie would be a better choice.

Twenty minutes out, they turned off the highway and onto the deserted two-lane access road that ran parallel to the highway along the barbed-wire fence marking the east border of the ranch. Relaxing her grip on the wheel, Gail turned to look at her mother. What caught her eye was the large tear-shaped opal dangling from Nora's left ear.

"Mother," she said, interrupting Nora in mid-sentence, "I bought the most stunning evening dress for the governor's reception this weekend–blue silk. You'll just die when you see it. Souzie

Schaeffer will be absolutely green. You simply must let me borrow your Texas Teardrop earrings for the party. They'd be perfect with my new dress."

"Honestly, Gail, you haven't heard a word I've said. You can thank the business Daddy worked so hard to build for your lavish lifestyle. The foundation was his dream, a payback to the state he loved so much. And to think neither of his daughters cares a hoot about it." Nora's eyes welled with tears. "It was so important to Daddy for us to be charitable."

"I care. I just have no business sense." Gail looked to see her mother's reaction to what she had said. Nora had turned her back to Gail and was looking out the passenger side window.

"I remember the night your father gave me these," Nora said, touching the gold Texas-shaped supports that anchored the earrings to her ears. She turned to face Gail. Her voice softened. "We struggled for years, just getting by. Then suddenly everything started going right. Daddy made a windfall profit, and it just kept getting better. He said 'You've earned those earrings, Nora, for all the years and for all the tears you never let me see.' Apart from you girls, these earrings mean more than anything to me."

"And you will let me borrow them, won't you, Mother?" Gail said, offering Nora her most winning smile.

Nora shook her head. "I 'm sorry you and Olin have no children. That may have taken some of the selfishness out of you and given him someone else to dote on."

"Anne Marie has children."

"Anne Marie has a nanny and a housekeeper who, thank God, pay some small attention to those children." Nora waved her hand to the right. "Here's our road. Let's hope the bridge is above the water when we get there." Gail turned the car onto the unmarked dirt road that wound its way for nearly five miles through scrub oak and open range to the brick gateway of the family compound.

The "Rockin' B" was a 10, 000-acre spread, a gentleman's estate. Expertly run by hired hands, it was home to a small herd of champion Longhorn breeding stock. After John Breen's death, Olin Morgan, wealthy in his own right, bought out neighboring ranches and expanded his father-in-law's hobby into a globally lucrative side business.

The ring of Gail's phone startled Nora from her thoughts. "It's

Olin," Gail said, reaching for the phone.

"Watch the road, Gail. You're going off the road."

"Hi, Honey."

"Hi, Sugar. Where are you? I've been calling, but your phone kept going directly to voicemail."

"I guess the signal was out. I was in town picking up Mother. We're almost home. Where are you?"

"My meeting is running way over. I'm stuck in Austin for the night. I was going to call you tonight, but I got to worrying. It's raining like crazy up here."

"Here, too. I can hardly see the hood of the car, but we're crawling right along. Should be home and dry in just a bit."

"That's my girl. I just talked to Jake. He and the boys are still out rounding up the last of the herd–wants to get em to high ground for the night. My guess is we lost a few already. The creek should be busting its banks. You drive careful, darlin', you hear? And call me when you get to the house."

"I promise. Bye, Olin." Gail put the phone down and peered out at the road. She bit down on her lip. The rain was coming hard, and the wind was picking up. As they rounded the curve, she could see water swelling over the wooden bridge, just how high the water really was she could only guess.

"You're not going to try to get through that, are you?" Nora twisted the ends of her scarf. "You should have brought the truck."

"It'll be just fine. If you're afraid, close your eyes." Gail shifted from second to first gear and inched onto the narrow bridge. She could feel the planks sink under the weight of the car. The wind was driving the rain in sheets against the windshield, and she couldn't see through it. The side window wasn't much better. She opened it, and a blast of wind and water hit her face. Looking down the side of the car, she could barely see the edge of the bridge. It rose and fell with the water cresting beneath it.

Nora sat rigid. Only her hands moved. She was grasping and releasing the knotted end of her scarf like a worry bead. "Dear God, save us," she whispered.

The car sputtered and died. Gail tried to restart the engine. She put her foot on the clutch, turned the key and frantically pushed on the gas pedal. Nothing. "It won't crank," she said. She pumped the pedal and tried again. Nothing.

"We have to get out of here," Nora shrieked, as she tried to push the door open.

The sound of the bridge breaking muffled her next words. A rush of water lifted bridge and car like a rubber raft and swept them together into the creek. The car hit the water and careened like a pinball across the creek into the far bank. Gail was lifted from her seat, and both her knees slammed up against the steering column. Nora was thrown up against the car roof, then forward. Her head cracked the windshield, and she fell, slumped forward against the dashboard.

Gail pulled Nora back against the leather seat. She knew enough not to try to open the car door against the water. She reached over Nora and rolled the passenger window down. She boosted herself out through the driver's side window and clung to the outside of the door. Submerged to her neck in the raging water, Gail began edging her way around the back of the bobbing car. The strength of the current kept flattening her against the car. She lunged for her mother's door handle and missed. The car left her behind, as she fought to stay afloat. "Mother," she cried. The word broke apart, as a wave of water filled her mouth. Choking and coughing, she struggled to regain her breath.

A distance ahead, the car whipped through the violent water like a tilt-a-whirl run amok. She watched in horror as the end of Nora's yellow scarf flapped out the open window. It hung momentarily in the wind, then fell wet and limp against the door panel just as the car disappeared around the bend.

Gail struggled to keep afloat. She grabbed at a dark dense shadow passing to her left. It was a dead steer. Gail dug her fingers into its hide and then moved her grip to its foreleg, leaving pieces of acrylic nails behind. The lifeless buoy dragged her behind, as they catapulted down the swollen creek. Past the bend where the car had disappeared, the steer crashed into the bank with such force it ricocheted into a stand of half-submerged scrub oak and lodged between two trunks.

Gail managed to crawl up over the carcass and onto a low-hanging limb. Above the water, the wind jabbed chilling rain against her, so sharp it seemed to pierce her skin. She was too numb to move, her throat raw from the water that had forced its way back through her clenched teeth and up through her nose. Gail sobbed uncontrollably. Her mother was gone. It was as though Nora had taken off on some ghastly motoring holiday, waving good-bye with her scarf from the window.

By daybreak the wind had stopped, and the rain had softened to a drizzle. Gail raised her head thinking she heard a sound in the distance, then voices. She waved her arm at the horsemen moving along the bank. "Here," she yelled. "Jake, over here."

The ranch hands had been skirting the creek looking for signs of her. Jake snatched the rope from his saddle, slung it over his shoulder and plunged bootless into the creek. A strong swimmer, he was soon by her side. "Now, don't be scared, Miss Gail. We'll have you out of here right soon." True to his word, Jake carried her up the bank just as a helicopter landed. Olin jumped from the door and rushed toward them.

"Olin. Mother—she's gone. She was here and then gone. You've got to find her." Tears rolled down Gail's eyes as she looked back and forth between the two men. "Jake? Olin?"

"We found her Gail," Olin said. "I'm so sorry."

Jake swung up into the saddle. Reining his horse to the right, he tipped his hat and led the rest of the men downstream.

Olin held Gail against his chest on the helicopter ride to the hospital. He stroked her back, trying to calm her racking sobs, trying to control the tears that welled in his own eyes. Nora had been his friend, his biggest supporter.

After the doctor cleaned Gail up and stitched a nasty gash on her thigh, Olin took her home and tucked her into bed. While she rested, Olin moved about the house mechanically arranging his mother-in-law's funeral. As shaken as he was by Nora's death, Gail was inconsolable.

"I just can't do this," she said over and over. I can't go on without Mother."

"You have to, Sugar. You must be strong," Olin said, drying her eyes with a corner of his linen handkerchief.

"I'll change, I swear, I'll change. I'll do what Mother wanted. I'll be just like Mother." She blew her nose into the offered hankie.

"That's not what Nora wanted, Gail. She wanted you to be the person she knew you could be—intelligent, compassionate, and strong."

On the day of the funeral, a sudden aura of tranquility surrounded Gail. She stood greeting neighbors and friends, accepting condolences and supporting both Olin and Anne Marie through the service and burial.

Two weeks later, Gail was propped in her bed, pen in hand, papers scattered around her when Anne Marie appeared in the doorway.

"Oh Gail, what will we do without Mother? I can't believe she's gone." Anne Marie cupped her hand over her mouth. Tears smeared her makeup.

Gail opened her arms, and Anne Marie rushed to be hugged. "Now, now," Gail said. "Don't cry, or you'll start me going again." Anne Marie sat up, her hand resting on a ledger.

"What are you doing with Mother's books?"

"I'm taking Mother's place at the foundation. I think I'm ready for it."

"How utterly boring, just what Mother would want."

"No, it's what I want," Gail said, getting up from the bed.

"You can't mean it." Anne Marie moved from the bed to the dressing table. She picked up the Texas teardrops and held them to her ears. "I suppose you'll take the best of Mother's jewelry."

Gail took the earrings from Anne Marie fingers. "Only these," she said. "Someday, I hope to earn the right to wear them."

WAR GAMES

James Gaines

When I turned ten in 1959, the world was worried about new Soviet satellites hurtling around the Earth and unseen nuclear missiles that made alert sirens sound every so often, making us dive under our desks at Bingham Elementary School for protection against atomic fallout. But after school, in the precious hours of freedom, no one on Albion Street in Somerville, Massachusetts, was worried about Reds or Communists. Instead, we refought the War to End All Wars against the real enemy of mankind, the Yellow Peril. There was no discussion about why the Japanese had to be the enemy, rather than the Germans or the Italians – it had always been that way, probably ever since previous generations of Somervillians had heard about Pearl Harbor. And while the city had a few German-Americans like myself and forty thousand Italian-Americans, there seemed to be no Japanese-Americans anywhere in its borders to take offense. Like professional wrestling, our war games made villains of those who weren't present. On Albion Street, we were fortunate to have a cruel, exemplary, and cunning enemy in the person of Charlie McSweeney.

Charlie was a genuine Juvenile Delinquent, suspended from school countless times and held back two grades. Rumor had it that he acted as a lookout for Butchie Molloy's gang when they stole hubcaps or shoplifted from the stores in Davis Square. For this reason, Charlie was already *persona non grata* at Papadopoulos's grocery on the end of the street. Apart from these natural qualifications, Charlie had everything he thought he needed to portray the ideal "Jap," a vision of history he got from watching *We're Coming Back to Bataan*, *Sands of Iwo Jima*, and *Halls of Montezuma* over and over again. First came an ant-like swarm of followers to be his troops. The oldest of five McSweeney boys, he could also count on the four Cousin McSweeneys who lived in the walk-up tenement one floor above him, and the Cotter brothers, and the Morrisons, and four or five friends from Alpine Terrace. Moreover, Charlie McSweeney worked hard at being a "Jap," and he loved it. He would tape up the corners of his eyes with Scotch tape and smile in a buck-toothed way, using wax Halloween teeth. He insulted everyone and strutted around with a swagger stick like Sessue Hayakawa in *The Bridge on the River Kwai*, even though the stick was just part of a broken umbrella. He actually had a sort of uniform, consisting of a stiff kepi cap and a faded khaki jacket he had found in an Army-Navy store. In true "Nip" fashion, he attacked only by surprise, so we Americans had to be on guard any day after school, ready for their onslaught.

Our Marine unit consisted of myself and my best friend, Tommie De Lucia, Ernie Gubbio and his little brother, the Pulsifers, Phil Billedoux, and our leader, Mikie Milano. As soon as we got changed after school, we usually ran directly to our base in De Lucia's back yard. Although dangerously close to Alpine Terrace and the lair of the McSweeneys, it was a mighty and impregnable fortress, surrounded by ten-foot, wire-topped fences on three sides and by Grandma De Lucia's porch on the other. Any "Nip" with half a brain would rather face that barbed wire than risk getting within range of Grandma and her broom. Back in our base, we would go through a brief boot camp, which consisted of Mikie making us do jumping jacks. Then we would collect ammo.

The rules of war were simple, and there were two kinds of ammo: little pebbles the size of your thumb nail for bullets, and grenades, which were actually mud balls. Our Marine-issue mud balls were made only from regulation sticky clay found in Pulsifers' back yard. The Jap grenades were, predictably, much less trustworthy. Chuckie Cotter was the chief "Japanese" munition-maker and claimed to be an expert on mud balls "because he was Irish." He would always shout out as he heaved a grenade, "Hey Joe, here comes one with a surprise in it!" This usually meant a roofing nail or a wad of gross, Cotter-chewed gum. However, Chuckie was also rumored to put pieces of dog turd in his mud balls, a form of germ warfare deplored by all the Marines as being typical of "Nip dirty fighting." The De Lucias, Milanos, and Gubbios took this so much to heart that they invented a new term for dog turds and called them "Irish surprises" whenever they saw them on the street. Some of us called them "Cotters" when Chuckie wasn't around.

Having made up a good supply of ammo, we stockpiled it back in the base, which was watched over by little Al Pulsifer, who was asthmatic and really wasn't supposed to play, and Tommie's sister Teresa. Teresa doubled with Al as a medic and also as guard for any prisoners we took. She was the subject of much criticism from the "Japs," who mocked us for using a girl guard. However, she was a specialist in hand-to-hand combat and her vicious nails were more than a match for any unarmed captives left in her care. Actually, she almost never had to resort to violence because our prisoners were well cared for. Grandma De Lucia would always come out to cast a suspicious Sicilian eye over any that were assembled in the back yard, and if Teresa assured her they were being good, Grandma would give her a tray of chocolate cookies to pass around. Very unlike the treatment *we* got. If we were caught, we were stuffed into a huge, ill-smelling refrigerator crate called the Hoosgow that sat in McSweeneys' back yard. In summer, Charlie would pour in jars full of red ants to torture the victims. Sometimes, he and his brothers would jump on the box to squash any prisoners inside. To avoid getting flattened by Charlie's giant rear end, I worked out an effective way of getting all the prisoners in the Hoosgow to sway together and tip the box back, causing our tormentor to land on the ground. At the same time, we moaned and shrieked to make him believe he had really done some damage. Otherwise, he would keep on jumping just out of spite.

Mikie always chose either Phil or me as the Scout. I loved this job, which involved concealment and sneaking around, but in truth it was not very hard, because McSweeney and his "Japs" showed a total lack of imagination and could always be found assembling in his back yard or the playground next to it. Mikie, who was actually a terrible officer, would always give the same orders if they hadn't moved yet: form a line and attack! This was of course in the brave Marine tradition, but it never, ever worked, because we were outnumbered two to one, and the enemy had some fine pitching arms bombarding us with mud balls. Charlie McSweeney himself was a formidable foe, firing out "bullets" at a furious pace and insisting on leading their human wave charges in person. You held your plastic or wooden rifle in your glove hand and used your throwing arm to sling pebbles, which were bullets. Pebble bullets could wound but never kill. To count a "kill," the combatant had to advance within reach, like a Sioux warrior taking coup, and fire three imaginary shots, pronouncing "Pow! Pow! Pow!" The "killed" soldier had to admit to being killed and immobilize himself, but he was allowed the histrionics of a death scene, which in some cases, like that of Phil Billedoux, assumed the proportions of Laurence Olivier. Phil could writhe and clutch for five minutes; by comparison, Richard III merely died in his sleep.

Under the hail of mud balls, we crouched behind hedges or trash cans, enduring the long-range artillery and the taunting that inevitably came with it. Just like in the movies, the "Japs" would call out to try to get us to show ourselves: "Hey, Joe, tonight you die! Death toooo Marrr-iiines! Die Yankee pigs!" Once Ernie Gubbio got so flustered by these calls and by the surprise-laden mud balls exploding on his plastic helmet that he actually went a little crazy with fear, like Robert Wagner in *Halls of Montezuma*. He ran over and surrendered himself to Charlie's gang, who immediately led him to the Hoosgow.

Sometimes as we "dug in," we would speculate on strange, philosophical subjects.

"I wonder if it would be better to be fighting real 'Japs'?"

"Real ones would not be as bad as Charlie."

"They're plenty bad in the movies."

"Those guys in the movies are not even real Japs. My uncle told me they're all Albanians or something with makeup on. All the real Japs were in jail."

"No, they weren't. They were in Japan, stupid."

"If the real Japs were here, we couldn't call them Japs unless we really wanted to insult them."

"How do you know? Maybe that's what they call themselves. Or maybe Nips? Isn't Japan the Japanese name for Nippon?"

"If real Japs were here, they wouldn't be mad at us, they'd be made at Charlie McSweeney."

"I have a feeling they'd probably be mad at us, too."

One day at the end of summer there was considerable commotion on the playground, and Al Pulsifer came to tell me that Charlie McSweeney had something real important to tell me about the start of school. Ordinarily I did not even talk with the McSweeneys outside of military conflict situations, but school was considered such a menace to the common good that it outweighed ordinary practices and prejudices. I went to hear what Charlie had to say. He leered at me, savoring the bad news he was waiting to unleash.

"Hey, Gainesey, you got a new teacher in your grade and are you gonna hate it, 'cause he's a Jap!"

"You're crazy. That ain't so."

"Is so, so! I seen him myself."

"How could you see anything like that? School doesn't start till Monday."

"My mother had to take me in early on account of getting my suspension lifted from last spring, and I saw him right there, and he was definitely a Jap, just like in the movies. Old Adolph probably brought him in specially to help him." I had to concede that this was a logical conclusion, given the commonly held idea that our principal, Mr. Buckley, was really Adolf Hitler, who had escaped after the War and was hiding out in Somerville, though he didn't take the trouble to shave off his characteristic little moustache, almost the only one in the city. The possibility of a new Axis alliance was not out of the question.

"You're lyin'," I retorted, unwilling to give McSweeney any credit. "Anyway, my teacher is somebody named Walker."

"That's probably some spy name he gave, but I saw him. You're gonna get flunked by a sneaky Jap!"

"I don't believe you, and I ain't gonna flunk. I don't care if the teacher is Fu Manchu." As I walked away, I heard him taunt me from behind, "Ha! Gainesey, tonight you die, Joe, you get F."

The trouble was that Charlie was at least partly right. When I showed up in fifth grade on the first day of school, there was definitely an Asian-looking man at the head of the class. It turned out when he wrote his name on the blackboard that it was not Walker, but Waka, though the pronunciation in suburban Boston was identical. Like most of the class, I was pretty stupefied and kept quiet the whole first week. Outside during recess, the catcalls started, as the McSweeneys, who had yet to get their first suspension of the year, jeered, "Hey Mr. Waka, you want some flied lice?" or "Tojo, you surrender now?" But Mr. Waka had a true poker face, and it was impossible to tell if he even heard these insults. Everybody was just waiting for him to do something to prove how sneaky and deceitful he really was, betraying his true nature by participating in one of Mr. Buckley's beloved caning sessions or ratting out somebody for fighting on school grounds.

Ironically, it was I, a Marine, who first got to see what he was really made of.

On the second Wednesday after Labor Day I was engaged, along with about four other young thugs, in the innocent prankish activity of holding the basement exit door closed so the kids coming from the lunch room couldn't get outside for recess. All at once, my co-conspirators (who I later realized were all McSweeney affiliates) bolted from the door, leaving me all alone against an irresistible force that turned out to be none other than Old Adolf himself, cane in hand, looking for the culprit. I took off like a scalded dog, hoping he hadn't seen my face, raced around the side of the building and in the first-floor door, looking for someplace to hide, but he was hard on my heels, tromping up the wooden steps only seconds behind me. With all other avenues blocked, I sped for the music room, but pulled up short. There was Mr. Waka right in front of me. I could see it all: the gleeful and treacherous denunciation ("Here he is Mr. Buckley. I got him for you! Shall I hold him while you apply the cane?"), the two of them leading me off to have the backs of my hands caned before the class and then the embarrassment of my parents coming for me ("Is your son raised to be a hoodlum, Mrs. Gaines?"). In Chuckie's words, I was gonna die.

But instead of blocking me or grabbing me, Mr. Waka deftly swept me in the music room door and closed it before I realized what had happened. Outside, he was quickly confronting Mr. Buckley.

"Oh, hello, Arthur," Mr. Waka's voice said in a deadpan tone, "Were you going in to use the piano? I didn't know you played."

"Of course not," Buckley's rat-like voice shot back. "I was after one of those little creeps who was holding the door shut. Did you see a boy come running up here?"

"Nobody ran past me," said Mr. Waka, which was technically true, since I hadn't quite run past him. "I was probably too wrapped up in my *étude* to hear all the commotion."

"Hmphh," snorted Buckley. "Well, next time try to keep

an eye open and help with discipline around here. Stop fooling around with piano tunes and help us get these animals under control. Sometimes I think I'm the only one trying to maintain a little order and dignity in this damned place."

I waited behind the door, listening to Buckley's receding footsteps and an instant later heard a couple of light knocks on the door signaling, I supposed, all clear. When I peered out, no one was there.

Now that I had become personally involved and was actually beholden to someone who may be a "Jap," I had to get to the bottom of things. I waited until the class was empty at the end of school and approached Mr. Waka's desk. He paid no attention and went on grading some papers. I cleared my throat and began: "Mr. Waka, is it true you're a.....Where are you from?"

"I'm from Oregon, out on the West Coast," he answered, matter-of-factly, turning over another paper.

"Well, I didn't think you were from around here by the way you talk." I thought I'd better find out more. "Were you ever…in the army?"

"No, actually, my dad was a Unitarian minister and so I am what you call a conscientious objector, which means I didn't fight, but I was in the medical corps for a few months in Korea."

"Oh." I imagined him alongside Teresa De Lucia tending the wounded, but the idea seemed too ridiculous. I was running out of things to say. "Well…do you know karate or anything like that?"

Finally, he made a wry little smile and said, "I'm really not any good at it. How about you? Do you play the piano?"

"Oh, no, Mrs. Phelps in third grade said I couldn't play anything. Last year at the hearing test they marked me deaf, but that was only because they didn't explain I was supposed to raise my hand if I heard that bell sound."

"I'm glad you're not deaf. At least you can enjoy listening to music."

"Thanks," I muttered. I wasn't sure if he knew what I was thanking him for, because he acted like nothing had ever happened. I was feeling too awkward to try to say anything else. But from that moment on I decided I was going to enjoy his class.

The next morning at recess I confronted the McSweeneys on the playground.

"You can't make those catcalls about Mr. Waka anymore."

"And why not? Ain't he a Jap?"

"Nope. He's from someplace out west, and he was on our side in the army."

"He wasn't in no army! He fight for Rising Sun on Iwo Jima."

"That shows how much you know, you stupid oaf! He was in the army fighting Commies."

This caused a lot of murmuring among the McSweeney's, who had recently heard about Khrushchev and Stalin from some radio program, since they certainly couldn't read a newspaper or a real book. Mr. Waka's status as a "Jap" could not go on if he wasn't really a legitimate villain.

Charlie turned to me and tried one last ploy to rescue his pastime of Jap-baiting. "I bet you're full of baloney. How come we don't know he's just a jerk?"

So, I told them the story about what happened at the music room door. Actually, I exaggerated it a little bit, too. I said Mr. Waka stood in Buckley's way and shielded me from his swinging cane. McSweeney jaws were dropping as I described the scene.

Charlie resisted, "Oh yah? How do I know that's true?"

"He called him Arthur." This left my interlocutors dumbfounded. I don't know what perplexed them more: the idea that someone could treat Mr. Buckley, Der Fuhrer himself, on a first-name basis, or the possibility that he wasn't Adolf, after all. I saw my advantage and decided to go for the final point. "I think he threatened to give Buckley a karate chop." There was nothing more to say. I walked off and could practically hear the rusty gears grinding in the McSweeney heads behind me.

For most of that fall there were no more after school or weekend games of War. The McSweeneys were left without an identity, dolts without a country who could no longer play the role of Japs with any hope of verisimilitude. They also stopped the catcalls and watched Mr. Waka closely, interpreting any remotely graceful gesture as a secret karate move. Instead, they infuriated Mr. Buckley so much with dialectal playground calls of "Hey, Ahh-thuhhh!" that he shaved off the moustache to try to change his image. He was too embarrassed to cane anyone any more.

Charlie McSweeney was at a loss what to do. He couldn't bring himself to restyle the gang as Krauts, because he couldn't stomach taking on the personality of Hitler, even though Mr. Buckley had apparently vacated that role. A brief hint that the villains might be restyled as Wops led to a massive and definite veto from Mikie Milano, the Gubbios, and especially the De Lucias, who threatened to tell Grandma. This scared Charlie more than anything.

The problem was finally solved by Mother Nature, when a November storm swept down out of Canada and dumped a couple of feet of early snow on Greater Boston. We emerged the next day after the plows had done their work and found they had heaped up a giant mountain of snow right next to the McSweeney residence in Alpine Terrace. The ant-like horde of followers was busy at work making an arsenal of snow grenades. Of course, we knew that a lot of them would have cores of dirty ice or other Cotter inventions. On top of the pile stood Charlie McSweeney, defying the world. Gone were the faded khakis, the kepi hat, and the taped-up eyelids, replaced by a big, ratty fur coat, a moth-eaten pair of ear-muffs, and a size 12 shoe that he pounded and pounded on the snow packed in front of him, ranting just like Nikita K at the UN.

"Americanski svine, ve vill bury you. Ve vill send you to Siberia. You vill freeze in our Red Hoosgow. Ve vill stuff ice down your Yankee troats. Hey, Joe, tonight you vill die!!"

SPRINGTIME IN CHICAGO

Judith Fournie Helms

Roberta was scheduled to meet up with Shalondra Smith at the grocery store in Sandberg Village, an upscale housing enclave just east of Cabrini-Green. She waited outside the door, clutching a small notepad and pen. She had shoved her bus fare and apartment key deep into her jeans pockets. She wore a simple muted green pullover sweater to avoid attracting attention. Since her hair color often did just that, she'd also tucked her hair into a black ski cap. She felt ridiculous wearing a wool cap in late May.

A slender black girl, in her mid to late teens, approached her. The girl was wearing a short black skirt, black flats, and a yellow sweater. She had a medium length Afro and wore large gold hoop earrings. She extended her hand and said, "Hi. I'm Shalondra. You must be Roberta."

Roberta shook her hand, laughed, and said, "Yeah, I thought I should dress down."

"Well, you succeeded. But not much you could do with that white face anyway." She smiled and added, "I think you'll be fine. It's broad daylight. The best time to sightsee in the projects. My granny is expecting you, so we should get going."

Roberta fell into step with Shalondra, and the girls walked south on North Larrabee then west on Chicago Avenue. Roberta noted that the streets, sidewalks, and buildings were fading to gray. An odor permeated the area. *A broken sewer line?*

Shalondra stopped at a mid-rise building, identical to the others, and went in the front door followed by Roberta. "My granny lives on the fifteenth floor," she said. Roberta scanned the concrete floor, painted cinder block walls, and a section with tiny mailbox slots. There were two green elevator doors painted over with graffiti, and a door marked "stairs".

Roberta said, "Should we take the elevator?"

"The elevators don't work."

"You mean now, or generally?"

"I mean, the elevators never work."

"Really? How old is your grandmother?"

"She's actually my great-grandmother—but we all call her Granny. She's seventy-two."

"And she walks up fifteen flights to get home, after shopping, or visiting, or whatever?"

"Yeah. Since she can't fly."

Roberta made a quick note on her pad. Following Shalondra into the stairwell, she recoiled at the stench. She could see the gray sky through the barred, glassless windows. The stairway was poorly lit but she could make out graffiti covering the walls. What was most striking was the stench. Roberta asked softly, "Why all the urine?"

Shalondra responded as they walked, "Well, the CHA doesn't get to repairs for a while. So, if the toilet doesn't work, people have to go somewhere. Better the stairs than the apartment. See what I mean?"

"Good point. But how long does it take the Housing Authority to respond?"

"You'd have to get that from them. But I'd say a couple of weeks. That's a lot of urine in the stairs. Some of it goes down the kitchen sink, if that's working. The other business can be thrown down the garbage chute. You don't want to open one of those doors."

"Holy shit," Roberta said and made a quick note on her pad.

"If that was supposed to be funny, it wasn't."

When they arrived at the twelfth-floor landing, they came upon a group of young men, all shirtless, playing a dice game. One of the boys looked up. Shalondra said, "Hi, Li'l Mike."

"Hey, Shalondra," replied a heavy-set young man with tattoos on both shoulders. Then he glanced behind Shalondra and saw Roberta. He ignored her and turned back to Shalondra. "Who's your friend?"

"Roberta."

"Well, she shouldn't be here."

"It's cool, Li'l Mike. She's just visiting Granny. She won't be here long."

"Whatever. It's her neck."

"Yeah. Thanks for the advice. Catch you later," said Shalondra.

"What did he mean, 'shouldn't be here'?"

"Just that you're in enemy territory."

"Is that really how you think of me?"

"I don't know you. Don't especially want to. But Travis has helped my family, so it's the least I can do for him. You've got twenty minutes with my granny. That's it. Then we go. Believe me, you don't want to be here when it starts getting dark. I live here. I know what I'm doing. I can't protect you though."

"Seriously?"

"Yeah. But I'll try my best..." She smiled and added, "...for Travis."

Roberta thought, *I'm dead. Oh well, I've had a good life. Kinda. Let's get this over with.* She focused her attention on the steps in front of her and completed the remaining three flights. Shalondra then led her to a door, which was labeled 1504 in neat adhesive numbers.

Shalondra knocked softly. Roberta tried to catch her breath. They heard a muffled sound from within and Shalondra yelled, "It's me, Granny. Shalondra."

"I'm coming, I'm coming," they heard through the door.

Roberta heard a chain lock undone, maybe more than one, and then the deadbolt scraped heavily. The door opened slowly to reveal a plump black woman in a floral print dress and mid-heel pumps. She had short gray hair and a comely face. Roberta wondered whether Shalondra's great-grandmother had dressed up for her visit or for Shalondra's. Or maybe this was her usual daytime attire.

The girls went in, and the woman reached up to hug Shalondra. She pushed her back gently to look at her again, and said, "Sweet girl, you are looking so pretty... just so pretty." She stared at Shalondra for some time before shifting her gaze to Roberta.

"Hello, Roberta," she said. "Tyree called to tell me all about you. Now you really must take off that ole hat so I can see the red hair he tole me about."

Roberta smiled and pulled off the ski cap, allowing her hair to fall around her shoulders. She said, "It's wonderful to meet you, Mrs. Green."

"Who's Mrs. Green?" Shalondra's great-grandmother looked around.

Shalondra spoke, "Roberta, when Tyree changed his name to Travis, he also changed his last name to Green. I think Smith seemed too ordinary or something. Anyway, I'm pretty sure the

Green is like a joke about his being from Cabrini-Green." She laughed, "Well, if he'd taken 'Cabrini' for a first name we'd know for sure."

Roberta smiled and turned back to Travis's grandmother. "Oh, I just assumed you had the same last name as Travis, I mean Tyree. I'm sorry. How would you like me to address you, ma'am?" asked Roberta.

"Well, ain't she polite?" she responded, looking at her great-granddaughter. "Roberta, you can call me Granny Smith."

"Like the apples?"

"Yes, dear. I've heard decades of apple jokes so don't even try to come up with a new one." She laughed. "I just have a studio now that I'm all alone. So, let's go into the living room/bedroom/dining room area." She chuckled again. They sat around a small round table in a corner of the room. Roberta made a mental note of the neatly kept space: small kitchenette to her side, counter clean, canisters orderly, a twin bed made up with a pink and green floral spread, a Naugahyde recliner to the side of the bed, facing a tiny television sitting on a small table covered with a deep pink tablecloth. The room smelled of air freshener, floral, a little over-powering. There was something else. A bakery smell. It was all a relief after the urine. Granny Smith offered the girls tea and warm cornbread. Shalondra declined. Roberta felt it would be rude not to accept. The tea water was hot, and in just a few minutes Granny Smith had set the two cups of tea and one small plate of corn-bread on the table. She had also placed a stick of butter on a saucer next to the cornbread.

Roberta smiled and said, "Thank you so much. You shouldn't have gone to the trouble." She spread a small amount of butter on her piece and took a bite of the cornbread. It melted on her tongue, sweet and flavorful. "This is so delicious."

Granny Smith smiled, and then sipped her tea slowly while Roberta finished eating. Then she looked at Roberta and said, "So, what did you want to ask me? Tyree said you have some questions about Cabrini-Green."

"Would you mind if I take some notes? I'd really like to be as accurate as I can."

"Certainly, dear. Can't see why you want to talk to me specially. But go ahead."

"Thanks. So, I'll just dive in. How long have you lived here?"

"Oh, going on fifteen years." She nodded, as if confirming her own math.

"Have you seen changes here over that time?"

"My yes. When I first got here everything felt new, and people were excited to be out of their falling-down houses. Neighbors would barbecue on the back lot on Sundays. There was grass in the yards then. But they done took it out and put in blacktop a few years later. But it was a good time."

"Well, what do you think of it now?"

"Now, girl, I know you're not blind. It's terrible. The young men have no jobs, quit school, and hang out. The walls are all covered with their gang things." She paused and looked at her tea-cup but did not take a drink. "The CHA ignores us. The elevators don't work. Most of the lights are out in the stairs and outside in the parking lots. The plumbing doesn't get fixed. Well, anyone can smell what comes of that. One time, it was in 1970…just two years ago. Well, the garbage chute backed all the way up to my floor. That's fifteen floors!"

"Oh my. Well, what happened to make it change so much?"

"Well, let me think. fifteen years is a long time, dear. I've thought about it, of course. But let me think how to say it to someone who's not from here."

They all sat silently. Granny Smith stared at the kitchen cabinets. Roberta smiled slightly at Shalondra, who did not acknowledge her. Granny Smith began to speak, slowly, deliberately. "Nobody moved out. The children went to school, but a lot of them didn't get what they needed. So, they'd drop out of school to get away from the stress. I can understand that. Always bein' made to feel small because you can't do the work. They couldn't get any proper job without that diploma, so they just hung around. Then one day, somebody tole them that they can be a big man if they just have a gun. They can have money if they just take it. They can have friends if they join the gangs. And it worked. Money, girls, friends. The police tried to stop it. But they offered nothin.' Those young-sters can't do this kind of business out in the world. Just here. So, they never leave. Then the drugs came. Now that real money. The little ones see a choice. Work hard in school? Why? They think they have a better chance selling drugs."

"But they can't all make a lot of money stealing and selling drugs, right?" asked Roberta.

"That's true. Some of the top gang guys flash a lot of money around. Most the boys just get enough to get along. A lot of them get sent to jail. And they come back meaner. If the young ones had work, well, I think it would all be different. But they never can get work without them doin' good in school. And very few can do that without the right teachers, and without their kin doin' right by them. But their families don't know how to give 'em what they need 'cause they never got it themselves. Believe me, they have lots of problems besides their youngsters. And we prob'ly haven't had enough right teachers all these years. A few, yes, a few. But now who would want to come here to teach? They think it ain't safe. And they right."

"Well, may I ask you how Travis, I mean Tyree, managed to do so well out in the world?"

"Of course. I love to talk about my grandbaby. You see, he was a special boy. Real smart. He was talkin' in sentences when he was eighteen months. Imagine that." She turned to her great-granddaughter. "Did you know that, Shalondra?"

"No, Granny. I didn't know. But it doesn't surprise me. I know Travis is real smart."

"So, when Tyree got to school, he was always the star pupil. You know, I think he got extry attention because he so smart. Then this white church lady came to school in the beginning of the school year and tole the children… well, it was for fourth through high school… that they can earn a week at summer camp in Wisconsin if they read ten books by the end of May. They had to do a book report on each one to prove they read 'em. Tyree went to camp every summer from fourth grade on. It was at Lake Geneva, Wisconsin. Oh, that boy loved it so much. He tole me once that the best thing about it was bein' with boys from all over the country. Well, I just think that got his heart set on getting out into the world. So, he did real good on the test for college and got a scholarship to the University of Michigan. You know, the whole amount was paid for. He studied business and theater." She paused for a sip of tea and sighed.

"The truth is he never did come back. He sends his brothers money, and calls me oncet a month for a nice chat. I'm really happy for that boy. But I'd be lyin' if I said I don't miss him." Granny Smith leaned back in her chair and pushed it out from the table. "I have a scrapbook on Tyree, if you want to see it." She looked at Roberta.

"Oh, I'd love to," said Roberta. She was intrigued at the chance to see a picture of Travis as a child.

Granny Smith walked to her bed, sat down near the nightstand, and opened the bottom drawer. Roberta saw there were many books crammed into it. Granny Smith pulled out a blue scrapbook and ran her hand over the cover. She returned to the kitchen table and sat between Roberta and Shalondra, setting the book between them. As she opened it, Roberta saw that the edges were yellowed and frayed. The first page was a birth certificate. The name, Tyree James Smith, seemed off…not close enough to Travis Green to be the same person. But Granny Smith turned the page to a 5 X 7 picture of a beautiful little boy, maybe a year old, sitting on a rocking horse and smiling at the camera. The dimples and tiny cleft in his chin were giveaways.

Tyree's grammar school report cards filled the next few pages, mainly A's, for all eight years. Roberta said, "It looks like Tyree was pretty much a perfect student. You must've been very proud of him. He didn't have perfect attendance too, by any chance?" She laughed.

"Roberta, I know you kiddin', but the truth is, he did. I told him not to go when he was feelin' poorly, but you just couldn't stop that boy. He had such determination. It was all from within hisself. I tried to get him to slow down, but I never could."

Roberta said, "Well, he definitely puts me to shame. I probably missed the maximum number of days allowed as long as I can remember. But, then again, Tyree had something I've never had."

"Yeah, right," said Shalondra. "I'm sure he had tons of things your parents couldn't afford for you."

Roberta was surprised by the hostility. Granny Smith simply turned to Roberta and asked, "What was that, Roberta?"

"Motivation."

Granny Smith nodded and smiled. Shalondra looked away. Granny Smith turned the pages silently. They were filled with certificates and awards. The last page had his high school graduation picture on it. He had a medium length Afro under his mortar-board, and a big smile. He was so handsome that Roberta thought he looked like an advertisement for black academic success.

Granny Smith slowly returned the scrapbook to the nightstand drawer. She turned to Roberta and said, "Oh, dear, I'm really feelin' kinda tired all of a sudden. Is that enough for you, dear?"

"Oh yes, Granny Smith. Thank you so much for your hospitality and for sharing the…" She searched for the right word. "… information with me."

The girls rose and Granny Smith walked them the few steps to the door. She hugged Shalondra tightly and said, "I love you, girl." When Roberta stepped forward, Granny Smith smiled and stuck out her hand to shake. She held onto Roberta's hand, looked into her eyes and said, "Be safe, dear." As they turned to descend the stairs, Roberta heard the metal against metal of the locks being placed back into position.

The girls didn't talk on the way down the stairs. The group of boys was no longer on the landing. When they reached the bottom, Shalondra said, "I know it's none of my business, but why exactly did you want to interview Granny?"

"I'm just trying to get into a journalism program at my college. And when I found out Travis had lived here I thought I'd try to put together a story from what I could learn from an interview and a little research. I mean, it's not for publication or anything. Just for school."

Shalondra looked at her and said, "Hm."

"Why? Did it bother you?"

"You really want to know?"

"Yeah."

"It felt wrong. Like you were some kind of voyeur. It's like the stories of Cabrini-Green should be told." She paused. "Just not by you."

After a long pause, Roberta responded. "You're probably right. Why don't you do it?"

"Hm."

Light rain had started to fall. As they stepped out of the building, Shalondra looked around at the nearly empty street. There was a group of boys on the corner ahead. "Let's cross the street here," she said. They were halfway down the block when the boys crossed and began to follow them. "Roberta…"

"Yeah?"

"Hold my arm and let's get to the next corner."

"Sure. Is something wrong?"

"Not necessarily. It's just that I don't recognize those boys."

"Oh, okay." Roberta remembered that she hadn't put her cap back on but had just squeezed a corner of it into her back pocket. She thought she might've attracted attention which may've put them in danger. She felt her chest tighten.

They heard, "Hey, ladies," and the whistles.

The girls walked more quickly. Not running. The boys caught up and were now within a few feet of them. A black sedan rounded the corner in front of them at a fast clip. It braked as it came alongside the girls.

"Get down!" yelled Shalondra. She stepped forward between Roberta and the car. There were shots. Pop. Pop. Pop. Then more. Pop. Pop. The car sped off. Roberta looked to her right and saw through the drizzle that the boys were running off. They were half-dragging one. She felt a wetness spreading over her left arm.

"Shalondra, you okay?" she said. Shalondra pivoted to face her. Roberta saw that Shalondra was holding her stomach with both hands. A dark stain was spreading over her yellow sweater.

"I'm shot, Roberta," she whispered. "You okay?"

Roberta lied. "I'm fine. But we need to get you to a hospital." She looked around, desperately scouring the area for someone who could help. She saw no one. She tried to cry out, but terror had frozen her vocal cords. In a few minutes Roberta heard the sirens. *Thank God.*

Two police cars pulled up, one after the other, and four officers were upon them. Roberta pointed at Shalondra, and then stepped back to get out of the way. In moments, an ambulance screeched to a stop in front of her. In a blur, Roberta saw Shalondra placed on a stretcher and whisked away as a second ambulance pulled up. Medics were on her and helped her onto a stretcher. Her notepad fell to the sidewalk and her notes bled to gray under the drizzle. The ambulance sped off. It was still light out. She remembered what Shalondra had said, "...broad daylight. The best time to sightsee in the projects."

SWEPT AWAY

Jody Hobbs Hesler

R oger had been in the middle of his morning shave when he heard the news about the rogue wave on the radio. Hardly two hours later, he was halfway through security at Dulles. One person swept into the sea from billions on earth, from millions in the San Francisco area, from however many legions of visitors to Point Reyes Seashore each year. What were the odds that the person—yet-to-be identified—had been his daughter, Mina? It was crazy, he knew, to hop on the first available flight from Dulles to San Francisco for fear that his twenty-five-year-old daughter had been swept into the sea, crazy not even to call ahead in case she wasn't there, afraid what her absence might mean.

But Mina had mentioned, in an e-mail or birthday card he remembered from years ago, that she'd spent time at Point Reyes, so it wasn't impossible that the person he'd heard about on the radio was his daughter. Non-zero odds were enough to speed Roger's heartbeat, to keep him jerking his head toward his watch, cursing the people in front of him, as if his impatience could make the line move faster.

"You seem nervous this morning, sir," the security officer said, pulling him out of the regular line, running a wand up and down his arms and legs.

"What's next?" Roger snarled, "the cavity search? Or can I get on the plane?"

"We're just being thorough, sir."

Be thorough with the terrorists, Roger felt like snapping, but they kicked people off planes nowadays for being hostile. So Roger took a deep breath. "You're right. I'm sorry. Just worried about my daughter."

The officer looked at Roger several beats past normal, maybe trying to measure whether Roger was a nut job or just a sympathetic man in his middle-fifties with a bona fide daughter off somewhere suffering.

Eventually, he nodded. "Good luck with your daughter, sir."

§

Everything else this morning had happened in a blur: hearing the radio article, thinking of Mina, throwing his GPS and an old letter with Mina's address on it into a bag, speeding to the airport in the half-dark of early dawn, getting hassled in the security line. But now he faced a six-hour flight, cramped against the seat in front of him.

The flight attendant demonstrating drop-down oxygen masks at the front of the plane looked like a twenty-years-earlier version of his first wife, Janet: petite, brown hair curling in toward her face, breasts and ass straining slightly against her uniform, giving him something to think about while she pattered on about what to do if the plane crashed.

Jesus, if the plane went down in the middle of the country, they'd all be as dead as that person who got swept out to sea. Roger squirmed. They weren't even in the air yet. How many more emergency procedures could there be? He tugged at the neck of his oxford shirt, feeling choked.

You don't even know if she'll talk to you.

The words came as clear as if the flight attendant had spoken them, but she was holding up the airplane seat-cushion-cum-life-preserver, explaining how to grab onto it if they plunged into a body of water. So many ways to die.

The flight attendant was right, though, even if she hadn't said it. Roger had no idea if Mina would talk to him, if it turned out she was alive.

With the safety instructions over, the plane was no longer taxiing but hurtling forward on the runway, lifting, lifting. To prevent anyone else from telling him he seemed nervous—or seeming to tell him that his daughter might reject him—Roger plugged the airline earbuds into his ears, clapped his arms across his chest, shut his eyes. He only looked up whenever the sexy flight attendant walked by. He even bought a mini-whiskey to keep her near for a few extra seconds.

Janet still looked this good back when Roger had divorced her, when Mina was only four and had stood crying while he packed his things to leave. Having the not-Janet standing next to him now—her flowery scent hanging thick in the air as she planted the whiskey on his tray table—reminded him of why he'd fallen for the real Janet all those years ago, before she'd overheard that raunchy phone call with Lizbeth, who eventually became wife number two. That had been bad luck. Bad luck that Janet had overheard that call. Bad luck he'd rebounded into Lizbeth's waiting arms. Bad luck Lizbeth eventually thrust an onyx paperweight into his eyebrow at the end of an argument, leaving him with his next divorce and a scar that made him look a little post-mafia even now.

Roger belted back the whiskey, clamped his hands into his armpits, forced his eyes shut again. He didn't want to be bothered by anybody, past or present. He just needed to get to his daughter.

§

At SFO, he made straight for the Avis. The line was long. When the clerk finally got to him, it was only to say that all their rentals were taken. Roger's watch said six-thirty. Bleary-headed from travel and weighing hours on the plane against the time change, he got confused about which direction he should adjust his watch. The fog outside made it impossible to judge by sunlight. Regardless, his trip had taken too long.

At the third rental car kiosk, when it was Roger's turn, he begged, "I'll take anything. Please? Anything." This clerk handed him keys.

Inside the runty rental car that smelled of wet-dog-mixed-with-peanuts, he untangled his GPS, found the socket for the cord, entered the return address from the envelope he'd packed, and stuck the GPS onto the windshield. As he was leaving the lot, the GPS thumped to the dashboard for the first time.

Even when the display screen *wasn't* facing the floor, it was hard to follow the prissy voice's directions in the midst of unfamiliar, fog-shrouded roads. By the fifth time the GPS fell, Roger was lost. He pulled over and, this time, licked his fingers and rubbed the spit against the suction cup to keep the thing in place. When he looked up, he found himself in a parking area off a Pacific Coast beach.

Roger had traveled up and down the East Coast, back and forth to Europe, but he'd never seen the Pacific, and it surprised him. His head still murky, he suddenly felt as if Cherise, his most recent ex-wife (number four), was there exhaling beside him. *Well, what did you expect?* With her, no matter what he'd expected had been wrong.

He got out of the car for a better look. What *had* he expected?

Sunshine, maybe? A surfboard under every arm?

Not this, anyway, the bullet-grey grimness of the Pacific, a thick muff of fog, spitty mist hitting his nose. Waves, slowly gnawing their memory into the shore: they would eat anyone's young alive. Why not Mina, then? What would protect her?

§

Back in the car, the spit trick worked, and this time the GPS stayed put. It took Roger most of an hour to get back into the city, and even more time for him to decipher which building the GPS meant when it began to insist he'd reached his destination. Then he had to figure out where to park. He only hoped his daughter was still living here.

It was a lousy building, but Roger was sure the funkiness of this part of town was what had attracted Mina. You could hear Middle-Eastern music from a restaurant half a block away, and across the street was a Balkan bakery, closed for the day.

On the porch, paint from the woodwork was curling off in chunks. Roger brushed a coil of it aside while he searched mailbox labels for Mina's name and the apartment number from the corner of the envelope.

When he found 2E, he didn't recognize the names below it. If he pressed the button there, someone inside would say, *Who is it?*, and even if that someone turned out to be Mina, *It's your father,* would sound strange. It would take more than that to explain why he was here. But as soon as he pressed the buzzer, another buzzer sounded at the building's front door, letting him in.

He trudged up a dank stairwell and down a dark hallway across ugly, threadbare carpeting. The distressed plaster walls were painted a drab green. Maybe at one time the green had not been drab, or maybe it wasn't drab in the light of a clearer day, but in the foggy dimness of an early fall evening, walking down that hallway to learn if his daughter was still alive, it was so drab that it leeched the last vestige of energy from Roger's legs, which fell heavy and stump-like toward what he hoped was still her door.

When he came to 2E, the door stood ajar. He could see bangs and eyeballs through the slit between door and doorframe. The eyes saw him, widened, stayed wide. Clearly, she hadn't been expecting Roger, but she didn't turn him away.

It was Mina: five foot two, short black hair, bangs cut in a severe straight line, black eyeliner making her eyes severe as well. It was cold, but her feet were bare. Her toenails were a creamy red. She wore toe rings. She was alive.

"Dad?"

He nodded his head, but words wouldn't come yet. His throat had tightened into a fist, but inside his head he was crowing: Mina! Good God Almighty, you're alive!

She said his name again, then dropped her hand from the open door and stood back to let him in. It wasn't a welcome, but at least she had talked to him.

Inside, there was a lot of purple: Chinese-style paper light shades, Indian fabrics on furniture and hanging on walls or from doorways as curtains. Everything smelled like cloves, and crowds of plants seemed to reach for Roger. Mina seated him in her tiny kitchen at an old Formica table. It was clean, but damaged. Any-place else, it would've looked like trash.

She padded over to the stove, fiddled with a kettle, set it to boil. "I only have herbal," she said, opening a cabinet and revealing a stock of tea boxes daintily printed with soothing names arranged across tigers and lily pads. "You look like hell. No offense."

"None taken. I feel like hell." They were silent until the kettle clattered to a boil. Mina prepared some orange-smelling tea and set it in front of him, along with a spoon and a plastic bear full of honey.

She then took the seat across from him and shook her head while she studied his face. "Dad, Dad, Dad. What the hell are you doing here?"

The straight-up answer sounded stupid in his head: You wouldn't believe me if I told you! I was shaving at six this morning when I heard this crazy bit on the news. Next thing I know, here I am! So instead he said, "What are the names on your mailbox?"

Her stark makeup accentuated the narrowing of her eyes. "What kind of question is that?"

"It's just that this apartment looks too small for roommates."

The kitchen they sat in was small, and it looked out toward a small living room. One doorway probably led to a bathroom, the other to a bedroom.

"I don't like people knowing I live alone, so I left the old names up. A little protection for a woman on her own."

"Not much protection," Roger said. He was still thinking of the bitter Pacific Ocean, not far enough away from them here to make him feel safe again. "And you didn't even ask who I was at the door just now."

"It's broken," Mina said. The tone of her voice indicated that any patience she might have had for her father was thinning by the second. "It automatically opens any time a button gets pushed."

"Jesus! That's so dangerous!" He could feel his eyebrows lifting high into his forehead, his heart rate amping up.

"Why are you here?" Mina asked again. When he didn't answer a second time, she gave up. She returned to the counter and fixed herself a cup of tea. Her metal spoon clanged against the mug.

When she sat back down, Roger couldn't read her expression. He almost flinched when she reached a hand toward him. "Your hair," she said, lifting a curl, "it's all grey. When did that happen?"

"I prefer saying silver," he said, and laughed. She dropped the lock of his hair, and it tapped against his forehead. "It wasn't like this the last time I saw you?"

Mina cupped her tea in both hands, hunching herself over it, keeping her eyes from his. "Do you even remember when you saw me last?"

If he had imagined Mina asking such a question before he was sitting here in front of her, the words would have roared, her face crinkled in reproach. But when she looked up again, her face was all soft lines, her eyebrows creased more with pity than with blame.

"A couple of years?" he said, guilt clenching his belly.

"Six," Mina said. "I haven't seen you in six years, Dad." The soft lines on her face hardened a little at this. Somewhere in that time frame her college graduation had happened, to name just one thing, though he remembered sending a card for that at least.

It had started over the phone when Mina, then nineteen, had told him, "I'm cool with you getting married again, Dad. It's just that I'm a grown-up now, you know? This won't be a person I'll ever know that well. So I don't want to be a bridesmaid this time. Not to be cruel, I just don't want to be in the wedding party." Roger could tell the words had been hard for her to say. Her voice had shaken; he'd heard her swallow in the middle, interrupting herself.

It was useless now, ridiculous even, to explain how hurt Cherise's feelings had been, especially since Cherise had been gone from his life for a year already. At the time, he had said Mina was busy with finals, so couldn't she come to the wedding as a guest instead? But Cherise said if Mina wasn't a bridesmaid, then she didn't love her father enough, didn't love Cherise enough. So she uninvited her to the wedding, stopped answering the phone if Mina's name showed up on caller ID, didn't notice or mind when it stopped showing up altogether.

At first Roger had called, written cards, sent an e-mail now and then. Now and then became less frequent. He still sent money on her birthdays.

In all the time since Cherise had left, no one had stopped him from calling his daughter. So he knew it wouldn't explain enough for him to say, I guess Cherise was some kind of rogue wave! Sucked me in and that was that. You know me, Mina: always a fool for a pretty girl!

"I heard on the radio this morning," he said, suddenly feeling the toll of all the hours since morning, as though each one had taken a year off his life. "I heard about this rogue wave off Point Reyes."

Mina nodded, looking at Roger even though he wouldn't look at her, and waited for more.

"A rogue wave in the ocean. You've heard of those?"

Mina nodded again and offered a simple definition of the phenomenon that must have happened the night before, which explained some number of disappearances along the Pacific coastline each year. "It can happen anytime, no matter the weather."

"Huh." Roger couldn't bring himself to drink the tea that smelled so pleasant. He wasn't ready to be soothed. But he kept one hand on the mug, letting it warm him a little. "It could've been anyone." He'd been looking down at his own clumsy hands while Mina was looking at him. Now he met her gaze. "It could've been you."

Six years. He had to look away. His head felt too heavy on his neck. She had asked him when he got there, "Why are you here?" And why would she want him to be? But now she laid one of her hands across one of his on the crummy little table. "Aww, Dad," she said. He was surprised at the tears beading in the corners of her eyes.

He straightened in his chair, laughed an embarrassed laugh. "I guess I better be off then," he said and stood up. "It's been a crazy long day!"

Mina stayed seated, tea in hand, and blinked at him as though someone had just aimed a very bright light at her face.

"Yeah, I'm so tired. I better hit the hay! God only knows if my car's where I left it. It's probably getting towed right now! I don't understand this city at all!"

"What are you doing?" Mina said.

"Getting out of your hair. I don't want to be a bother." Standing in the kitchen, trying to figure out what to do next, he felt cumbersome and ridiculous. Thank God she was alive, but she couldn't want him to stay.

Mina started to laugh. He wasn't sure what her laugh meant, how many feelings mixed into it. But it kept going. A lovely sound. How long had it been since he had heard it?

Finally Mina caught her breath and said, "You mean to tell me, you hopped on a plane first thing this morning and came all the way out here just to see if I was *alive?*"

He'd known all along it was a stupid thing to do, but he'd never thought of it as funny. "Well, yes."

"And now, you're just going to leave? Before you eat supper? Drink your cup of tea? Have a freaking piece of toast? Three thousand-some miles and not even a slice of toast?"

"Toast?" Roger echoed. Then he said it again. And again, and then over and over, and they laughed until tears came. Suddenly, everything about toast was hilarious.

Mina was the first to regain composure. She wiped her eyes with her thumbs, took a deep breath. "Dad? Where are you planning to go right now? Did you even book yourself a hotel?"

Roger shook his head, and they fell into laughter again. But the feeling of laughter gave way to something different this time.

"I'll have to pull out my couch for you," Mina said, gesturing to the futon in the tiny living room. "It's just twin-size, but you won't find a hotel this late in the day."

"I hadn't thought of that," Roger said.

"I'll get you some sheets." Mina stood up. Roger was still standing in the middle of the little kitchen, suddenly not needing to leave but still at a loss for what to do next, so for a moment they stood there in each other's way. When Roger finally stepped aside, he glimpsed a sad, lonesome look on Mina's face. He must have missed the cue for whatever he was supposed to have said or done to prevent such a look. Now, the chance had passed him by.

Roger watched Mina disappear into what must be her bedroom. Rather than continuing to stand oafishly in the kitchen, he decided to freshen up in Mina's bathroom while she got the sheets. He did his best to straighten his clothes and ran fingers through his "silver" hair. Somewhere, maybe even right now, while Roger washed his face with lavender-scented soap and dried off on plush, smoky purple towels, somebody else's father was learning it was his child who had been swept away.

Mina was sitting on the futon next to a pile of fresh, folded sheets when Roger came back out. There was something in the way she looked at him that made him stand very still. She said, "You don't know how to apologize, do you?"

"What?"

Instead of answering him, she mimed a phone in her hand, punching a number in. "Hello, kiddo!" she said into the imaginary mouthpiece, practically hijacking the booming quality of Roger's voice. "It's your old man! Risen from the virtual dead!" She paused for effect, pointing to the imaginary phone, mouthing, *It's my daughter*, to Roger. "Hey, I was a real asshole and I'm sorry as hell! I flew all the way out here to see you!" Another pause. "That's right, I'm in the Bay City as we speak! Wadda ya know! How about I take you out for a nice supper, Sunshine? Your favorite place!" Another pause. Roger smiled, but when he started to speak, Mina covered the mouthpiece with one hand and shushed him. "That sounds great, Sunshine. You know, it's great to hear your voice again."

This time, instead of trying to speak, Roger walked over to Mina and pulled her to her feet. He tucked her into his chest, wrapped his arms around her and said, "I'm so sorry, Mina. It really is great to hear your voice again, and your laugh. Did I ever tell you how much I love your laugh?"

"You're telling me now," she said.

He clutched her close to him, her hair tickling his nose. "I was so afraid I'd never see you again."

"But now here you are," she said, and she held him a little tighter.

Back at the kitchen table, Roger finally took a sip of the now tepid tea. He closed his eyes, and relief washed over him like water.

UNCOVERED

Linda Hudson Hoagland

By the fifteenth month of the drought, the lake no longer held her secrets. The skeletons of deeds gone badly could be found encased in dried mud.

As each and every day passed, the drought worsened, and the fear in Lisa's heart rose to the point that it had become panic.

What will I do when they dig it out of the dried mud? This should not be happening.

Lisa jumped into her car to drive to her fate. She had to go see for herself what had been uncovered. She didn't want to just believe the rumors.

Maybe they were wrong. Maybe they hadn't found anything of importance.

As she was driving, she had to come up with an explanation.

She climbed slowly out of her car and started walking to the area that used to be the beach.

"Oh my God," she whispered. "No wonder everything on the bottom of the lake can be seen."

The shore line had receded about five hundred feet from the sandy, man-made beach.

There it is. It's shining like a beacon of bright light. What can I do? How can I explain it?

***

Lisa was standing in the center of her living room crying as she pondered her next step.

She was working as many hours as she could each day, but it wasn't enough to pay her rent, utilities, insurance, and babysitter. Feeding the three of them and sometimes the babysitter became a begging proposition where she would enter the local food banks, dragging her two sons with her, so the people in charge would feel sorry for her and give her a bag or two of food. That free food was what they had to live on, no questions asked.

Then it occurred to her amidst the falling tears that her car was worth some money, but only if something happened to it because she had always managed to pay the full coverage insurance premiums. If her car were stolen, she could collect a couple thousand dollars. She could always walk to work or bum a ride when the need arose.

I need to find someone to steal it. How would I do that?

The tears weren't helping her one little bit. Her bright idea of collecting insurance money for the survival of her and her two sons started with her leaving her keys in her car every time she parked her car in a parking lot.

She made it as easy as she could for the future car thieves of America to ply their trade short of posting a 'steal me' sign.

Nobody took the bait. Nobody wanted to steal her car, not even for parts. The idea that her car could be chopped apart and sold in pieces wasn't nearly as bad as the three of them having to go to a homeless shelter.

"Come on, boys. We're going to go walk around the mall," she said as she tried to get her boys to get out of the car.

"You want me to lock the door?" asked Jimmy, the four-year-old grown-up.

"No, you can leave it unlocked. We won't be gone very long," she answered loudly so anyone in the area would hear her.

The boys ran around the mall like excited, uncaged animals. They didn't visit the mall very often because Lisa didn't have any spending money. Joey was only two, but he was running along trying to keep up with his brother.

Lisa's heart swelled with pride when she watched her sons run, play, and be happy.

Lisa's anger appeared when she thought of their father who didn't care if they lived or died. He made that fact known when he wouldn't pay his small pittance for child support without another round in the courts.

Lisa rounded her boys up and started for the car that she hoped wouldn't be there.

"Look mommy, our car is the only one in the lot," shouted Jimmy.

"Yeah, I know," Lisa answered sadly.

All three of them climbed inside the car for the trip home that was only about two blocks.

"Can we go by the water?" asked Jimmy.

"Okay," Lisa said as she thought about what she should do next.

Because it was summer, the days were long, and they could see the rippling water as the setting sun glinted off the tiny waves making the whole area sparkle like diamonds.

That's when it occurred to Lisa. The water was deep, and there as plenty of it. There was a wide pier extending out toward the center.

Would it hold the weight of a car?

"Come on, boys. We will go for a walk on the pier," Lisa shouted to her excited sons. "Jimmy, hold my hand. Joey, you get on the other side and hold my hand real tight. I wouldn't want you to fall in the water and drown," Lisa said sternly.

They walked to the end of the pier and peeked over the edge. There was a removable barricade erected to prevent accidents. Lisa inspected the obstruction to determine if she could remove it herself. She certainly didn't want to ask anyone else to help her take it down.

It didn't look too complicated. She lifted one board to gauge the weight and she slide it a little to see how movable it was.

"I can do that," she said, as she slid the board back to the position where it had formerly been.

Her boys were getting tired so she ushered them to the car, and they headed for home.

As soon as the bathroom duties were complete, they all headed for bed. Lisa had to get up early to be at McDonald's by seven a.m.

Lisa jumped off of the bed as soon as the alarm rang. She knew she had a busy day ahead of her so she needed to start it out by being totally awake, which was hard to do, because her sleep had been interrupted many times with nightmares that kept repeating over and over again.

As soon as the babysitter showed up, Lisa was on her way.

She would work from seven to noon at McDonald's, then she would go to the Dollar General, and work from one to six. After getting home, she needed to get her plan into gear.

She played with her boys until they were completely and thoroughly tired. She needed them to go to bed, when the time came, and sleep through the night.

She was going to have to do something she didn't like to do and that was leave them alone in the house while she took care of the car problem.

She figured it would have to be after midnight before she could put her plan into action. Then she would have to go home and get some sleep so she could work the next day.

Lisa worried about being caught.

What would happen to my babies if I went to jail?

Then…

What will happen to us if I don't get some money from somewhere?

"I have to do this," she whispered harshly.

Lisa watched as Jimmy and Joey were getting so tired and sleepy that they couldn't stay awake. She picked up Joey, removed his jeans, shoes, and socks before gently placing him on his twin bed. Next, she carried Jimmy into the same room and followed the same routine for him.

Lisa stood in the doorway and gazed lovingly at her two beautiful sons.

She returned to the living room, turned the volume of the television to a low hum to soothe her sleeping sons.

When she was sure they were sound asleep she walked out to the car to remove all of the personal items belonging to all of them, just in case this little trick didn't work. Lisa removed toys, papers, and shoes from the interior, stowed them inside the house where she placed them in the closet for future use.

She checked on the boys, pulled up the light blanket on each of them after giving Jimmy and Joey each a kiss on the forehead.

God, I love them so much.

She left the bedroom pulling the door closed about halfway. The sonorous sound of the television with the dim variations of emitted light should make her boys feel safe.

When Lisa returned to the car, she started it up, backed out of the driveway as quietly as possible, and drove toward the lake.

The park surrounding the lake was deserted as it should be at one in the morning. She sat in her car with the engine idling as she thought about all of the possibilities that could ruin her life.

"It's now or never," she whispered as she climbed from the car. She needed to remove the barricade at the end of the pier.

Thankfully, the moon was almost full, and the stars were lighting up the sky. She could faintly see what she had to remove from the end of the pier.

Lisa removed the first piece of wood by sliding it aside and lifting it from its groove. When she moved the second one she had to balance the base piece to keep it from falling into the water as she slid the bar of wood from its moorings.

When she had everything moved to the side, she ran to her car, and drove it onto the pier. She stopped the car as close to the end of the pier as possible. She threw the gear into neutral, climbed out, and shoved the vehicle into the deep, deep water.

She found herself crying from her loss as she replaced the barricade. She wiped her eyes and started walking to her home. She crawled into her bed and stared wide-eyed at the ceiling for at least an hour before she fell into another fitful sleep.

It was seven in the morning, and someone was knocking at her door. Lisa was startled for a moment as she was trying to figure out where the sound was coming from.

"Mommy, mommy," shouted Jimmy, as he and Joey dived onto her bed.

"What?" she asked.

"Someone is hitting the door," said Jimmy, as he tried to hide under the covers.

"Let me up so I can see who it is," she said, as she tried to move the boys away from her.

Lisa grabbed her robe, pulling it onto her body as she ran to the door. She looked through the peephole and discovered that it was the babysitter, Kathy.

"Oh my God," Lisa screamed, as she scrambled to unlock the door. "I must have turned off my alarm this morning. Come in, I'll call McDonald's and tell them I will be there as soon as possible. Come on in and I'll get dressed."

"Where's your car, Lisa?"

"What? My car? It's parked in the driveway, isn't it?" Lisa asked Kathy with the utmost sincerity. She had forgotten what she had done during the wee hours of the morning with all the confusion racing through her brain.

"No, it's gone," said Kathy. "Did you let someone borrow your car?"

"No, I never let anyone else use my car, ever," Lisa said as the events of the night before flashed through her mind. "Maybe I'll call in to work and let them know I won't be there today," she said, as she reached for the telephone.

After telling the manager that she was having car problems, she ran into her room to get dressed.

"Kathy, go with me outside to see if I can find out what happened to my car," Lisa said, as sincerely as she could muster.

"It's not here, nowhere around here," said Kathy, as they walked out to where the car should have been parked. "What happened to it? Do you think it might have been stolen?"

"Yes, stolen, that's it. I guess I should report it to the police so I can notify my insurance company," said Lisa.

A policeman named Martin Dennison took down the information after checking the area for any evidence and said he would be in touch. That was the first and last time Lisa talked with the legal authorities in person except for getting a copy of the police report to send to the insurance company

Lisa was so excited when she received her insurance check because it allowed her to buy another much older used car, pay some bills, and have a little extra as a reserve.

Guilt laid heavily on her heart but she felt she only did what she had to do to survive. At least, that was what she kept telling herself so the words could ease her mind a bit.

***

The car was there, covered with dried mud, but she knew it was her car because she had pushed it in what used to be the deep water.

She knew when the police checked the VIN they would find out that it was her missing vehicle.

Then what?

She waited every day for the knock at her door. She envisioned the policeman, Martin Dennison, cuffing her and taking her away from her sons.

To this day, that knock has never happened.

Soon, the statute of limitations will expire, and it won't matter legally.

It will forever matter to Lisa.

OLD SUKIE AND ME

Lois M. Holden

Yessir, young feller. You see that man over there with that camera. He just took a picture of me. Yes, he did. Couldn't believe it myself. But he just walked up to me and asked if he could. With me leaning up against this here wall. I asked why he wanted to and he said I was an interesting character. Can you believe that? Me. An interesting character.

Well, I have seen some remarkable things in my time. Maybe that's why I look like an interesting character. What do you think? You probably think I'm just a crazy old man talking to the air. That's all right. You just go ahead and walk away but maybe I'll be famous someday and you'll tell your lady friend, "Hey, I seen that old man one day in Merced!"

Young folks don't have time to talk to us old timers. But I could tell you a thing or two. Years ago I had the gold fever real bad and Old Sukie and me wandered them hills together for years looking to strike it rich. Never struck it big but we did find a little gold on my claim. Yessir, Old Sukie was a fine companion. Some folks say mules are dumb and stubborn, but not Old Sukie. She was by my side when them claim jumpers tried to run me off. But we was smarter than they thought. I could read that paper they wanted me to sign. Old Sukie knew they was bad 'uns, too. She kicked one in the back side when the other tried to force me to sign. Gave me time to get my gun and send them on their way. Don't know why they wanted that parcel. I never did find much gold there—just enough to get by.

See that girl over there? The one with the dark hair? She reminds me of my Lily. Only Lily was much prettier and her hair was black as pitch and her eyes green as new grass in spring. Couldn't believe it when she said she'd marry me. Her mama had a boarding house and Lily helped her with it while I was out on the claim. We built a little cabin out there and Lily would come with me in the spring. Mostly, I stayed in the valley in the winter, though. Lily and me had ten good years except we couldn't have children. We lost two at birth and the doctor said Lily shouldn't try to have any more. One of the saddest days of my life. Lily loved children and after she lost the second baby, she started teaching Sunday school. Seemed like she always had a bunch of kids around her like butterflies to a flower. Doc Parsons would take her on his rounds when he had to go to a place with children. One day while I was out at the claim, Lily and Doc went to see the Rose family. Doc heard that Mrs. Rose was bad sick and her no-count husband was out drinking and gambling leaving Mrs. Rose with five young children. She was so happy to see Lily she hugged her and kissed her. While Doc was tending to Mrs. Rose, Lily pitched right in cooking and baking and washing. Mrs. Rose's sister finally came later that day and Doc and Lily left. Mrs. Rose died a few days later with the typhoid fever. Weren't long before Lily took sick. Her mama sent word to me that Lily was real bad off and I hightailed it back just in time to bury her.

I hate it when the wind kicks up and puts dust in your eyes and makes them water.

Anyway, I left the valley for good, I thought. Me and Old Sukie went back to the claim and worked it for nigh on to thirty years. Just me and my mule. She was a great comfort to me and the best friend I ever had besides my Lily.

Then one spring day me and Old Sukie was down at the river panning for gold. Spring time is a good time for panning with all the snow melt. All of a sudden I heard a roar and looked up at a wall of water coming at us. I was able to scramble up the river bank but Old Sukie's legs couldn't make it—she'd been getting real feeble. I could only stand there and watch that flash flood carry away my best friend.

There goes that wind again making my eyes water.

After that, the gold fever left me. I didn't have the heart to stay out there all alone. I sold my claim to some city slicker who thought he was going to find the mother lode. Maybe he will, who knows. So I came back down to the valley and got me a room. Now I do odd jobs around town. Seems somebody always has a job for me so I'm able to keep body and soul together.

Well, that feller with the camera is packing up so I reckon he don't want another picture of me. Even gave me five dollars to take it. Told me his name. Adams, I think it was and he had a funny first name. One I ain't heard before.

I wonder what he's going to do with that picture. Said he was a professional photographer. He sells photographs and even put out a book. Imagine that! Be funny if one day it ends up in a fancy place in Frisco or somewhere and people walk along looking at me. What would my Lily say about that? Imagine. Me bein' famous and not knowing it!

But I sure wish Lily was in that picture with me. And Old Sukie.

Originally published in *2013 Writer's Eye* anthology

MIXING WITH CHARLIE

Esther Whitman Johnson

I was thirteen, in eighth grade, and my friends and I were sneaking around, drinking, smoking, acting big for our britches. It was the year of the big party. And I gotta tell you, one thing my mama and daddy could do was throw a party. Mama was the general and we kids were the army. Being the oldest, I got to order around the younger ones.

My daddy hired colored orderlies from the hospital as bartenders. Big Charlie—I called him *One-Eyed Charlie*—was my favorite, partly because he was spooky, looking at you with that one glass eye looking someplace else. Partly because since I was a little girl he'd fixed me a 'Charlie special', a Virgin Mary with celery to tickle my nose. And once, when I was about six and nagged Mama to death, she let me go home overnight with him and Queenie, and they took me to church, and I told everybody I was theirs.

Anyway, since the party was already big, I got to invite a few friends, our stuff set out not far from where One-Eyed Charlie manned the grown-up bar.

Things started simple. I sauntered to the bar with a Coke. "Hey, Charlie, how about a teeny weenie shot of Virginia Gentleman?" I stuck my glass in his face, looking straight into his good eye, the one that moved.

"I don't know 'bout that, Miz Clarice. Your mama and daddy might not like you drinkin' at your age…And me helpin' you might not be too good."

"Come on, Charlie, I'm thirteen, old enough for a little swig. Tell you what, put the bottle at the end of the table, go fill your ice bucket, and I'll pour it myself. You won't be involved."

Big Charlie did like I told him but didn't look too happy about it. Three or four more times I visited the bar, pulling the same stunt. Charlie was too busy with the guests to notice, I guess.

Then my friend Smitty, who was fourteen, way prettier and more popular than me, had this brainy idea. "Dare you to get us a bottle. We can go over to my house, drink and smoke while our parents get shit-faced here."

Charlie was super busy when I sneaked back to the bar. Smitty's mama was ordering him to mix her something fancy, being snotty about it, if I say so myself. She had on one of those mink things where the mink mouth chomps on another mink's tail or maybe its own tail—I don't know. She was keeping One-Eyed Charlie real busy, so he never saw me take that unopened bottle of bourbon from under the table. Least I don't think he did. With that one eye looking in odd directions, you never knew.

We went to Smitty's house, got shit-faced, and watched a movie on TV. Only kid in the neighborhood with a TV in her own room, color at that. On the way home, I went behind a bush and puked my guts out. I gotta tell you Virginia Gentleman tastes even worse coming up than it does going down. But no one saw I couldn't hold my liquor, especially Smitty.

When I sneaked back in, the fur coats and minks biting their tails were gone. The party was over, Mama was in the kitchen directing the cleaning, and Daddy was on the sofa waiting for Charlie to stack empty bottles into cartons.

"There's a bottle missing, Charlie." My daddy stood up, not smiling like usual with Big Charlie.

"No suh, Dr. Billy, can't be. I ain't done nothing with no bottles. Must be here somewhere."

"Charlie, that was a full case when I bought it, and now one's missing. I always give you a bottle, but I won't have you drinking on the job or pilfering, especially after putting in a good word for you with my colleagues."

Charlie saw me then, behind my father's back, standing at the doorway. He turned his head away from me and looked down at his feet. I almost interrupted Daddy to confess I was the culprit and get One-Eyed Charlie off the hook. But I hesitated, my heart beat fast, and I pictured my father angry. Then it was too late.

"Yes suh, Dr. Billy," said Charlie, "I guess I done drank up that whole bottle of whiskey on the job. Didn't think it was that much, and I'm awful sorry about it."

"I'm sorry, too, Charlie. You'll never work bartending again."

"No suh, I guess I won't." One-Eyed Charlie lifted his glance from his feet and turned in my father's direction, but I felt he was looking straight at me.

Still, I see my reflection in that dark glass eye.

(Originally published in *Longleaf Pine* "Truth or Dare" issue/ Spring 2016/Midwood Press, Charlotte, NC)

A LONELY BRIDE

Urmilla Khanna

Year: 1963

I am a lonely bride. I love America. I do not quite know why I love America.

I like Krishan. I like the name. Though everyone in America calls him Kris. I am not in love with Kris, for I do not know exactly what that means. I have not known Kris for more than a fortnight, at best. I am certainly committed to him. I look at a bright future with him. He is very nice to me, in his own way.

Kris is oblivious of my loneliness. He has lived in America for three long years, studying for his PhD. Now he has brought me over from India as his prized possession, his bride. He is a proud and happy man. He has a job. His boss likes him very much. He is productive in his research. He has a wife.

He has no need to be lonely.

I am very lonely.

I like him so much that I feel I cannot tell him, I am lonely. That would break his heart. I do not ever want to break his heart. He is such a good man, in his own way.

A letter to India takes better than a fortnight to get there and that does not help my loneliness. I realize, that by the time I get a note of comfort back I am long over that bout of loneliness, and actually, exuberant about being in America. The words in that letter seem so redundant that I rip it to shreds as being meaningless.

I tell Kris that I would like to call my family in India. I know it will be costly. I ask anyway. He is very agreeable and I go through the ritual of placing the call.

To call my mother in India I have to first dial a double zero on a rotary phone. I reach the international operator in New York.

"Which country, please?" The voice is sometimes friendly, at other times indifferent and sleepy.

"India, please," I say, smiling into the receiver with hope.

After a wait of a few seconds, the voice from India comes through. That itself gives me closeness; I feel I have already touched my mother's bosom.

The operator from India: "Which city, please?"

"Durg," I say, "Durg in Madhya Pradesh." I try to help her locate my mother.

"Not listed, madam, Durg not listed. Is there a city it is near?"

"Yes, yes," I say hurriedly. I do not want to lose the connection and start all over again. "Try under Raipur."

She has obviously found it. Time is of essence, so she immediately goes to the next question "Phone number, please?"

I give her a number and then add, "Make it pp, particular person."

"Ye—ss" the voice drags. "Name of pp please?"

"It is for Kamala Khurana," I say and she spells it back to me using the Indian vernacular. K as in *kala bazzar*, a as in *aam ka achaar*, m as in *mandir ke haar*…Everything Indian makes me exuberant.

"Call placed, madam," she concludes.

I have made the call a pp-call only, because my mother does not have a phone in her home. She has given me the number of her neighbor who is a cloth merchant and has managed to get a phone using his connections to get through the red tape. When he will receive the call, and appreciate it is coming from America, he will drop anything he may be doing, rush across to Mother's and hurry her back to his house. I can quite envision the commotion created by this call and the pride with which Mother will talk to him after the call. "That call was from my daughter. She is married. She lives in America."

After the call is successfully placed, there is nothing to do but wait. The return call could transpire at any time; could be a minute, highly improbable, but a chance I cannot take, or, not until twelve or twenty-four hours. Therefore, I sit by the phone and wait.

I wait and I wait.

If I get too restless, I start an enquiry process. The operator tells me my call is active and has moved up to seventy-seventh in queue.

"It will come through any time now, madam," she says with confidence.

"Soon…?" I ask.

"Yes, very soon."

The fact that her voice has traveled all the way from India into my hungry ears reassures me.

I wait some more…

It is two a.m. The shrill ring-tone of the telephone jolts me awake. I have been in deep sleep, the kind that has always followed the most gratifying interludes I have had with my husband, whom I hardly know. I untangle myself from his arms, rub sleep off my eyes, and stumble to the switch of the bedside lamp.

I realize I am in America, a happy and satisfied bride.

I pick up the receiver and start with a long drawn-out "Hello?" I have to talk so loud that I am afraid I will wake up my neighbor. In the three minutes allotted for the call, I manage to ask how things are at the other end, and how Daddy is doing. There is so much echo in our voices that the only thing I hear is my own voice in return. May be a small streak of, "And how are you baby?" comes through.

Three minutes are over, and I plead with the operator for an extension. Extensions are given in increments of one minute with a maximum of six-minute talk-time. By the time I am assured that the extension has been granted, I have only thirty seconds left. I say to the receiver "keep talking, Mummy." All I hear is the echo "keep-talking, keep-talking, keep-ta…." and the line is dead.

Kris is half-asleep, his reassuring hand gently rubbing my back. I sit at the edge of the bed and look at his face, so peaceful, so full of hope.

I mutter softly, "I am not lonely. I am a happy bride. I am in America."

COLD FEAR

Julie Leverenz

She thought they always came in pairs. But the burly man standing before the reception desk had to be at least six five, and even without the regulation haircut, black suit, white shirt and muted tie, his stance screamed Federal Agent. Maybe they only needed one of him.

"Miss Winston?" *Yikes,* Hannah thought, *even his voice is huge.*

She nodded, her heart sinking.

"Special Agent Frank Holman, FBI." He flashed his badge. "Do you have a moment?"

Do I have a choice? Hannah struggled to keep her expression neutral. "May I see your identification again, please?" He reached over and held out his badge wallet. Hannah removed her big Jackie O-style glasses, cleaned them with a tissue, then pretended to study the badge while she steadied herself. Her deep brown eyes, magnified by the glasses' thick lenses, were cool as she looked up at him. "I can take my break; let me just tell my boss." She felt the man's eyes boring into her as she knocked on the connecting door to the Dean's office. Somehow, she doubted he was appreciating how nicely her soft angora sweater hugged her 34Cs.

A few minutes later, Hannah closed the door of the faculty conference room behind her and announced, "You're here about Bel Dorin Restoration."

Agent Holman registered a flicker of surprise before his face returned to its original granite. From the tinge of gray at his temples, Hannah figured he was probably in his late thirties, early forties. She wondered if there was a human being in there somewhere. She didn't see a wedding ring, so probably not.

"Yes Ma'am," he said. "Mr. Doring told us where we might find you."

Hearing Ed Doring's name flooded Hannah with a mix of regret and gratitude. She would never forget Ed's words as he put her on the bus: "Go on, Hannah. Forget Bel Dorin. Forget me. Be safe. Be happy."

"How is Ed?" she said, doing her best to match Agent Holman's level gaze.

"He is well. And cooperating fully."

Hannah gave him a tight smile. "Then I will, too."

Agent Holman set a tiny tape recorder on the conference table and spoke into it. "This is Special Agent Francis Holman of the FBI Cheyenne Resident Agency. Date: November 28, 1978; location: University of Wyoming College of Agriculture, Laramie; purpose: interview Miss Hannah Winston in regard to Bel Dorin Restoration, Incorporated, particularly as regards Gino Belvidere. Miss Winston, would you state your full legal name, please."

Hannah leaned toward the machine. "Hannah Lorraine Winston."

"Date of birth." Hannah hesitated; she would just as soon not have it on record that she was 31. She glanced at the agent, who clearly didn't give a damn. Hannah sighed.

For the next half-hour, Agent Holman quizzed her about her two years as a secretary at Bel Dorin Restoration in Bethesda, Maryland. She told him about the sloppy records that took her two months to straighten out after the bookkeeper quit, and how she found overcharges on multi-million dollar Federal contracts. Gino Belvidere, Ed Doring's business partner, was charging the government for chauffeurs and mistresses, lavish parties, drugs, and personal travel. She was careful to tell Agent Holman that Ed, the technical expert in charge of the restoration work, was as horrified as she was when the extent of Gino Belvidere's fraud came to light. Ed confronted Gino, but Gino just blamed the previous bookkeeper and brought in a new one.

Agent Holman made some notes on a small spiral-bound pad, then set his pen down. "Do you recognize the names Angelo Grasso or Mike Bruno?"

A chill snaked down Hannah's back. "No. Should I?"

"We have evidence that the new bookkeeper was connected to organized crime and may have been the mistress of one of those two men."

"Theresa was Mob? Did she say that?"

Agent Holman's steady gaze faltered. "I am sorry to tell you that Miss Pirello died last month. Under suspicious circumstances."

Hannah slumped in her chair, stunned. Then the full impact of the agent's words hit her. "Am I in danger?"

"We don't think so. But we may need you to testify. In that case, we will provide an escort."

Hannah understood immediately—if she testified, she could be in danger. "In that case," she said, "I hope you won't need me to testify." She looked out the conference room window at the brilliant blue sky and snow-capped Medicine Bow range in the distance. She had no stomach for getting sucked back into this mess, and hated the thought of returning to the traffic, noise, and pollution Back East. She turned to Agent Holman, who had raised one eyebrow. Raking her fingers through her thick, wavy brown hair, she said, "But... yeah. Okay. I will, if I have to."

§

For several days after the interview, Hannah looked over her shoulder and jumped every time the telephone rang. She told no one; she hadn't made any close friends in the ten months she'd been in Laramie, and she preferred it that way. Gradually, however, her jitters faded, and after spending a ghastly Christmas with her quarrelsome parents in Arizona she was glad to return to her little log cabin on the cold, crisp, high desert plains. In the evenings, curled up with a book in front of a crackling fire with her shepherd-husky mix, Sarah, snoozing at her feet, Hannah felt safe, comfortable, and in control. She had cut the firewood herself, and the freezer was stocked with antelope hunted with her own rifle. Never mind that the antelope was a flat-out lucky shot, taken blind after she sat on her glasses; she had gutted and dressed the beast, hadn't she? Come Spring, she would plant vegetables, help out at the ranch on weekends in return for a break on her rent, and ride Bridget, her sorrel mare, into the mountains. She was happy.

Weeks passed. She never saw the man watching her. He kept to the shadows, waiting for instructions.

The subpoena arrived on a Monday afternoon in late February, served by a grizzled, self-important Special Agent in a hurry. She read it, then her eyes scanned her windowless office—locking onto the University seal on the wooden side chair and the spiffy new IBM Selectric on her desk—as if the sensible, practical surroundings could make this not be happening. Every ounce of her screamed, "No!"

She phoned the FBI office in Cheyenne and demanded to speak to Agent Holman. When he answered, she blurted, "What the hell is this?" without identifying herself. "It's Monday, and this thing says I have to be in Washington on Wednesday." She poured on the sarcasm. "Thanks for the advance notice. Just how the hell do you expect me to get there?"

"Miss Winston," Agent Holman said in his deep, maddeningly contained voice, "your testimony is requested in Washington on Wednesday. The Bureau will furnish transportation. Can you arrange your schedule?"

"Do you mean that, or are you just being polite? I have to tell you, I really don't want to do this."

"I understand. But you said—"

"I know what I said," Hannah snapped. "I have to clear it with my boss. Give me your direct number." She jotted it on a pink While You Were Out pad, then slammed down the receiver and put her head in her hands.

The phone rang—a professor calling for the Dean. While fielding four more calls and answering questions from two hapless graduate students, Hannah concocted a story about a family emergency. Fortunately—or unfortunately, she couldn't decide which—the Dean bought her story without question. She called Agent Holman.

"Thank you," he said. "An agent is en route from Washington to accompany you. He will pick you up at your home at—" he paused. Hannah could hear papers shuffling. "—seven thirty tomorrow morning. He will brief you on the plane."

"Nothing before then?" Hannah hated how frightened she sounded. *They killed Theresa*, she thought.

"We believe the risk is minimal," he said. "I have been informed that all of the principals are either in custody or under surveillance."

Hannah snorted. "'Minimal' is not zero. Basically, you're saying I'm on my own."

"Is there someone you can stay with tonight?"

Hannah rolled her eyes, imagining the hassle of telling the story to a well-meaning coworker; never mind the gossip. "I'll manage. Tell your agent I'll be waiting. And he'd better bring ID."

The rest of the afternoon passed in a blur. Hannah deliberately stayed late, typing a thesis until the last evening class ended. Trailing a cluster of students to the parking lot, she saw a figure on the far side of the quadrangle duck out of the light of a street lamp. Hannah moved faster and smacked down the locks on both doors as soon as she jumped into her pickup truck.

Snow began to fall about thirteen miles west of town and, by the time she turned off the state road into the ranch, the ground was lightly covered. The forecast called for snow showers, with overnight temperatures hovering near zero. That suited Hannah just fine—snow meant telltale footprints and tire tracks, and that kind of cold could be fatal to mobsters from Back East. *Hell, it could have been fatal for me my first week here,* she thought, grateful again for the neighboring rancher who happened upon her old Camaro in the white-out of a sudden ground blizzard. She hoped she was smarter now.

Sarah barked and bounded over to meet the truck as Hannah parked next to the cabin. With the dog underfoot, Hannah hurried inside to feed them both, careful to set the deadbolts she installed after Agent Holman's visit last fall.

Sometime after midnight, Sarah's barking awoke her from a restless sleep.

Instantly alert, Hannah whispered, "Good girl, Sarah." She reached for her glasses, then for the rifle she had propped next to her bed, and squinted at the pale backlit clock dial: 3:15. Sarah padded over, tail wagging. *Bark, damn you, Sarah. Keep barking.* But Sarah sat down and leaned companionably against her leg.

Leaving the lights off, Hannah stole to the bedroom window, her bare feet soundless on the cold wooden planks. Peering through a narrow gap in the gingham curtains, she saw steady snow falling outside, glinting like ghostly dust motes in the beam from the ranch's tall yard light. Nothing stirred between her cabin and the barn, 100 feet away. The only sound was the propane-fired furnace growling down the hall as it staved off the chill outside the cabin's thick log walls.

She was shouldering into her soft fleece robe when a sudden, sharp CRACK plunged the room into darkness. Someone had shot out the yard light. Gripping the rifle, she dashed to the kitchen, where she fumbled for the telephone. The line was dead.

Oh jeez, ammo. Hannah scurried back to her bedroom, took ammunition from the bedside table, loaded the rifle, and filled the pocket of her robe. Then she sat on the rumpled bed and quickly pulled on heavy socks. Sarah stayed close. Hannah rested her hand on the dog's head and automatically stroked Sarah's soft muzzle with her fingertips. *Okay*, she thought. *Breathe, Hannah.*

In her mind, she reviewed the layout around her cabin. The front room, with the stone fireplace wall at one end and kitchen at the other, looked out on her tiny yard. Beyond the yard's low, decorative, useless picket fence was a dirt lane, then a deep ditch and the sparsely-traveled highway. Her truck was parked on the side, under the kitchen window. That window looked down the lane to her landlord's house, but he and his wife were in Florida. Out back, the mudroom door led to her dormant garden, which sloped down to a stand of cottonwoods lining the frozen Branch River. On the now-dark farmyard side, the barn stood between her and the ranch hands' shacks. The ranch hands liked their booze; Hannah knew she couldn't count on any of them being a light sleeper.

She gave the fine bristles on Sarah's head a final pat, tightened her grip on the rifle, and stood up. *We can do this.*

The furnace cycled off. Hannah heard the faint rattle-hum of an engine on the cabin's far side. She crept back to the kitchen, leaned low over the sink, then peeked above the windowsill. A black van stood on the other side of her truck, silhouetted against the rapidly-gathering snow. She retreated to the doorway between the front room and narrow back hall, then felt her way into the mudroom and pulled on her boots. Soundlessly, she moved the mudroom's straight chair into the back hall and set it where she could see the windows in both the front and back doors. She sat down and waited, straining her eyes for shadows against the faint brightness of the falling snow, and straining her ears for any sound other than Sarah's breathing at her side.

Minutes passed, then Sarah's ears pricked. Hannah heard it, too—a shuffle, then a click at the mudroom door. Sarah jumped up and started barking. A shadow crossed the mudroom door's window.

Moments later, Sarah directed her barking at the front door. The dog trotted across the front room, barking happily, her tail wagging. "No, Sarah, come here," Hannah hissed. *Stupid dog.* Hannah could only hope that the shadow outside couldn't tell the difference between a friendly bark and a warning bark.

A bright yellow light flashed across the living room's picture window and over to the front door. *Flashlight.* A gunshot splintered the doorjamb. Hannah heard Sarah yelp in pain, but stifled the urge to rush to her dog's aid. She raised the rifle and, as the shadow bashed in the door, she fired.

"Holy fuck," a man's voice yelled, and a figure staggered into the room. The flashlight skittered across the floor and stopped, its beam focused on the dog pinned under the shattered door. The man's face was covered by a ski mask; clutching at his leg, he raised his pistol.

Hannah fired again. She felt as cold and steady as the rifle in her hands. The man crumpled.

Keeping her rifle trained on the man lying face down on the floor, Hannah went over and kicked his pistol away. She nudged him with the toe of her boot. Nothing. She bent down and felt for a pulse. Nothing. With her eyes fixed on the body, she heaved the door off of Sarah and used one hand to stroke the dog's head, sides and limbs. Sarah whimpered when Hannah touched her hip and left foreleg. "Shh, there's a good girl," Hannah said. "Stay, Sarah."

As she stood up, an arm circled her neck from behind. Before it could tighten, Hannah whirled around and jammed her knee into the man's crotch, registering another ski-mask-covered face and a pistol in his other hand. The man grabbed her hair as he doubled over, pulling her down backwards. As she fell, Hannah gave her head a violent shake, causing her glasses to fly off, but she had made him lose his grip. Hannah wrested free, seized her rifle, and scrambled to her feet. A bullet grazed her sleeve as she darted out the gaping front door.

Hannah sped around the farmyard side of the cabin, silently thanking her father for forcing her to take a self-defense class. She didn't know how much time she had before the man came after her. Probably not enough time to make it to the barn, she thought. She skidded down the embankment to the frozen river, then scuttled under the wooden bridge that led from the farmyard to the pastures. Crouched under the bridge to catch her breath, she became aware of the searing cold seeping through her bathrobe and thin pajamas. The snow and cold that she thought would keep her safe were now her enemies.

The image of the dead man sprawled on the floor flashed into her mind. *I killed a man.* Hannah pushed the thought away and forced herself to see only Sarah, injured and in pain. After a moment, she crept over and peeked out from under the bridge. A flashlight beam rounded the corner of the cabin, followed by a dark blur. *Shit. My glasses.* This was no antelope; she couldn't count on a lucky shot. And a miss would just advertise her location.

Fueled by adrenaline and fear, she hurried out the far side of the bridge, keeping low behind the cover of the embankment and cottonwoods. The Branch River was only ten feet wide at the ranch, but its frozen pools were slick and littered with rocks and branches. The embankment was steep and treacherous.

By the time she saw the barn looming over the bank, her fingers and face were numb. Every wheezing breath brought more painful, freezing air into her lungs. But she knew the ranch hands' cabins weren't far, now. Looking over her shoulder, she saw the flashlight beam scan the pilings under the bridge, then point directly at her. She ducked her head, praying for the camouflage of her white robe. A shot careened off a tree branch over her head. Hannah ran.

When she was even with the back of the barn she scrabbled up the bank and raced for the barn's cover. Halfway there she heard a shot, then felt a fiery stab in her arm. The rifle fell out of her unfeeling hands. Another shot whizzed by her ear. Abandoning the rifle, Hannah flew, gasping, into the dark shadows behind the barn.

A powerful arm clamped across her chest, pinning her elbows. A rough, leather-gloved hand covered her mouth, stifling her scream. She kicked, but she might as well have been kicking a tree trunk. Tears of helpless frustration filled Hannah's eyes. *So this is it*, she thought. *A third man.* She wondered when—if—her body would be found.

"Are you hurt?" the deep, resonant voice whispered.

Agent Holman. Hannah's terror drained away, taking what was left of her strength. Even her brain went limp.

His whisper became more urgent. "Miss Winston, are you hurt?" He lifted his hand from her mouth.

She nodded, unable to speak. He leaned his head down. She managed to squeak, "Arm." With an effort, she added, "I'll live."

She heard sirens approaching on the highway. "About damn time," the agent growled. "Stay here." He released her, then strode around the corner of the barn. She heard a shot, then another; a yell and a thump. Hannah sagged against the barn, shaking uncontrollably.

Agent Holman carried Hannah to the cabin and set her in a chair that faced the fireplace, away from the body. He retrieved her glasses. Hannah looked at him vacantly, as if seeing him for the first time. The ambulance medics came and warmed her limbs, declared her arm a surface wound, and wrapped it in bandages. They cheerfully tended to Sarah as well—extracting an enormous splinter from her leg and opining that the hip was just bruised. The police took pictures, peppered Hannah with questions, and rousted a ranch hand to slap plywood over the front door and broken mudroom window. The coroner carted away the body bags. Through it all, Agent Holman stood by, speaking when spoken to, a solid, comforting presence.

When at last the others had gone, Hannah stared at the floor. Agent Holman watched her. Finally, she said, "So much for 'minimal' risk, huh." He said nothing. Hannah looked up. "So what made you come, anyway?"

He grimaced. "I got a call from the Denver Field Office; they tracked a shooter up here. I just wish I'd gotten the call sooner." He rubbed both hands over his haggard eyes. "We didn't know there were two shooters. You're a brave one, Miss Winston."

It's time you called me Hannah, she thought. But she couldn't bring herself to say it.

The snow had ended and the sky was brightening over Sheep Mountain when Agent Holman washed the last of the breakfast dishes. Hannah had rallied when she heard him rattling around in the kitchen, and rather enjoyed instructing him while he made coffee and oatmeal. Now he checked his watch and said, "Seven thirty. Right on time," as an official black SUV pulled into the lane. Agent Holman looked sideways at Hannah. "I warned him he'd better bring his ID." Hannah thought he almost smiled.

The two agents drove Hannah in convoy, first to the vet's and then to the airport. Hannah's eyes widened when she saw the waiting government helicopter. Agent Holman walked her across the tarmac. "Give 'em hell, Hannah," he said, giving her good arm a gentle squeeze. As the helicopter lifted off, she watched his towering shape grow smaller until she could no longer see his hand, raised in a sharp salute.

FROM THE STARS
EXCERPT FROM CHAPTER 8: RETURN

Bethany Lortz

"What do you mean they disappeared?" Azia cried when I told her what I had heard.

"That's what Agent Wight said. He didn't know how else to explain it." Aiden informed.

I had told him earlier.

Nina had been absent from school that day for whatever reason. We all knew she wasn't sick. It was probably her parent's doing like it was almost every time.

"Great!" I yelled, "Now we might have giant robots running around!"

"And you call me crazy." Azia smiled, "People are gonna think you're crazy by the way you're talking.

"I'm still in shock." I admitted, "I just can't believe it."

"I can!" Azia butted in. "If they come back we should help them."

"Yeah." Aiden agreed

My mouth dropped open. "I've created monsters." I moaned

"I think you caught the girl bot's eye, Dominic." Azia's eyes sparkled with a troublesome glint.

"Don't even go there." I demanded waving my hand at her.

"I like the yellow bot." Aiden decided. "Even if he took my matchbox car."

"You mean, Nyein." Azia corrected, "I liked Haleem. He's a rocker. I could tell right off the bat."

I blinked a couple of times then looked at Aiden. "Wasn't that matchbox car from your dad?"

Aiden nodded.

His dad wasn't around as much as Aiden wanted. He always out traveling like Nina's dad, only Aiden actually missed him. Nina didn't expect much from her parents since they didn't do much for her.

I looked up at both of them. "Do either of you notice that

Alvira had scars on her back?"

"Hey, Haleem had some too!" Azia cried

"I'll bet Nyein had them too." I replied with a nod. "They looked a lot like whip wounds."

"Where would they get those? They're huge! Nothing can be big enough to hurt them." Azia thought aloud rubbing her chin.

"My thoughts exactly. If they come back, I want some answers." I declared.

Azia nodded her agreement.

Aiden shrugged. "Maybe my car was better in Nyein's hands than mine. He might need it more than I do. I mean, at least I don't have to worry about being beat up."

"Guess we'll never know now, will we?" I added with a sigh and putting my hands into my pockets.

Aiden nodded his head sadly peering down at the ground.

Azia perked up. "Maybe we can."

Aiden and I looked up at her with confused expressions.

"What if they teleported out to protect themselves from the government?"

I shrugged my shoulders. "Why would that change anything?"

"What if they went back to the same place we found them?" Azia's eyes shone brightly.

"You're crazy." I said simply shaking my head.

A ringing noise came from Aiden's back pack.

"What's that?" I asked as Aiden pulled off his backpack.

Aiden got his computer out of his backpack before sitting down on the curb.

"Don't keep us in suspense, Aiden! What was that?" Azia demanded peering over his shoulder.

"I have an email." Aiden pulled it up then cocked his head. "I don't know who this is."

Azia gasped.

"What? What is it?" I asked a little alarmed.

"Read the subject." She squeaked

I squinted to read the small text.

Nyein, Alvira, and Haleem

None of us spoke for a full five minutes.

"Is it from them?" Aiza said finally

"I don't know." Aiden breathed slowly. "Should I open the

email?"

I couldn't bring myself to answer him.

"Go on!" Azia said so suddenly that I jumped.

Aiden clicked on it and we each read it silently to ourselves.

"Dominc, Aiden, and Aiza,

We know of the eventful night you three had last Friday. You met three very special bots that night, didn't you? Their names are the ones that appear above. Do not worry, they are safe and have not betrayed you. They are strong, but I'm sure you already know that. I will not tell you everything that has happened. I'm sure you have noticed some of their scars and numbers that come before their names. You are curious and full of questions. Good, we are counting on it. Humans might be just what the Outcasts need to recover. Time is short. All you need to know are these three things: Nyein, Alvira, and Haleem will return, they will appear in the same place you found them, lastly there will be more of them. I wish all three of you the best of luck I can offer. Know this, they need you, all four of you."

Right after I read the last sentence it vanished off the screen.

"What happened?" Azia cried

"I don't know! It looks like it deleted itself!" Aiden said frantically searching for the strange email.

I blinked and tried to make sense of the strange email. Where did it come from? Who was is from? Did they know the Outcasts? How did they know us? What were we supposed to do?

Azia ceased her panic and looked both of us in the eyes. "They're coming back."

Neither of us grasped it for a second.

"They're coming back!" Azia squealed throwing her arms up into the air while jumping. "Let's go! They could be there right now!"

Before we could stop her, she grabbed her bike and started unlocking it hastily.

Aiden followed her lead after a while. When they both got them unlocked they looked at me expectantly. I sighed heavily, then stepped toward the bike rack to do the same.

FIRE DRILL IN MOTHERHOOD

Michelle McBeth

Given the advances made in prenatal care over the past few decades, I should have been more surprised that I didn't deliver a healthy baby boy. I mean, how could they have missed this on the ultrasounds? Were so many pregnancies so routine these days that doctors just didn't pay much attention? There's a heartbeat; it's moving around; it must be going well. How else could they fail to notice the wings and tail that had formed, or the oddly shaped skull with sharp, pointy teeth? At what point had things started to go awry? Surely to undergo such a transformation from a human baby would have taken at least a few weeks.

Through my epidural haze only a few things stood out as strange. The first was the ease with which the baby emerged. There was no intense pushing. The slender body simply slid out. I remember preparing myself for hours of pushing, but the whole thing was over in about three minutes. I wondered why I had heard so many horror stories. It must be to prepare you for the worst, I thought. In reality, it's no sweat. I thought I must have just become a member of a secret club—I would tell the story of my labor, the hours of grueling work and exhaustion, hiding the smile on my face that knew the truth.

The second thing that struck me was the confusion on the faces in the room. No one screamed, as I would have expected had I given birth to a monster. It was more bewilderment. They must have also been wondering: How could we have missed this? My husband smiled in awe. The doctors shrugged and handed my son over with a look that said, "Well, here you go."

I expected the sound of a baby crying, but the wail had too much of a growl to it. A tear rolled down my husband's cheek as he brought the bundle of blankets towards me. "Honey," he said, leaning down so I could see my child, "it's a dragon." The last thing I remember was a puff of smoke billowing from a rough-skinned nostril before I passed out.

§

I only tried to nurse once. There was a lot of screaming on my part and some blood. He didn't seem to understand bottles either, and tore through the rubber nipples. But when I pumped and left a bowl of my milk on the floor, he lapped it up readily.

We agonized over a name for weeks. "Steven" no longer seemed appropriate. We tried to pick a famous dragon to name him after, but most famous dragons are considered monsters or have less than pleasant endings to their lives. Trogdor was a silly name. We didn't like the hippy connotations of Puff. He didn't look like a Falcor. In the end, we settled on Sheepstealer, from a George R.R. Martin novella. Sheepstealer's fate was undetermined at the end of the book, and that was good enough for us. When Sheepstealer turned out to be too much of a mouthful for a quick attention call, we resorted to simply calling him Sheep. But for a scolding, Sheepstealer Benjamin Writhe had a nice ring to it.

The first thing I let Sheep burn was the book *Babies for Dummies*, that had proved incredibly useless in my situation. It was a mistake. Not the book choice, but the fact that we allowed him to burn anything. His excitement was endearing as he scattered the burned bits of paper with his tail, then stumbled and slid his way across the hardwood floor, his talons leaving scratch marks in the surface. Endearing turned to frightening as he tried to ignite the dishtowel hanging from the oven handle. He tried to make sense of our admonishment. Clearly, dishtowels were off limits, but books were okay. He pranced and slid out of the kitchen, his wings flapping vainly for purchase of air and assistance in prancing in search of more paper. My husband caught him a few minutes later in the study, a hardback copy of "Wuthering Heights" had been pulled from the bottom shelf and splayed open on the floor. Teeth marks in the edge of the cover betrayed where he had grabbed it, the edges of the first few pages curling slowly inward as the red line of fire worked its way across the surface.

Over time, we somehow managed to convey that food and things in the fireplace were the only things he was allowed to burn. We built a fire pit outside in the back yard, and objects in there were added to the list of allowable kindling.

Our expenses skyrocketed. First, it was the fire extinguishers. Two in every room, and we used one at least once a week. When a two-year-old child has a tantrum, he breaks the living room vase. When a four-month-old dragon has a tantrum, he burns the living room drapes to a crisp.

Once he had outgrown milk, it turned out the only food Sheep liked was meat. We purchased an additional freezer to keep in the basement just for him, and frequently went to Costco to fill it with the cheapest packs of meat we could find. He was not picky, and the cuts of beef sold for stewing were often the least expensive choices.

Thankfully, we were able to use our strange situation to help fund his diet. We were constantly offered our own reality TV shows, which we turned down. We did agree to a Ken Burns documentary that only involved a few hours of filming every month, and I started a blog about my experiences raising a dragon. Mediaeval décor companies and tourist castles clamored to advertise on my site, but we stopped short of allowing our son to become the celebrity endorser of any products. We wanted him to have a normal childhood. As normal a childhood as a dragon was meant to have.

He grew incredibly fast. The proudest day of my life was when he finally lifted himself off the ground. I watched as he gradually and awkwardly rose and fell, gaining a little more air with each flap of his wings. The down current blew a beautiful swirl of sparks from the wood he had just lit in the fire pit. About twenty feet up his wings hit the branches of an overhead tree and he tumbled back to the ground in panic. Dragons are not like cats. Dragons do not always land on their feet. Thankfully, his hide and bones were strong and the soft grassy ground absorbed much of the impact. He wailed and approached me, so I stroked the scales between his eyes and down his long neck while making reassuring noises.

When we finally started turning a decent profit, we bought a castle. It seemed appropriate, and the property came with an enormous wide-open grassy area for him to practice flying. He had grown to fifteen feet long in just over a year and needed more space. It also afforded us more privacy, as neighbors and young ladies dressed like Daenarys Targaryen had liked to linger in front of the house to try and get a glimpse of Sheep through the curtains.

I liked to spread out a blanket in the grass of our enormous lawn and lie down, an unobstructed view of the sky above me. I watched as he swooped and climbed and dove, over and over again, and gradually doze off. I enjoyed the feel of his shadow sometimes passing over me, breaking the warmth of the sun.

I tried not to scream the day a half-burned lamb landed with an explosive thud a couple dozen yards from me. Sheepstealer had lived up to his namesake. He landed with a light prance near his prize and nudged the mass of bloody wool and bones towards me. He sat and curled his tail around his body, obviously pleased with himself and his offering to me, as I tried to wipe the gore off my arms and clothes.

Nothing is worse than scolding a child who is so proud of what he has accomplished. I laid a tarp out in the bed of our truck and commanded Sheep to put his prize in the back. He halfheartedly flew behind as I drove to the neighboring farm to return the mangled sheep. The owner promptly vomited as Sheep hung his head in shame, and I wrote an excessively sized check to pay for the lamb and some emotional distress. It hurt beyond measure that Sheep couldn't muster up the energy to fly back home, but rode in the bed of the truck instead. I sent him to bed without dinner.

A few days later the farmer put his property up for sale at a steal. We quickly purchased it, along with all the livestock. I rode with Sheep in the bed of the truck as my husband drove us around the perimeter of our several hundred-acre land acquisition. Any time his attention wandered to something outside our land, I reprimanded him and explained which side was ours. After two circuits, he seemed to understand the boundaries. The next time he landed in front of me with a sheep, I trusted it was one of ours as he tore into the flesh.

§

Sheep stopped growing after two years. At full size, his body was twenty-two and a half feet long. When we included his neck and tail, forty-nine feet. His scales had grown into a beautiful scarlet color, though his belly remained dark gray.

One day he landed beside me and crouched down, extending his head out next to me. He did this when he wanted my attention. I reached over and rubbed the scales on the top of his head for a moment. He extended his head backwards and looked at his back, then back at me. I stood up and stroked the length of his neck to the ridge where his back began. As I stood there he bumped me towards him with his head, then looked at his back again. Understanding dawned on me.

I went horseback riding exactly once. This, I thought, would be a million times more terrifying.

I awkwardly lifted a leg over his neck and wriggled backwards so I was seated between his shoulders. There was nothing to hold onto except one of the spikes that lined his neck, so I grabbed a hold and said, "Gently now."

It was not as bad as I had anticipated. His shoulders kept me centered and he lifted his head high to keep me from sliding forward too much. We circled the perimeter of our property a few times and I marveled at the view. The air was cooler up here, and the wind made a mess of my hair. I was not frightened like I thought I would be. Somehow, I knew, Sheep would not let me fall.

Even at this slow speed, it took only a couple minutes to make the circuit, a trip that had taken an hour in the truck. I realized how little space Sheep actually had to fly about. On the third circuit, he pulled out of our space and flew away for a few moments before turning back to his regular path. He did this repeatedly before I finally realized what he was trying to tell me. This was not enough.

I patted the base of his neck and we circled back down to the lawn. He crouched down again so I could easily dismount, and I walked around to touch his face. "Wait," I said, and held up a finger.

When my husband came home, I explained the situation. We took an old sporran and put the state issued ID the government had forced us to get inside it, along with a note explaining who Sheep was, a DVD copy of the Ken Burns' documentary, and a photo of the three of us taken shortly after he had taken his first flight. We belted it into place at the base of his neck.

Most parents get at least seventeen years with their child before sending them out to fend for themselves. We had only gotten two and a half. We cried together as we watched him fly out of reach. I absentmindedly rubbed the growing mound below my stomach, uncertain if I wanted it to be another dragon or a real child this time.

To this day, I still sit out in the grass and feel a little flutter of hope every time a cloud shadow passes over me. We did well, I tell myself. As well as any parent can hope for their child.

SMILE A MIGHTY JESUS

RJ McCarthy

Alhambra Charles lived her life tired, and at 32, she already glimpsed what 64 would feel like—if she made it that far. She believed in keeping her options open, one of her few surviving beliefs after her preacher tried to seduce her.

Bamba—a childhood cousin's quaint name crunch—shouldered the cleaning cart through the halls of Warm Comfort Nursing Home, an endless hill with no down. The cold, steel bar in her work-punished hands pushed back. The smell of resignation—urine, gardenia, disinfectant, repetition, and more urine—added drag to her soul fatigue.

As she labored toward Wheeler "Roy" Seltry's room, a glance at a beveled hall mirror revealed a span of hips winched wider by time, natural hair in need, and a fling of freckles under no-quarter hazel eyes. Bitterness clawed at those eyes, but Bamba clawed back, probably why people largely avoided her.

She halted at Seltry's door, the hesitation more than fatigue. His sister, Dud, was already in there, chatting away, riffling the air with the nonstop patter of a caffeinated DJ. It was something about those old country-cracker accents that ground at the fillings in Bamba's teeth, crow-pecked her last nerve. The kind of accents that used the N-word comfortably the moment she was gone, she'd just bet on it.

Thank God for weekends, she thought, and snorted at the contradiction.

At the moment, she clung to the hair-reclamation promise of her Saturday appointment at Curl Caress, along with a mani and a pedi, foot massage included. She'd budgeted tightly for this rare indulgence, and her eyes filmed at the anticipation

Bamba lingered at the door listening to the *conversation*—mainly a monologue—between Roy and Dud.

"He was always the thinker," Doris Seltry'ed described her brother to Bamba. "Me? Comes to talking, I can't find the off-tap."

Got that right.

The Seltrys were Lincoln-lanky, affable people with trowel-long, work-tormented hands. Patches of red still poked through tabby-gray hair, original paint clinging to weathered barn siding. Life for them had been an endless procession of double jobs, tag-teamed between a modest country store and the daily lint-storm of a cotton mill.

"Worked anything that paid," Roy'd said. Work equaled survival, leisure an alien concept.

According to Dud, "Roy" was the gentling of "Roister," his childhood nickname. "Seems like it won't but a day ago he was out raising Cain."

Bamba distrusted the affability.

At 78, Roy was unable to reclaim his physical independence after a bout with spinal meningitis.

"I damn!" Bamba'd heard Dud say. "I thought that doctor was saying you had 'smile a mighty Jesus.' I'm thinking, that don't sound so bad."

For someone who'd suffered "I-ticulitis," attended Cousin Mozelle's "remorial service," and referred to her neighbor's son Jeremy as "Jermeny," it sounded about right to Bamba.

Roy'd looked at Bamba when Dud's attention was elsewhere, pointed to, and cupped his ear.

Dud's beehive hair-do reminded her of the Bride of Frankenstein in an old movie, the primary difference—the marijuana residue she smelled in Dud's hair. Bamba finally understood Dud's red eyes and two bowls of Frosted Flakes every morning at Roy's bed-table.

You old cracker! A spliff?

Dud was 74 or 75, depending on her birth certificate or her mother's memory. "Come to it, I went with Mama."

Bamba took a deep breath, and rapped on the jamb of Roy's room. She required courtesy of herself, a means of preserving what was left of who she'd wanted to be.

She entered the room at Roy's invitation, only to freeze, as if someone had hand-checked her. Every surface of the room – his bed, desk and dresser, floor included, was covered with baseball cards. Her stomach plummeted.

"Mr. Seltry," she said, her voice quavery, "y'all making it hard on me. I got to clean up."

Glancing up from his wheelchair, Roy said, "I'm sorry, dear heart. I thought maybe I'd look through this mess again. See if I couldn't find something I ain't sure I had in the first place. Sounds like I believe in magic, don't it?"

Dear heart?

"Miss Bama," Dud said, her head shaking sympathy. "Miss Bama," she always repeated it, and never correctly. "Whyn't y'all just skip the cleaning today. We won't tell nobody, will we, Roy?"

"No, ma'am."

"What y'all looking for?" Bamba said, a tendril of curiosity holding her.

"A gen-u-ine 1959 Stan Musial," Roy said, his smile rose-blushed with embarrassment. "I was always partial to Stan the Man. You believe it's the onliest one in the set I can't lay my hands on? Least not for no seventy dollars, what they selling for in *good* condition, never mind mint."

Bamba thought, *who?*

"Ain't that something?" Dud said. "He got steak taste on baloney money. But seeins he be 79 come Saturday, we been looking anyhow."

Your birthday?

"June 6th," Roy said, as if reading her thought. "You know, 6-6. Musial was number 6."

If you say so.

Bamba quietly slipped from the room, doing her best not to step on the flock of cards.

It was break-time, and she plumped into a hall chair beside Seltry's room. She could still hear the Seltrys conversing – well, Dud talking and Roy grunting an occasional acknowledgment. He tended to root himself in his daily newspaper, while Dud crocheted and chatted. It struck Bamba that the thrum of Dud's voice was their music.

But now it was Roy talking. He was speaking about the renewal of The Civil Rights Act, noting that several Supreme Court Justices questioned its continued purpose.

Unable to stop herself, and risking exposure to one more racial slur, Bamba leaned closer.

"It helped us all grow up a bit, what it did," Roy said. "Taught us to think a little before we spoke. Some of us still learning, that right, Dud?"

Dud hummed a one-note tune.

§

Saturday washed in on rumpled rain clouds, the sky lavender at the margins, dove gray overhead. But within Roy Seltry, light overflowed his heart, spilling into every corner of his room.

Bamba listened just outside the door.

"Come look!" Roy said, wonder thickening his voice.

"What is it, brother? Oh, my Lord, it's the Mus-al card, ain't it? Who's it from?"

"Why it's from Nurse Charles! My Lord, what's she gone and done?"

A nurse? I wish.

"What's the card say, Roy?"

Seltry read it slowly, as if treasuring the sentiment as much as the Musial.

"Condition – *good*.

How's that for bologna money?

Happy birthday, Mr. Seltry."

"Well," Dud said, softly. "Well."

Bamba thought she heard sniffling, the scraped pull of a Kleenex, and the muted *honk* of a blown nose.

"I damn!" Dud's wintry voice livened with admonishment. "She be done gave you the Mus-al, and *you*—you done gave her nothing but grief, what with all them baseball cards falling out of ever'where."

Bamba looked at her cracked nails, and smiled.

Not true, Ms. Seltry. Not true.

JUST DESSERTS

Greg C. Miller

Elmeara sat up as a scratching noise reached her ears. *What could that be?* She leaned forward and peered through the taffy curtains. Two hunched forms lurked near the porch.

Rotten little vandals are ruining my beautiful sweet home! Her blood pressure peaked, and a swift rush of inspiration ran through her. Sadly, the feeling quickly drained away. The ax was dull, in the basement, and her knees weren't what they used to be. *Oh to be young!*

She heard them again, the uninvited shin kickers. From the sounds of it, they might be pulling the gutters off.

Blast it all! If she didn't stop them, the holy terrors would damage all her hard work. With a thud she dropped her carving knife and whetstone, slipped through the back door and around to the front yard. There they were—a boy and a girl, sitting on the stoop, gnawing like a pair of demented beavers.

The boy squatted in baggy, low-riding pants as black as his Metallica T-shirt and greasy hair. She wasn't sure what was more revolting, that his underwear leered at her from his droopy drawers, or that his arms and clothes glistened with chocolate stains. He was positively drooling on himself.

Elmeara rolled her eyes. *Bah! Not surprising, teenage boys do that naturally.*

The girl was marginally better, dressed in short shorts and a mid-riff baring shirt. Then she spied the Christmas tree collection bits and bobs that flashed and glittered from the girl's navel, ears, eyebrows, and lips.

Egads! The King of the trailer park must be missing a princess! A steady clicking noise came from the girl as she licked the candy cane down spouts.

Newt eyeballs! This one had a tongue piercing. She was going to take forever to prepare.

They looked up at her, eye's widening. *No doubt they are more embarrassed at being caught, than ashamed of the damage they're causing. But, as her mum used to say, "When life hands you a stray chicken, get out the gravy."*

So, with as much saccharine as she could muster, she asked, "What are you doing to my house?" *As if they don't know, but I might as well let them explain themselves. No need to appear too vindictive, yet.*

"I'm hungry," the girl whined. The slack-eyed boy stared while chewing with an open mouth. More chocolate dripped off his chin.

Elmeara shivered. *Disgusting!* "Why didn't you just ring the bell," she said, pointing toward the door, but blanched at the hole in her door frame. The teenage termites apparently ate that, too.

She struggled to keep her voice controlled. "Ahem, well, if you had bothered to ask, I would have given you something." *Seriously, you little pests! It takes real skill and time to bake a gingerbread two-by-four.*

"We're sorry," they chimed, giving her puppy dog eyes. *Nice try, you little manipulators, but I have jars of those in my basement.*

She resisted a grimace. *Phooey, they are baiting me, still I need to take the high road.* "What are two beautiful, scrumptious children doing alone, in the forest? Did you get lost?"

The girl answered with a flip of her long blond hair. "Like, our step-mother, totally frizzed out, when I asked for a ride to the mall. She told us to WALK! I couldn't believe it. It's like forever a mile away. So, I said, like you gots a minivan, sista, so why don't you just take me there already! But the hag went all Tom Cruise and pushed me out the door."

Ah yes, the old tired and overused "mean step-mom" routine. Elmeara shook her head. *Some animals eat their young or should at least consider it.* She studied at the boy, and he stared back with one eye, the other hidden behind a clump of long hair. "Have you been victimized for the same reason?"

"Huh," he said, dullness disappearing from his eyes. "Sort of— the step-witch pulled the plug on my X-box, and right in the middle of a wicked round of Grand Theft Auto; I'd just iced a cop and..."

"Poor thing," Elmeara interjected. *That unfortunate step-mother ought to be given a medal, or at least a shovel and a shaded backyard.*

"Well, my sweet things, why don't you come in and make yourself comfortable."

The boy perked up. "You got wifi?"

"No."

He stared sullenly at the ground, as another bit of railing dribbled down his chin.

"Oh no," the girl whined looking at the strange rectangular

device in her hand. "I've got no bars."

A smile crept across Elmeara's face. *Heh, heh. I do—in my basement.* The girl noticed her staring. *Uh oh, better play along.* "Little young to be hanging out in bars, aren't you?"

With a shake of her head, the girl rolled her eyes. "No, duh! I'm talking cell signal." She held out the box and waved it at her.

Like that is going to help you, hehe. "Sorry, no signal here. I receive a letter every now and then, but no phone calls."

"Wow, how prehistoric!" The girl said, incredulously.

Prehistoric, eh? I'll outlast you, dearie. "How quaint, my dear. I've got some tasty lemonade inside, we can talk more there."

"Okay. Come on, Hans, we're going to chill with granny in her crib." With a bang, she threw open the front door with such force a couple hard candies popped out of the door frame.

"Mmmmmppfhh," Hans drooled, dropping the masticated porch railing with a plop on the ground.

Elmeara darted for the door. *Phooey! Drooling Dudley beat me to it.* She hesitated before grabbing the glistening doorknob.

Ack! It would have been cleaner if he had licked the thing. So she dug into her robes, searching. *Let's see: ice pick, scalpel, bottle of ether, gauze, bone separator—nope, no salad tongs. Guess I'll risk it.* With a grimace, she grabbed the knob and rotated the candy coated mess enough to swing the door open, and followed her meals on heels to the kitchen.

By the time she caught up with her dumplings, they were already poking around the kitchen. The boy stuck his head into the refrigerator. "Wow, you don't eat much, do you?"

"Well, yes, I haven't had victims...um...made a trip to the store in quite a while."

The girl pawed at the giant meat cleaver on the butcher's block. "I take it you're not a vegan?"

Elmeara managed a weak grin. "No, not exactly."

The girl scrunched her face up in disgust. "I could never eat meat. It is so disgusting."

How disappointing. Vegans are always bony and tasteless—I'll save her for last.

The boy gave her a smirk. "Not me, I love a good steak, but not too raw. It can't be mooing."

Elmeara gave him a congratulatory grin. "Me too," she said,

resisting the urge to pinch his arm. "Pink and juicy for me."

"OMG!" The girl shrieked. Elmeara's heart skipped a beat. With concern, she followed where the girl pointed at an oven in the corner. The youngster exclaimed, "That is huge! You could cook a horse in there."

Not a horse, my little dumpling, believe me. They tend to run off before you can properly season them. "I like to cook large animals. They tend to last longer."

"Bleh," the girl said, with an exaggerated expression.

"Before we do anything else, could I have your names?" *Not that it mattered, but it sure made labeling leftovers easier.*

"My name is Gretel, and this is my brother Hans. What's your name?"

"Elmeara."

"That's odd. How about we call you Elly?"

How about I call you dinner? Stupid children. These two were definitely not grade A material. Let's see, is it the bitter ones are sweet, or the sweet ones bitter? Oh well, it didn't matter, that's what condiments are for, so on to business.

"How about some lemonade my sweeties?"

Hans perked up. "You got any Red Bull? I need to get jazzed."

That's all I need, my dinner full of caffeine. "No honey, but the lemonade is sweet. Will that do?"

He rolled his eyes and shook his head. "Oh, I suppose so."

She pushed a glass toward him. *That should make him drowsy. I just need to deal with the broccoli eater now.*

"What can I do for you, my dear?"

Gretel stared at the floor, hair shrouding her face. Slowly, she started swaying, her hands clenched and arms flaying.

Elmeara scratched her head. *Is the girl having a seizure?*

"YEAH! Put a ring on it, uh-huh, put a ring on it," the girl shrieked to the floor.

A ring? What is she talking about? Elmeara jumped back to avoid Gretel's dry-heave dance moves. Thin white cords trailed up the girl's sides and into her ears. That, combined with the glazed expression made her look as if she'd been freshly lobotomized.

Elmeara waved a hand in front of Gretel's face and yelled, "DO YOU WANT SOMETHING TO EAT?"

"Yeah, I'll have a seat," she answered, sashaying on a stool next to the butcher's block.

Elmeara's eyes widened. *At this rate, I won't be able to eat until after sundown, and that always gives me indigestion. Plus, children seldom taste better the second time around.*

She grabbed the girl by the shoulders and shoved her through the pantry door. "Search the top shelf, there should be a delicious can of peaches in there." THUMP. The lock clicked into place.

Gretel's voice drifted through the door. "Hey! There's no light in here!"

"There's a switch on the wall; keep looking for it." Turning around she found the boy, his head bopping and swaying, eyes glazed over. *Ah, the lemonade was working. Now to the oven.* She danced over to him. "Come, my dear, you must be tired. Time for a nap."

"Wwwwha…" he stammered, spittle dripping on his shirt front.

She grabbed his collar and pulled him toward the oven. With her other hand, she tugged open the heavy iron door.

"Uh oh," he said.

Elmeara tensed. *Had she made a mistake? Had the lemonade not taken effect?*

"I'm gonna…"

Suddenly he bent double and sprayed the butcher's block with predigested porch railing. Elmeara cringed. *Blasted child! It took me weeks to clean from my last meal.* His jerky movements threw her off balance, and she teetered too. His head thumped off the surface of the butcher's block and recoiled toward her face.

Oh no! Too late. Stars filled her eyes as his knobby noggin dented her forehead. She rocketed backwards as the world quickly faded to black. Somewhere in the distance, she heard the loud thump of the oven door slamming shut.

§

Hans woke up a few minutes later, only to find himself staring at the kitchen ceiling. As he sat up, pain pounded at his temples. "Oh man, I ain't felt like this since…uh…last weekend."

Thumps erupted from the pantry door. "Hey, let me out of here!"

He rolled his eyes and shambled to his feet. "Keep your panties on."

Pulling the door open, Gretel glowered at him, a glowing

iPhone in her hand. "Granny told me there was a light switch in here, but I couldn't find it."

"She probably forgot. You know how they always forget their teeth and pills."

"Yeah, whatever."

She attempted to brush past him. "Ewwww, you reek. What did you do?"

A quick sniff of his glass confirmed it. "I think granny gave me some loaded lemonade. You know how I can't hold my Jack."

"Why would she keep that in her fridge?"

"Maybe she's a booze hag, or she uses it for arthritis. You know, oldies can't walk anywhere without screaming in pain." His face lit up. "Oh man, I had a killer idea!"

"What?"

"You know how old people are always popping pain pills? I'll bet she's got some Vicodin or Percocet around here."

"Sweet!" Gretel's brow furrowed. "Wait, where is she? We don't want her catching us."

"Beats me. She probably fell asleep on the crapper."

Gretel looked at the mess on the butcher's block. "Then again, she probably went to find a mop, puke boy."

So, they searched, but not finding Granny, they quickly crushed and huffed her prescription meds, as well as emptying her liquor cabinet.

§

Elmeara woke up in complete darkness. *Where am I?* Her fingertips brushed against cool metal with raised ridges. She tried to stand, but bumped her head on the ceiling. Tracing the boundaries, she quickly tallied up the dimensions. *If this is a closet, why isn't there a door hand handle?*

§

Hans sat on the kitchen counter. "We should head back home before the step-witch sends the five-oh after us."

"Oh, she wouldn't do that."

"Sure, she would. She'd like nothing more than to put us in juvie."

Gretel nodded. "Okay, let's go. Strange, we didn't find granny."

"Yeah," Hans said, wiping pill dust off his upper lip. "I kinda feel bad about taking her stuff. Maybe we should do something nice for her."

Gretel pointed at the butcher block. "How about cleaning up that mess you made?"

"Nah, too much work," he said, yawning. His eyes drifted around the kitchen before settling on the oven. "I know what to do. Let's go!"

With a shrug, Gretel whipped out her iPhone. "Hey, I got GPS," she shouted, walking out the front door.

"Cool." Hans stepped in front of the oven and searched the display. "Thanks, granny," he said, punching the button marked "Auto-Clean."

§

Light erupted from the walls, quickly turning from brown to red. As it increased so did the heat. Realization came to Elmeara, like the sweat on her forehead.

Oh, how I hate children!

THE OAK TREE ON THE OLD POST ROAD

Frank Milligan

Soon's I walked into that doctor's office, I knew things was finally going to start going my way. That Dr. Samuels, he a fine handsome young man, remind you of Carey Hatcher's first born, young Winston. He so cute, trying to look all official and everything.

He says, "Mrs. Quarrels, do you understand the purpose of our session here today, why you're here?"

So, I answer him straight out and truthful just like the public defender say I should. I say, "Yes sir. I here cause the judge remaindered me here."

I know I be OK now. Was the way he smile at me clinched it. He have that kind of smile go all the way up into his eyes, just like young Winston. He asks me how old I am, tells me it says in his papers, "around seventy-nine." I tell him that's right. He says, "Well then, when will you be eighty?" I tell him probably never. Been around seventy-nine for a couple of years, probably going to be around seventy-nine for a couple more.

He says, trying hard to look doctorly, "We'll be taping our session, if you don't mind. For the record, you're here because the Chief Judge, Williamsburg, and James City County District Court, remanded you for psychiatric evaluation to determine if you're competent to stand trial for the murder of Mr. Rawley Semans, bulldozer operator."

Remembering what the lawyer told me, I says, "Yes sir, that's right. I kilt him all right, but like I been telling everybody, it was self-defense. He was going to kill my tree."

So, he ask me to tell him bout my tree and I start telling him, but then it hits me, maybe now things not going so well as they was, cause I start blatherin on bout my tree, and I see this look come in his eyes like he thinks maybe I am nuts, but I got to tell it to him, so I keep going.

I tell him about how that old oak was probably already a hundred years old the day I was born there in my Daddy's house out on the Old Post Road. And I tell him bout how when I was a little girl I'd stand there next to that tree after a rainfall and drink in the smell of that heavy, sweet black soil, and dig my toes in, and share a drink of God's goodness with that tree, knowing it would make me grow up big and strong just like it. And then I told him bout how I first met Henry there, the year of the big drought.

I was sitting in the swing Daddy'd hung from a wide low branch and I see this swirl of dust coming up the Old Post Road, long before I can see what's causing it, and don't it turn out to be Henry, tall and strong and handsome, just moved in with his aunt, and for all of his twelve years old, in all that heat, peddling his bike like the hounds of hell nipping at his heels.

Well, don't he take a notice of me sitting in that swing, and bring that bike to a skid and cause a cloud of dust make him look just like that fella in the magic show, appears out of a puff of smoke. He asks, can he push me, and I say yes, and before long there's Henry's initials next to mine inside a big heart carved into that old tree and you can still see'em today if you know where to look.

And I told that doctor how I'll never forget the night Henry asked me to be his wife under that same tree. It's a warm spring evening, and there's a full moon peeking its light through the leaves causing Henry's eyes to sparkle like they was full of thousands of little diamonds just like the one he's slipped on my finger. And when I tell him yes, all of a sudden a gust of wind comes and sweeps through those branches, and it sounds like the tree is sighing just for us, and we both laugh, and then Henry kisses me.

I guess I must have got to daydreaming for a minute there, and the doctor noticed it, cause he says, "Please continue, Mrs. Quarrels."

So, I tell him bout all the good years in that house, and the bad ones too, like that cold wintry day near the end of the war I was out there filling up the bird feeder, when up the Old Post Road, which was paved now, comes the Western Union truck, and I'm praying like I always did when I saw that truck on the Old Post Road, "Keep going. Please God, keep him going." But don't he stop there and give me the telegram, right under that old tree, and I sit down on one of its big old roots and read that telegram over and over like somehow if I keep doing it enough, my eyeballs passing over it will erase Henry's name off it.

That spring we had another drought, and the leaves come in all stunted and the branches had a bad case of droop. That was the saddest looking tree I ever seen. It took a very long time, but that's a strong tree with good roots, and little by little, season by season, it came back to its old self.

So, I told that doctor all about the holiday picnics, the christenings, and the family reunions we held in the shade of that old friend, and about how that tree's the first thing I see out my window when I wake up in the morning and the last thing I see at night when I go out to check on the animals.

He just taking it all in, and now I'm thinking, uh-oh, and I'm starting to get scared, cause the lawyer tell me they think I'm crazy there be no trial. Just put me away somewhere, and that the end of the story. I get a trial, at least I have a chance. And I know I must be doing something wrong, cause he been smiling at me through most of it but now he not smiling, and he says, "Mrs. Quarrels, tell me what happened that morning, out by the tree." So, I take a deep breath and tell him the whole sorry tale.

I tell him bout how the county want to condemn my land... condemn it, like they was God Almighty Hisself. They talking bout condemning my land, cause they want to widen the Old Post Road, let them new people get in and out of their big fancy houses, get them down to the highway, so they can get to work faster. And my tree smack in the middle of things, in the way of progress.

I tell him bout all the public hearings and the court hearings I got to go to cause I tell the county I don't want their money for my land and ain't no way they gonna cut down my tree, but the county say they gonna take it anyway. And I tell the doctor how surprised I am that them new people be on my side, least ways bout the tree, cause they don't want to see it come down either. They put it in the newspaper, and take up a collection, and hire a lawyer to save my tree.

Make a long story short, the judge go ahead and condemn my land, but get the county to agree they got to use "all possible means," his exact words, to save my tree. Now the county people be all sweetness and light cause hell, they got most of what they wanted anyway, and they tell me they gonna put a little bend in the road right there, take care of everything. So, I thinking things okay now, and I get a little bit of money from the county for the land they condemned, things looking pretty good.

But then I wake up that morning, and the hairs on the back of my neck standing up like a porkeypine. Something wrong. Ain't no birds, can't hear no animals. Nothing.

All of a sudden there's this god-awful roar, like the earth tearing itself apart, and I look out the window and down there by my tree there's this flat-bed truck on the Old Post Road with this giant bulldozer backing down a ramp off it. And there's these fellas out there with hard hats and big rolled-up plans and they looking at all those colored ribbons and little stakes the county put there. and I can tell from their arm motions and so on, they after my tree.

So, I throw on my housecoat and go running out there, but then I think, what if these fellas don't wanta listen to me, so I run back in the house and I call the lawyer and tell him to get over here, and I grab Henry's old hunting rifle, and I go on over to my tree. I talk to the boss-man, and he tells me he looked at the plans, and it just ain't gonna work with that little bend in the road, so the tree's gotta go.

I tell him all about the judge and what he said, and he tells me the judge gave those orders to the county, and he's the State Highway Department so he ain't bound by no agreement the county made. So, I ask him to wait till the lawyer come, we get this cleared up, but he tell me he can't wait. Got a schedule he gotta keep— time is money and all that. So, I tell him he gonna kill this tree, he gonna have to kill me first, and meantime this bulldozer fella sitting up there on top of that monster, watching us and laughing like this the funniest thing he seen in his life. And then he get this nasty look on his face, like he looking at everything ever troubled him in his lifetime, and he yell over the sound of his engine, "Get out the way old lady, or I gonna doze you into the ground along with this old tree." And I yell back I ain't going nowhere till the lawyer get here, but don't he slam that monster into gear and come right at me with it.

"What did you do?" the doctor said.

So, I answer straight-up what I done, just like the public defender told me to. "I shot the son of a bitch."

Well, I don't know what was so funny bout that, but it sure seemed to tickle that doctor. He says, "You shot him. Just that simple?"

"Simple? Wasn't nothing simple bout it. I'm shouting at him, 'Wait for the lawyer, wait for the lawyer,' but he ain't listening. He still coming, and I'm backing up, and all these things racing through my mind…all them years, and my Henry, and I can't bear the thought of that tree being killed. But still he don't stop.

"And he's looking right in my eyes and I'm looking back in his and I can see there's an evil in him, cause he laughing and carrying on like maybe he's hoping I'm not going back off, like maybe killing me and this old tree just be mighty fine to him. So, I close my eyes and squeeze the trigger, figuring it'll scare him off, and next thing I know the dozer stops so I'm saying, 'Thank you Lord for making him stop.'

"But something still ain't right.

"I look up there at him and he sitting there leaned back, his shoulders slumped, his hands hanging straight down past his seat, his chin resting on his chest, like he taking a nap or something, and I'm thinking, what that fool up to now? Then, it hits me. Lord a mercy, I must of shot him. The foreman fella, he climbs up there, and sure enough, that dozer man dead as dead can be. Got this dead-man switch they call it, shut the dozer off soons his hands come off the controls, and that's what saved me and my tree."

The doctor gets real serious again, asks me am I sorry for what I done? Again, I answer truthful. I tell him I'm awful sorry that man be dead, but awful glad the Lord seen fit to guide that bullet, save me and my tree.

The doctor tells me our session all done, and that he'll be seeing me at the trial, which was just what I wanted to hear, so I got out of there fast, fore he could ask me any more questions.

He telephoned the other day, asks could he come out just to see how was I doing, and he'd like to see the old oak for hisself. I tell him come on out any time, and we'll sit under my tree, and sip some lemonade, and I'll show him where them old initials are, and he says thanks, he'd like that very much.

The Oak Tree on the Old Post Road was originally published in Harboring Secrets: Tales and Reflections from The Chesapeake Bay Writers, 2013, an anthology of work celebrating the 20th Anniversary of the Chesapeake Bay Writers. I own the reprint rights.

VISIT TO A WRITERS GROUP

James W. Morrison

(The scene: A writers group meeting. William, a first-time visitor to the group, has been reading aloud for ten minutes from his manuscript. Others in the group have been reading along silently from paper copies William has provided.)

William. *(concluding his reading)*

Thinking, 'And if he is going all the way to
Jefferson, I will be riding within the hearing
of Lucas Burch before his seeing. He will
hear the wagon, but he wont know. So there
will be one within his hearing before his
seeing. And then he will see me and he will
be excited. And so there will be two within
his seeing before his remembering.'

(William lowers his manuscript) Well, I think I'll stop there.

Jack *(the group leader)*. Very nice reading, Bill.

William. I prefer William.

Jack. Why, certainly. As I started to say, William, I enjoyed your reading. It's not easy when you come to a writers group for the first time and read.

William. I've read aloud to others before.

Jack. OK, but our group is unique. Some say we're too critical, but our goal is to help people become better writers—assuming, of course, that they have talent.

William. That's very noble.

Jack. We try to be positive in our criticism, without sacrificing honesty.

William. Honesty is good.

Jack. All the members of our group have been writing for years, and we have lots of experience to share.

William. Have your members been successful with their writing?

Jack: Successful? Well, we're modest, but, yes, I'd say each of us has been successful—in his or her own way.

William. Success has many definitions.

Jack. Indeed it does. Well, perhaps we should open the floor to specific comments on William's story. Does anyone have comments?

Shelton. I certainly do. Now, William, you open your story with "Sitting beside the road, watching the wagon mount the hill toward her, Lena thinks…" Now, William, the beginning is very important. Just read any good book on writing. If you don't grab the reader with the first sentence, you'll lose him. Beginning with a participial phrase--"sitting beside the road"--is not good. Participial phrases are weak. And you begin with two participial phrases--"sitting" and "watching." The whole opening is weak and extremely passive--Lena is sitting, watching, thinking. You need action and hard-hitting verbs.

William. You mean that after people have bought the book or checked it out of the library they will stop reading after just a few words or sentences?

Shelton. Well, they might. More importantly, an agent might stop when he looks at your manuscript. Agents get so many submissions. They won't read past the first paragraph if it isn't a grabber.

William. Is that so? What a pity—to be so hard pressed for time.

Martha (*squirming in her chair*). William, just look at that first paragraph. I hardly know where to begin my comments. I want to ask the group to look at the text as I read it. (*All the other group members pick up their papers and study them. Martha reads aloud.*)

> SITTING beside the road, watching the wag-
> on mount the hill toward her, Lena thinks, 'I
> have come from Alabama: a fur piece. All the
> way from Alabama a-walking. A fur piece.'
> Thinking *although I have not been quite a
> month on the road I am already in Mississip-
> pi, further from home than I have ever been
> before. I am now further from Doane's Mill
> than I have been since I was twelve years old*

Harold. If 'a fur piece' is meant to be funny…

Martha. Harold! I was speaking. Now, Harold is right. 'A fur piece' is not funny. It demeans the character, and it's repeated twice!

Irma. I must say, William, this story needs a major editing. First you enclose Lena's thoughts in single quotation marks. One is supposed to use single quotation marks only within a quotation, but there is no quotation. Then you switch and put Lena's thoughts in italics. You need to be consistent.

William. Let me explain. I was…

Martha. Really, Irma, must you interrupt me, too? I was going to make the inconsistency point.

Harold. Jack, will you exercise some control here. Martha has already had more time to comment than all the rest of us combined.

Jack. OK, OK. Does anyone have specific comments on William's story?

Ruth. Yes, I do. Some may think this is nitpicking, but William, in your opening paragraph alone there are two or three incomplete sentences, there is an extra space before the italicized words, and …

Martha. And there is no period at the end of the last sentence.

Ruth. Damn it, Martha! I was going to say that!

Jack. All right, folks, let's cool down now. Well, William, we're out of time now, but you can surely see that we care passionately about writing.

William. Yes, I can certainly see that.

Jack. Tell us, do you have a title for your story?

William. "Light in August."

Jack. Well, I hope you'll come back. Maybe we can help you refine your story enough that it might, heh, heh, see the light of day. It was good to meet you, Mr….,uh, Mr…,uh, Mr….

William. The name's Faulkner—William Faulkner.

"VISIT TO A WRITERS GROUP" was published originally in *THE VIRGINIA WRITER*, the newsletter of the Virginia Writers Club (VWC), July-September 2007 edition, and later in *VOICES FROM SMITH MOUNTAIN LAKE,* an anthology of the Lake Writers, a sub-group of the VWC and literary arts arm of the Smith Mountain Arts Council, 2013.

REST IN PEACE

Becky Mushko

We buried Paw for the last time yesterday, and I reckon this time it's for keeps. My older brother Darrell preached the funeral just like he's always done, but this time he really meant it. Darrell wanted to be a preacher ever since he was a little bitty fellow.

"Farmin's too hard," he always allowed. "Preachin's a heap easier. You git to wear a nice suit and people respect you for it, and you don't even work up a sweat unless the Spirit really moves you. Folks even invite you to go home with 'em and take dinner afterward."

When he was a kid, Darrell practiced preachin' funerals a lot on our little sister Dulcie's doll-baby, but Dulcie got right tired of having to dig it up every time she wanted to play with it, so she fussed to Rhodie, our oldest sister, who always took up for Dulcie on account she's the littlest. After Rhodie beat him up to make him quit, Darrell moved up to road-kill. Since we're on a dead-end road without much traffic, this meant that funerals were few and far between and limited to what our hound, Jeb Stuart, drug in.

Usually what Jeb Stuart brought home won't even a full corpse, and he won't much in the mood to share it. More often than not, he'd dig it up again and gnaw on it no sooner than the funeral was over. Once we buried the same headless squirrel six times in a week and, after about the fourth time, it won't real pleasant. That was when all of us ganged up on Darrell and told him we won't havin' no more truck with funeralizin' varmints.

Darrell worried that he'd get out of practice, but Clete and me—who always had to be pallbearers—held our ground. Sometimes, just so's he wouldn't lose his touch, Darrell would slip into the church graveyard and preach funerals of people who'd already been buried for a while. One time somebody's next of kin heard what Darrell was doin' and complained to Rev. Sullins, and that put a stop to it.

For a while there, Darrell was gettin' real desperate. Then Paw got hisself dead drunk.

One day on our way home from school, we found Paw layin' alongside the road. At first we thought he was dead, but then we got a good whiff of him and knew what it was. We figured we'd better get him off'n the road before somebody come along and seen him and told Maw.

Paw won't that big a man, so us kids didn't have no trouble at all draggin' him in the woods. Once we got him there, we was afraid he'd take cold, it bein' October and the nights gettin' real chilly, so we covered him up with leaves. Doggone if Paw didn't look like a fresh covered grave, so Darrell whipped out that little testament he always carried in his pocket and commenced to preachin' away.

"Lead us not into temptation, but deliver us from evil," he started up. "This man was led into temptation, O Lord, and has done fell into evil ways."

Darrell went on like that for a right good spell. He must've preached a good half hour on resistin' temptation and the evils of strong drink and how the flesh was weak when it come to such things, and then come right back to resistin' temptation again. Dulcie was startin' to get a mite restless.

"When we gonna sing a hymn?" she whined. "I wanna sing!"

"Hush!" said Darrell. "I ain't even got to the prayer yet."

"Well, I wanna sing!" She pouted for a while and then started off into "Shall We Gather at the River," which made Darrell have to put his hand over her mouth until he finished. This spoiled the overall effect some, but Rhodie and Clete and me told him it was just fine anyway. If we hadn't, he would've just started over again. Darrell could be real headstrong like that.

We went on home afterwards, and Maw wondered why we were so late. None of us wanted to lie to her, and we certainly won't gonna tell her the truth.

While we hemmed and hawed, Dulcie piped up, "We had to stop 'cause I wanted to sing," and Maw allowed as how it was real sweet that we let Dulcie have her way.

She held dinner for a spell waitin' for Paw to get home. "I wonder what's takin' your Paw so long?" she said. "I thought sure he'd a'been home afore now."

"He's dead," Dulcie said.

"Ain't no such thing!" Maw said. "You ain't to tell lies like that, Dulcie. I've a good mind to—"

Before she could finish, Rhodie whisked up Dulcie and took her outside. I don't know what she said to her, but Dulcie was real quiet when they come back in. Finally we gave up waitin' and et.

Paw came in late at night after us kids was all in bed. Maw had waited up for him. I heard her light into him no sooner than he came through the door.

"Jes' look at you all covered in leaves and smellin' to high heaven!" she hollered. "I know what you been a'doin'—don't you think for a minute I don't. You been so dead drunk you done passed out in the woods! Don't you tell me you ain't! Now what if the kids seen you? Ain't you 'shamed?"

Paw knew well enough to admit what she said was the gospel truth and begged her to forgive him. He promised not to do it again, just like he always done. He told her won't no way us kids could've seen him. Darrell and Clete and me stuffed our fists in our mouths and played like we was asleep so we wouldn't laugh out loud.

We didn't tell nobody what we done, but about a month or two later the opportunity arose for us to bury Paw again. This time it was a Saturday. Maw and the girls had gone over to a quiltin' and wouldn't be back until supper.

Darrell, Clete, and me had stayed home to chop out all the cornstalks from the field in preparation for next year's plantin'. Well, no sooner than we'd about finished, but here come Paw staggering along the road. He keeled over right in the corner of the field nearest the house.

Darrell looked at me and Clete and picked up his hoe and commenced a'diggin'. Won't long before we had us a respectable lookin' shallow grave, so we rolled Paw right in. I run and fetched a dried cornstalk that was hollowed out. We put that in his mouth so's he could breathe and then scraped the dirt all over him. Darrell about outdid hisself a'preachin' that funeral so's we could get done before Maw got home.

We was settin' at the table waitin' when she and the girls come in. She asked if Paw had got back, but Clete got around tellin' a lie by sayin' he seen him in the yard earlier but didn't think Paw had come in the house.

"Well," said Maw as she set supper on the table, "I reckon he'll be back directly. Darrell, would you say the blessin', please?"

Darrell was more than happy to do it. Since his blessin's tended to run long, I opened my eyes and looked out the window to kindly relieve the boredom. There was Jeb Stuart a'diggin' Paw up! I kicked Clete under the table and motioned him to look. He did, and his eyes got just as wide. About that time, Darrell got to the "A-men," and we "A-mened" along with him. Maw and the girls were on the side of the table with their backs to the window, so they didn't have no idea what was happenin'.

When Ma got up, she saw what was goin' on. "Y'all boys been buryin' squirrels again?" she asked.

We shook our heads. "We ain't buried a squirrel for a long time," Clete said.

Jeb Stuart didn't finish diggin' Paw up until well after dark.

The third time we done it—buried Paw, that is—we caused so big a commotion that we vowed never again to do it. What happened was that Darrell had got real taken with different styles of preachin' and never missed a opportunity to watch a new preacher. In early summer, the foot-washin' Baptists was havin' a week-long revival down near the river, so naturally we all snuck out to watch on the first night. Maw wouldn't have cared for our goin', us bein' Methodists and all, but Darrell just had to see how they done things. We managed to find ourselves a space in an old brush arbor that they had used the year before, and we could pretty near see most of what there was to be seen.

One thing that impressed Darrell was how the preacher would suck in his breath every few words. While we walked home afterward, that first night of the revival, Darrell started practicing. "Brothers and sisters—uh," he said, "we are gathered here—uh— to praise—uh—His name! A-men, yes!—uh," and so on like that.

Clete and me tried to tell Darrell it sounded downright foolish, but Darrell said that it was probably how the big-time preachers did, and what did we know anyway. He also took to carrying a handkerchief so's he could whip it out and wipe his face ever' few minutes regardless of whether he was sweaty or not. He played like he was loosenin' his tie even though he didn't wear one. He was determined to get this big-time preacher thing down pat.

It won't long till Darrell decided he could practice better if he got right up in the place where the revival was being held and preached there, so we slipped out Saturday morning and went down by the river. Clete and me didn't much want to go, but Darrell needed us for the congregation. We left Rhodie and Dulcie at home, for there was no tellin' when Dulcie might say something that would cause us all to get whupped.

Anyhow, no one was around, so Darrell launched right into one of his best hellfire and damnation sermons with a lot of hollerin' and sweatin' and breath-suckin' and pretend tie-loosenin' ever so often. He was so good that Clete almost got Darrell to save him again right then and there—and Darrell would have—except we heard somebody comin' along the road.

We hid in the brush, and before long, here come Paw and Jeb Stuart. They'd been out coon-huntin' the night before and neither one had been back home yet. Paw had him a demijohn of likker, and he sat right down on the mourner's bench and drank it down. Then he passed out.

Well, it won't two or three hours before the revival people would be comin' and it takes Paw considerable longer than that to sleep off a drunk.

"What we gonna do with him?" said Clete. "We cain't leave him here."

"Lessus bury him again and have us a funeral!" said Darrell.

Darrell was still fired up with the spirit hisself, but at least it won't the kind of spirit that was Paw's undoin'.

Good thing the ground was real soft on the riverbank, and there was a shovel and some other tools tucked back behind one of the benches. Somebody must've kept them tools there in case they had to make repairs to the preacher's platform or somethin'.

Anyhow, we soon got a shallow grave dug and put Paw in it. Darrell got a reed and stuck it in Paw's mouth so's he could breathe. We covered him up with that red riverbank clay and patted it down just as nice as you please, and Darrell purely outdid himself in preachin' the funeral. I held Jeb Stuart so he wouldn't dig Paw up and ruin the funeral. Won't long till folks started arrivin', so we went into the brush and hid. I had a little piece of balin' twine in my pocket, so I tied Jeb Stuart to a tree.

On this Saturday evenin' service, that big-time preacher really pulled out all the stops. He was prayin' and hollerin' and moppin' sweat and suckin' breath to beat the band. The congregation was pretty loud theirselves, and they was A-menin' for all they was worth. I was a mite worried that Jeb Stuart would commence to howlin', but he must've been runnin' hard all night and was too tired to do much.

We had planned on Paw sleepin' through the revival, too, but I guess all the commotion sobered him up quicker than usual.

The preacher was hollerin' somethin' about resistin' the devil and his ways, and he was prayin' fast and furious for everyone to come forward and get saved. Not many people was takin' him up on it, so he tried a new trick.

"If the devil—uh—be in these parts—uh, I challenge him— uh—to show hisself—and pit—uh—hisself—uh—against the power—uh—of Al-uh-mighty Go-ud!" the preacher hollered. He loosened his tie like he was fixin' to do battle.

That was when Paw stood up and called Jeb Stuart. "Heah- heah-Heah!" he hollered. "Heah, Jeb, heah!"

Ever'body's eyes turned toward Paw. He looked right fearsome with all that red clay coatin' him, and he was walkin' none too steady. They must've thought he was the devil hisself. Ever'body screamed 'cept the preacher, and he just stood there with his eyes bugged out. I reckon he thought the devil had took him up on the challenge.

The screamin' must've woke up Jeb Stuart 'cause he howled one of those deep fearsome howls he uses when he's bayin' at a treed coon. Paw called him again, and Jeb Stuart broke loose from the balin' twine and went runnin' right smack through the middle of the crowd.

"The hounds of hell is loose!" I heard a fat lady holler right before she fainted.

I guess she was partly right for it seemed like all hell did break loose. Some people dropped to their knees and prayed, but most ran ever' which way. There was plenty of screamin'. This must've confused Paw, especially when the preacher yelled, "Get thee be- hind me, Satan!"

"Satan? Where?" said Paw, just before he run off. I reckon he thought he'd died and gone to hell. Him and Jeb Stuart went run- ning up the road, one baying and the other hollering. Darrell, Clete, and me figured it won't a good time to go home, so we might as well stay hid and see what happened next.

It took a while, but finally everybody either come to or settled down, except for a half dozen speakin' in tongues. The preacher more or less got everybody under control and decided to make the most of it by makin' another altar call, and danged if folks didn't near about push each other down rushin' forward. I bet more got saved that night than had been saved in the ten years previous.

At the baptizin' next day, they had to start early and didn't finish till well after dark from what I hear. Me and Clete and Darrell didn't go to it. We figured we'd seen enough and had best not push our luck.

Well, there was a big difference in Paw. From that day on, he never touched another drop of likker. He was a changed man. He wouldn't come right out and say why, but he allowed he seen things that no mortal man ought to look on and still be alive. Maw was just tickled at the change in him. He even started goin' to church with her ever' Sunday.

We heard talk around the town that a lot more folks had changed besides just Paw. Word was that the earth had opened up and the devil hisself walked out amidst fire and brimstone. There was some dispute as to whether the flames was red or blue, and a couple boys got into a fistfight over it. Some folks said the devil had pointed to certain ones and claimed them as his own before he run back to hell.

Darrell was right worried over these stories that was goin' around, and he wanted to confess what really happened. But Clete and me did some real fast talkin' to convince him not to.

"Look at the good it done," I said. "Paw is a changed man. Lots of folks give up their evil ways and found the Lord. Lessus not undo all those good works."

"That's so," Darrell finally allowed. "The Lord does work in mysterious ways."

We agreed then and there not to ever mention it again. And we didn't—not for the last twenty-five years. We grew up and went our separate ways and, sure enough, Darrell become a real preacher just like he intended. Maw was real proud when he said he'd preach the funeral after Paw had his fatal stroke.

But I'll tell you, I was doggone tempted to tell it yesterday when we buried Paw again.

JFK, DADDY AND ME

Deborah Prum

Late at night, in my small bedroom, by the soft yellow beam of my father's flashlight, I used a blue ballpoint pen to scratch out a story about a band of orphans who were stranded on a gorgeous tropical island—a place very different from New Britain, Connecticut, the grimy factory town where I lived.

Meanwhile, Ma and Daddy screamed at each other in the kitchen. They'd fought before. Plenty of times. But never this bad. For several weeks, my father had been coming home late from his dispatcher job at the police station.

"Where you been, Mick? Four hours past supper." Ma banged a pot.

"Ha! But I'm damn early for breakfast." Daddy slurred his words.

"You're dead drunk. What's that smell? You stink."

"I stink? This apartment stinks of garlic. Reeks." I heard Daddy fall onto the chrome kitchen chair, knocking it over. "Marrying into an Italian family—I'm cursed with a lifetime of garlic." My father seemed to be giggling.

"Beer and smoke." Ma paused. "And her cheap perfume. You can't fool me. I can smell that, too. A stench like disinfectant."

My father never drank that much, sometimes one beer on Friday night. After that, he'd sing some Irish tunes—crazy songs—one about a girl so skinny she slipped down the bathtub drain. Once, he sang that Elvis hound dog song and wound up howling which made even my grumpy mother laugh a little.

A scrape and a bump, maybe Ma picked up the chair then set it against the Formica table. I couldn't tell. I prayed that God would stop the fighting. I waited, hopeful for a quick answer. But no, if anything, my parents shouted louder, hurling violent words at each other.

Did other families fight like this? Not on *Leave it to Beaver* or *My Three Sons*. Every show, those people disagreed about something—but no screaming and yelling. And, by the end, always lots of smiles and jokey talk.

I tried to go back to writing my story. I forced myself to picture a starry night and happy orphans—children not tortured by fighting parents—those lucky kids, stirring a delicious stew over a warm campfire. Not one word came to mind. So, instead, in the margin of the paper, I sketched a picture of myself: curly black hair, green eyes behind blue-rimmed glasses. I tried to make my face look happy, but the mouth came out all wrong. More words. This time Ma saying that despite all his promises, all his big talk, they were getting nowhere, still stuck in a rat hole.

Rat hole? At least that's what I thought I'd heard. My mother tended to exaggerate. My room had a comfortable bed, red plaid café curtains, a wooden roll top desk, a narrow three-legged bureau, a pile of books forming the fourth leg. Not much, but not a rat hole either. My mother complained —to Nonnie, my grandmother and to all our friends—how we were going nowhere fast, how she'd had bigger ideas for her life. Once I overheard my parents talking about sending my mother to accounting school. My father said something like, "Angie, I'll work my way up in the department, you'll see. The minute I do, it's off to school for you."

I wished someone would show up at the apartment door—specifically an angel. An angel who behaved like a tooth fairy, someone who could wave a sparkly wand and undo the mess. Presto! My father would come home on time and sober, with an arm full of flowers for Ma. He'd give her a big smooch. And Ma, well, she'd smile, then hug him hard.

But no angel, no tooth fairy, no nobody. I buried my head under the pillow. Didn't matter. I could still hear them.

"You got a woman, don't you? Go stay with her." Ma's voice sounded raw. I couldn't stand it. I hit my head with the flashlight, little thunks, but hard enough to hurt. Somehow, that pain helped me get through the ache of listening to my parents shred each other.

"A woman? A woman!" Daddy's voice battered the air. He started laughing, laughing and sobbing at the same time. "Maybe I will leave. And I'm taking the money. I earned it. Every bloody dime."

My parents tried to put aside a little cash each month, hoping to buy a tract house in Hazardville, tiny and square, only two bedrooms but with a bit of grass out front. "Anywhere away from the tenements." Ma would say. Nonnie owned the building we lived in. Both Ma and Daddy wanted to get out from under her thumb. But every month, they had to dip into the savings—a flat tire on the Oldsmobile, new uniform pants for Daddy, fillings for my teeth.

More yelling. I couldn't make out the words. Why didn't God make them stop? Maybe I should pray to a saint. Was there a Patron Saint of Fighting Parents? I never paid attention in catechism. Then again, maybe God gave me these arguing parents to punish me for being such a bad Catholic.

A door slammed. Their bedroom door? Pounding. Ma screaming, "No....Mick...stop."

I jumped out of bed, throwing covers aside, rushing into the kitchen. I saw them, kneeling by the stove, struggling over the small metal box where they kept their money. Finally, my dad gave up and left.

The next two nights I kept watch for my father, staring out the window by my bed, hoping I'd see the light on at his workshop behind our tenement. Usually, after working a day shift, my father would gobble down dinner, then head down to the shop, repairing radios, toasters, lawn mowers, whatever the neighbors brought—although they'd been bringing less and less.

But my father never showed. No call. No nothing. Ma said she didn't care, good riddance to bad rubbish, but I heard her crying at night.

A dull ache filled my chest. Each morning, I considered skipping school, heading to the station downtown, seeing if I could talk to my father. I knew exactly which bus to take there. But Ma had never let me ride the bus on my own, saying eleven was a little too young for that.

Even if I did go, I wondered if my father would hate for me to barge in at his job. He never once had brought me inside the station. Maybe he felt ashamed that he only answered phones or maybe he wanted to protect me from all the sadness. I don't know.

I did consider calling him. Almost dialed him several times. I knew the emergency number, but I worried about my mother catching me. The phone sat dead center on the kitchen counter. I'd never get away with it.

Bone-tired and heartsick, I dragged myself through one last

day of school before the weekend. I had gym seventh period on Fridays and could play outside. Thank God for that, but to be honest, I was furious with God. I pictured him in the left-hand corner of the universe, standing with his back to me.

We kids bundled into our winter jackets and braced ourselves against a brisk November wind. As we filed out onto the schoolyard, Mr. Sweeney, the P.E. teacher, told us to line up for alley soccer. Each child sprinted toward a chalked-off section of the asphalt court. No one dared disobey him. He'd gotten injured in the Korean War and came back a hero. Unless the students misbehaved, Mr. Sweeney hardly paid attention to any of them, spending most of every gym class with a mint green transistor radio glued to his ear.

Right off, I got hold of the ball and started dribbling down the alley toward the goal. But a boy named Pete tripped me as I tried to make the shot. My bare knees skidded on the pavement. Worse yet, I missed the goal. Within seconds, Pete had kicked the ball clear toward the other side. Blood dripped down both my knees. I glared at Pete as I sat next to my teacher on the sidelines.

I checked the dial on Mr. Sweeney's watch. One-thirty. Nonnie and Ma would be looking at *As the World Turns*. My father once said Nonnie would probably come back from the dead every afternoon just to keep up with the story.

A few minutes later, just as a child made a goal, Mr. Sweeney yelled, "Holy Mother of God!" This made no sense. He never cared about who won the games. I saw him hold out the radio in front of him, looking at it as if it were dripping with poison. Then, covering his face, he put the radio back to his ear.

Mr. Sweeney kept shaking his head. At last, he said, "Everyone go inside. Our president has been shot."

The principal sent all us kids straight home. I arrived to an empty apartment. When I went upstairs to my grandmother's, I found half the people from our tenement squished into Nonnie's parlor watching Walter Cronkite. In our block, no one but Nonnie owned a television.

Sitting on the floor, I could barely see the screen, but I noticed that the newsman didn't have his jacket on. Strange. Mr. Cronkite always wore a suit jacket on television. He also kept taking his glasses off and repeating himself, about how there were three shots and maybe President Kennedy was dead, but maybe not.

Another reporter, one in Texas, was talking about a man who killed a cop. I didn't understand. Wasn't it the president who got shot?

Mrs. Domkowski, Mrs. Kaufmann, and Mrs. Perez all squeezed on the same sofa together which was something. Most days these women squabbled about parking spaces, garbage cans, noisy kids, you name it. None of them spoke English well, which also didn't help. Daddy said that those people stepped off the boat and right into Nonnie's apartment building. Of course, after that they headed to the factories to work. Nonnie's tenement was not far from Stanley Tool and Fafnir Bearing. Everybody was welcome at the factories: long hours, low pay and no English-speaking skills necessary.

Mrs. Perez ran her rosary beads through her fingers, one by one. Click, mumble, click, mumble. A cigarette dangled from Mr. Assaryan's mouth, the ashes fluttering down to the carpet. I wondered who was running his store on the corner and why Nonnie wasn't getting him an ashtray.

Then, just after 2:30, Mr. Cronkite announced that John F. Kennedy had died. Was he wiping tears from his eyes? I had never seen a newsman cry on TV.

The set stayed on all day and into the evening. Some people came and went, but most just stayed. Folks left food on the kitchen table—provolone cheese, salami, bread, olives, empanadas, chicken cutlets, stuffed cabbage, angel wings dusted with sugar. The neighbors picked at the food, but didn't eat as much as you'd have thought. All day Saturday went the same way, everyone staring at the sad scenes on the screen. When the Rutgers college boys sang a requiem with the Philadelphia orchestra playing behind them, even Mrs. Kaufmann cried. And that was something. She was a hard one. Never a smile or nice word. Ma said the woman survived a war camp and still had a number tattooed on her arm.

Every time the back door opened, I jumped up, hoping it'd be my father. But no Daddy and no word from or about him. I felt bad about John Kennedy—he was young, handsome and Catholic. A Catholic man in the presidency. Our whole church celebrated back on election night. Yes, I was sad about JFK, but I remember feeling guilty that I was way sadder about my father being gone.

On Sunday morning, no neighbors showed up. Each family went to their own church, not Mrs. Kaufmann, of course. The priest at my church read a statement from Pope Paul. The pope said he was profoundly saddened. I felt profoundly saddened, too, by every damn thing. I could have thrown a chair through a stained-glass window I felt so sad. I wondered if God felt sad too, or if he cared at all.

People wept and blew their noses and wept again. This reminded me of my Grandpa Padric's funeral, years ago. Oh, how I wished I could be sitting on that wooden pew, snuggled under my father's arm. But my father was nowhere to be seen. I knew it was a sin for him to miss Mass. That much I remembered from catechism. I wondered if God planned to send my father to hell.

Back home after church, my family ate our usual Sunday lunch—chicken soup with orzo, roasted chicken and potatoes, spaghetti and meatballs, always followed by a cake covered in whipped cream and soaked in rum. This day, though, we didn't gather at Nonnie's dark wooden table, and we didn't quite make it to dessert.

We sat in the parlor, balancing plates in our laps, staring at the television. At first the screen showed President Kennedy's coffin traveling down Pennsylvania Avenue. But then, the picture changed to Oswald being taken out of the Dallas jail. As Oswald came out into the parking area, in the lower right corner of the screen, I saw a man's back, then heard a shot. Lee Oswald gasped and fell to the side. Then the screen filled with scuffling bodies, pushing down the shooter.

I jumped, sending the plate of pasta to the floor. No one seemed to care about the mess. A stretcher carried Oswald away. Not much later, a newsman announced that Oswald was dead. The neighbors must have heard the news on their radios. Within minutes, Nonnie's parlor filled to overflowing.

The shooting at the police station terrified me. My father worked at a police station. Was he safe? I went downstairs to our apartment, to my room, and crawled under the covers. I pushed away my fears about my father and the police station. Instead, I tried to picture the day last summer when my father taught me how to ride a two-wheeler. He ran by my side for hours, red-faced and breathless, making jokes the whole time: *If Ireland sank into the sea, which county would never go down? Cork, of course.* Later, my father and I lay with our backs against the small grassy hillside behind the school, discovering fantastic stories in the clouds overhead.

No school that Monday. All morning we watched famous people arrive for the funeral—Prince Philip, General de Gaulle, Haile Selassie. As the television showed the Mass given at St. Matthew's Cathedral, I noticed my mother crossing herself with the parishioners on screen.

At the end of the Mass, as little Caroline left the church, the Cardinal leaned down and kissed her on the cheek. Big tears rolled down Nonnie's cheeks. I realized I'd never seen my grandmother cry.

As the pallbearers lifted the casket, John-John fidgeted at his mother's side. I pitied the child, losing his father so young. Jacqueline Kennedy whispered to him and took a paper from the boy's hand. Then, John-John saluted his father. The picture shook, maybe the cameraman was crying, too?

I could not hold back my own tears. I ran down the wooden porch steps and sat down on the cement stoop at the bottom. I knew I had to talk with my father, to see if he was all right, to try to make him come home. Would the buses be running today? I didn't know. If I wanted to take the bus, I'd have to go inside and steal the fare. Too big a risk. I decided to walk to the station. Ma and Nonnie wouldn't miss me. Not today as they watched the funeral.

So, I headed downtown, trudging into the bitter wind, getting lost once, asking directions twice, but finally arriving. I paused in front of the heavy wooden door, frightened to go in. Through the large side window, I could see my father sitting by a counter, talking on the phone. Would he be angry?

My father jumped up from his chair and scooped me into his arms, holding me close for a long time. I burrowed into his hug, never wanting to leave.

"Where have you been? Your mother just called. She's worried sick. Go ahead. Sit down now. I've got to let her know you're okay." He pointed to a wooden bench then dialed my mother.

My father turned his back to me, cradling the receiver, talking quietly into the phone. I couldn't hear the words, only the tone of the words, quiet reassuring murmurs. He spoke much longer than it would take to convey a simple message. I dared to hope.

After my father hung up, another cop came by. "Mick, go on.

Your shift is almost over anyway. I'll cover for you."

My father grabbed his hat, scarf, and jacket from a locker, and we left out the back door.

Once outside, my father asked, "Jemma, how in the world did you get here?"

"Walked." I lowered my head, bracing for a lecture.

Instead, my father grabbed my shoulders. "Good lord, girl. Five miles?"

"I had to see if you were all right."

My father pulled me into another hug. He shook a bit as he spoke. "All right. Yes, I'm all right. But sad and very ashamed."

The wind picked up. Daddy wrapped his scarf around my neck. "Buses aren't running. Let's get going. Your mother will be waiting."

I shook my head. "They're watching television. The funeral."

"Even still. I know she's anxious to see you. Let's try to get home before dark." We started down Main Street, going past one closed shop after another.

I looked up at my father. I hated to ask, but needed to know. "Do you have a girlfriend?"

"No, darling, of course not. Your mother is the only woman for me."

Did I believe him? Not quite. I knew that adults lied, parents even. "Where have you been staying?"

"I've been sleeping in an empty cell at the station. Not too comfortably."

I couldn't let it go. He still wasn't making sense. "But why have you been so late all those nights?"

"They cut back my time at the station. The chief's nephew— they gave the boy half my hours."

"That's not fair."

"Ah sweetheart, if life were fair, JFK wouldn't be dead now, would he?" My father kissed the top of my head. "So, I took a part-time job as a janitor at the high school. Cleaning toilets."

"The perfume. I heard Ma yelling about perfume."

My father gave a sad smile. "Yes, 'perfume like disinfectant' was actually Clorox."

I suppose I should have felt relief, but instead I was furious. Why did my parents have to be so dumb? "Why didn't you just tell her?"

"She didn't intend to marry a janitor. We've been hoping I'd get on the force, maybe make detective someday. Instead, I was pushing a mop. I couldn't face her or your grandmother, either."

"But why were you so drunk?" If my father had been my child, I'm sure I would have punished him for pure stupidity.

"Felt depressed. Guess I can't hold my liquor."

"I'll say." I didn't want to be disrespectful, but it was all I could do to hold my tongue.

We paused by a shop full of televisions. Even though the store was closed, several of the sets were on, replaying scenes of the funeral. We watched for a minute. Without sound, I especially noticed the faces, all sad, all in shock, all holding questions with no answers.

Finally, my father tugged at my sleeve. We continued in silence for a while. Then he said, "It may not look like it, but your mother and I, we're trying." He paused. "I'm not perfect, Jemma."

Not perfect? Not by a long shot. My *scream first, ask later* mother wasn't perfect, either. And Nonnie, God help anybody who crossed her. "I know. Nobody's perfect."

Come to think of it, for the first time, it hit me that maybe I wasn't perfect. I was no big expert on running the universe.

I squeezed my father's hand and said, "Well, I guess you're perfect enough."

The sun started to set. As we made our way, the cold November sky bled red and then purple into the horizon.

If I'd had the power to write my life like the stories I wrote by flashlight late at night, I would have gone ahead and given myself a happy ending, right there and then. But I didn't have that power and knew I never would. Instead, on that saddest of sad days when the whole world seemed to be weeping, I held my father's hand and walked slowly toward home.

WHAT HEIDI KNEW

K. P. Robbins

When I answered the phone, the voice on the other end said, "Woof," and hung up.

I got the message. Al was calling to tell me Heidi needed another walk. Ten minutes later, Al pulled into my driveway. Heidi squirmed and yelped in excitement as I climbed into the Jeep. She knew we were heading to her favorite place, the C&O canal path on the other side of the Potomac River from here in Harpers Ferry.

"How are you, Heidi?" I said, as I patted her large head. Her name conjured up pictures of blonde girls in pigtails, not this black dog in the backseat.

"She's raring to go today," Al said. It still amazed me how attached Al had become to this mutt he rescued from the local pound after his wife died from breast cancer two years ago. We'd been friends since college, but I'd never known him to own a dog until then. None of his family lived close by, and I guess he needed more companionship than neighbors like me could supply.

The dog walks gave us an excuse to get together at least twice a week, and I welcomed the break from my work-from-home office routine. We didn't have a set schedule, but tried to avoid weekends when families and bicyclists crowded the canal. On weekdays, we were often the only visitors.

Al crossed the Potomac into Maryland and turned right onto a narrow road that wound downhill to a parking lot paralleling the canal and river. "Ah, smell that fresh air," I said, as Al fastened the leash to Heidi's collar. Although it was early November, the weather had not yet turned cold. Gold and orange leaves crunched under our feet as we walked over a short wooden bridge to the canal trail.

The Potomac flowed before us on our right, and on our left, a deep, grassy ditch, the remnants of the famous canal. Heidi strained the leash, her nose leading the way. "Smell is that dog's number one sense," Al said. "We humans rely more on our eyes, or maybe our ears, but with Heidi, the nose knows."

I'd heard Al make that same comment many times before, but couldn't disagree. With her tail upright and wagging, Heidi plowed ahead, nose to the ground, stopping every now and then to sniff a particularly interesting weed. "She's got the all-black coat of a lab," I said, "but maybe there's some bloodhound in her, too."

Suddenly, Al began to cough, a deep heaving sound from deep in his chest. "Are you okay?" I asked.

"Yeah, yeah. Just a little tickle in my throat lately. Maybe it's allergies. Maybe I'm allergic to the dog."

But the dog looked terrified. She had crouched down and was staring up at us with alarm in her eyes. "What's wrong with Heidi?" I asked.

"Don't know," Al replied. "She does that sometimes if I cough. I think whoever owned her before abused her and must have had a smoker's cough. The same moron who would name a black dog Heidi. I thought about changing her name, but then I thought, what the heck, she doesn't know the difference."

I laughed. It was a gorgeous day. The sun cast a spotlight on the rushing rapids of the river and shone through nearly naked trees shed of their few remaining leaves. Geese in V-formation honked as they flew overhead, a few stragglers heading south for the coming winter. Heidi paid them no mind, as she continued to investigate the smells along the path.

Over the next few weeks, Al's cough got worse, as did Heidi's reaction. The coughing frightened her badly. She'd cringe, slink away, and occasionally whimper. Once, when we were sitting in Al's living room and his coughing began, she came right up to me, put her head on my knee, and let out a sigh, like she was urging me to do something. I told Al he needed to see a doctor, but he always came up with the same excuse: "Doc will just tell me to give up my cigars, and I don't want to." I didn't buy Al's reason, but in a way, I couldn't fault him for wanting to avoid the medical profession. I'd seen him suffer through his wife's debilitating decline after rounds of radiation and chemo.

In December, Al experienced a particularly violent coughing spell during our walk. Heidi lay down on the trail, lowered her head into the ground, and refused to budge. Her body shook. "You're scaring your dog," I told Al. "It's just the cold that's making me cough like this," he said, but I guess the dog's reaction got to him, because he finally made a doctor's appointment. His doctor ordered some blood work and a chest x-ray, and when the results came in, ordered more tests. Al had to go to the hospital for a needle biopsy of his lung, a procedure that scared him, and left him sore. Finally, his doctor told him he had to see a specialist and referred him to an oncologist in Washington, DC, sixty-five miles away.

I could tell Al was anxious about seeing the oncologist, so I volunteered to drive him to that appointment. On the ninety-minute trip through heavy traffic, we didn't talk about his cough. Instead, we stuck to our usual topics of conversation, the news, sports, and Heidi. Neither of us wanted to confront the obvious questions facing us.

I stayed in the waiting room while Al consulted with the doctor. Finally, he emerged, looking stunned. I knew he hadn't been given good news. He didn't say anything and neither did I until we were settled into my car. "Lung cancer. Stage four," he announced.

"Wow. I'm sorry, Al. What's next? What's the treatment plan?"

"Not sure. Maybe chemo. Maybe nothing. It's pretty far along, apparently."

I guess I was in denial, because I thought Al would get some kind of treatment and be around for a few more years of dog walks. But three weeks later, he ended up in the hospital, where he died within days.

Al's brother Paul travelled to West Virginia from Indiana to settle up his estate. I helped him clear out Al's belongings and find a real estate agent to put his house on the market.

"What do you want to do with the dog?" I asked. Heidi had been living with me since Al died. There was no one else to care for her.

"Keep her or give her back to the pound," Paul said. "I can't take her. My kids have allergies."

So, Heidi became my dog, an easy adjustment for both of us since we both missed Al. I soon learned why Al had become so attached to the animal. A loving companion, she rarely left my side. We still went on river walks a couple times a week, and I thought about Al and wondered if Heidi did, too. In the evening, she slept beside my chair as I read while the television droned in the background.

Then one night, a TV news story caught my attention. Researchers at some foundation in California discovered that dogs can detect disease in humans. The reporter said our breath emits minute particles of organic compounds that dogs, with their acute sense of smell, recognize. The research study proved that dogs can identify patients with many kinds of cancer—bladder cancer, breast cancer, or lung cancer like Al had—by the smell of their breath.

"You knew, Heidi, didn't you?" I said aloud.

She sat up and plopped her head on my knee. I scratched her behind the ears, the way she liked.

"You tried to tell us, and we didn't understand. But you knew."

A WELL-KEPT SECRET

Madelyn Rohrer

Jack Marshall had wanted to be a pilot in the British Royal Air Force ever since he was ten years old. That was when his father and mother took him to an Air Force base in Southern England to visit his uncle. That was when he fell in love with the planes—the De Havillands, Armstrongs, and floatplanes. He set his sights to be a pilot "someday" and now, fourteen years later, he stood proudly in a line of new pilots, all waiting to receive their wings.

Mindy, Jack's bride of just one year, was off to the side of the staging area with Jack's parents and dozens of other spectators. Her heart was almost bursting with love and pride as she had watched her husband march by in formation with his fellow graduates up to the ceremonial platform.

But while one part of her was excited and happy for Jack, another part of her was apprehensive. She knew Jack's parents felt the same way.

It was 1942. World War II was in its third year, and the 1940 and '41 bombings of Britain by the Nazis were still fresh in their minds. Even now when the air raid sirens sounded, they never knew if it was a test or a real bombing. They would hurry to the shelters, knowing that the Air Force pilots would be scrambling to their planes to protect Britain's airspace. Now Jack would be one of those pilots. But wartime or peace, Jack's dream had come true—he was an Air Force pilot.

It was June of 1943 when Jack's squadron received news that they were going to be relocated to another base—away from London; *closer* to Germany.

It was a difficult good-bye for Jack and Mindy. Mindy was expecting their first child, and they both knew that Jack would probably not be home when the baby was born. They shared a kiss, an embrace, and Jack was gone. He never saw the anxious tears that fell behind him.

The pilots received a longer-than-usual, in-depth briefing in London the morning of their departure, before packing up their gear and heading out to their new home base.

It was a time of true international camaraderie as Jack's squadron shared quarters, lunch tables, and fitness areas with the Canadian and American pilots who were also assigned to the same base. They traded stories of families back home, traditions and memories, and pulled out pictures.

"My baby hasn't been born yet," Jack told them good-naturedly, "and someday I'll have a stack of pictures in my wallet, too. But meanwhile, let me show you a picture of the most beautiful wife and mother-to-be in the whole world!" They all laughed...and agreed. The petite brunette with big brown eyes and captivating smile *was* beautiful!

§

Jack was an excellent pilot and quick in reacting to any threat in the air or on the ground, but on a regular nighttime bombing run over the Ruhr Region, Jack's Lancaster was shot down. He escaped from the burning plane, only to become an unwilling "guest" of the Third Reich—a prisoner of war.

He was young and muscular and, with his good military training to sustain him, weathered the interrogations and harsh treatment of the POW camp as well as any of his comrades. He followed his instructions from the London briefings on what to expect, what to do, and how to survive as a prisoner of war. He did as he was taught, especially taking careful note of everything and everyone around him. One of the most important instructions was...try to escape if at all possible and get back to England.

His chance for escape came four months into captivity. A fire in one of the buildings drew attention of the guards, and he was able to maneuver through the barbed wire and into the woods. He had a small compass, as all the pilots did, cleverly hidden inside one of the buttons on their uniforms.

Although Jack did not know where he was, he was sure he had to go northwest to get to the English Channel. He stayed in the woods by day, crossing fields and roads only at night. But it was winter. The wind was raw; nights were bone-chilling. Several times he heard the yelping of patrol dogs in the distance. Although physically exhausted and weak from hunger, sheer determination and the thought of home pushed him forward.

It was to no avail. Without a map, food, warm clothing, or transportation, it was more than his body could endure, and the dogs tracked him down.

Being *recaptured* by the enemy was brutal. Jack mentally steeled himself against pain after receiving the first of many deep gashes inflicted upon his face and arms, followed by the crushing of his collar bone and broken ribs from boots and the butts of Nazi rifles. The bumpy ride back to the POW camp on the cold metal floor of a truck did little to cool the heat of searing pain in his body. His 'home" was now a small, solitary concrete cell where he was pushed in and left alone to heal and survive as best he could.

Winter seemed like a bleak eternity. Cold and dampness permeated the concrete walls and floor of the building and never left until spring. His wounds and broken bones had healed, although a persistent achiness pervaded his chest and back.

Jack knew his body was weak and that he had lost a lot of weight. His rations consisted mostly of bread and water, sometimes cabbage or turnip soup, and once in a while a small piece of meat – *probably to satisfy the Geneva Convention,* he thought wryly. It was barely enough to live on, let alone maintain energy.

Spring brought with it a small resurgence of energy as he thought about England, Mindy, his baby, his parents. *Will I ever see any of them again,* he wondered? He could only hope, of course, but the one thing he did know was that he had to somehow keep his mind and body fit!

He walked around his cell, ran in place, did push-ups and any other exercises he could do in cramped quarters. He recited everything he could remember – people's names, events from history, lessons from school—anything at all to keep his focus on living and staying alert. He often looked up at the small, barred window at the top of his cell and wondered what was happening in the world beyond. *When will the war end? Can I survive until it does?*

Spring gave way to the heat of summer, and finally to the moderating temperatures of fall. Jack regretted not keeping track of the number of days since his capture. He only knew seasons by the change in temperatures and the partial tree he could see from his window. Its leaves were changing to brilliant autumn colors, which would have been beautiful if he were any place else on earth, but in the POW camp, it meant the imminent arrival of another cold winter—one he doubted he couldn't survive. A year and a half of confinement and meager rations had taken its toll; he was physically and emotionally tired.

"Hope," which was all he had left, was diminishing. He no longer felt an urge or even a need to exercise his mind or body as visions of freedom and reuniting with his family faded more each day. Any thoughts of escape gave way to the reality of simply trying to survive.

"Besides," he bitterly concluded, "where would I go even if I got out and had the energy to run?" Escape was no longer possible for Jack, and he knew it.

Fall was gradually turning into winter. Jack could feel the cold seeping into his concrete building once again. His bones ached from the dampness; his mind blurred from loneliness. He knew that unless the war ended soon, this was where he would die.

With physical and emotional strength drained, Jack found solace in the only strength he had left—prayer.

Prayer and church had always been a part of his family life, and he had prayed continually since arriving at the POW camp. He had prayed for strength to sustain his body and mind. He had prayed for his family back home, his country, his fellow prisoners, and for freedom. But tonight, he dealt only with reality as the remnant of spirit remaining within him reached out with a desperate plea.

"God, please help me! You know I cannot survive another winter here. If it is never meant for me to see England and my family again, then I beg you to not let me linger here any longer. Please take me to my Heavenly home. Please, God. Take me away from here!"

The light of day was fading outside his solitary window, as he slowly pulled together the small pile of straw that was his bed, wrapped the thin blanket around him which was all he had for warmth, and laid down on the straw. He didn't expect warmth or comfort. He didn't expect to sleep—only to rest until death took him to a better place. The only question was…how soon?

His mind gently pulled him away from the ugliness of where he was to his cozy apartment in London…to his beautiful Mindy. He thanked God for the two short years of happiness they had enjoyed together, even as busy as they were with him attending flight school and Mindy the university. He could see her sitting on the chesterfield in the parlor with a baby on her lap – *their* baby.

"Did we have a son or daughter, Mindy?" he asked her silently.

"I'm sorry to leave you. Take good care of our baby. I know you will."

He thought about his "growing up" years, his parents, and all they did to encourage him to learn and always be the best he could be. Early memories played through his mind like a movie film, his favorites being holidays at the ocean, family picnics, and Christmas. "I'm sorry to leave you, Mom and Dad, after all you have done for me. Please look after Mindy and your grandchild. I know you will."

Jack was so deep into enjoying beautiful memories that he scarcely noticed the strange sensation coming over him until it engulfed his body – *warmth!* He suddenly realized he was starting to feel warm!

He knew what that meant, or what he *hoped* it meant! He knew that cold sometimes turns to warmth just before a person dies. Maybe, *hopefully*, this was his night, the night he would leave this earthly prison forever and ascend to a beautiful place.

Thud!!

The floor of his cell shook, shattering his reverie and false sense of warmth! His eyes flew open. A guard was walking away, and sitting on the floor a few feet away from him was a box—a carton.

Jack bolted upright and stared at it. "Licensed Victuallers Prisoners Relief Fund" was stamped on the box. *Who are they? Why would they send a package to me,* he asked himself? He squinted at the box once again. It didn't have a name on it—just "Prisoner of War."

He stood up and looked around at his cell walls to make sure he wasn't hallucinating, then looked down again at the floor. The box was still there. It was real. He reached down and, with his cold, thin hands, pulled it open.

The first thing he saw right on top was a blanket – a dark colored blanket was all he could see in the fading light. He picked it up and felt it. Ah, yes! It was refreshingly familiar—warm and woolen like the ones back home. He wrapped it around his shoulders and almost immediately he could feel it starting to hold in his body heat. How comforting it felt on his back!

"Thank You, Lord!" was all Jack could say over and over again as he savored its warmth.

Daylight was disappearing from the high, barred window, and with the last slivers of light, Jack looked again into the carton of gifts. Sitting right on top was something he quickly recognized—a can of Spam! It was that American invention that Mindy had fixed for him a couple of times. He hadn't thought much of it then, especially when compared to his favorite gammon steak, but right now it was beautiful! He pried the can open and ate every bit of it.

It wasn't long before his stomach started to hurt, and he knew why. It was the same kind of hurt he experienced the few times he was given a small piece of meat to eat. It was protein, and his body was not used to protein or solid food any more. But Jack didn't care...it was a "good hurt." He laid down on his shallow bed of straw with his new blanket wrapped around him and, with a full stomach, slept better than he had for a long, long time.

Jack greeted the new day with an energy he hadn't felt for a long time. He was anxious to explore the rest of the treasures in his package. *Whoever these people are, they are wonderful,* he decided.

There was another can of Spam, more canned meat, sardines, raisins, beans, a toothbrush and toothpaste. He couldn't remember the last time he had been able to brush his teeth! There were thick woolen socks, gloves, a knitted hat and scarf, a deck of cards… and something on the bottom of the box that made his heart skip a beat!

A surge of electricity went through him as he stared into the box. It jolted a memory from that last briefing in London. They were told that IF any of them should become a prisoner of war, and IF they were to receive a box from a charitable agency, it MIGHT contain a game of Monopoly. And IF they were in an area where *escape was possible*, it would be a *special* game of Monopoly—one that could help them escape!

On the bottom of the box was a game of Monopoly!

As his trembling hands moved to unseal the package, frightening thoughts flooded his mind: *If escape is possible, do I want to attempt it? If I'm captured again, it will certainly mean death. But last night I wanted to die. Well, do I want to die, or don't I? How much longer can the war last? How long will this supply of food last? Can my body even survive another escape? Maybe it's just a regular game of Monopoly, and I won't have to think about it anymore.*

Jack's heart was pounding so hard that his chest hurt. He carefully unfolded the game board and looked for the "Free Parking" space. There it was – a small drop of red ink in the corner of the square! To anyone else it would be nothing more than an inconspicuous drop of red printer's ink, but to Jack it meant escape was possible!

He carefully and ever so gently slightly pried the two layers of the game board apart, and out spilled two slender rods of metal that screwed together to form a file.

His mind struggled to recall all of the significant game pieces, but as he gazed at the board and the array spread out before him, they started coming to life:

The Scotty dog. He took it apart, and yes, there was the compass. He had thrown his button compass away when the dogs tracked him down, as he had been told to do. Now he had another one.

The red hotel. He took the top off and pulled out a small, thin silk scarf – with a coded map of the area printed on it. To an untrained eye it was just a design, but to Jack it showed exactly where he was and places where he might find help. He carefully folded it back up and placed it between the layers of the game board.

What else? He tried to remember. Oh, yes—the money. He opened the sealed package of Monopoly money and there, in the middle of the pile, was *real* German and French currency.

Jack knew he had everything he needed to escape and get back to England…except strength and the right opportunity.

§

He rationed his food, eating just a little each day. Exercise became more important than ever before in his life. He exercised quietly in his cell by day while sweet thoughts of family and home filled his dreams at night. As his body grew stronger, so did hope. He prayed to God that if escape was His will, the path would be opened up before him. He waited.

An unexpected diversion in the camp provided the opportunity he needed to once again slip undetected through the barbed wire and into the woods. But this time was different. *This time* he knew where he was, where he needed to go, and how to get there.

One week before Christmas, and with the help of many hosts along the way, Jack arrived back at his home base in England. It was beautiful, and so was England…and so were the planes he fell in love with many years ago! His fellow pilots made sure he was delivered to the front door of his apartment on Christmas Eve.

It was the very best Christmas of Jack's entire life...home with Mindy, his toddler son, JJ – Jack Junior, and his parents!

§

Jack was free to talk about almost anything that had to do with his ordeal as a prisoner of war, with the exception of the special game of Monopoly. "Monopoly" was top secret—indefinitely, protected by the British Official Secrets Act. It would remain that way for the next 63 years of Jack's life, until 2007, when the special game of Monopoly was officially declassified by the British government.

He chose December 26, 2007—Boxing Day, to share the "extended" story of his escape from the POW camp with his family. (Boxing Day is a special day of thanks in England...a day when British families traditionally get together to show appreciation for their gifts by boxing up their used clothing and toys for delivery to needy families.)

Jack's family listened in amazement as his awesome story unfolded – the story of a time and place and escape that *could only be imagined* by his children, grandchildren, and great grandchildren.

"So if you should ever doubt whether God really hears your prayers," Jack concluded, "let me tell you for certain that He does. He hears you no matter where you are or how hopeless you think a situation is. After all, who else but God could have heard my prayer for freedom from a concrete prison somewhere in Germany and brought me home with a game of Monopoly!"

§

Notes:

In 2007, the "special" game of Monopoly was declassified by the British Secret Service, and the former prisoners of war who had been keeping the secret hidden for decades were finally at liberty to talk about how they really escaped.

The time had also come for the British government to publicly acknowledge and thank the Waddington Company. At the time of WWII, Waddington Ltd. was the only company in the U.K. licensed to make the British version of Monopoly. Equally important, it was also the only company in the U.K. that had mastered the art of printing on silk. Waddington created the very special silk scarf maps – those maps that made no noise when they were opened or closed; that didn't smudge or fall apart if they got wet; and could be wadded up and easily concealed in a boot or the corner of a pocket. During WWII, the Waddington Company had a secret room where just a few dedicated employees assembled the special sets of Monopoly. For the safety of the prisoners of war and the Waddington Company, secrecy was of utmost importance. No one other than the few employees who worked there knew the location of the secret room or its purpose. As the special games were created and sealed, the same group of employees personally delivered their precious stock to another group of equally dedicated people who made sure the special sets got into certain cartons and delivered to the correct prisoner of war camps. After the war, all remaining special Monopoly sets were quietly destroyed.

Of the 35,000 English, American, and Canadian POW's who escaped German prisoner of war camps during WWII, it is estimated that approximately 10,000 were aided by the special Monopoly games and silk maps.

§

Historical facts and information are from multiple internet sources, including:

Warhistoryonline.com

Armedforcesmuseum.com/monopoly

Snopes.com

Newser.com; January 15, 2014

Theatlantic.com; January 9, 2013

THE CENTERPIECE

Richard L. Rose

Colonel Charles Holburn hadn't been much of a hero, but he was the only one the town had, so Clysta Holburn-Follette was not about to have him again turned into a stack of dominoes like the hideous sculpture that Arne Coleman had made for the waterfront plaza. As she pierced a block of Oasis with the fresh-cut Forsythia stalks she had forced to flower for the monthly meeting of the Holburn Historical Society and Garden Club, she rehearsed aloud what she would tell the others about Millie Coleman before the woman arrived.

"We can count on Millie to be late. She always expects us to do her bidding, but how often has she ever arrived on time for one of our business meetings? She expects us to give our blessing to that ridiculous statue of Colonel Holburn, just because her husband received a grant from the Town Council to make that obscene statue of the Colonel. Now they're trying to get another grant for a statue in front of our library. Why, it's just a stick figure with blocks stuck here and there. It doesn't look like a human being. Even a child could have done better. We certainly don't need another one."

Clysta placed the Forsythia arrangement in a green vase on her dining room table. The table was still cluttered with name tents, pamphlets about the Society and stacks of petitions to select a different design for the statue□something that at least resembled a human being rather than a bent coat-hanger hunched over Lego blocks. Arlington had the Custis-Lee Mansion; Alexandria had Mount Vernon and the Washington Masonic Temple. Surely Holburn could have a real statue of her ancestor.

Clysta tried to calm down by turning on the radio, but the music was too loud and disturbing□a pounding beat that sounded like lids being slammed down onto jam jars flying by on a conveyor belt. Victor hadn't helped. He always had some reason to return to the office whenever it was her turn to host the meeting. She always did it by herself. None of the other officers ever turned up to help before the meetings. Everyone assumed that the hand-outs, refreshments, and speakers appeared by magic. If she hadn't been a Holburn on her mother's side, she would never have stayed a member. But it was her responsibility to see that the Colonel was properly remembered, even if her own husband wouldn't help.

She finished clearing the table, set out the appetizers, and went upstairs to dress. The members would begin arriving promptly at 4:30 p.m. They were mostly elderly ladies who didn't drive at night and expected the meetings to begin and end on time. Because Colonel Holburn was better remembered for his rose gardening than his war exploits, the meetings provided an opportunity for the gardeners in the group to swap stories and advice. But Clysta hoped to steer the conversation away from American Beauties and climbers to the petition drive for a real statue. Every officer was to bring a newcomer. Clysta had told them this explicitly. If they did so, there would be more than enough of them to blanket downtown Holburn with petitions. Of course, Millie would try to throw them off-track.

This was going to be one meeting that was not about Millie. As far as Clysta was concerned, Millie was spiteful and jealous of Clysta being a real Holburn. Several members had told her as much. Jacey Connors, the wife of a retired Air Force colonel, had told her in the grocery store that Millie Coleman seemed to resent how Clysta organized everything.

"Let her do it, then!" Clysta said.

If Millie wanted to do things her way, she was going to be very surprised at this meeting. Just in case Millie arrived early or had some idea that she was going to interrupt and take over the proceedings as usual, Clysta had set aside a special drink to quiet her down. Victor would never miss the medicine. He hardly even knew when he ran out of medicine, because it was Clysta who made the calls and picked up the prescriptions from Mr. Pinder at the drugstore. As a matter of fact, she had saved up fifty of Victor's little pills for this occasion, and Mr. Pinder hadn't said anything about it when she told him she'd lost a bottle. The whitefish *hors d'oeuvres* would provide a plausible reason for choking, she thought, and she doubted that any of the elderly club members could perform a Heimlich maneuver. It should be finished up early in the meeting, leaving plenty of time to discuss the petitions.

Guests began to arrive promptly at 4:30 p.m. They were surprised to receive agendas as they entered the house, but the older members knew that Clysta was in one of her organizing moods.

"Best to let her get on with it," whispered Clarisse Pettiford, a tiny octogenarian with quick, sparrow-like movements. She was the oldest member. She sat beside Jacey Connors, an auburn-haired, middle-aged woman only slightly larger than Clarisse.

Jacey nodded warily. "When I saw her yesterday in the store, she was worked up about having to do this meeting by herself. I almost reminded her that she had turned down the help volunteered at our last meeting but decided that she only needed to vent."

Clarisse nodded. "The sooner we get on with it, the better. Otherwise we shall have to watch what we say for the rest of the evening."

Clysta called the meeting to order while everyone was still on the appetizers. She made a few carefully chosen comments about Millie Johnston before delegating responsibilities for handing out petitions. Then Millie arrived.

Always fond of theatrical entries, Millie had brought two props to heighten the effect, a cake topped with orchids and an arrangement of roses. These immediately set the gardeners to talking about their leaf spot, bone meal, and latest tea hybrids. Not only was Millie's arrangement twice the size of Clysta's Forsythia centerpiece, it was bright, showy and imaginative. As Millie set her arrangement beside the other one for comparison, Clysta took the little cake into the kitchen and threw it into the trash compactor

Clysta poured a generous helping of Victor's tiny pills into Millie's tea and also made her a special plate of the whitefish appetizer. When she returned to the dining room, Millie was talking, as usual.

First, she had to tell them about all her winter pruning and how this was the best time of year for hawthorns and privets but one must wait until February for yews, "if one must prune the yews." She preferred to leave yews and Forsythia to grow naturally. She thought they were so much more beautiful outside than in the house. Of course, she concluded with a nod toward Clysta's centerpiece, "decorative greens were welcome at any time of year."

Just when Clysta thought that Millie had finished, another

discussion broke out between Millie, Jacey, and other newcomers about persistent weeds and the best times of year to attack them. No one at the table was paying any attention to the agenda. Some of the petitions had fluttered to the floor. Meanwhile, Millie talked incessantly, never touching her tea. Finally, it was too cold to drink.

Millie finished up the evening with a lecture on the proper herbicides to use around roses. She noted that one can never be too careful, as many were toxic even when absorbed through the skin.

"Of course, I've been known to use even Dalapon and Bensulide together full strength on persistent grasses. What we won't do to keep the weeds away from our babies!" She laughed, stood up, and thanked Clysta for "doing everything, as always."

Everyone stood with her, cheerily put on their coats, and headed for the door, leaving the petitions and dirty dishes on the table.

When they had all gone, Clysta poured Millie's tea down the drain, returned to the table, and seized the rose-arrangement. As she jammed it into the trash compactor, a small balloon at the base of the arrangement burst, puffing a nasty mist into her face.

Driving home, Millie Coleman planned her centerpiece for the next meeting of the Holburn Society. Not roses, she thought, but lemon leaves, statice, and simple daisy mums would suffice. So many babies could grow once you cleared out the weeds.

A RIGHT OF PASSAGE

C.A. Rowland

It wasn't that we were mean kids. Or even that we hated or disliked Derrick Wilder. He was different—just a bit slower at swinging the bat in softball, a bit more awkward in P.E. class, and he stammered when he spoke to any girl he liked. He was stocky and stood around five feet five, a bit shorter than all the other boys in his class, but you wouldn't guess he's different until he smiled, then you knew. A crooked little smile. Not that we were cool or anything, but everyone was cooler than Derrick.

In 1975, our junior year was drawing to a close. Anticipation of steamy days spent water skiing on the nearby lake, where a breeze dismissed the sweaty smell of being out under the beating sun for hours. Weekend jam sessions at Luckenbach and two-stepping with your favorite girl at Gruene's Hall electrified the air. We read-ied for the last party, chomping at the bit for our freedom and already feeling the glow of being a senior, our mouths watering at the thought of free food, while I our bodies already yearned at the thought of a possible kiss from that special girl.

Special privileges like lunch off campus and early dismissal on Fridays came to those soon to graduate in our small high school. Everyone had at least a learner's driving license, except Derrick. Some had old beat-up junkers like me, while other parents bought their kids shiny new cars. Wheels were golden, no matter what the age, and even in our one stop light town, no one missed out on draggin' Main St. from one end turnout to the other, honking their horns at friends.

The morning of the big party, Derrick's mom stopped by my house. We lived in a small subdivision, where all the one-story ranch houses mirrored each other from the red bricks on the outside and the narrow gardens graced with flowering plants that circled the perimeter to the small grassy front yards bordered on one side by a concrete driveway and another by the sidewalk. A quiet neighbor-hood where a backyard bar-b-que was a big event.

"Jeremy," she said. "I need you to watch over Derrick. He wants to go to the party by himself. The only way that works is if

I'm sure he has someone to bring him home safely. Will you do it?

My face must have fallen, since she added, "You've always been his friend. I'm so grateful to you."

How could you refuse with that kind of guilt trip in front of you? Plus, I knew my mom listened from the kitchen. I wasn't ever sure why Mrs. Wilder asked. Derrick was almost grown.

"Sure," I said. "We're going to be at the gym. Probably Bobby or Jim's house afterwards."

Bobby was blond, tall, lanky and played baseball—just like me. He wasn't a jock really, cuz only football counted, unless you're a girl, and then it's basketball. Jim was all legs and ran hurdles but wasn't fast enough to qualify for regionals. Still, exercise kept them both in shape and allowed them, and me, to hang out with the jocks when all the athletes got together. My other claim to fame was chess. My father had taught me. Semi-finals at state gave me a bit of respect but nothing compared to the adulation heaped on the quarterback and receivers.

"I know," Mrs. Wilder smiled. "I guess I'm one of those moms everyone laughs at. But you know Derrick doesn't have his license, and we like to make sure he's in good hands. He can't know I asked, okay? We'll say you are giving him a ride instead of me or his dad."

My daydreams of making out with Susanna were dwindling fast. How on earth would I get her alone if I chauffeured Derrick?

"What time are you leaving?" Mrs. Wilder asked.

"About 8 o'clock."

"I'll be sure he's here. Thanks again."

My responsibility for Derrick began the day he was born. He'd lived next door to me all his life. Best friends, our moms had been pregnant together. When Mrs. Wilder had problems with the birth, my mom had stayed by her side until she and Derrick left the hospital. She'd once told me how hard that time had been to have me, a perfect little boy, while her best friend's child struggled.

"Jeremy," my mom called as she walked into the front room. "I'm proud of you. I know this party is special. Do you have clean clothes?"

My ever-practical mom. "Yeah, I have some jeans and a shirt," I said knowing she wouldn't stop asking until I answered.

§

"Derrick's here," my mom yelled up the stairs.

I was still taming a few hairs. I gave up and pulled on my cotton blue shirt, buttoning it. I took the stairs two at a time.

"Hi, Jeremy," Derrick said.

"Hey. Ready?"

Derrick smiled. Why did I ever agree to this? All I could think of was Susanna's long blond hair, her curvy figure, and soft green eyes.

At the party, Willie Nelson and Waylon Jennings' songs mixed with the sounds of ZZ Top and other pop tunes. My entire class showed up to celebrate with cokes and pizza, and few forbidden drinks. Derrick followed me around a lot. Every time I talked to Susanna, he seemed to be there.

She and I danced to "Get Down Tonight," "Jive Talkin,'" and "Fame," but it was the slow dance to "Mandy" that made me want the song to go on forever.

Afterwards, she asked, "Can we go for a ride in your car?"

"Can I come too?" Derrick had magically appeared again. I would have stared him down, but I knew he wouldn't understand what I was trying to tell him. What I wouldn't give to have his mom picking him up right now. Inwardly, I groaned but I couldn't think of a good solution.

"I'd really like to, but I can't tonight," I said to her. "How about we go out tomorrow night? I promise we'll take a long ride on the back roads."

"Maybe," Susanna said. "Call me tomorrow."

I wanted to kick myself for not saying no to bringing Derrick with me.

§

"So, what now? It's only 11 o'clock," Bobby asked.

"I wanna see the Albino Bull," Derrick said.

I sighed. Derrick only spoke up strongly when it was something he truly wanted. He had been asking to go since he first heard of the bull. I'd always said no. Bobby and Jim looked at each other, then turned to me.

"Why not? It's late enough. Old Man Thompson will be asleep. It's a good night for a visit," Bobby said with a smile.

"Oh, yes. I really, really want to go," Derrick said.

I'm not sure if it was because I didn't get to spend more time with Susanna, or I just figured Derrick could handle it, but I said, "Okay."

Everyone piled into Bobby's Chevrolet Malibu. Beat-up and second hand, the car took the hill country back road curves like one of the hot rods at the local track. Dust flooded the air, and we all stifled our coughs as if it didn't affect us.

Earth, Wind and Fire radiated from the speakers. With the windows rolled down, a warm May air laced with a whiff of manure aftershave swept through as we flew along the road to Old Man Thompson's land. Bobby stopped the car by a field of low grasses, weeds, and boulders. The area was deserted.

We climbed out. A clear sky with a full moon and a raft of stars greeted us.

"So, where's the Albino Bull?" Derrick asked. He enunciated every word. He was nervous.

"See the house on the hill?" Jim asked, pointing north.

Derrick nodded.

"Halfway in between is the bull. The only way to get there is to climb over the barbed wire fence and head up that way. You'll find it," Jim said.

"What if the bull charges? Can't we get closer?" Derrick asked.

"Nope. Now that you're here, you have to go. See the mass of white in the middle? That's where you'll find the bull," Bobby said.

Derrick looked uncertain. It was scary, but that was part of the thrill.

"Oh, and you have to be quiet, cuz if Old Man Thompson wakes up, he shoots at trespassers," Jim said.

"Wha... I don't know that I wanna do this," Derrick said.

I shook my head. "He doesn't have to do it if he doesn't want to," I said. I was regretting not saying no earlier.

"That's fine, but everyone knows we were coming out here. If you chicken out, they're all gonna know," Jim said.

We weren't bad kids. It was just somethings you do or don't do – and you have to accept whatever comes from it. I'd had my turn and a pair of ripped blue jeans to show for it.

Derrick hesitated. Jim and Bobby walked back to the car and reached into the cooler in the back seat. They each popped the top on their cans and lazed against the car.

"Up to you," Bobby said.

"I'll go," Derrick said.

"Good. Hop on over the fence and head out. Careful for rabbit holes and snakes out there," Jim said laughing.

"Don't listen to him," I said. "You'll be fine. Go straight out to the white mass and then come right back. The barbed wire fence is the worst part."

Hopefully, he was listening to me.

Derrick walked to the fence, placed his hands on the top wire and began to climb over. His pant leg caught on the top, but he freed his blue jeans without falling. Derrick disappeared into the night. Part of the fun was figuring out the Albino Bull was just a large white rock formation in the shape of an animal. Jim and Bobby gave him about five minutes and then headed to the trunk of the car.

"Maybe we shouldn't do this," I said.

"Nah, we have to. If it was me, and I found out there was more, I'd be mad," Jim said.

"You worry too much," Bobby said.

The boys reached in the trunk and pulled out two metal garbage can lids. They beat on these with metal pipes to make noise. Bobby reached in and started honking the horn. Lights flickered on in the house on the hill.

The front door opened. A figure stepped out, his rifle illuminated.

"Get off my land. You're trespassing," Old Man Thompson roared. I was always amazed how far his voice carried in the night.

He lifted his gun and fired a warning shot.

"Get off my land, now. And don't come back. And you down by the road – get outta here now."

Jim and Bobby laughed. We were too far for Old Man Thompson to reach us.

My eyes strained in the darkness for Derrick.

"I'm leaving," he screamed.

Sounds of someone running through the brush reached my ears.

"AHHHHH," Derrick screamed. We heard a thump like something fell.

A weaker, "Help me" followed. Sounds of what were whimpers or cries drifted to us.

"Damn. We never should've brought him," Jim said. "Now someone's gotta go get him."

"I'm not doing it. He's not my responsibility," Bobby said. "Besides if Old Man Thompson gets my license number, my dad will take away my car."

I stared at Jim. He shrugged his shoulders.

"Help me…Please?"

On the hill, the figure moved across the front porch.

"Crap, he's going for his truck. We've gotta get outta here," Bobby said. "Derrick will be all right. The farmer will help him."

Jim crawled into the back seat while Bobby jumped into the driver's seat. I sat in the front seat. Bobby started down the road.

"Stop," I said.

"No," Bobby said.

"Dammit, stop. I can't leave him," I said.

Bobby looked over at me and hit the brakes. "I'm not coming back for you. And you can't tell anyone we were here. You got it?"

I nodded. I opened the door and stepped back on the road.

Bobby gunned the motor and threw up dust and dirt. I coughed and waved it away. I ran to the fence and climbed over.

"Derrick, I'm coming," I yelled. "Holler out so I can find you."

I stopped and listened.

"I'm here, over here."

I headed to the spot and found Derrick lying on the ground.

"How bad are you hurt" I asked.

"My leg. I fell. I think I stepped in a hole."

"Okay. I'm gonna help you up. We're gonna get you to the road and then we'll find a ride."

"Where're the others?"

"They had to leave. Now listen. This is important. You can't tell anyone who was here, okay?"

"Okay. It's our secret," Derrick said

"Can you walk if you lean on me?"

"I think so."

Derrick and I hobbled to the road. He whimpered and cried out a few times. His ankle was at best twisted, and, at worst, his leg was broken. Whatever it was, we had to get to the road so I could find help. He stumbled a few times, and I did my best to keep him upright with no pressure on the bad leg.

As we approached the fence, lights flashed in our eyes. Old Man Thompson and his truck sat facing us. He'd turned on the headlights. We shielded our eyes.

"How bad are you hurt, son?"

I felt Derrick tense and begin to shake. We had all heard the rumors about Old Man Thompson's temper, not to mention the stories of how he'd killed at least one man. I wasn't sure if Derrick was shaking from pain or fear. But at least he had an excuse.

"It's my leg, sir," Derrick said as he sniffled.

I felt Old Man Thompson's stare as he sized up the situation.

"Well, it's gonna hurt gettin' you over the fence, but I reckon you already know that."

Derrick nodded. I left out the breath I had been holding.

I helped lift Derrick, trying not to lose my grip on his sweaty arms and back. Old Man Thompson reached over and hauled him up like he must have done for a hundred calves—across in a quick movement that was likely the most humane way to handle him.

"Ahhhh…, Derrick cried.

I winced, but there was nothing I could do to ease his pain.

They moved to the truck while I climbed over the fence. Old Man Thompson lowered the tail gate and Derrick slid his way back into the bed of the truck, breathing hard. I followed him.

Old Man Thompson ignored me as I whispered, "Sorry about all this." The gate slammed shut, and minutes later we were on our way. Derrick leaned against my shoulder and sobbed off and on as we headed to the hospital twenty miles away.

§

The white walls and antiseptic smells seemed claustrophobic to me. I sat in a chair across from Old Man Thompson and got my first good look of him. He sat with his back against the chair, the blue jean clad legs strewn out in front of him, and his straw hat pulled down low. Wrinkles lined his leathery tanned face. Each time someone would walk by, he'd raise his right hand to the brow of his hat. Must have been his way of acknowledging them without saying anything. He hadn't said a word to me since we'd arrived.

All I wanted was to go home and crawl in bed. And for Derrick to be okay. When the door opened, my parents entered. Right behind them, Derrick's parents rushed in. The nurse rescued me by asking for information about Derrick. His mom and dad followed her behind her station. My mom stared at me with sad eyes.

"What the hell were you thinking?" my dad asked.

I had no answer. I lowered my head, staring at the floor. We waited.

Derrick's dad emerged from the back room. "He's going to be fine. His ankle's broken, and the doctor is casting his ankle now."

He paused. "But what I don't understand is what the two of you were doing out there."

I sucked in my breath. "It's a dumb thing. Everyone does it. The Albino Bull."

Mr. Wilder's eyes widened. He turned to the farmer. "I hear you're the one that brought my boy in."

"Yes sir, I did."

"I can't thank you enough," Mr. Wilder said offering his hand to Old Man Thompson.

Turning back to me, he said, "But how did you get there? Where's your car?"

"At the gym."

"So, who else was there?"

I remained silent.

"Jeremy, we've known you a long time, and you've always been good to Derrick. Tell me who else was there."

"No one. Just me and Derrick," I said.

My dad spoke. "Tell us now, Jeremy, or your car will sit in the garage until hell freezes over."

I took a deep breath. My shoulders sagged. Derrick was going to be all right. So was I.

"I'm sorry Derrick was hurt, and I'm real glad he's gonna be okay. But I can't tell you."

Mr. Wilder and my dad stared at me.

Behind them, I watched Old Man Thompson straighten up from his chair. He raised his head and looked right at me. My eyes widened as he raised two fingers to touch his hat's brow before he moved to the door.

A Right of Passage originally published in The Virginia Writers Club 2014 Virtual Anthology, 2014.

NUN RUN

Elaine Ruggieri

My Aunt Carmen liked bars. I found out when she asked if I'd go with her to drive two nuns to a convent near Philadelphia. Her kids were in school, and I was on college break. I hesitated. Nuns!

"Won't take long. We'll drop them off, and then we'll go to a nice bar I know," she said. Carmen's knowing a Philadelphia bar sounded as strange to me as transporting nuns.

Will I have to pray, I wondered, thinking of the rosary, bead by bead? Nuns and men with round white collars intimidated me. I didn't go to Catholic school, but I still feared the parish priests and the nuns, especially the good sisters of St. Joseph. They drilled the Catechism into us public school kids during our required, after-school classes two days a week, and they taught us more lessons after mass on Sunday. Sister Ann Marie would often ask why I didn't go to Catholic school and didn't I want to be a nun like her? How does an eight-year-old tomboy honestly answer? My mother doesn't want us hit with a ruler, and I like playing baseball with the boys?

I hadn't talked to a sister of the cloth since my confirmation ceremony, another nun-dreading event when Reverend Mother clicked her cricket to make us genuflect in unison. We had to impress the bishop on cue and answer Catechism questions as His Excellency walked among us. We trembled in our pews, suppressing acid reflux, and praying "Spare me, Lord, and I'll never lie again." The man in the miter came close but interrogated the kid next to me. That marked the end of my instruction classes. Once confirmed, I forgot all about Catechism and Sister Ann Marie.

My aunt Carmen didn't go to church either except for family ceremonies like weddings and funerals, but she sent her kids to the parochial school with bursting collection envelopes, so I guess she was pardoned. Carmen was also my Godmother, sworn to look after my Catholic upbringing. I couldn't blame my religious lapse on her neglect of duties, or, worse, expose hers to the church.

"Okay, I'll go with you," I answered without enthusiasm. "But where do I have to sit?" I was dreading the backseat next to some pinch-faced nun who would stare at my too-casual clothes, my painted fingernails, and orange lipstick.

Carmen laughed and told me "they" always sit in the back and are usually silent. "If they had asked me earlier, I could have gotten us tickets to see the Phils game."

Carmen was a big baseball fan and followed the Philadelphia and New York teams of the early 1950s—the Athletics, Phillies, Yankees, Dodgers and Giants. During the season, one of these teams was usually on her black-and-white TV. As she watched, she smoked Camels and ate Baby Ruths.

"Instead we'll stop at Guido's Bar. The best Philly steaks and pizza in the city! Not to mention the Manhattans. And, the Phillies might be on television. Be ready around one. Can't be late."

She sensed my uneasiness. "Take a book and say you have to read it for college. They'll leave you alone." Good advice, but the book I had to finish was *Madame Bovary*. Convent drop out, French adulterer, defective mother, Church scofflaw. Suppose they asked what I was studying. I couldn't lie. I promised the Lord. However, I could honestly say it was assigned reading and not my personal choice.

"Relax," said Carmen. "They read the Bible, don't they? Where do you think all that adultery stuff started?"

"Can we talk? To each other, I mean. Just you and me?"

"No vows of silence, but they'll be listening, honey. Better you read, I drive, and they pray."

I was dreading their questions. Did I go to church every Sunday? Did I go to confession? Are you a member of the Newman Club? "Yes" to only the last one, but they wouldn't like why. I joined the Newman Club, because that's where so many, good-looking Penn State football players went on Thursday nights.

"What's your favorite at Guido's?" I asked. The thought of a good Philly cheese steak sandwich briefly calmed my anxiety.

"All delicious, and the Manhattans are the best," said Carmen. "Guido's is the fun part of the trip. You'll see." She looked at me. "Relax, Nina. And, be grateful for all the blessings we'll get from the holy sisters. Can't hurt."

Carmen was my father's sister. He never went to church much

either, often disparaged priests, but contributed money for special collections. I overheard him say once to Carmen, "Sure, I don't go to communion. Who knows where that priest's hand's been?" My mother, a faithful, sinless Catholic, didn't actually lie when the parish priest paid a yearly visit and asked when my father last received Holy Communion, but she'd shake her head to mean "who knows, or, yes, he's going straight to Hell, Father." My brother, like most young men his age, hardly ever talked about religion and went to mass only by habit.

Carmen was prompt. We parked before the gray stone convent beside the gray stone church beside the gray stone school. A fortress! As a kid, I wondered what the nuns did in there. I would get as far as the front door, delivering an envelope with cash or a cake for a bake sale, and happy to be dismissed with "We'll thank your mother in our prayers. God bless her." I'd turn and run home.

We walked to the front door that immediately opened, and, holy Hell! There was my old instructor, Sister Ann Marie, showing a few wrinkles, made deeper by her wimple, with a nun I didn't recognize. Carmen introduced me. Sister Ann Marie nodded, fake-smiled, and introduced the Reverend Mother as she eyed me. I pinched my lips to hide the orange glow.

"I remember you, Nina. You and your brother came for Catechism. I suppose you're in college now?"

"Yes, Sister. Penn State. My brother, too." She looked as if she could still flatten a student with one swing of a ruler. I never saw her do it, but I heard the tales. "Let me carry your bag, Sister." She handed me hers and Reverend Mother's, identical valises in black leather with crosses embossed on the sides. They didn't weigh much. The nuns didn't own much.

"How long will you be staying?" asked Carmen.

"Just overnight, Mrs. Pinto. We have a ride back with Father Dolan. Bless you for helping us today."

"No trouble, Reverend Mother, happy to do it. And, I get to spend some time with my favorite niece." I knew all five of her nieces were her favorite, but I appreciated the compliment with Sister Ann Marie in earshot. I smiled at Aunt Carmen's support.

They settled in the back, valises on the floor, and we drove off. Carmen's husband always had the newest car in the family, usually a Plymouth. It was a treat to ride in luxury and sit on shiny seats.

Our 1947 Chevy had dents, rusted fenders, bald tires, and frayed upholstery.

The Reverend Mother noticed. "This is such a lovely car, Mrs. Pinto!"

"Yes, so comfortable," said Sister Ann Marie. Then, she asked, "Do you like the book, Nina?" Carmen shot me a glance.

Turning slowly toward the back, I said, "Just something I have to finish. Assigned reading. I'm not very far." I knew that didn't answer her question and feared she would persist.

"It's *Madame Bovary*, isn't it? I saw it when I got in." Why didn't I cover it up? Carmen was smiling like the Cheshire cat.

"Yes, Sister." I said and turned toward the front, hoping that would end it.

"I had to read it, too. Long time ago. Emma is a woman who does bad things and then pays for her sins." She didn't have to add, "And let that be a lesson to you, young lady."

I wanted to say I just couldn't *wait* for Emma to do "bad" things, but I turned a page instead and feigned interest in Emma's boredom with country living in 19th century France.

"Speaking of reading, we have some to do, don't we, Sister?" Reverend Mother said as she pulled a notebook out of her valise. "Unfortunately, this is not a pleasure trip."

"Yes, Reverend Mother," said Sister Ann Marie in a deferential tone. She quickly retrieved her notebook and opened it.

Carmen, looking straight ahead, gave me a quick thumbs-up down by her knees.

For the rest of the hour-long drive, we were silent except when Carmen asked if anyone wanted a mint. There were no takers, but Reverend Mother said, "We don't want to spoil our appetites. The sisters at Villanova have prepared refreshments just for us. They insisted they treat you."

My heart sank. No Guido's? I looked at Carmen. "That's so nice of them, Reverend Mother, but I really should turn right around and head home to my husband and kids," Carmen said.

"Oh, they would be so disappointed, Mrs. Pinto. We won't keep you long, and they are so looking forward to your visit. We don't entertain often."

"Well, I guess we can. Just not for long."

I wondered what the refreshments would be. Tea or coffee

would be nice. I was getting drowsy.

"Park right in front, Mrs. Pinto," said Reverend Mother. "It's usually saved for visiting priests, but you are special today."

Carmen stopped the car, and we both hopped out to open the doors for our backseat passengers. I took their bags again, and we walked toward the front door of the gray stone Villanova convent. Before we could knock, two nuns opened the door and greeted us, thanking the Lord for our safe journey. Reverend Mother handled the introductions. She said Carmen was a dedicated, loyal member of their parish, and I was her niece Nina on a holiday from Penn State.

"Welcome, welcome. Please come in. We've prepared some refreshments for you so you won't drive home on empty stomachs," said Sister Margaret Agnes. There goes Guido's now, I thought.

We were shown into a small sitting room, plainly decorated, with a wooden crucifix over the mantel, brightly colored pictures of Jesus and the Madonna on the walls, and a statue of St. Joseph placed in a bay window. I noticed the afternoon sunlight glinting off his head like a halo.

"Isn't that just the perfect spot for our patron saint, Nina?" Sister Ann Marie asked.

"Yes, Sister, it is." I then looked at the coffee table and the prepared refreshments that would tide us over—a tray with six Nabisco Mallomar cookies, those chocolate covered marshmallows with graham cracker bottoms, and six glasses filled with an amber liquid.

After a short grace, they passed the cookies and drinks. "Oh, what a treat!" said Carmen. "These are my favorites." She took a napkin from the tray and placed one cookie on it. I followed her lead, and said, "Thank you, Sister. I am a little thirsty." I hoped Sister Margaret Agnes didn't see the tremor as I held the glass.

"We thought and thought about what to prepare for you, and Sister Catherine Clare suggested that cookies and ginger ale would be perfect," said Sister Margaret Agnes.

"And, she was right," said Carmen. I envied her ease in talking to nuns. I could hardly swallow. I nodded and nibbled at the cookie, pretending it was indeed stemming my hunger. To avoid looking at Sister Ann Marie, I concentrated on the diminishing Mallomar.

After a short conversation on how I liked college, what my

major was, and how Carmen's children were doing in school, Carmen rose and said she was sorry to eat and run, but she knew they had things to do, and we had to get on the road. After many thanks from the sisters to us and us to them, the nuns, with their black skirts swishing and their rosary beads rattling, walked us quickly to the door and recited their many blessings for a safe trip.

"Finish the book," whispered Sister Ann Marie. She looked directly at me and clasped my hand with her bony, but strong fingers.

"I will. I have to, Sister," I said with a little smile.

"I pitied poor Emma. I felt sorry for her at the end. You'll see. May God bless you, Nina." As we walked to the car, I turned, thinking I might wave good-bye to Sister Ann Marie, but the nuns were making the sign of the cross before walking inside.

We were silent until Carmen pulled away. I was feeling ungrateful after their hospitality and prayers for our safety, and a little ashamed of my childhood judgment of Sister Ann Marie. "May God bless you, Nina," she had said with such warmth. I didn't even say "thank-you."

"Does this mean no Guido's?" I asked.

"Are you kidding? After that sugar high, I need a drink and some solid food," said Carmen, who started to giggle.

"We shouldn't laugh," said Carmen, still doing it. "They had to pay for those treats with their own money, and they don't have a lot. Six cookies and six drinks. What a feast!" It tickled her. "And, now I can smoke!"

Guido's was one of those corner bars at the end of a block of brick row houses in a mixed neighborhood of residences, small grocery stores, restaurants, and bars. In these local taverns, the owner usually tended bar, and his wife or another family member cooked.

"Carmen! *Benvenuto*! Where you been?" Guido greeted us. Carmen had told me Guido was old Mrs. Regalli's son and his in-laws owned this bar for years. Now, he and his wife were running it, and had changed the name from Gianni's to Guido's. In that neighborhood, the name change needed no explanation.

"Just did another nun run, Guido. No game today but got some points in heaven. This is my niece, Nina."

"*Bene, bene*! So, you can see the Phillies here. Now what do you beautiful ladies want?" He stared at me. "Nina, are you of age?

You know, I have to ask." He hunched his shoulders showing he didn't make the rules.

"Twenty-one," I said, and showed him my driver's license, even though Carmen was nodding that I was okay. A priest once gave me severe penance for lying with fake IDs, but I continued the sin until I hit the legal age.

"We'll split a medium pepperoni pizza and a cheese steak each. And, Guido, I want a large sausage pizza and three sandwiches to go. My family will be waiting at the door," said Carmen.

"And, now? A Manhattan for Carmen, right? Nina?"

"A draft," I said, wondering how the beer would mix with the ginger ale and Mallomars.

"No, give her a Manhattan, too," said Carmen. "Guido mixes a good one, and I'll drink yours if you don't like it. You college kids drink too much beer."

Carmen was studying the television, small by today's models. The Phils were beating the Giants. "They should win this game," she said.

"Yeah, but they could still screw up," said Guido. "Just like the other day. I'm sticking with the Yankees."

"Can't go wrong there," said Carmen. I was a Yankees fan too, but didn't follow baseball the way Carmen and my brother did. I left Carmen and Guido talking about Joe DiMaggio and went to the restroom.

Seated at the bar were three men also staring at the game, drinking beer, smoking. An older couple sat at a table eating pizza and drinking the house red. They all smiled as I walked by. Immediate acceptance was nice. The smell of sausage, tomato sauce, and cheese came from the kitchen. A radio was playing Puccini arias, just audible above the baseball game. I liked this place. Carmen did know bars.

"Isn't this nice? I love bar stools. Nothing better than a friendly bar in the afternoon. Good drinks, good food. I like to treat myself every time I'm in Philly," said Carmen.

She was sipping her Manhattan between drags of a cigarette. "How's yours?"

"Stronger than I'm used to," I said. "Lot stronger than ginger ale." We both laughed.

"Do you think we left too soon? Was it rude?"

"No. Nuns have work to do, prayers to say, papers to grade. I never stay too long. The six cookies and six glasses were a message. No seconds and no time. Maybe, no money too. Just sip the Manhattan, and you'll enjoy it more."

"Did you notice how Reverend Mother changed the subject of Madame Bovary in the car? She saved me."

"She's not *Reverend Mother* for nothing, you know. She was afraid Sister Ann Marie might discuss Madame Bovary's sinful ways, and put you on the spot. You don't antagonize your benefactors or their relatives."

The pizza and the sandwiches arrived. "*Buon appetito!*" said Guido.

"Smells so good!" said Carmen. "I'll tell your mother I stopped in. She raves about this place all the time."

"What can I say? She's my mother!" said Guido, smiling. "Want another Manhattan? The couple over there's treating. Anniversary."

"How can I refuse?" She looked at the couple, raised her glass, and drained the rest of her drink. They returned the toast, saying "*Salute.*"

"Mine's not sitting too well with the Mallomars."

"You drive home, Nina. These Manhattans are loaded, and I couldn't turn down the freebie. Wouldn't be nice."

On the ride back with the savory smell of the to-go pizza and sandwiches wafting from the backseat, I drove while Carmen slumped. I thought about Sister Ann Marie. What made her become a nun? Where did she read *Madame Bovary*? How old was she when she taught us catechism? What did she do before taking the vows?

"Carmen, did you notice how Sister Ann Marie kept staring at me? I felt so guilty. Like I was Madame Bovary or something!"

"Oh, don't dwell on it. She said she felt sorry for her."

"Didn't expect that. By the way, did Mom suggest that you take me today?"

"No. Why?"

"Well, I've been avoiding religion like a drunk uncle, except for going to the Newman Club. And, a friend of mine told Mom on Parents Weekend that she knocked on my door every Sunday to go to mass, but I slept in. Nuns and priests still make me feel so sinful, you know?"

"They're supposed to. Look, your mother warned me you might say no. That's all. I just wanted your company. And, kill the guilt. You can't be Madame Bovary. You're not even married."

I was silent, thinking how routine it used to be to study the Catechism, go to mass, get smudged on Ash Wednesday, give up watermelon for Lent, go to confession with made-up sins; observe all the Catholic rituals. I didn't question my faith then. I just resented the time it took. I looked over at Carmen, still slumped with eyes closed. I hoped she didn't have two Manhattans every time at Guido's.

"Going to mass or not is your business. You're old enough. Oh, I know they tell us it's a mortal sin to miss mass, but to me mortal sin means sin committed by mere mortals, us sinful souls! Not mortal as in 'fatal' and 'straight to the Devil with you!' As I said, what would they do without us sinners?" said Carmen.

"Spoken like a true Godmother," I said, making Carmen laugh. "I never knew you liked bars. And, Manhattans."

"We grew up right after Prohibition ended. You uncle and I would go to bars on Saturday nights. Drink, dance, smoke, play poker. Fun! Not Sister Anne Marie's kind, but most of us would get up and go to mass the next day. Maybe a little hung over," she said, looking at me now with a wink and a smile.

When we arrived in front of my house, I leaned over to give her a hug and to thank her. "You all right to drive home?"

"Oh, sure. That solid Italian food soaked up all that alcohol. If only that couple hadn't bought a round. Made me sleepy."

"And the nuns?" she asked.

"Umm. Surprising. Scary, but nice. Real nice. Never thought I'd see Sister Ann Marie again. She still got me with those stares."

"Forget the guilts, Nina. Or, go to confession. You'll feel better. And, remember, she gave you a personal blessing."

"Yeah, I know. Can't hurt. Right?"

Carmen saw my mother on the porch, and yelled to her, "Hey, I think Nina wants to go to church with you on Sunday." She laughed, blew the horn, and drove away.

Nun Run. Originally published in Skyline 2015, Prose and Poetry by Central Virginia Writers.

PRAIRIE WINDS, THE LEGACY

Ann Skelton

I get the willies during summer storms. Yesterday, standing on the porch watching black thunder clouds roll toward me over the prairie, I found myself back in Nebraska reliving a nightmare. Oh, I don't hide under the table and whine like Scotty, but I clench my fists until my fingernails dig into my palms. Don't go thinking I'm just a dramatic actress here because in those days everyone was frightened. Even now, twenty-five years later, I can close my eyes and see the black clouds rolling across the prairie. Still, when the storms started, we Flanagans didn't understand that we were witnessing the disintegration of the life we knew.

The Flanagans were farmers in Greeley County for three generations. Grandfather homesteaded in Nebraska—but that's another story. In the early 30s, before we felt the full blow of the Eastern depression, our family was prosperous. Dad was proud and confident, a muscular man with keen blue eyes and the gnarled hands of a working farmer. More than a few cautious folk thought him a mite quick to take up newfangled devices. Dad was up to date, that's for sure. Was the first in Spalding to get a tractor with rubber wheels. Decided to give pesticides a try after the experts in Lincoln said they kept the fields clear of weeds right up to harvest. Best of all, we had a fancy Philco radio, that plugged right into the wall socket. Those who knew Dad well understood he was a natural born mechanic—could fix anything. Most Saturdays we'd find a neighbor in the yard lugging some piece of equipment for Dad 'just to take-a-look at.' I don't mean to brag, but he could make most any motor run with a dab of oil or a screw he just happened to have in the shed. Did I mention he was a proud man? Polished the chrome of his Model T 'til it shone. Refused to call it a *Tin Lizzie*.

Looking back, the four of us kids made up a happy family—that was before Mama got so sick and Dad so quiet. Before the black clouds, thick with soil, and grit and seeds descended onto our prairies choking everything in their path. At first, the winds shocked us, frightened us. Finally, we began to understand those relentless clouds of dust were changing our lives. Until then, determination and hard work were the hallmark of the farmer; but no amount of determination could overcome those black winds. I know. I had a ringside seat to watch the beginning of the Dust Bowl. Still have the scars to show.

1934, Early Spring – The Beginning

We didn't know it yet, but our luck began to turn one day when Dad drove into Spalding to meet with Mr. Thornton at the bank. I only figured out much later how important that meeting was. I found the paper on washday, neatly folded and tucked into the bib of his overalls. I showed it to Anthony. He read it twice over before telling me he'd put it beside Dad's bed. We were in a drought at the time, but that was nothing new for Nebraska. We just waited for the rain we knew would come.

We waited and watched, but that spring the rains didn't come. Dad never stopped fretting about the weather. He'd stand on the porch looking up at the horizon, supposing he felt some drops, listening for the weather reports. The day the giant cloud rolled out of the sky, Dad was out checking the fields for signs of sprouts. The cattle were restless, lowing fretfully all morning. They put us all on edge. Anthony and I were nervous as the animals—only we didn't moan. I was darning Dad's socks, and Anthony was whittling when Johnny called us.

"Peggy, hey, Anthony, come look at this."

We had seen dust clouds before, but nothing like the black cloud that stretched from the highway way up into the horizon. Anthony was the first to react.

"Let's go, Little Brother. We'll tend the cows. Peg, close up the windows fast as you can." Anthony always knew exactly when to take charge.

The boys took off running toward the holding pen. Dad must have seen the cloud because shortly the tractor pulled up, and he scrambled from the cab shouting orders. Bethy and I were stuffing the windows with newspaper and trying to watch the boys move that nervous herd into the barn. What with the grit and pebbles hitting the glass, little Bethy started crying. I made a game of singing silly nursery rhymes while we went from one rattling window to the next, stuffing the sash with paper. Some game. It calmed Bethy, but my stomach was churning. I knew it was silly, but I kept wishing Mama was here.

Watching Dad wave his arms and gesture was like a dumb show at the circus. I could see he was directing the boys to catch the lead rope of any nearby cow. They just needed one to move for the rest to follow.

I almost could hear his shouts: "Anthony, whup that *damnable* cow."

"Johnny, get the calf. Daisy will follow you, then." What a plucky little kid. Just past ten years old, but he slapped that calf's rump and pulled its ear until the little critter followed him to the barn. When Daisy followed her calf, I found myself breathing again. Despite the dust blowing and whipping branches and pebbles every which way, the animals finally trotted one by one into the barn.

"See, Bethy, the cows are playing follow the leader."

Dad and the boys bent their heads into the wind and sprinted for the house. As they hit the first step, I opened the door, and in they raced stumbling to the floor. Later I saw their discarded kerchiefs so embedded with grit they were stiff as cardboard.

"Dad, I think those stones can break the windows."

"Here, come on closer to me, Johnny. We're safe in the house. It's just damn noisy." Dad hardly ever swore, but no one noticed this time. He put his arm around Johnny. "C'mon close to me, Son, you are the *shiveringest* boy I ever seen. You know, you did fine today with Daisy's calf. It's almost as big as you are."

Aftermath

Dirt and debris lay in mounds around the barn and piled up against the front steps. A sycamore branch lodged in the windmill frame. Dad stepped over a dead jack rabbit that lay in the path, smothered; dead birds littered the yard. The dust was so high along the fence we could walk over the top. Not much of fence at that point.

Inside the house, a fine layer of dust had seeped in despite our efforts to block the spaces around the windows. It covered everything. Earlier when Bethy and I set the table, we turned the dishes and cups upside down to keep the dirt off. I remember I was wearing Mother's old flowered housedress while sweeping dust into piles here and there in the kitchen. Dad scooped up Bethy and twirled her around making light of the storm, I guess.

I just watched.

"Well, you're a tough one, aren't you, Peggy? But what's this little tear running down your cheeks?"

"Not tears, Daddy. Dust got in my eye, that's all. That wind was so loud I couldn't read to Bethy. We just curled up together in the corner."

"Well, funny thing. That's just what I wanted to do," Anthony said. "Curl up with the cows," and he poked me in the ribs.

We sat down to supper exhausted. Bethy fell asleep in her chair. Dirt and pebbles tapped the windows in a staccato rhythm.

"Bless us oh Lord and these thy gifts…"

Hastings Tribune, May, 1934 United Press: "A gigantic cloud of dust, 1,500 miles long, 900 miles across and two miles high buffeted…almost one-third of the nation today."

I learned later the worst news I had since Mama got sick: news traveled across the telephone lines. Like most rural folk, we had a party line. Our ring was two longs and a short. Everyone listened in regularly to conversations—everyone expected it. It was how we learned the news. It's how we learned the Kane family was selling their farm, lock, stock, and barrel, and moving out west someplace.

I felt angry and hurt that the Kane's were leaving. I took it personally. First, Mother dies. Now, Mary Louise, my best friend, going away. That's good as dead. At thirteen I was too old to cry, but I learned how to feel sorry for myself. Tried to punish the world for my loneliness.

Anthony just kept on with his teasing ways, imitating my long face, making loud sighs, until he finally made me laugh. I was still sad, but, as it turned out, so was Mary Louise. She wrote me once. From California, I think it was.

We Flanagans hung on. All that year and the next. We believed that gentle spring rains were soon to come. Luck was bound to change. Wasn't it?

Then one evening after dinner Anthony provoked Dad something awful. He learned something from that piece of paper I found in Dad's overalls, but never raised it for these many weeks until now.

"Never did ask you, Dad, things going okay at the bank with Mr. Thornton?"

"Fine, fine, Son. Decided we should plant wheat next cycle. Gets a better price than corn.

"How about Mr. Thornton, Dad? Did he change the terms like you wanted?"

"Oh, he changed them alright. Wanted a good bit more of a guarantee than I expected."

"That right? What exactly?"

"We'll go into it later, Son."

Through the spring and summer, as the news worsened, we seemed to lose the habit of conversation. Evenings became quiet, except for Johnny who reported the neighborhood news. One evening Dad dropped into his rocker, the Lincoln paper in his lap. He dug through his shirt pocket for tobacco. I could see the weariness in his slumped shoulders. Dad seemed to study the faces of the boys: Anthony, tall and more muscular than most sixteen-year-olds, seemed to know how to calm the frantic cows with his crooning—a natural born farmer. Skinny little Johnny, with his thatch of red hair not much taller than the cows.

"You'd be that proud 'a these kids," Dad murmured.

"Is Dad talking to himself again, Peggy?" Johnny asked.

"Not to himself, Johnny. He's talking to Mama."

"But that's creepy."

"Well, I talk to her sometimes. When Jimmy Hemple says something mean."

"All we have to do is hold on. This old homestead will be Flanagans for some time to come." Dad's shoulders slumped as he rocked.

When I heard a snore, I stepped over and took the half-burned cigarette from his hand, mindful not to let the ash fall on the floor.

1935, March

Headline: *Daylight Turned into Inky Blackness*

Hastings Daily Tribune: "Snow came to this region today in the wake of the worst dust storm in years.... Snow obligingly obliterated the unsightly piles of dust heaped up by a 60-mile-an-hour gale which struck with tornadic fury Friday night.

Luck changed, all right. Only it got worse.

"Mind if I sit here awhile, Dad?" Anthony perched on the

piano bench with his penknife, working on a block of pine.

"Sure, Son. Just want to see if the *Trib* has any news besides the weather."

Dad peered over the top of the paper fascinated by Anthony's nimble fingers. A tugboat no bigger than his hand, topped with smokestacks, emerged from the wood.

"That's like magic, Son. Where'd you ever see a boat like that?"

"Found a picture in Mom's encyclopedia. Dad, mind if I ask you something?" Anthony watched his father's face. He knew more than all of us that Dad was quick to take offense and his words could bite like an angry wasp.

"What's on your mind?"

"Well, it's just I've been thinking. Don't be mad now, but maybe we shouldn't take any more loans from the bank. What with the drought and the wind and all."

Dad spoke quietly but through his teeth. "Young cub. What do you know about the business side of farming? What made you suddenly so smart?"

Anthony, still gripping the little boat, peered sideways at Dad without raising his head.

"I'm not so smart, Dad. Just that we heard the McGuffins' were selling out, leaving Spalding. Their little Ruby got the pneumonia. From breathing the dust…"

"Think I don't know that? Think I haven't heard the reports? Prayed for rain? But we're holding on, Anthony; we've got pluck. The Flanagans don't give up."

"Well, against these storms, plucks' not worth a toot – as Mom used to say."

At the mention of Mama and her famous common sense, Dad dropped into reverie, probably thinking of the family's migration to Nebraska. Anthony didn't need to hear about those early days again. All us children knew that the farm had been Dad's life from childhood. We knew how Grandfather Henry took the family from Pennsylvania to homestead in Nebraska.

"Sure, that was risky, Dad, even brave. But planting wheat in the middle of a drought—well, it's a gamble, Dad. It's near-to foolhardy."

"Mind your tongue, Youngster, and recall who you're speaking to."

Listening to their strained voices, I crossed my fingers that they wouldn't have an ugly quarrel.

"We can't give up, Son. Got to hold on. The wheat's due to germinate any time. In just a few weeks, we'll be solid."

"Yes sir. That's if it rains—a big if."

Thankfully, salvation came from the kitchen. Johnny, his mouth full of a left-over biscuit called, "Almost time for the *Lone Ranger*, Dad." Johnny sat cross-legged on the rug so he could tune the station during the show. "C'mon, Bethy, sit beside me."

Dad closed the *Tribune*, but I could see he only pretended to listen. I guess his mind drifted back to early days on the farm. He told us the stories often: the endless journey to Omaha from Pennsylvania with his brothers to make a homesteading claim. What an adventure. His mother loved the long train ride. She chatted and laughed with the passengers, never minding the noise of the tracks nor the soot that blew in the windows and got in their eyes. She was the adventurous one alright. Said she left County Cork for America with nothing more than a clean shift. Told everyone who'd listen that she'd do it again in a heartbeat and glad of it for a good piece of Nebraska farm land.

Johnny hushed everyone "Quiet everyone, it's starting," and we heard the announcer's sonorous voice.

"*...and now: The Lone Ranger.*"

"*Hi Ho Silver. Away!*" had just faded when the program was interrupted:

News flash: This just in from the extension service in Lincoln. The final report on wheat yields is grim. A total of five million acres of wheat has been lost. All the wheat crop in Nebraska is gone along with half of that in Kansas and a quarter of the Oklahoma acreage.'

"What?" Dad's face was ashen. "Did he say the whole state? Can't be... Anthony, did he say the entire wheat crop? All of it?"

Indeed, the entire Nebraska wheat crop was carried away. Across the state farmers walked their barren field unable to understand what had happened. We held on. Planted another cycle. But after each visit to town Dad became more silent. Until, the Friday before Halloween we were together in the kitchen reading ghost stories aloud. Dad interrupted just as the headless horseman approached Ichabod. We were impatient. Until he began, "I'm glad Mary isn't here to see this..."

And then we knew.

Handbill

Printed on or about November; distributed through Swenson's general store, Spalding, Nebraska.

PUBLIC SALE

At my place 7 miles south of Spalding, Hyway 281

Monday, January 6, 1936

6 Head of Horses

16 Head of Cattle

25 Head of Hogs

Farm Machinery, Etc.

Will Flanagan, Owner

Usual Terms. No property to be removed from premises until settled for.

Lunch Wagon on Grounds

Scott Baker: auctioneer

The morning of the sale, Dad lay still in the dark, still wearing yesterday's flannel shirt.

He crawled from under the quilts, and picked his way down stairs to put on the coffee, trying not to wake us though Anthony and I had been up for an hour putting aside things we could save as personal. Dad fingered the Rosewood clock on the wall above the kitchen table. "Mom's fancy clock" we kids called it. Dad just sat the window with his black sugared coffee. It would be hours before people began to arrive. We could hear the whoosh of the windmill and the creak of the old tractor tire swinging from the beech tree.

I know now that Dad was still young in 1937, just gone fifty years of age; but he looked gray and weather-beaten, staring out into the dark. As the winter sun rose, and shapes emerged from the shadows of the barnyard I could hear his voice—still hear it today: "There's the cultivator, the John Deere corn planter, the cream separator, the good McCormick-Deering Seeder."

He pulled a paper from his shirt pocket and reread the hand-bill, though he knew it by heart: *16 head of cattle, 6 head of horses, 25*

Head of Hogs. "Sounds like the goods of a prosperous farmer, not someone dead broke."

"What are you thinking, Dad?" I asked.

"Oh just, I'm glad Mary isn't here today. And, how I loved to see her drive that team of black mares, sitting straight and tall as she snapped the reins. Mary would have been sad about the horses."

That evening after the sale, after the auctioneer's hypnotic song had faded, Dad paced. The farmyard, only a few hours ago cluttered with equipment and furniture, was now bare. Almost everything sold. A few old tools remained on a hay bale along with Mama's Rosewood clock. "Still ticking," he said to the empty barnyard. He stood alone and still in the cold night, watching the activity inside the kitchen, no doubt struggling with the words, thinking of how he might comfort us.

I was at the work table under the window making biscuits for supper, sobbing and kneading, tears running down my cheeks and watching Dad out in the cold. I'd been crying since they led Blackie out of the barn, prancing. Thought I was strong until then. Outside I saw Dad shiver, pick up the clock, and press it against his stomach. I watched his slow walk across the near empty barnyard to the warmth of the kitchen. The two boys were staring out the window into the empty barnyard.

"You okay, Dad?" Anthony asked when the door slammed.

Dad put the clock back where it had always hung and turned to Anthony, "Tony, I want to say I'm sorry."

"What's that, Dad?"

"About the wheat. You were right. I was stubborn."

Bethy broke the tension. She took Dad's hand and asked the question that we all were thinking, "Daddy, are we poor?"

"Listen to me children. Look around you. Think of a picture you want to hold onto." He waited. "Do you have one?" He looked at each nodding head. "Let's hear it."

I started. "Mine is riding Blackie pell-mell across the pasture."

Anthony hesitated. "Mine is the prairie sky with the Sandhill cranes flying by."

"The sky with all those white puffy clouds, so quiet." Johnny added.

"What's your picture, Bethy?" Dad asked.

"Remember the day I climbed up the windmill, and Anthony had to save me?"

"Well you see, with those memories we're not poor. Not on your life."

The next day when everything was loaded into the car, Dad walked through the empty house listening to his footsteps. Only the Maytag washer remained in a corner waiting for a neighbor to collect it. "Doesn't seem like my house," he said to the empty room. I watched from the door, unable to enter the now strange house, as he walked from room to room. He smoothed and edge of the lilac wallpaper, stood long before the corner shelf he built for Mama's books.

"Mary, can you hear me? Where are you? Don't you know I've needed you here beside me, your hand on my shoulder?" He stood listening in the silence for a long moment. The only sound was the creaking of the windmill.

Finally, Dad turned on his heel and walked out into the bitter Nebraska January wind leaving behind all we had known to that day.

WAITING

Brenda Gates Spielman

It rose out of a high mountain lake early one morning as dawn was still only impending. The woman at the side of the deep, cold water did not notice what had been lifted from the depths out in the middle of the lake; she was too absorbed in her own thoughts.

They had come here to start over, to renew their marriage. Or so she had thought. Actually, he had only come to give her a "rest" so that she could recover from her "delusions." She had realized this the night before, realized that nothing would change because he did not want to change, and that she could not go on as it was. She had come to the lake intending to walk into the deep, deep water until she felt no more pain, for she was more afraid of being alone than of dying.

She did not notice what was in the middle of the lake, almost reflecting the beginning dawn, but she did notice the peace, the silence broken only by the sounds that belonged there: birds, the rustling of squirrels in the new leaves, the tiny voices of insects. In that silence, she found a strength she had forgotten she had, found that she was not that afraid, after all. As she watched the dawn break in splendor from behind the sharp, pointed mountains, she decided that she could continue, though not as before. But she never did see the light of the thing that was now fully out of the water and drying in the air.

A bird flying across the lake saw it with sharp bird eyes and flew down to investigate but soon flew away in search of something less shiny but more tasty. Fish, shiny themselves, swam in gentle dance around it as if in convoy before attending to the urgencies that motivate the lives of fish. Even the breeze seemed to swirl in investigation for a moment and take on the softer touch of summer rather than the sharp chill of early spring.

Two boys down from the nearby village for an early-morning adventure saw it and swam as near as they dared, but told no one else, for their presence was strictly illicit and had been contrived by climbing from bedroom windows. There was no reason for them not to swim at the beach at a more reasonable hour, but to boys of their age there was much reason to swim at a forbidden time. They both knew what they saw, for to them magic was still real, but they both were at an age where secrets were a prized treasure, so they looked, and talked, and told no one.

A young man who walked by the side of the lake on his way to work saw it, recognized it, and doubted first his sight, then his sanity. It frightened him because he wanted his world ordered and sure, so he ran instead of looking closer. But, later that evening, he proposed to the girl he loved instead of the one who had a wealthy father.

Finally, though, it was seen, talked about, and discussed. On the third day, it appeared on the back page of a newspaper, which was lacking for excitement or news of import. Everyone saw the picture. It was very clear: a woman's hand out of the water only to the wrist, holding vertically a sword that glittered, even when shadows lay on the lake, and the sun was no longer striking it. The newspaper thought it was a clever illusion, probably a promotion trick of some advertising agency, but it adequately filled up a blank space on their last page, that owed its existence to the fact that world leaders had not promoted any major tensions that week, nor nature any disasters. No one paid any attention to the photographer's story, that he had tried to touch the sword but could not. That is, no one paid any attention to it until others had tried, failed, then talked about it.

The next story was on the front page, and more people began paying attention. A distinguished scientist refused to talk to reporters about it, and referred them instead to a local fortune-teller. Another scientist, equally distinguished, came with equipment and assistants to take measurements and form theories, but he, too, was silent—or, at least, muttered things that no newspaper could print—when his instruments told him that the object his eyes saw was not really there. An evangelist denounced the sword as evil and the work of devils, while another, with just as fanatical a following, proclaimed it a divine sign. One government called it a political trick and accused the United States of being behind it, but most governments found it wisest to make no official statement. Some sent an agent or two to look at it and decide if it were a danger, and two congressmen came to investigate because they thought the lake a nice place to spend a week or two in early spring. Slowly, a crowd did begin to gather, built of those who had time and money to waste, and a number of those did not. And among the crowd, one word was whispered over and over: Excalibur.

The chief of police was not concerned about the sword. He considered it a cute trick, probably caused by some of the college-aged children home for spring break using lasers or computers. He was concerned about the crowd, because he knew that too often the morality of a crowd fell to its lowest common denominator, but they were surprisingly well behaved. There were no fights, no thefts, no mounds of trash left by the wayside. Instead they simply watched the sword and waited. Letters were sent to London news-papers suggesting that the Prince was the obvious one to go to the lake and take the sword, but the Palace made no official announce-ment, though rumor did get around that he was certain Excalibur would appear only in a British lake.

For those who could not watch from lakeside themselves, the major networks set up cameras so that every evening after the news of the word (which was, as always, bad), they would close with another view of the sword, still glinting, still unclaimed.

A man, or perhaps something that might at one time have been a man, decided to make a statement for what he believed to be his side in one of the perpetual conflicts on this tired planet by blow-ing up the lake. He managed, with much ingenuity, to slip into the lake with a load of explosives (only a small load, for plastics can do much damage for their size), but he was never heard from again, and the lake remained quiet save for small chewing and swallowing noises from a large Beast that no one heard except the Lady.

The two evangelists both came, one to exorcise, the other to bless. Nothing changed. Businessmen manufactured toy swords, T-shirts with swords inked on them, letter openers that looked like swords, and so on, in lists unending. Divers tried to get a picture of the rest of the woman, but their film showed only schools of fish swimming in fishy precision. So the people waited. There was no countdown clock such as comforted those awaiting the birth of the space-shuttle *Columbia*, no similar explanations, and in the end no similar exaltation.

The sword was there a month, watched, blessed, cursed, and photographed. But not touched.

No one had seen the sword rising from the water, but thousands and, with the aid of cameras, millions saw it slowly vanish inch by inch back into the deep blue of the water. The people stared at the empty lake in silence, hoping it would reappear, but knowing it would not. Finally, in a gathering dusk that had the texture of velvet, they started leaving, strangely silent, speaking only in whispers as if in the presence of Death.

The cameras were packed and the people went home, not as happy as when they came, but not wholly despondent either—for if magic did not live again, they knew it was neither totally dead—which was something, at least, to cling to in a mundane world.

But at the deep bottom of a different lake surrounded by a land whose people called it Scotland, the Lady whose Domain was the Lakes of the Earth wept against a large scaly side that itself was cold and unyielding, yet which nonetheless covered a heart that was warm with comfort.

"He didn't come," she wondered. "Why didn't he come?"

Waiting was originally published in Fantasy Book March1984

IN OTHERS' WORDS
THE BEWILDERING CASE OF SHARIFA AL-GHOSAIBI

William E. Sypher

She exploded into my consciousness a year ago last spring. I had taken over a writing course for a professor who had quit at mid-year. As the first class got underway, I was talking about the importance of honesty in writing when one student held up her hand and asked in native speaker-quality English, "Do you think reality is only in the imagination?" I tried to conceal my surprise and suggested that, while this is a good and ancient question, it was beyond the scope of the class. She huffed in disappointment, and the class proceeded on the more mundane course I had set. It was to be the first of many such encounters over that semester and continuing into the spring of the following year.

Sharifa al-Ghosaibi is medium tall, rail thin, and deathly pale; she has the look of one chronically ill and, as I later learned, had been seriously ill last year and missed almost a month of class. But one feature overwhelms all others: her luxuriant eyebrows, thick, black and grown together over her medial brow, form a furry black visor. With this naturally darkened brow, artificially darkened eyes, and wan complexion, it is a face too sharp with contrasts; it looks unreal. She is confident, utterly at ease in American-accented English, but projects little warmth, only a sly smile.

Throughout the semester, she blurted out more standard philosophical questions: "What is the meaning of our life?" "What is truth?" These could be launched like rogue rockets at any time, generally unrelated to the topic and discussion ongoing in class. She seemed to be hosting a furious interior dialogue, which simply burst, periodically, geyser-like, to the surface, beyond her control. Occasionally, her questions were political, or equally worrisome in this context, religious. In the midst of a discussion about gender-prescribed roles, I had taken the standard progressive position that it is hard to think of any job a woman cannot do.

She sprang like an endangered Arabian leopard, "Sir, our Prophet, peace be upon him, [the obligatory honorific], said that women cannot do the same jobs as men. What do you think of that?"

I had lived in Sabaquan too long to take such bait. "Sharifa, we are advised not to discuss religion in class."

She was undeterred. "Why not? How are we to learn if we can't discuss some ideas?"

The class tensed at this prickly and potentially risky challenge to classroom orthodoxy, which requires vigilant self-censorship. I had to reply; what could I say to mollify her?

"If I disagree with your Prophet, I could be accused of criticizing Islam. I must be careful."

"But the Quran encourages us to read and to question. We are required to do this."

"Sharifa, that may be. but you are a Muslim, so you can do this. Anything I say could be considered as anti-Muslim."

She wouldn't quit; she just wouldn't quit. "No, sir. That is wrong. You can say what you want."

I scanned the class, which was clearly apprehensive. I fell back, lamely glossing my reluctance as politeness. "I am a guest in your country. It is not right for me to comment on your religion or your prophet."

Sensing my weakness, she ratcheted up the attack. "We should be able to discuss anything. That's the purpose of a university. We are curious and we want to know your opinion."

I was out of defenses. "Sharifa, if you want to change the rules, you must talk to the president, but please do not mention my name."

"I will," she said. I had no reason to doubt her.

Two days later she came to my office to pursue the conversation. "I went to see the President," she said coyly and paused.

"And?"

"He said it was all right to discuss such things."

I thought to myself: "No, Sharifa, it would not be wise to discuss such questions in a sensitive, developing region that does not encourage free interchange of ideas, a place where almost any criticism could be seen as a direct and intolerable threat to the religion, government, or the culture. Sabaquan is fragile as a glass slipper." I quickly changed the subject.

As the semester proceeded, she continued to ask provocative questions, which I parried more or less successfully. She was intriguing, uncommonly bright and inquisitive, a rare bird here aloft in the endless desert, flying wherever she wanted and delighted in learning for learning's sake. Her writing was abstract, her vocabulary impressive, her grammar flawless. I now realized why a colleague had called her the Little Professor.

Her writing was also unfocused, florid, bombastic, over the top, a style befitting a court poet in 11th C. Baghdad, but alien to the spare, academic writing I was obliged to teach. I began to push her to simplify and steered her toward Thoreau and E.B. White. She was showing off, not showing, but she couldn't or wouldn't change. Here's a sample, first of bombast and then of losing her way. "*Her* [the sea] *furious turmoil can bend the will of even the strong. Rolling mountains of fluid strength can break the bow and crush the spirit.* Then, in an essay on animals dying out of view, '*It is a masterpiece of science writing that should be read by anyone seeking to renew or reinforce their sense of biology.*" She could say nothing simply nor stay on topic. While I did not succeed in getting her to change, she was so far above her classmates that she would earn an A, although I poured a flood of red ink on each of her papers. I took the time because she was worth it. She might become someone quite important in her society. Perhaps I could influence her in some small way.

I saw her rarely in the fall, but she was keen to enter my writing class the next spring, and she did. The first assignment was to write an essay answering two questions: What makes you angry and why? The students were intrigued that they could get academic credit for venting. When the papers came in, Sharifa's was eight pages and handwritten, in defiance of my requirement that all papers be typed and properly formatted. Hers was a rambling, mewling account of a failed romance and engagement. The word "anger" appeared only once on page seven, as if, nearing the end, she had suddenly recalled what the assignment was about and dropped the word in. I returned it to her as unacceptable. She defended it. "It's all related, "she said lamely. I wouldn't budge. "Re-do it," I said. A week later, the re-do came in, equally bereft of anger, and I rejected it. Her defense changed: "I can't do it. I can't write about what makes me angry because I do not get angry."

I was flabbergasted: "I don't believe you."

"But it's true. My parents raised me not to show anger."

For a moment I thought I was talking to a Stepford wife, but she wasn't married and this wasn't Connecticut. I told her to come see me in my office, an invitation I later regretted. When she did come, she steadfastly defended being psychologically unable to do such a paper. In exasperation, I told her to choose another topic; she brightened and said she would.

The next day, on my way from a class to my office, I saw her sitting on a curb surrounding the formal flower garden that separates our college from the neighboring one. She was eating an ice cream bar and didn't notice me, or so I thought. Seeing a local girl, sitting so casually on a curb licking away on a messy ice cream bar in this utterly formal world where everyone notices everything and comments on it, shocked me. At that point, I knew she was more than just academically different. She showed up in my office in a few minutes to say that she would not be re-doing her paper and would grudgingly accept her C. She was changing gears faster than a NASCAR driver, but I was glad to be spared additional grading.

The next assignment was to be a live report of any activity in places as ordinary as shopping malls, cafeterias, street corners, family dinners, or evenings in the dorm. The idea was to render something seemingly commonplace into something revealing and significant. Try to capture small, revealing details or actions or snippets of conversation, I told them. In a previous course, this assignment had produced some spectacularly fine reports, especially of village life (weddings, celebration-of-birth parties, dinner preparations), which were unsparing and often funny.

Sharifa's submission was a flowery panegyric to nature, complete with recurrent breezes and butterflies. I rejected it. It was not a report of any human activity and whatever it was, it was tediously over-written, a pattern that was beginning to gall me, and I told her so. She defended it as "activity" but where I come from, breezes and butterflies are not activities and not human. She said she could not rewrite it. I was tired of arguing with her; I told her to forget it; I would base her grade on the other four papers. I was clearly being unprincipled, treating her as a special case, being too forgiving, but, damn it all, she was interesting, as eccentric and stubborn as Melville's Bartleby the Scrivener, but so capable of writing superior prose that I did not want to crush her spirit. Looking back, I wish I had leaned harder on her then when she deserved it.

The third assignment was to interview someone old in your family or neighborhood, perhaps a grandparent, and fashion it into a narrative. This assignment generated visible excitement among the students, even more than the anger paper had— love of and reverence for elders is ingrained in Sabaquan. Sharifa's submission was an affectionate description of her grandfather, with memorable lines like "His head and wrinkled neck came out of his robe like the head of an old turtle coming out of its shell." I read it to the class—without mentioning her name—to illustrate what fresh writing is. Unfortunately, the lesson was lost on them. To them, it seemed to demean the elderly. These village literalists could not get beyond the turtle.

She described his old shoes in crisp, loving detail: dried mud and tiny rocks caught between the layers of the soles that had been crudely repaired by simply gluing or nailing on additional soles. It was the kind of acute perception of minute detail that distinguishes fine writers from wannabe's.

Still, the paper said virtually nothing about her grandfather's interior, his passions, doubts, longings, regrets. It was a paper of surfaces, and I told her so. It did not seem to be the result of interviewing him, but of staring at him. I commented pointedly at the end of the paper: "Are you a writer or photographer? This is a writing class."

But what stood out was the last page. She quoted her grandfather: *"Ahmed, when he was seventy, fell passionately in love with a girl of eighteen. And Hassan, who survived until last year, is supposed to have sent telegrams of courtship at the age of seventy, too."* Who were these men, Ahmed and Hassan, who suddenly appeared, un-introduced, undefined, and then disappeared? They just showed up like carbuncles, unwanted and troubling. Could it be that this was not her writing? Unthinkable. She wouldn't need to do anything like this. She's too good. I'll let it pass and simply advise her to re-interview her grandfather and draw out the man instead of just drawing him. But the carbuncle spread over the last page, festering and painful. I could not ignore it. Something was not right. Her description of her grandfather and his quotes was disjointed, a puzzling patchwork. It was time to think the unthinkable. It was time for Google.

I nervously typed in one of the above lines and in 0.27 seconds, Sharifa was wriggling on a hook. There it was, almost word for word, except that Goethe had morphed into Ahmed; Henry Miller into Hassan; Modigliani's Portrait of a Woman into that of an unknown woman, and Tokyo into India. The source was curious, a poem called "Hole in the Heart" by a Korean writer, Su Kang, which appeared on a Sogang, (Korea) University website. Sharifa was an accomplished plagiarist, who naively thought that an obscure source would be undetectable. Ah, my dear, the Internet is a ruthless, uncultured robot; it does not distinguish between Grub Street and the grand.

Still, I anguished. I could not simultaneously believe that this talented writer was a plagiarist. I either had to reject the evidence as coincidental or inadvertent plagiarism, thus preserving her image, or conclude painfully that the evidence was inescapably damning, and she was a fraud. Cognitive dissonance is not easily resolved. The brain has two competing models of reality and one must win, if sanity is to be preserved. I decided I could risk my sanity for a few days until her next assignment came in.

It was a definition paper in which she chose to define a storm at sea and a shrimp boat's struggle against the storm, or something like this. She incongruously called it, "The Poetry of Life," which turned out not to be incongruous at all. The first page showed the old Sharifa at work, over-writing with a fury. Listen to sentences like "*Frothing with white anger, she bares her will for all to fear. Beyond this, the thunderous proclamations of warning spell the awaited destiny.*" I had become so weary of this extravagance that I wrote, "Sharifa, you are wallowing in words. How many times do I have to say it? Simplify!" Still, I am a teacher, so I was obliged to struggle through the thrashing waves to see if it got better.

Page two began crisply. "*The sun is down, the night is dark, the stars are in the sky.*" "Hmmm, she's grasped simplicity," I thought. Then the second line: "*The sea is running past the mark where the dry sands lie.*" Would she, could she, know the nautical phrase, "running past the mark?" I was immediately suspicious. Then the next line: "*They drop their nets and hopes below into the sea and turn their bow into wind, while the engine groans in agony.*" Now, little red warning flags were flapping furiously in her stormy prose. I decided to look at the next two lines: "*Then they cinch their lines onto the cleats and the lower the booms about. While seas rise and the engine bleats, they stay the course throughout.*" No, she would not have such specific nautical terms, and I commented on her paper, "Which is it, groans or bleats? They differ dramatically." Dim-witted and trusting, I had missed the obvious: this was a poem rendered in prose to disguise its form. "Sky" rhymed with "lie; "sea," jarringly with "agony;" "about" with "throughout." The poem continued to masquerade as prose, her prose, for the next four pages. Her paper title, "The Poetry of Life," was revealing. I had had enough. Come, Google.

This time she had used two sources. The first was an unheralded poem by one Bill Orr called "The Shrimper," which he had vanity published in a newsgroup on the Internet. Her conclusion had been taken verbatim from an Amazon.com review of renowned poet J.D. McClatchy's "Poetry of the Sea." Cognitive dissonance was resolved: Sharifa was at least a two-time plagiarizer. I wasn't angry, just sickened and disappointed. I wrote at the end of her paper, "This is one of the saddest moments of my teaching life." Underneath that lament, I inscribed the obligatory F.

A person who plagiarizes once might do it again. If twice, "might" switches to "likely will." I had no other papers from her, but I did have a journal, which seemed unlikely to produce further evidence. After all, journals are a chance to write freely, unencumbered by concerns of spelling, grammar, punctuation. Students are encouraged to react spontaneously to what they've been reading and discussing in class. They can sound off; relieve their frustration about readings they don't like, or challenge comments classmates or I have made. The journals are unedited and typically blunt and, for that reason, highly valuable both for the students learning to express their emotions in prose and, for me, as honest feedback on the class. If any form of writing seemed least likely to be plagiarized, journals would be it. What would be the point? But I had to see.

Her third and final journal was entitled "Dr. Sypher's Classes," which I gathered would be about what had been said in class. But the first few pages were a review of a book she had read recently and obviously liked: <u>The Seven Habits of Highly Effective People</u>. She said she was reading it to solve a mystery and that the "connection might not be clear between the mystery and Dr. Sypher, but his classes have been the reason for reading it." Groan, once again Sharifa was not doing what I had asked but doing what she wanted or could cadge and forcing it like sausage meat into an undersized casing. My comments at the end of her journal were blunt: "Again, Sharifa rides her own train, not the train she is asked to ride. Am

I just a stubborn old coot who refuses to acknowledge your brilliance or am I perhaps a true teacher who is offering you honest
feedback, not false praise?" The other parts of her journal were a
rambling, largely incoherent discussion of religion, motherhood,
the West, frustrations of living in Sabaquan, you name it, it was
in there. I gave the journal a generous score of two out of five.
Students typically get 4s and 5s.

But now I was looking at it differently, not whether she had
done what I had asked, but whether it was **she** who had done it.
Google convicted her quickly: part of it came from an online journal called "A Family in Baghdad," written in March by a mother
and her three sons.

Oh my. Already a convicted three-time plagiarizer, she likely
had been doing it throughout the course. I called my Department
Head who quickly summoned Sharifa to a meeting at which she
had cried and admitted her guilt. After they talked awhile, I was
invited to join. Sharifa was obviously distraught and acutely embarrassed. She said, "This is the worst day of my life," and lamented
out loud again and again, "I want to know why I did it." I suggested campus counseling. She continued, "Everyone hates me now." I
assured her that no one hated her, but we are disappointed in her.
Perhaps for one who tried so hard to live up to the expectations of
others, telling her we were disappointed was not comforting, but
to me it sounded better than hate. I asked her if my course was the
only one in which she had plagiarized. She said, "No, there were
others," including one time in my course with her last spring.

Her once promising academic career was in shreds. She coveted a government scholarship to study abroad. That will not happen. I advised her to take a semester off, to visit her two sisters
studying abroad. The change of scenery would help her to heal
and start anew. I felt conciliatory and reminded her that she is
young and can have a good, productive life. She said, "I am glad I
was found out." I left her, and the Head to continue the discussion.

In about one hour she came into my office, extended her
hand—uncharacteristic behavior for a Sabaquan woman—and
when I took her hand, expecting her to remove it quickly, she held
on for at least half a minute--truly uncharacteristic. Then she said,
"This is the happiest day of my life." An hour ago, she had said,
"This is the worst day of my life." Could a transfiguration take

place so quickly? She thanked me and went away, and I was left to wonder if this line, "The best day of my life," while obviously in the public domain, had, too, been lifted for the occasion.

Postcript

The next day she dropped in to ask, "Have you told others?"

"Yes, of course," I said. "It's important for other professors to know."

"Can you tell me their names? I want to apologize to them."

"You need only apologize to the professors whose courses you plagiarized in. You said there were others."

"No, yours was the only one."

Clearly, problems remain.

PICTURE OF GUILT

Larry Turner

When Lambert heard the rapping on the classroom door and saw the two policemen through the glass, he walked over with resignation and opened the door. His shoulders fell as he saw the sketch they carried; anyone could recognize him from it.

"Okay, Lambert, come with us," said the older policeman, round-faced and round-bellied.

"Have a heart, guys," Lambert said. "This is the sixth time you've picked me up this year." He laid the chalk on the groove under the chalkboard covered with chemical symbols and formulae. "How are these kids ever going to learn the difference between an ether and an ester?"

"You should have thought of that before you exposed yourself in front of those two schoolgirls this morning," the younger policeman said in a high-pitched voice, looking down at the sketch. He appeared little older than the students sitting in rows of school desks, some relieved that class would end early, others irritated, but none surprised by another visit from the police.

"Now, Tom," chided Al, the older policeman. "Even a pervert like Lambert here is innocent until proven guilty."

Experience had taught Lambert it was pointless to resist. He stuck his head into the principal's office as they went by.

"The police are taking me downtown again," he said. "You'll have to find someone to take my classes." He knew the principal was getting tired of finding substitutes every time the police picked him up.

Lambert followed the others into the dimly lit room. Then a light blinded him, and he realized he was in a police lineup with a teen-aged pizza delivery boy, an old woman, and a uniformed policeman.

"You can sit down, Tom," Al told the younger policeman. As he did so, Al told Lambert, "It's his first lineup." When Lambert didn't acknowledge the honor, he added, "We've been criticized for not following proper procedure."

The delivery boy turned to the old woman and muttered, "The things you gotta do to get a tip here."

"I don't know why you're complaining," she hissed back. "I just came in to report my cat was lost."

The light had slowly tilted down on its clamp, and Lambert could see the venom in the faces of the four parents, each grasping a copy of the sketch. He recognized Mr. Venuti, the butcher, and shuddered at the thought of being alone with him in the butcher shop some time.

The other father was Mr. Fortner, editor of the local newspaper; his retaliation would be less dramatic, but more public.

The two girls sat in chairs in front. Angela sat stiffly, her hands folded over the sketch, wondering what was expected of her. Vicki sat in boredom, swinging her leg and every so often thrusting out her lower lip to blow her blonde bangs off her eyes. She had added a mustache, goatee, and cigarette to the sketch and then turned it over to draw horses on the back.

Al Parker stood behind Lambert and put his hand on his shoulder. He asked the girls, "Do you see the man?"

Angela looked at Lambert, then quickly looked down. She licked her lips nervously and said nothing. Vicki stared at his face steadily for ten seconds, and then turned her gaze to the policeman and said, "That's not him."

"Are you sure?" Al asked her. "He sure looks like the drawing."

Vicki scarcely looked back at Lambert and answered, "No, that's not him."

Angela repeated softly, "No, that's not him."

Back in the squad room, Tom asked, "Can we drive you back to the school, Mr. Lambert, or would you like to go home?"

"To the school, please. My car is there."

"Sorry about all this, Mr. Lambert," Al said, "but we were only doing our job."

"Yes, I know, I know. But the police artist—"

"He's doing his best, Mr. Lambert."

"Yes, but dammit, just because I modeled for that drawing class he took, can't he draw anybody's face but mine?"

"Like I said, he's doing the best he can," Al replied. Then he looked at the sketch and chuckled. "It sure does look like you, though."

GENGHIS AND THE .55 MAGNUM

A farce

Rodney Vanderhoof

On a bright Saturday in early spring, a dapper John Huntington Hardwood donned his Armani shirt, grey denim trousers, crested blue blazer, and fancy deck shoes. *I am indeed elegant and debonair,* he thought, *and so handsome.* He adjusted his yachting cap to a frisky tilt and was now ready for the annual Richmond Powerboat Show.

As Hardwood stepped toward the front door, his wife shouted, "Be careful, John. Predatory salesmen are everywhere at those boat shows." She worried about her impulsive husband.

The Richmond Show exhibited scores of watercraft, from luxurious yachts to tiny car-tops. These craft came in every configuration a customer might want, including V-hulls, tri-hulls, pontoons, flat bottoms, and every type of engine. All were displayed with eagle-eyed salesmen at the ready.

Soon after arriving, Hardwood spotted a powerful, tri-hull inboard. *Look at those sleek lines,* he thought. *That baby can fly.*

A salesman wearing too much aftershave spotted Hardwood and, grinning like a barracuda scoping a swarm of succulent baitfish, he stepped forward. "Hi, I'm Slick Wilson… and you are?"

"John Huntington Hardwood."

"Isn't this a beautiful craft, Mr. Hardwood? It has an innovative polyethylene hull. It's strictly state-of-the-art."

"State-of-the-art?"

"Right, the special polyethylene prevents algae and other water growths from sticking to the hull. Without the accumulation of these growths, the boat skims the water at an amazing speed. The big engine takes you from zero to fifty in mere seconds, great for water skiing and thrills."

Hardwood walked around the boat inspecting every square inch. "This boat is magnificent," he announced, as he climbed in and ogled the instrument panel. Grasping the wheel, his eyes closed, and he envisioned himself navigating heavy seas: *Suddenly, he was slammed by a violent squall. He squinted steely-eyed into the stormy onslaught. Against all odds, he steered his craft skillfully from wave to wave, constantly adjusting engine torque by using the tab adjuster to get the steering just right. From minute to precarious minute, hour after hour, he fought hurricane force winds but refused defeat, even against the mighty gods who rule the sea.*

"Ooh, yeah!" he shouted, causing the people at other displays to stare. Who was this pompous prig creating the ruckus? Wilson noticed Hardwood's reaction, too, and smiled.

"Do you want to take delivery of this fantastic boat today, Mr. Hardwood, before someone else snaps it up, or would next week be better?"

"Well, it is a terrific boat and I'd like to be on the lake this afternoon…" He paused, but only for a moment. "Yes, I'll buy it right now."

"Oh, one more thing," Wilson added, "You need to fasten the registration decals on the hull, near the bow. If you don't, the game warden will give you a hassle."

"So why don't you put them on for me?"

"The guy who does that is visiting his sick grandmother."

Hardwood hesitated. *How hard can it be to put number decals on the hull? I'll do it myself.*

He gave Wilson a check when the paperwork was complete. The boat and trailer were fastened to the hitch on Hardwood's Cadillac Escalade, and he was off.

At his lake house, Hardwood changed into his Burberry all-weather jacket and trousers, and a baseball-style cap bearing the Lake Jefferson Boat Club logo. Next, he tended to the registration numbers.

He placed the decals on the hull, but they held for only an instant before sliding off. He tried twice more with the same result. Nobody told him he needed a few quick licks from a small blowtorch to warm the polyethylene surface; then, and only then, would the numbers stick. Being naturally cautious, he knew he shouldn't go on the lake without visible numbers; on the other hand, it was early in the season, and no other boats were out. Surely, no one would care.

Hardwood's first task was to break in the new engine at slower speeds, with only brief bursts at full throttle. After twenty hours, the engine could be revved to full power for as long as Hardwood chose.

He whistled for his faithful canine, a mischievous pit bull named Genghis, and went out on the lake. Genghis hung over the bow, his nose in the air, inhaling the delectable scents of deer, rotting compost, and putrid carcasses of dead fish. For Genghis, this smelled of dog heaven; for Hardwood, it smelled of sheer boredom.

Hardwood drove for an hour in big circles: first clockwise, then counterclockwise, and then back again. He did figure eights until totally stupefied, then circled until inspiration struck: *I'll head across the lake. It's several miles, but I can cruise in a straight line.*

The county boundary ran right down the middle of Lake Jefferson, so when he arrived at the other side, he'd left Malvern County and entered Chocataw County. He was now in the legal jurisdiction of the infamous lady judge, "Lock'em Up" Llewellyn.

To say Judge Elsie May Llewellyn had a vicious streak was an understatement. Elsie May found a man guilty of loitering in front of the county courthouse and gave him six months at hard labor. This included mopping the jailhouse floor each morning, mowing the judge's lawn three times a week, and washing the Sheriff's patrol cars every day. But we'll return to Judge Llewellyn later in the story.

Hardwood's powerful craft was bounding over heavy waves like a crazed porpoise, when a fast-moving police cruiser zoomed in with siren blaring and blue lights flashing. A uniformed lawman stood at the helm in all his law enforcement glory. *He wants my help in tracking a criminal,* thought Hardwood. *I'll cut my engine.*

As the cruiser pulled alongside, Hardwood saw bold, black letters along the side that read, "Game Warden." The nametag over the officer's shirt pocket read, "Rufus Crane." A sidekick in plain clothes dropped rubber bumpers over the side, then helped the game warden secure the two boats together with grappling hooks.

The warden was a giant who could have played defensive line in pro football. He had a buzz cut of carrot-red hair and a beer belly that sagged over his too-tight cartridge belt. If he'd flown the Jolly Roger and gritted a dagger in his teeth, he could not have been more menacing.

Leaving his engine idling, the warden boarded Hardwood's

new craft. He squared his hat and made a big show of adjusting his sidearm, a huge revolver with pearl handles. Hardwood had never seen such an imposing weapon.

"You seem fascinated with my gun," Crane said. "It's a Colt .55 magnum, custom-made just for me. The bullets are armor-piercing and can go right through an engine block."

"Amazing."

"Now, let's get down to business. I need some identification." Impatient with the delay, Hardwood jammed his driver's license into the lawman's hand. Crane noticed the rudeness.

"So, Mr. John Huntington Hardwood," he snapped, "where's your boat registration number? It's supposed to be visible on the hull. That's the law."

"The numbers fell off. Since no one was on the lake, I didn't think it mattered."

"Without numbers on the hull, I can only conclude that you haven't paid your boat tax, or, worse yet, the boat is stolen," he said. "The law is important. Can you imagine the chaos we'd have without the rule of law?"

"Yes, but the numbers wouldn't stick. I just bought the boat this morning."

"Where's the sales slip?"

"In my lake house, over there," Hardwood pointed. "If we cruise over, I'll run in and get it."

"I'm not going there, not for an unscrupulous scofflaw," said Crane, "I'm placing you under arrest."

"Go ahead and arrest me if you dare, but the governor is a friend of mine. I'll have your badge on a platter, you backwoods bumpkin." *He doesn't need to know I've never met the governor,* thought Hardwood.

"That settles it, you bag of Lake Jefferson muck," Crane said. "I've heard all that before. Turn around and put your hands atop windshield." Frisking Hardwood for weapons, but finding none, he said, "I'm taking you in."

"How dare you arrest me, you six-gun, back-country buffoon, I've never broken the law in my life."

"That's what they all say, Jerkwood," said Crane. "Okay, put one arm through the steering wheel and put your wrists together." The officer snapped on the handcuffs and placed the boat ignition key in his pocket. "I'll fasten a line to your bow cleat and tow you to the landing. We can't have *criminals* like you on the loose."

"I am *not* a criminal, you Paleolithic boob."

"You violated the penal code, you half-fried catfish. That *makes* you a criminal."

Genghis was riled by the shouting and was skittering from side to side, yapping and snarling.

As Officer Crane climbed back into the police boat, his feet became entangled with Genghis, so Crane kicked him.

Genghis retaliated by jumping into the lawman's boat, going straight for the officer's leg, and locking on with his jaws. Crane screamed and tried to pull the pit bull off, but Genghis just bit down harder.

In desperate pain, the officer drew his gun and fired. He missed Genghis and, instead, hit his own foot, blowing off his big toe. The bullet went through Crane's shoe and through the hull. Water began to gush into the cruiser. The shot frightened Genghis who let go, then chased Crane's sidekick who dove overboard.

"Come, Genghis!" Hardwood shouted, but the pit bull paid no attention.

Crane fired another shot but missed the dog and blew a gaping hole in the engine compartment, hitting the engine and causing it to stop. Gray smoke oozed out. Crane fired a third shot but nailed his own gas tank, dead center. Gasoline spurted from both front and back of the tank onto the floor and into the engine compartment. Gas fumes permeated the air.

Crane hollered to the shackled Hardwood, "Jump, fish ball, before she blows!"

"I can't, you slobbering eel," Hardwood yelled back, "I'm cuffed to the steering wheel."

Crane dove over the side, and Genghis followed in hot pursuit, nipping and barking the whole time.

Although fastened to the steering wheel, Hardwood stretched forward with his leg and kicked off the front grappling hook with his foot. He did the same to the hook at the back and began drifting away from the police boat. He hunkered down on the floor below the instrument panel and the driver's seat, just as the explosion rocked his watercraft with a force that left him senseless.

The blast rattled windows in homes all along the shores of

Lake Jefferson and was heard, like a sonic boom, for miles. Rafts of ducks and Canada geese scattered airborne. Workers at a distant marina scanned the sky for thunderclouds and impending rain flurries, but were mystified when they saw nothing.

When Hardwood awakened, a mushroom cloud was rising. The police boat was destroyed by the explosion and, except for a few floating remnants, was on the bottom. Game Warden Rufus Crane and his sidekick were splashing in the lake and screaming for help. Since Crane still had the ignition key, Hardwood could do nothing.

Along the shore, a homeowner heard the explosion and saw rising smoke. He launched his boat and rescued both the game warden and sidekick.

Meanwhile, Genghis was back in his own boat sitting next to Hardwood. Using his forepaws, Genghis had climbed onto the swim platform at the stern and made an additional jump that landed him in the boat. He shook the cold water from his fur, spraying it all over Hardwood. Genghis was wagging his tail and having a wonderful time.

"Bad dog!" Hardwood scolded. Genghis put his tail between his legs and whimpered, but Hardwood smiled: *the game warden got what he deserved.*

Once aboard the rescue craft, the warden and sidekick fastened a line to Hardwood's bow. Crane had his Game Commission pickup and trailer at the boat landing. Hardwood's boat was winched onto the trailer, while the rescuer returned home.

Officer Crane's sidekick drove them to the Chocataw county seat and left Crane at the Emergency Room for treatment of his missing toe and dog bite. Genghis was deposited at the animal shelter, and Hardwood's speedboat was impounded.

Hardwood was booked for verbally abusing a law officer, stealing a boat, and operating an unregistered watercraft. He was fingerprinted, photographed, and thrown in the slammer.

A few hours later, a bedraggled Rufus Crane arrived from the Emergency Room and limped over to Hardwood's cell. He was teary-eyed. "My gun is in ooze at the bottom of Lake Jefferson. I'll never see it again."

"Oh pity."

"All of this is your fault, Klutzwood. I lost my magnificent Colt

.55 magnum, your dog bit me, and my big toe is gone. I'll drown in paperwork for six months trying to explain all this to the Game Commission." Crane turned to go but stopped and came back.

"Lock'em Up Llewellyn will handle your case early next week. I'll be in the courtroom as prime witness. You'll be cleaning jail-house johns and mopping floors for a long time. I'll enjoy every moment of your misery."

On Monday at eight sharp, Hardwood was marched into court past his wife who was a spectator. She handed him the sales slip for the boat.

Judge Elsie May Llewellyn wore a black, dignified robe. Her hair was long and dark and her lipstick, bright red. *She is attractive,* thought Hardwood, *but looks can be deceiving.*

"Mr. Hardwood, how do you plead?"

"Not guilty."

"Officer Crane, please describe what happened." Crane presented his version of events with the proud confidence of a law-man accustomed to winning his cases.

"And what do *you* say, Mr. Hardwood?"

"Here's my sales receipt, your honor." Hardwood handed it to the judge. She examined it.

"Officer Crane, this receipt shows that Mr. Hardwood paid the boat tax and is the owner. Why did you arrest him?"

"I didn't believe him and, well, he acted guilty and called me a 'slobbering eel.'"

"What say you, Mr. Hardwood?"

"Officer Crane called me a 'half-fried catfish.'"

"You two should be ashamed," she said. "If you were school-boys, I'd wash you mouths out with soap." The two men stared at the floor.

"The case against Mr. Hardwood is dismissed. Bailiff, release him."

"Officer Crane, according to your own testimony, you kicked an innocent little dog named Genghis. Then, you repeatedly tried to shoot him. As Chairwoman of our local Society for Prevention of Cruelty to Animals, I detest your behavior. You are a disgrace to the uniform."

"A disgrace?"

"I hereby place you under arrest," she said, scowling. "Bailiff, book this man for extreme cruelty to animals and place him in a cell. I'll deal with *him* later."

As the bailiff escorted Crane from the courtroom, Hardwood heard the judge mutter, "Besides, the shrubs around the courthouse need pruning."

True justice prevails, thought Hardwood. *Is this a great country or what?*

This fiction was published in the *Rappahannock Review*, Riverside Writers, a chapter of The Virginia Writers Club, 2011. All rights reverted to the author.

FLY

J. Elizabeth Vincent

Mariah bent down and gathered up yet another sharp scrap of iron from the floor with her long, slender fingers. It was smaller than the length of her little toe, so she threw it onto the scrap heap. That seemed to be the last one. She grabbed the broom and began to sweep the stone floor, starting at one corner of the room and moving foot by foot to the edge and over to the door until all of the coal dust and tiny flakes of metal were on the ground outside. Row by row, she swept until the gray stone was smooth and clear. Magnus insisted that it be so, even though they both knew that by midmorning, it would be covered again.

Sweat dripped down the sides of her face and down her back beneath her woolen dress and cloak, even though the air blowing in through the open doors of the smithy was biting. She resisted the urge to stop and rub her back like a bear up and down the nearest wooden support to get at the spot between her shoulder blades. It itched like mad whenever she was too warm. The smith wouldn't have that kind of behavior, so she ignored it and propped the broom up back in its corner, breathing in the smells of burning coal and the ghost of molten iron as if it were life.

The fire in the brick forge was starting to fade against the cold wind. So, despite her own discomfort, Mariah pulled one of the wide doors closed. The temperature in the room started to increase as she moved to the bellows. She grabbed the hook overhead with her calloused palm and maneuvered it up and down with ease, feeding air into the fire. She could hardly even remember a time when it had been hard to reach and more difficult yet to pull. As she moved, she double-checked the room around her.

Magnus's tools were all hanging neatly on hooks on the side of the forge. The cooling tank was full of fresh water, and another full bucket waited nearby. Although she carried the water up from the stream every morning in the gray light of dawn, her shoulders still ached. They twitched, and feathers brushed her calf. Still working the bellows, she quickly looked down, checking the ends of her floor-length dress and cloak. She sighed in relief. Her wings were still safely concealed. The binding across her chest was still snug, uncomfortable even, so she knew it was still in place. Raising her head, she continued her visual inspection of the room.

The anvil was clear. Had she checked the holes for bits of metal? She nodded. There was also extra coal in the wheelbarrow just inside the room. *The hammer!*

Mariah let go of the overhead crank and searched the room for Magnus's favorite hammer. He had left it on the stone table near the side wall. She hefted it up and carefully laid it on the edge of the anvil.

The slamming of the house door startled her, but she scuttled back over to the bellows, working the crank with one hand and running the other through her short, silvery hair.

She expected to see Magnus's hulking form come through the door at any second, but instead she heard her mother's voice.

"Think about it, darlin'. You can't go on like this."

"Maybe I can let Mariah try somethin', a short sword to start. Then she can work her way up. Once she's got a handle on things, she can help me with the longer blades."

Her heart jumped in her chest. Her father had let her work on hooks and chains and arrowheads but never an actual weapon. Weapons for the crown were his stock-in-trade.

"We both know she's not strong enough to take your place. Besides, who would buy weapons from a slip of a girl barely old enough to marry? The king? I don't think so. Girls might be servin' in his army, but smithin' is a man's trade."

The edge of her father's foot appeared around the edge of the smithy door. Ashanya continued, her voice pitched low, but even with the roar of the fire and the whoosh of the bellows, her mother's voice was clear to Mariah's keen ears.

"With all of Eaglespire's boys heading off to Glenley, there's no one to apprentice for you. How will you supply King Rothgar with swords for the war when your shoulder keeps seizin' up? That girl can't do it all for you, Magnus, and you know it. But she can serve us...and serve the crown if you only..."

"Ashanya," his voice was a low rumble. "You promised. We promised we'd keep her safe."

There was a long pause. "We made that promise when you

were still bringin' in enough coin to feed us all. If you can't work, we'll all starve."

As if in response, Mariah's stomach growled fiercely, but she ignored it.

There was silence outside the smithy for a few moments. Then, she heard the squeak of the back door. Her mother must have finally gone back into the house.

Mariah shook her head. Her mother couldn't possibly mean it, but her heartbeat sped up anyway. Her back muscles twitched, and her wings brushed against her legs again. She longed to fly, to escape the ice that had suddenly filled the middle of her chest. Maybe she had misunderstood.

"What's wrong with you?" Magnus's basso filled the space.

Her head shot up. Her father's face, as big as the rest of him but lined from all of his years at the forge, was drawn. One hand rubbed his shoulder as he walked over to check the fire.

"That's good for now." He walked to his table and started sifting through the long billets he had already shaped. "Now, answer my question."

She let go of the crank and lifted his favorite pair of tongs off their hook as he brought the long metal bar around. "I heard, what you and Mother... Father, I..."

"Don't go listenin' to Mother. She's always overworryin'. Nothin's going to change."

Her smile came naturally, but it was strained. *Nothin's going to change.* She handed him the tongs, and he used them to push the billet into the fire, holding it there until the metal began to glow. It was like the sun at sunset, all blazing yellows and oranges. *Nothin's going to change.* Her wing twitched again. *Mother's right about one thing. No one would trust a girl as a smith, so I'll just keep helping Father, like I always have.*

Magnus moved the hot metal to the anvil and picked up the hammer with his free hand. Clanging filled the air as he began to draw it out, pounding the hammer down again and again. The sound soothed Mariah's nerves, and her smile brightened. *This is good work.*

"Grab one of the short ones." Magnus gestured with his head toward the pile of metal he had left on the table. "I want you to try a hunting knife this mornin'."

Mariah's eyes widened, and her heart, which had only just begun to slow, began to race again. There was nothing she could do to stop the stupid grin that spread over her face as she moved over and began to sort through the billets. Her father had faith in her, even if no one else did. She would forge the best knife anyone in Eaglespire...

Time slowed as the clang of metal hitting the anvil in quick succession ceased. It was followed by a soft thud and her father's scream. By the time she spun around, the blade Magnus had been shaping was sizzling on the cool stone floor with the hammer lying nearby. Her father was still by the anvil, but he had stepped back, and his meaty hands clung to either side of his thigh. She had never seen such anguish on his face. The fabric of his trousers had been burned away in a clean line across his thigh, and the smell of searing flesh filled the air. The white of bone peeked through her father's bloody flesh like an unwelcome guest.

"My shoulder, it...it...Garrett. Get Garrett," he croaked. His eyes fluttered closed, and his body crumpled.

Mariah reached out, barely catching his head between her hands. His fall pulled her to her knees, but she kept his head from hitting the floor. She laid it down as softly as she could manage.

Then she was up and out of the smithy, running for all she was worth down the cobblestone road toward the healer's cottage.

§

Mariah paced her bedroom, ever aware of keeping her footsteps quiet. She was down to her shift. In her nervousness, her wings had kept twitching, threatening to rip through their bindings and her dress as well, so she had locked her door and stripped down. Her mother would forgive her that more than she would a ripped dress.

The scene replayed over and over in her mind, every action from the second her father had walked into the smithy, but she didn't see a way they could have prevented it, unless she had been the one working the sword. His bad shoulder had apparently seized up as he brought the hammer down, and the molten hot sword had slammed into his leg before bouncing onto the floor, where it could do no further harm. That one moment on his leg had been enough.

Her father had been injured at the forge before. Even she had a multitude of small scars from flying sparks. But nothing could compare to this. How could a person go on walking if their flesh was burned away to the bone? How could he avoid infection?

Garrett was with her father now. Mariah prayed silently that he would be able to save him.

She paused in her pacing and stretched her wings, their black tips touching the walls of her small room. She let their complexity distract her. They were long and nearly straight when extended like this. The feathers were silvery on the bottom, matching her hair, and black on the top and around the edges. She shook her head, again amazed that someone like her, Ceo San, could have come from her mother and father. Ceo San supposedly had the ability to become animals like the ancient, mythical gods of Whitelea.

Those gods, if they existed, had a mysterious sense of humor. Why give wings to a blacksmith's daughter? She had heard that there were others similarly cursed, but she had never met one. Instead, she had spent her whole life hiding. After she was born, her parents had told neighbors that she had a deformity of the back. It had been excuse enough to keep her in the house as a baby and a toddler and to explain the lump under her clothing. Her eyes still filled with tears, she stifled a giggle, remembering her father recount tales of how hard it was to keep her on the floor, because once she had learned to walk, she had also learned to fly.

At his insistence, she had been one of the few Ceo San in Varidian to be raised at home. As she understood it, most children like her were sent to be raised in Glenley, to be put into service to the kingdom as soon as they were old enough. His majesty, King Rothgar, had strongly encouraged this practice since he had taken the throne shortly before her birth. Less than a year ago, he had declared it law. All Ceo San, whatever their age, were to be sent to the capital city to be trained to serve in the king's army. Those who sent their children voluntarily received a hefty reward from the royal treasury. Those who did not risked imprisonment.

Her father had never liked Rothgar. Nor had he agreed that the king should be able to "kidnap" the kingdom's children to serve in his never-ending quest for world domination. Mariah had heard Magnus speak of it so many times, had watched her mother smile and nod whenever he went on one of his rants, always within their walls, of course.

"Mariah, open this door right now. Garrett is gone."

She snapped her wings closed before unlocking the door and pulling it open.

"Yes, Mother? Is Father okay?" She looked down at Ashanya. Her face was pinched, and her eyes were red. "Is he…?"

"He is alive. He is restin' but he needs a tincture, one that Garrett cannot make. I need you to travel to Glenley to get it."

"Glenley?" Mariah's mouth dropped open of its own accord. She had never been beyond the outer limits of Eaglespire.

Her mother handed her a sealed scroll and another piece of paper, this one with a hand-drawn map and directions to a shop on the outskirts of the capital. "Take this letter, and the alchemist will know what ya need."

Ashanya's steel gray eyes looked straight into her own blue ones. "You must do this if your father is to heal. Now, get dressed and say your goodbyes quick. I'll have a bag of supplies for you in the kitchen. Hurry!"

§

Mariah tried to rush, she really did, but her mind kept getting caught up in the newness of what was happening. In the nineteen years that she had been alive, her mother had insisted that she never leave Eaglespire and, in fact, had discouraged her from ever leaving the house. Her father was the one who had started sending her on errands around the village when she was eight. She had learned to enjoy that little bit of freedom, despite the odd looks because of her deformity, and eventually, although she had never been allowed to play with the other children, the townsfolk had gotten used to her and the "lump" that ran down the length and width of her back. And now, her mother was sending her to the capital, the very home of the man who thought that every Ceo San was born to serve him.

She buttoned up the front of her dress and threw on her cloak, tying it at her neck. She opened her door and started to go through, but she stopped and looked back at the simple space. A hard lump formed in her throat, but she pushed it down and shut the door.

Her parents' bedroom was across the hall. The door was open, and she could see her father lying in their bed.

The tears that had finally dried welled up again when she saw him.

His leg was wrapped in wet bandages and propped up outside of the blankets. Blood seeped through, and she could see the outline of his injury.

"Father!"

He opened his eyes. His black hair, peppered with gray, was damp with sweat, and his face was drawn, but he smiled. "Mariah, sweetheart." She had never heard his voice sound so weak.

She hurried to his side. "I'm going to help." She grabbed his large hand and folded it in both of hers. "Mother's sending me to Glenley to get a tincture. You'll see. Everything will be fine. We'll be together in the shop again before you know it."

"No, no, no," he shook his head, panic in his eyes. "Don't go! You must run! You must fly!" The movement must have caused his leg to shift, because he began moaning and trying to grab at it again.

She put her hands on his chest and pushed him back down on the bed. It was a struggle. Even in his weak state, he was so much bigger and stronger. "Father, you must lie down. It'll be all right. I'll be as fast as I can. I promise."

"Run," he panted. His eyes drifted shut. "Take…take my knife."

His prized knife. He always wore it. It was a hunting knife, but since he didn't hunt anymore, he used it whenever he could, even just for spearing his meat at dinner. The belt and scabbard were on a chair against the wall.

"Okay," she murmured. "I can do that."

His breathing slowed, and she used the damp cloth from the basin beside the bed to wipe the sweat from his face.

"I love you, Father." It would do her good to have a piece of him with her on her journey.

§

In a few minutes, she was in the kitchen with her mother, her father's belt wrapped around her waist twice with the knife tucked in its scabbard at her hip, all hidden under her cloak.

Her mother put a linen bag into her hands. Inside it was a water skin, two loaves of bread, and a few coins. "Mother, are you sure—" she began, but Ashanya cut her off.

"You must go, child. Hurry. Leave on the North Road and follow the map from there."

"Mother—"

"Go!" She didn't meet her eyes, only shoved her out the door. Her voice was oddly tight. "Your father needs you to do this, girl."

"Yes, Mother," she replied, but the door slammed, and she was talking to the air. Mariah looked up at the door, shaking her head, and began to walk, following the cobblestone path away from her house, away from the smithy where she had grown up.

Something felt very wrong. It was all too much, she decided. It had all happened too fast, and her mind just hadn't caught up. So, she would get to Glenley and return as fast as she could. It was a few day's walk from what she'd heard. She could be back within a week.

Steeling herself, she began to walk faster, turning after a moment onto the main road, which led to Glenley in north and Kilgereen and the Granite Sea in the south. The baker, her face knowing, nodded in her direction from inside the window of the bakery. The whole town must know by now of Father's injury. Mariah nodded back and turned to the road again.

Two men were coming toward her from the north gate, and the sight of them made that feeling of wrongness burn in her chest. They each wore black and gold armor with a dragon carved on the chest plate. What were King Rothgar's soldiers doing in Eaglespire? Their eyes were hard, and their hands were on their swords.

They looked straight at her, and their pace increased.

She stopped and stood still for a fraction of a moment, betrayal lancing through her, pain burning in her chest. *Mother!*

Her father's voice cut through the fog in her head. "You must run!"

She turned and ran. The sound of the guards' boots rang on the cobblestone, drowning the sound of her own fleet steps.

She had to make it to the south gate and to the forest beyond. She could hide there until nightfall. *Then what?*

All of her fears were confirmed when one of the guards shouted behind her.

"Ceo San! You must stop in the name of King Rothgar. Halt!"

Mariah stumbled. She could never come back. Her mother had condemned her.

She picked up speed, dropped her bag, and tore at the ties at her throat. The pressure of her wings pulled at the fabric of her dress. Her cloak came away and flew to the ground behind her. She could see the gate ahead. It was a small affair in a stone wall only a few feet high. She fumbled at the buttons down her front but ended up tearing them off, exposing her shift beneath. It was enough.

Mariah's wings snapped open, brushing one of the guards behind her and pushing him backward. Her wings knew what to do. She knew what to do. She pumped them hard and rose into the air and over the gate. She had never done anything like this before, although she had always wanted to. She spared a look down and saw that the guards were running in her direction, but they were quickly becoming smaller. She flew toward the mountains west of the South Road, grief and exhilaration warring for control.

Nothing was supposed to change. Tears fell and dried on her face within a matter of seconds. *Everything has changed.*

Her mother had turned her in. She must have done it days ago for the guards to have arrived so quickly. There were no words for the pain that lanced through Mariah's heart. Her father would need the reward for his recovery...if he recovered. Only his last words kept her from turning around and giving herself up.

He'd wanted her to run, to be free. He'd wanted her to fly.

A SLOW SPRING MUSIC

Erin Newton Wells

The clamor becomes too much. At their best, a group of bells can be a marvelous cohesion, honeyed and seamless. In ordinary hands, they are only so much brass. I come to the decision, both suddenly and slowly, traveling here all my life. Finally, I tell them.

It is an awkward place to stop. Already they are well into the big events of spring, all the rehearsals for Easter. Forsythia has bloomed. Dogwood begins. But I know what I must do. It is a matter of listening for interior music. When I hear it unmistakably, it is time to tell them and not look back.

"But you can't," says Hilde, who stands to my left. "You're the anchor."

"We need you," says Diane, who stands to my right. "You're tempo. You're the beat."

"There will be others," I tell them. "The beat will find you. All is well."

And I depart in peace.

From now on I will be quiet and slow. I will sing, if the songs are good. If not, I will be quiet. I will sing to myself. I will make harmony for the tunes, singing a lonely alto in the dark at night or when I work outside. Then, I will cease and let the song continue on its own. That is when the music knows exactly what to do.

Hilde calls several times, distraught, urging my return.

"Don't worry," I say. "Let someone new try. Wait and see."

I imagine the long, padded tables, the brass bells lined in swelling rows from tea-cup tiny to enormous buckets. In the middle is the gap where I stand. My spirit hovers over it, keeping tranquility. Others scurry to fill in when my notes appear on the page.

And then I imagine the piece played without my bells, an empty space at those notes, the brief silences. Silence spreads slowly left and right beneath their playing, a hushed substance that calms them. It is mellow, smooth, round, a warm and melting gold which curls into the ear, gives comfort and no pain.

Hank's gone, so there's just me. And in the afternoons, there's

Lollie. To most, I am Merle. To her, I am Moom, a name she formed for me when her small mouth was soft and new. It could not bend around sounds that take place farther back. She is so fresh and malleable, a chance to start over.

I walk to the school now to fetch her, as I've done each week-day this year. It helps Kate. She picks her up around five after work. It saves on childcare, better for Lollie. I get another chance to pass along what I know and maybe do some good. Such a messy divorce. In earlier times, we kept it hidden and soldiered on. Who's to say? The little ones bounce around more when the halves split.

Here she comes, skipping to the gate, and halts with the line of children. Security is fierce. Gone are the days when children walked home on their own, as Kate did. Now they are checked off to a recognized adult, the time marked, their small lives burdened early.

She spots me and raises her hand. I raise mine, the required salute. The aide scrutinizes me, smiles, lets Lollie through the gate. A sheep from the fold returns to my imperfect arms. Oh, Lollie, I think. I will surround you with simplicity these three hours each day, as long as I can.

"Moom!" Her small body hits me with a thud.

"Sweet Lollie!" I exclaim. I wrap myself around her, miniature backpack and all.

I am ancient among these late-model parents, the pitch of their voices still high, their faces fresh.

She shrugs out of the pack and hands it to me. Already, it is too full. She is only six. I try to spare her back. The bag is custom stitched with her name and a stylized lollipop. "In case you forget it's me," she explains on the first day of school. So far, this has worked. I slip into the straps, gingerly easing them over an achy shoulder. It is a reminder of when I first began playing bells and did not use the proper oval motion. Now and then, the left joint flares. You are mortal, it says, and flawed.

"I missed you!" she says.

"That makes two of us, because I missed you, too."

"All day?"

"Every second."

She grins and begins to skip, tugging my hand. The metal parts of the lunchbox inside the pack clank against me as we sail colt-ishly past the young mothers and dads. The grass fluoresces with its first green. Everything is April new.

"What will we do today, Moom?" she asks.

"What do you think?" I turn the question back, good Sopho-clean form.

"Let's gather something."

"Good idea. Snack first."

"Fuel for the journey." She repeats a phrase I use.

Gather is not a typical word for a six-year-old, or journey. But I have begun to enfold her with my odd, outdated speech. I smile to hear myself speaking from her small face. We often embark upon gathering journeys together.

"And what shall we gather, my fair young maid?" I sing. She giggles, which also happens frequently.

"Dewberries!"

"Ah. Would that we could. But too early for them. Not until summer."

She skips in her one-footed version, galump, galump, as she thinks.

"Let's search for the rare, perfect leaf of spring."

My heart leaps to hear this baby conversing in Elizabethan.

"Your wish is granted. Rare and perfect it is. Plenty of those where I live."

We pass the young dogwoods the school planted. They've just begun to bloom. Lollie stops.

"Look, Moom! Someone hurt them. Every petal."

We examine what appear to be burn marks on the ends of each white heart, and I say this is how they grow. Later, I will tell her the legend.

We move down the quiet street leading to my house. We stop to watch ants, squirrels, rocks, broken nut shells, a redbud frothed with mauve blooms. How compelling is this world the lower you are to the ground. I am in no hurry. There's time.

She finishes snack and is soon out the door again, pulling me with her. She's grabbed our floppy and misshapen journey hats from their hooks and adds the two good hickory branches we found out back. They are slender and resilient, stripped of bark and silky smooth.

Our property is large, extending a good distance back, a lot of it useless except for adventures. It's old farm land redone as sub-division. We head through the Bramble Briers, the Wild Ivy Patch, the Stone Gnome Homes, the Poor Dead Animal Place, which is the graveyard for Kate's childhood pets. Lollie has named all this.

She remembers our mission and slows to examine leaves, look-ing for the rare and perfect. I can see many. But she is quite par-ticular.

"No," she says, pointing to infinitely small deformities on each one.

By now we've reached the back of the wooded lot, beginning to be shaded again as trees fill out. It contains the old culvert from the farm road that ran through here, draining the land when it rains. It used to be fenced, but all of that rusted and fell away. The place is a hazard, and Frank was going to fix it. Lollie knows to be careful. She knows how far she can go.

I see her heading there but keep quiet. They are so protected these days. Let her experiment. I move closer, ready.

"Moom! I see it!" She points into the hole. "It's beautiful! Come see!"

Instantly, I am beside her as she squats to show me a lovely yellow-green leaf of a sapling that grows through the cracked wall of the drain. It rained yesterday. The concrete is wet, streaked with mud. Right here, the pipe goes straight down, then levels out. It's an overgrown mess.

"It's perfect!" she says. "I can reach it, okay?" She holds out her hand to me for support.

Alarms go off inside me. I extend my hand. She grips it. Her feet are straining at the edge, her other hand reaching for the leaf. She slips. I hear her smack the puddle of muddy water.

"Lollie! Oh, baby!"

What on earth was I thinking? She lies on her back and looks up at me, her eyes huge.

"Baby, are you broken? Can you move? Did you hit your head? Speak, honey."

"Moom?" A tiny voice. Her lip quivers.

"Are you hurt, baby?"

"I got my school clothes all muddy." She examines an elbow. "And this is all scrapey"

"We can fix that. Are you able to move around?"

She sits up and nods.

"Good. Then just stay there while we think."

"Moom? I'm scared. I don't like it down here."

"Can't say I blame you."

"I'm all wet and icky. Can you get me out?"

"I will. But you're a bit too far to reach. I'd slide down, too. Then we'd both be in a pickle."

"You could use the journey stick."

We'd talked about rescuing people this way when they fell into water. But with my bum shoulder, I'm not sure I can pull her up. The sides of the drain are too slick for her to scramble out on her own. I test the reach of the stick, but I'm afraid I'll drop her and make it worse. I look around for someone else, but I know the neighbors aren't likely to be home now.

"Lollie, I can go check next door for help."

"No, Moom! Don't leave me," she moans.

"All right." I sit on the edge where she can see me.

People are always leaving her. First, her Big Frank Pops. He loved that little girl, and the feeling was mutual. Then, her father. That left a big hole. She's been dropped off at daycare and now, these past two years, at school. This year, there's no dad to pick her up, and Mom needs to work more hours. That's where I come in. My real purpose in life right now, I've decided, is not to be absent for Lollie. She still clutches the leaf.

"Looks like you got a good one," I say.

She grips it more tightly.

"You still okay?"

She's quiet. Then, "I'm scared, Mooms." Tiny voice.

"Well, who wouldn't be, in a predicament like this? But I suppose it's all for a reason. We just have to figure out what."

She considers this. I can see her face thinking.

"Like it's our journey?"

I brighten. "Exactly. What a brilliant child you are. You already found the perfect leaf of spring. That was the first part. Now we just have to figure out this second part."

I lie down and stretch out.

"Moom?" she says nervously.

"I'm still here." I edge over so she sees more of me.

"What are you doing?"

"Looking at the sky."

"Why?"

"Because it makes me feel peaceful. Try it."

I hear her rustling. Then, she's still. Softly, I start singing her name to a wandering tune. I add words that rhyme with it. Polly, holly, jolly, kabolly. I make them up. She giggles, joins in. When we run out, she sings my name, then makes rhymes. The sky glides calmly overhead. I'm silent.

"Moom?"

"I'm listening to my interior music."

"What's that?"

"If I let everything go quiet in me, sometimes I start to hear a slow little tune inside."

She's quiet.

"I don't hear it."

"It takes time. You may have to wait awhile. But it's there."

"Inside everybody?"

"Yes."

She's quiet.

"Moom? What was your name when you were a little girl?"

"Same as now. Merle. Until you came along. Then I became Moom, too. But I'm still Merle. You could call me Moom Merle."

She giggles.

"What was your name before you were Lollie?"

"Shaneesy," she says, without hesitation.

"Ah. Your angel name."

"Huh?"

"Before you were born. When you were an angel."

"Oh. Yes. That's what it was. What was your angel name?"

"Nell. I'm pretty sure. It's been so long ago."

"You're Merle Nell?"

"I think it's Nell Merle, since Nell came first. Nell Merle Moom. That would be the right order."

She giggles. I do, too. The name sounds like a cheer. Sis Boom Bah. We laugh until our middles hurt.

"Silly Moom! I mean, Nell Merle Moom!"

"Shaneesy Lollie Holly Polly!"

Then she's quiet.

"I miss who I was when I was born," she says.

"Why?"

"Because Daddy would've been there. And I'd get to see him all the time."

I take a deep breath.

"I miss Daddy. I miss Big Frank Pops."

"So do I."

"Pops isn't coming back, is he?"

"No, Lollie."

The other question hangs in the air. I begin to sing all the angel names I can think of to fill up the space.

"Moom?"

"Still here."

"Don't leave me."

"Never."

We're quiet. She's lying on the soggy blue hat, her brown hair spread out.

"I hear it," she says.

"Good girl. What's it sound like?"

"It goes slow."

I don't correct the adverb.

"I like it. I think it's the angels. Like what I used to be."

There's a thought. We close our eyes and listen.

Then I hear something crashing through the brush on the slope, and here's Hank, our neighbor, standing beside me. Hank and Frank, I called them. Like two old housewives out in the yard, keeping up with whatever they kept up with.

"Merle!" he yells. Hank is hard of hearing. "You hurt?"

"Hi, Hank. What took you so long? Maybe you could give us a hand."

"I just got back, looked over, saw you lying flat out here. You all right?"

He reaches for me, but I brush him off and stand, putting my hat back on.

"Let's get Lollie out." I take him to look.

"Goodness, gracious, young lady! You okay?"

"Hi, Mr. Hank."

"Well, honey, I'm going to get you out there right now, don't you worry."

I suggest he use the stick, but he'll have none of it. He hustles off, comes back with a rope, which he ties to a tree, then dangles into the pipe.

"Now, you come over to the side, darling. Grab a hold tight. I'm going to walk you up the side till I can reach, then I'll pull you rest of the way. Think you're strong enough? You eat your vegetables today?"

She nods in amazement.

"Then, it ought to work."

He coaxes her up, her sneakers braced on the side, with me holding the rope behind him.

"Ready, now? Keep hanging on, both you young ladies."

When she's within reach, he grabs her, lifts her out, and starts to the house, carrying her like a baby.

"Mooms!" she cries. "I forgot my leaf!"

"Sweetheart," I call, jogging to keep up with Hank. "It's still perfect, no matter where it is. It's still spring. There's plenty more to find."

He places her, mud and all, on the sofa and waits to make sure she's okay.

"Going out right now, get that fencing like me and Frank was set on. Should've done it. Aimed to fix it come spring."

"Go for it, Hank. I'll pay."

"We'll see about that."

I get things to clean her, and an old shirt of mine for a dress, a bandage for the scraped elbow.

"Well, then," I say. "I guess that counts as an adventure."

"But could we not do that one again, Moom?"

"Well, if we did, you'd know how to handle it."

She nods. "I get quiet, and listen to my angels."

It took me a whole lifetime to learn that. Here she is, only in first grade.

It's nearly five. The phone rings. Hilde persuades me I should come to practice tonight. I remind her how she and Diane can two-in-hand the bells for a while, taking my part until they find a replacement. I tell her I need to step aside now.

"But you're coming back, after that?"

I say I've got other music I need to listen to.

"Merle. You're not switching to that group at St. Stephen's, are you?"

I laugh, assure her I'm not.

"Moom?" Lollie asks when I hang up. "You're not going to your handbells tonight?"

"No, dear."

"You'll stay with me?"

"Ever and ever."

The phone rings. It's Kate, saying she's running late, apologizing. I tell her it's my greatest privilege to keep Lollie a little longer, that we're engaged in some serious music.

"Okay, then. Everything go all right this afternoon?"

"The afternoon was perfect," I say, giving Lollie a conspiratorial look. "In fact, why don't you just let her stay here overnight. I'll get her to school in the morning."

Lollie gives a whoop, rushes to hug me. Nothing obvious is broken in her. I hand her the phone so she can talk to her mother. I see Hank backing into my driveway and unloading bales of fence wire and bundles of metal posts. Lollie is explaining the name Shaneesy, as if her mother ought to know this.

I go to the kitchen to start supper, selecting things that might please angels. The tune inside is slow, definitely about spring, because it grows more beautiful, more perfect with time.

("A Slow Spring Music" originally published in *Skyline 2016*, and the recipient of First Place in fiction in the *Skyline* spring-themed contest, 2015.)

EXCERPT FROM "THE KEY TO THE QUARTER POLE"

Robin Williams

Darcy's Dream was a train wreck looking to happen, even with a good jock like Alvarez Montegro in the saddle. A three-year-old filly whose breeding might best be described as "junk," Darcy's Dream had, throughout her life, been handled, broken, and trained by people who were well-meaning but remarkably ignorant of the sensitivity of horses. Accordingly, she hated the racetrack, she hated galloping, and she especially hated galloping with the two fillies alongside her this morning.

Teg, on the other hand, loved the racetrack, oved galloping, and loved horses, even a rank, nasty filly like Darcy's Dream. Teg was a gifted rider cursed with the same large rawboned frame that made Darcy's Dream look like she might be a racehorse. Good for a racehorse. Bad for a jockey. He rode races at sixteen, but Mother Nature began leaning on him almost immediately. At seventeen, he took up cocaine—for purely professional reasons, of course—made the weight and rode another year. But by the time he reached eighteen, not even a heroin habit could have kept him under 120, much less 110. So, he retired to exercising horses in the morning, keeping the coke habit for consolation.

Darcy's Dream, never a happy camper, was feeling especially cross this morning. She was coming into season, and her sides were tender, and she just wasn't in the mood to work. Although her owner paid the trainer for a regular shot of hormones to prevent her coming into season, her trainer used the money to pay the feed man, reasoning that Darcy's Dream was such a witch that it was hard to tell the difference anyway.

Teg was also having a bad morning. He misjudged his timing of the end of the party and the beginning of the workday, so he tried to compensate by having a beer before making his way from the dormitory to Barn Twelve. It seemed like once before, when his Uncle Pablo was pounding the steel drums in his stomach and the mariachi band was tooting in his head, that a beer had calmed things down. Or maybe it was a joint, but he didn't have a joint, so he drank a beer.

To make things worse, Teg had to borrow a saddle from the trainer he was riding for. Recently he had run up a tab with his supplier, and he had sold his saddle. Now, he was trying to find a tight seat on this piece of crap he found in the tack room, and the mariachi band was whooping it up in his eyeballs, and this filly who couldn't outrun a fat man in rubber boots was throwing her head around, trying to bust his face.

Darcy's Dream recognized the guy on her back: He had nice hands and a soothing way of crooning to her, but today, instead of sitting still, he kept hitching his knees forward and shifting his weight in the stirrup irons, causing the saddle to dig into her back just behind her withers. After jogging half a mile, she felt a raw hole growing in her back and a ragged edge on her temper. When the guy punched her into a gallop, the gouging in her back became sharper, and she threw up her head, trying to twist away from the pain.

As the three horses galloped around the clubhouse turn, Darcy's Dream saw ahead of her across the track, beyond dozens of horses coming and going and walking and cantering, the gap. The gap was the opening in the rail that led to the horse path back to the barn, back to the comfort of her stall. It was the escape route for fillies in torture, and she took it. First, she propped with her front legs, putting her head down, and jerking the guy forward. Then, she threw her head up as high as she could, bashing the guy in the face. As he loosened his grip on the reins, she bolted across the track, leaving the guy behind.

Directly between the filly and the gap was a lead pony alongside Alice's Restaurant. Both horses stopped short at the sight of Darcy's bucking fit. In the moment that it took for Darcy to stop galloping, buck, and bolt for the gap, Alice's Restaurant assessed the situation and decided to flee from the horse-eating monster that was obviously chasing the filly. But Darcy was already in full flight, and before Alice could take a step, the filly slammed into him broadside, knocking him down with a sharp crack. The gelding hit the ground hard and rolled over into the lead pony, who stumbled, and threw his rider.

Frightened by the horse's flailing legs, Darcy leaped sideways, then charged forward again, her anger changed to panic. The guy was no longer on her back, but the stirrup irons swung wildly, bouncing on her sweaty sides, urging her to run as though a cougar were on her back raking her sides. In her terrified flight, she saw other horses wheel and rear and scatter, some kicking at her as she brushed past. Their panic fed her own, driving her to greater madness as she galloped single-mindedly towards the gap.

By now the gap was clogged with horses and riders pausing in the face of chaos. Darcy's Dream's exit was closed when she got there. Never slowing, never flicking her ears to signal that she saw the obstacles in her path, Darcy's Dream drove towards the eye of a needle, a sliver of air between the corner post and another horse. The rider waved and hollered vainly to turn her. At the last moment, the filly shifted slightly to the right. When her shoulder hit the rail, Darcy's Dream was going thirty miles an hour. The rail stopped her body momentarily, long enough for her hind end to flip over her back, driving her head into the clay ramp, and snapping her neck.

Out on the track, Alice's Restaurant righted himself, organized his legs and climbed to his feet. As he became panicked by the turmoil around him—loose horses and shouting humans, an off-key siren, not to mention, somewhere, a horse-eating monster—he did what his ancestors had done in the face of danger for thousands of years: *fly*. No broken neck, no cougar, no monster for *him*. He could outrun the wind—at least for five-eighths of a mile.

Horses are creatures of habit, so as Alice fled, he worked his way through other galloping horses until he could hug the rail. Free of a lead line, free of a rider's hand on the reins, Alice indulged in the flight he was built for. Nostrils wide and sucking the humid air, he churned his hooves in the dirt and barreled down the backstretch towards the turn. But as the rail bent away from him on the left, he coasted across the track to the outer rail. He was still running hard about twenty feet from the rail, and he gathered himself to jump when a voice hollered *Whoa! Whoa!* Flicking his ears, he processed the *Whoa* and hit the brakes about six inches too late. Turning sharply in a half-rear and dragging his haunches, he threw up a rooster tail of dirt like a downhill skier. His right front leg about two inches above the knee that Louisa tended so carefully took the brunt of his weight as he slammed into the metal railing, which buckled but held. Alice scrambled a few steps and paused to let his windblown sides heave. When Bones, still hollering *Whoa*, reached the horse, Alice was waiting curiously for someone to lead him back to the barn. He'd had enough for the day and looked forward to his post-workout bath. And maybe some ice for his knee, which hurt like a sonofabitch.

excerpt from "The Key to the Quarter Pole"
2015 winner of the Best Unpublished Novel contest
sponsored by James River Writers and Richmond Magazine

ANDREW'S DECISION

John M. Wills

He rubbed his eyes and stretched. Despite being seven o'clock in the morning, semi-darkness bathed the room. Andrew hated winter because daylight hours were so few and the lack of sunlight seemed to make everyone grumpy. *Better get out of bed and get ready for school.* He reached over to the other side—*Oh no, it's wet.* He sat up. Younger brother, Stevie, was gone. This was not good.

Ever since their father left, six-year-old Stevie had begun wetting the bed. Even if the youngster made sure he had nothing to drink hours before going to sleep, he still lost control. Andrew's high school counselor told him his brother acted stressed because he missed his father. Wetting the bed was what she called, "...n outward manifestation of his worry and sadness. Once his father returned, the problem would likely cease."

Andrew didn't think that would ever happen. Dad left because their mom, Susan, was using drugs. *She used to look so pretty.* Despite all the sorrow she was causing, and the reality of her marriage crumbling, she persisted. When she lost her job and began spending the family's meager savings on her habit, her husband became infuriated. There were countless nights Andrew and Stevie glued their ears to their bedroom door listening to their parents argue. Dad would end each argument by threatening to leave. Finally, he made good on that threat. *How could you leave us, Dad?* That's when the real problems began.

For the last six months, Andrew had been functioning more as a father than a big brother. Susan was mostly gone, forcing Andrew to take care of laundry and meals, that is, when there was food available. Lately, he'd resorted to sneaking money from her purse to buy groceries. Some days, there was no money to take. On those occasions, the boys lived on soup and crackers.

He swung his feet over the side of the bed and went to the closet. Little Stevie sought refuge there whenever he'd had an accident. Andrew opened the door slowly and in the dim light saw his brother's feet sticking out beneath a pile of clothing. He knelt down and carefully removed the clothes, revealing the tearful little boy. He rubbed his little brother's head. "It's okay, Stevie, we'll get it cleaned up."

"Wh...what about V, V...Victor?" He rubbed his eyes and wiped his nose on his pajama sleeve. "He, he'll find out and then..."

Victor had moved in a few weeks ago. Mom told the boys her new friend was taking care of her, making sure nobody hurt her. Andrew was only sixteen, but he was pretty sure he knew the man was using his mother to make money. Victor was big and mean and said he didn't like kids. Andrew and Stevie stayed in their room when Victor was around because their mere presence seemed to upset him. When the boyfriend found out Stevie was wetting the bed, he told Susan he'd break him of that habit. He did so by administering a beating to the little boy when Stevie wet the bed. Since then, whenever he'd have an accident Stevie sought refuge in the closet, hoping to avoid punishment.

Two days ago, after another bed-wetting episode, Victor had taken his belt to Stevie's backside. When Andrew tried to intervene, Victor hit him so hard with his fist that Andrew fell against the wall, unconscious. When he came to, he heard his little brother's sniffles coming from the closet. The youngster was lying on the floor, unable to sit. After complaining to Susan about Victor, all she said was, "Try not to upset him." That's when Andrew began to realize their survival was in his hands.

"C'mon, Buddy, let's get ready for school." Andrew grabbed Stevie under the arms and lifted him off the floor. "We'll open the window and let the room air out. I'll put your pajamas and the sheets in a plastic bag—he'll never find out." He set the boy down on his feet. "Get dressed. I'll fix some toast for us."

"Okay, Andrew, I...I hope you're right. I, I...don't want h, h... him to hit m, m...me again."

Andrew patted his brother's head. "Hurry up; meet me in the kitchen." Lately, he'd noticed Stevie had developed a stutter. *Must be another one of those manifestations.* He opened and closed the bedroom door as quietly as he could and tiptoed past his mother's bedroom. Her door was shut—he didn't know if Victor was inside or not, and he didn't care to find out. His plan was to fix breakfast for the two of them and then walk Stevie to school. The breadbox had just three slices of bread. Looks like he'd have to buy another loaf today.

§

After bringing Stevie to his classroom, Andrew walked two blocks to his high school. The first bell had not yet rung, so students were hanging around in groups trying to stay warm while they waited for the doors to open. Andrew didn't really fit into any of the cliques—jocks, nerds, pretty girls and boys, and outcasts. He knew a couple of kids from each group, but lately his life had taken a turn from high school student to someone trying to survive life one day at a time. His main concern was Stevie. He was smart enough to know that if he went to the police about the abuse they'd both be removed from their home and possibly separated. He didn't think he or Stevie could handle that consequence.

A hulking presence seeped into the corner of Andrew's eye. "Hey, Dude, sup?" Known as "Chains" because he was famous for attacking his enemies with one, the six-footer had an intimidating presence. With thick arms sporting gang tattoos and profanities, he led the outcasts. Talk was he'd become your worst nightmare if you crossed him. Most people kept their distance.

"Uh, nothin', Chains. How's it goin'?"

"It's cool. See ya."

Andrew had become somewhat of a friend to the miscreant after he'd stuck up for Chains one day. The school resource officer had accused the troublemaker of threatening another student, but Andrew supplied an alibi that got Chains off the hook. Well, it really wasn't a "friendship" per se, since Chains demanded Andrew lie for him, or else. But ever since then, Chains had acknowledged Andrew whenever they saw each other. "You need somethin', anything, you tell me. I got yer back." Finally, the bell sounded, and Andrew followed the others inside the building.

§

On the way home, Andrew and Stevie stopped at the corner market for bread. "H, h… hey, can I get a pack o, o…of Gummy Bears?"

Andrew counted his money and quickly calculated he didn't have enough for both the bread and candy. "Man, I don't know, Stevie."

"P, p…please?"

Andrew walked back to the bread aisle and replaced the fresh loaf and then went to the day-old shelf and grabbed a cheaper product. "Okay, I think we'll have enough money."

Little Stevie eagerly grabbed a bag of his favorite snack from the display by the register, and Andrew paid. The wind began to pick up as they headed home, quickly dropping the temperature to freezing. "Wow, it's really cold out here. Let's go, Buddy, we have to get home so I can close our bedroom window."

The little boy, his cheeks as red as one of the candies, smiled and popped another Gummy Bear in his mouth. "Okay, A, A... Andrew."

The brothers arrived home several minutes later. "Hang up your coat; I'll go shut the window."

Normally, Susan and Victor were gone by the time the boys came home from school. Andrew planned on doing the laundry and putting the bed back together so no one was the wiser about his brother's accident last night. However, when he opened the door he saw the window had already been shut. *Uh, oh.* He looked underneath the bed where he'd stashed the bag with the soiled sheets and clothes. Gone.

Stevie walked in. "It's not c, c...cold i, i...in here."

"Yeah, I know. C'mon, I'll turn on some cartoons for you while I clean up." Andrew led him into the front room and turned on his favorite show. The little boy sat contentedly on the floor eating his candy while watching Bugs Bunny.

Andrew went to his mother's bedroom door. He didn't think anyone was inside, but he didn't want to take any chances. As quietly as he could, he turned the knob and slowly opened the door a crack. In an instant, the door flew from his grasp. Standing in front of him was the behemoth-like figure of Victor, and he was holding the bag containing the boys' bed sheets and Stevie's pajamas.

"Looking for this?" The man threw the bag at Andrew. "Where is that little bastard?" Spittle flew from the corner of the demon's mouth. He charged forward, knocking Andrew aside. As he lumbered toward the front room, Andrew watched him remove his belt. "So, you haven't learned your lesson yet?" Nostrils flaring, he wrapped the belt several times around his huge hand.

His eyes twice their size, Stevie stood and began backing away. He screamed. "A, A...Andrew. Help."

Instantly, Andrew jumped on the man's back and began pummeling him. He punched him repeatedly about his head and tried to wrap his arm around the man's thick neck in an effort to choke him. The enraged thug let out a thunderous roar and flung Andrew across the room. The teenager landed against the front door and crumpled to the ground.

Susan ran into the room. "Victor, NO, don't hurt my children!"

With a sweep of his heavily muscled arm, he struck her in the head causing her to collapse. "Bitch, don't you ever tell me what to do. There's only one person giving orders around here—me." He beat his chest, looking like a gorilla in the wild.

During the commotion, Stevie ran past the man to his bedroom. Mouse-like, he scurried inside the closet and began to cover himself with clothing.

Victor turned his attention from the woman. "Where is that little bed-wetting piece of crap?" He surveyed the room and then shook his head. "Never mind, I know where he is." He stomped off toward the boys' room and stood in front of the closet. "Get out here you little sissy and take your medicine."

Andrew shook his head to clear the cobwebs just in time to hear Victor yelling for his little brother to come out. *Must be in the closet.* He dashed into the room as the man was about to grab the doorknob. "No you don't." Big brother launched himself at the man turned monster, driving him into the nightstand. The behemoth hit his head on the edge of the table while falling to the ground. A tiny trail of crimson appeared on the side of his face as he lay still, stunned from the impact.

"What have you done?" His mother stumbled into the room. "He's gonna be mad as hell when he comes to. He'll kill us all."

"No, he won't, at least not me and Stevie." Andrew went to the closet and pulled the frightened little boy out. "C'mon, we're leaving." He dressed the little boy in his coat and hat and then slammed the door behind them.

The brothers walked down the street and turned the corner toward a friend's house. Stevie looked up at his older brother. "I want D, Daddy to c, c...come home, A, A...Andrew."

"Me, too, Buddy. Maybe someday, maybe—"

§

The shelter at the park was a meeting spot for the school's outcasts and local thugs. Chains held court there, making plans and meting out punishment to those who had dared to cross him. An eerie glow from the fire barrel bounced off the shelter's raised roof, making the spray-painted graffiti dance like pieces of art. Several aluminum garbage cans glowed like lanterns, as they reflected the fire's flames. They stood like sentries on the edge of the concrete slab that delineated Chains' turf. Swallowing deeply, the scene reminded Andrew of a wolves' den. He took it all in and slowly approached.

One of Chains' disciples, his hair sticking out from beneath a black watch cap, and a grill prominently displayed when he opened his mouth, quickly stepped in front of Andrew. "Whatch you doin', man? You don't come up in here less you invited."

"I'm here to see Chains."

"Ha, ha, ha." The hapless lookout bent over in an exaggerated laugh. "You here fo' Chains?" He turned toward the group warming themselves in front of the fire. "Hey, Chains, dude say he here to see you."

Chains squinted through the smoke. "Hmm, that you, Andrew?"

"Uh huh."

"Get out da way, let him pass."

Andrew moved tentatively toward Chains. "Hey, I need some help."

Several of those standing around the barrel began to laugh. "Dude say he need help."

"Shut up, fools." The pack leader's sneer quickly silenced them. "Sup, Man?"

Andrew glanced around at the wolves that now looked like little pups. He looked directly at Chains and set his jaw. "I need a gun."

For a moment, Chains' expression froze and Andrew wondered if he'd made a mistake. Then, to his relief, Chains flashed a smile and nodded. "Lil Bro, I got yer back."

§

Andrew dropped Stevie at school, but instead of heading to his own school, Andrew turned around and started toward what used to be home. Once there, he quietly entered through the back door and stood inside. He listened for several minutes, making sure no one was awake. Certain there was no movement, he crept slowly toward his mother's bedroom.

Several feet from the door, he heard coughing. He froze. *He's in there.* Andrew waited a few minutes before moving again. When it was quiet, he reached for the door, his hand trembling, but then stopped. *Can I do this?* He thought about Stevie and the beatings and then took a deep breath and grabbed the knob.

Victor was lying on his back, asleep. Andrew could see the bruised and swollen side of the animal's face, a vivid reminder of their last confrontation. As he crept forward, he reached in his jacket and pulled out the gun. Standing beside the sleeping nightmare, Andrew pointed his weapon directly at the man's head.

Suddenly, Susan awoke. "Andrew!"

The big man's eyes snapped open, and he stared in terror at the gaping hole of gun barrel just inches from his eyes. Andrew smiled and pulled the trigger.

Contributor biographies are available for download at

http://virginiawritersclub.org/Anthology-Contributors